The World at War

THE WORLD AT WAR

Mark Arnold-Forster

COLLINS
St James's Place, London, 1973

William Collins Sons & Co Ltd
London · Glasgow · Sydney · Auckland
Toronto · Johannesburg

First published October 1973
Second impression October 1973
Third impression November 1973
© Thames Television Limited 1973
ISBN 0 00 211952 8
Maps by Klonwood Limited
Printed in Great Britain by
William Collins Sons & Co. Ltd, Glasgow

Contents

CONTENTS

Maps

Preface

This book was written to accompany the television series of the same name; but it is not the book of the film. I have tried instead to write a general account of the war for everyone, and especially for those whose interest in it may have been sharpened or awakened by watching the television programmes. I have tried to fill in the gaps which even twenty-six hours of television must inevitably leave.

It was a long war and this is a short book. It is no more than an introduction to the history of a war which has already been meticulously documented and described by many careful historians. I have had the general advantage of writing thirty years after the event and the particular advantage of access to the British Cabinet records which were opened for inspection in 1972. They vindicate the judgment of those who wrote before their publication, and reveal no important decision that the historians had not already recorded.

But they do reveal – and I think valuably – the way in which decisions were reached. The Germans suspended submarine warfare in the Atlantic specifically because of centimetric radar. The map of Eastern Europe was redrawn in an afternoon at Teheran. Chamberlain and Halifax really did propose to give Malta to Mussolini in 1940.

I have also been able to draw upon many interviews with eye-witnesses which were recorded for television (but not used in full in the programmes) and which help to convey what it was like to be there. People who have not fought in a war may be shocked by the assumption that killing in action is forgivable. For nearly six years several million men, nearly all of whom would have been ashamed to maltreat a child, were prepared to kill other men whom they did not know. In my own experience the explanation of this is that when a total stranger shoots at you the incentive to shoot back is natural and powerful. So is the incentive to learn to shoot back better. Wars breed cruelty. But they also stimulate ingenuity and a determination to protect yourself and the group to which you belong – be it your regiment, your ship's company, or your nation. This is not the same as a determination to be cruel.

I have tried to convey an idea of what fighting the war was like to people who did not fight it. Those who did will not find many detailed descriptions of individual actions in which they took part. The accounts of particular actions are included as single examples of experiences that were common to many.

This book is a series of accounts of individual campaigns, not a chronological story. It would have been possible to write the story of the war chronologically, reminding the reader at every turn (irritatingly I think) of what was happening elsewhere. In fact each campaign is a story in itself; there is a chronology at the back of the book.

The legacy of World War II is still shaping the twentieth century. Many of the changes that the war brought about, or seemed to bring about, would probably have taken place sometime in any case. But the war was a catalyst which accelerated many important developments and nourished national and personal ingenuity. American mathematicians, impatient to break Japanese codes, developed machines which were the ancestors of the computer. In 1942 the Japanese captured the world's only source of quinine and forced the British to develop quickly a chemical cure for malaria; this alone made an immense difference to the post-war populations of under-developed countries. The Germans, beaten in the air, developed the V2 rocket to bombard London and introduced to the world the technology that put men on the moon. The British, having seen that unemployment and want could be cured in wartime, resolved to cure it in peacetime too, and to some extent succeeded. The legacy of World War II is not a precisely measurable thing; but it is impressive. And it does not consist, as did the awful legacy of World War I, mainly of cemeteries in France.

I have ruthlessly sought and been generously given a great deal of help. Miss Alison Wade of Thames TV has compiled the biographies and the chronology, has supervised the maps and pictures, and has carried a burden of verification, research and co-ordination which would have crushed me. Among many others Jerome Kuehl of Thames has offered welcome advice. So have Air Chief Marshal Sir Theo McEvoy, KCB, CBE, Wing Commander Ronald Kellett, DSO, DFC, Professor Sir John Randall, FRS, the Keeper of the Public Record Office, London, Mr J. R. Ede, and Mr A. Ford and Mr A. Harrington of his staff, the late Marjorie Wilkerson, Mrs Rosalind Mitchison, and Sir Geoffrey Cox, CBE. Alastair Hetherington, the Editor of the *Guardian*, has allowed me to exploit the paper's sabbatical leave system to its benevolent limit; my family has shown much forbearance; many have helped, but the responsibility for everything is mine.

Chapter 1

Beginnings

It comforts many people to suppose that Hitler's beliefs, his personality, and his power and influence over his compatriots were the only causes of World War II. After any catastrophe it is convenient to blame the dead.

But Hitler had become the ruler of Germany partly because of political, economic, diplomatic, and other circumstances that might have been prevented had the other world powers acted differently or more wisely.

Hitler's motives were not those of an ordinary dictator. He did not want simply to dominate his own country. He was convinced that the Germans – or at any rate the 'Aryans' – constituted a master-race. He sincerely believed that the Germans had been chosen to lead and dominate the rest of mankind. The racial theories that he put forward in his book *Mein Kampf* (*My Struggle*[1]) about the superiority of the German race were not simply slogans, they were true statements of belief and were the mainspring of his military policies of conquest.

Hitler saw himself as a medieval conqueror destined to subjugate at least a large part of the world (Europe to begin with) for its own eventual good, but mainly for the greater glory of the German Reich and people. He foresaw the Germans' destiny as that of proprietors of a European economic entity containing other subject races whose standard of education would be to 'know just enough to understand road signs so as not to get themselves run over by our vehicles.'

World War II would not have become the terrible experience for Europe that it was if Hitler, believing these things, had not become Germany's leader. And Hitler might not have become Germany's leader but for a series of misunderstandings and mistakes committed by the victors of World War I. Many of these mistakes were due to ignorance – ignorance about the capitalist system and the world monetary system (which no one at that time could control or guide, or even tried to control or guide) and ignorance about the Soviet Union. Tsarist Russia, defeated by the Germans in 1917, had been mysterious but explicable. The Soviet regime which followed it was an enigma which the Western powers failed to understand at all.

The Legacy of Versailles

The chief victor of World War I had been France, whose armies and people had suffered dreadfully during the four years that the war had lasted. The Treaty of Versailles, signed on 28 June 1919, eight months after the war ended, was a punitive treaty which forbade Germany to raise armed forces large enough to threaten the peace of Europe again. The German army was restricted to 100,000 men. The German navy was restricted to thirty-six warships. The German armed forces were prohibited from fortifying military installations within fifty kilometres of the east bank of the Rhine. Moreover, Germany would have to repay to the victorious Allies very large sums of money in reparation for the damage it had done.

The Versailles treaty was neither sensible nor enforceable. Under parallel and simultaneous treaties, the Hapsburgs' Austro-Hungarian Empire was dismembered. The Hapsburg Empire had never been as formidable a great power as it had seemed. But it had been big. Its elimination from the map meant that in spite of her defeat, Germany still was much the biggest and economically the most powerful State in Central Europe.

In 1918 the German Reich was only forty-seven years old, having been created by the King of Prussia and his Chancellor, Bismarck, through the amalgamation of a number of small German principalities and kingdoms after Prussia's defeat of France in 1871. Broadly speaking, the Versailles treaty left Bismarck's Reich untouched. France regained the territory of Alsace-Lorraine, which the Prussians had taken from her in 1871. Poland was granted a strip of German territory – the so-called Polish Corridor – to give her access to the Baltic Sea at Danzig which was made a League of Nations trust territory.

The peacemakers of 1919 believed, nevertheless, that this time the Germans had been subdued for ever. The French, who had suffered from German invasions in 1870 and again in 1914, were convinced that Germany could never threaten France again. The British concurred. The Americans, late but effective contributors to the Allied victory of 1918, were not quite sure. The American Commander, General Pershing, appreciated correctly an important flaw in the peacemaking and in the eventual settlement.

Unlike World War II, World War I did not end with the surrender of the defeated German army. It ended in an armistice under which the German army, nominally undefeated, but actually incapable of fighting any longer, remained intact as a military force. It was under these unreal conditions that the Versailles negotiations began. Pershing suggested that the Allies should insist on an actual German surrender so that there could be no doubt in anyone's mind that the German army had lost the war. Pershing was overruled; but he had been right. Generals and armies do not like to admit to having been defeated.

The German generals were able to argue truthfully that they had never actually surrendered and to contend, untruthfully, that they had not been defeated and could have fought on to victory. They argued they could have done this if only the German negotiators at Versailles had not been duped by the Allies, thereby betraying the German army.

This was nonsense. But the myth of the 'Versailles betrayal' was believed by many Germans and bred resentment among them against their own new Government of moderate statesmen whose main contribution to changing the nature of the German State had been to get rid of the Emperor, William II. He withdrew into exile in the Netherlands and the 'betrayal' myth persisted. It was one of the political factors which helped powerfully to bring Hitler to power later on.

American advice did not, in fact, weigh very much with the other victorious Allies. In World War I, the United States had played a minor role compared to France and Britain. In any case, the United States was reluctant to interfere in the affairs of Europe. America did not in the end agree to join the League of Nations, which was the hopeful, non-hostile outcome of the Versailles negotiations. The League was to be the international forum in which countries would settle their differences by agreement, if necessary by arbitration, but not by war. In fact, the League failed. It could not prevent World War II or even the minor wars which intervened between the First and the Second in Manchuria, where the Japanese conquered Chinese territory, or in Ethiopia where the Italians brutally enlarged their Empire. In spite of the devoted efforts of many wise and dedicated statesmen – notably Lord Robert Cecil, Philip Noel-Baker, and the French Socialists – the elected governments of the world still were not ready to surrender their sovereign power to make war. The League, tragically, was able to condemn war, but not to prevent it. Nor was it able to persuade the Great Powers to disarm.

America's withdrawal into isolationism and away from Europe was not

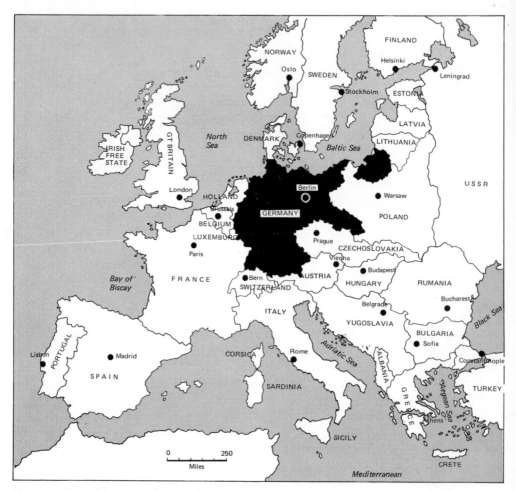

Europe after World War I

itself a cause of World War II. But the League would have been less weak if the United States had been a member.

When World War I ended, the Allies expected business to be resumed as usual. They also expected Germany to pay for the damage she had done. The popular slogan in Britain was that Germany must be squeezed until the pips squeaked. This was an impracticable aim. The German economy, like the French, was in ruins. Although Germany could and did recover economically, the payment of reparations on the scales foreseen together with the repayment of war debts incurred between the Allies involved

4

transfers of wealth which the international monetary system simply could not digest.

One of the delusions which still affected the Allies' thoughts at Versailles was that national currencies represented real wealth and that real wealth was gold. The accepted monetary doctrine was that a £1 note was as good as a gold sovereign and that national banks, the world over, would give gold in exchange for paper on demand. In fact, no national bank would have been able to do this. The so-called 'gold standard' was a myth already. Inflation on a scale that the world had never known was even then lying in wait to make nonsense of the Allies' plans that Germany should pay reparations in full.

Three years after the end of World War I the Allied Reparations Commission, dominated by the French, suggested that Germany should pay slightly less than £7,000,000,000 but said that this might not be all. Germany was thus asked to pay a fine the size of which was indeterminate. All that the Germans knew was that the total would be immense. The Germans never actually refused to pay their debts. The obligations had been acknowledged. But events prevented their fulfilment. In 1922, the fastest, most ruinous, and most spectacular inflation in history overtook the German Mark. Germans who had saved all their lives became penniless overnight. The price of a loaf of bread was measured first in thousands, then in millions of marks. By the end of the year the German Mark was wastepaper.

1922 was a year in which accepted doctrines fell like nine-pins. Hardly anyone wanted to look at the facts at the time. But the pillars of several temples developed evident cracks. Inflation on the scale experienced by the Germans was a spectre that a capitalist society had never imagined. It turned out to be untrue that money was the same as wealth. Promises 'to pay the bearer' were not to be trusted. Saving for the future could be the height of folly rather than the virtue known as thrift.

Diplomatic assumptions went by the board as well. On 16 April 1922 the Germans and the Soviet Union signed a treaty at Rapallo in Italy in which Germany and the Soviet Union promised to help each other and to renounce their claims against each other. As the Western powers saw it, Europe's two 'bad boys' – defeated Germany and revolutionary Russia – had formed an unholy alliance. In fact, the Rapallo treaty never produced effective results. But the signing of it came as a shock to Western statesmen. The illusion that the Soviet Union and Germany were diplomatically negligible had been disproved.

A third illusion also passed away in 1922, almost unnoticed. It had been assumed till then that although parts of the British Empire –

Australia, New Zealand, Canada, and South Africa – had been granted self government the whole Empire would automatically support the mother country in any war which the British Government in London thought advisable or necessary. In 1922, Lloyd George (the Liberal Prime Minister who had taken over in 1915 to lead Britain to victory in 1918) still headed a coalition government of Liberals and Conservatives and – for various and insufficient reasons – was determined to help the Greeks to acquire territory at the expense of the Turks who had been Germany's allies in World War I. In August 1922, the Turks, rejuvenated by their new leader Kemal Ataturk, attacked the Greeks in Smyrna, formerly Turkish territory. This brought the Turks close to a British outpost at Chanak on the eastern side of the Dardanelles.

The British were in Chanak to enforce the Treaty of Sèvres which had purported to settle the outcome of World War I in the Middle East in which Greece and Turkey had been involved on opposite sides. Lloyd George, strongly pro-Greek, decided to declare war on Turkey. He assumed that the Empire would endorse his decision without hesitation. This did not happen. Only New Zealand responded automatically and at once.[2] The Australian Prime Minister rebuked Lloyd George in the strongest terms for suggesting that Australia should join in a British war with which Australians were not concerned. The South African Prime Minister Jan Smuts responded with the equivalent of a diplomatic illness. He would not be able to reply to the British Government's request for troops to be used against Turkey until after his return from a visit to the Transvaal which would take at least a fortnight. The Canadians prevaricated too. The then powerful India office in Whitehall, strongly supported by the Viceroy, argued that it would not be possible to expect the Indian army, largely Moslem, to take up arms against another Islamic country – Turkey.

None of these disputes was publicly acknowledged at the time. But the Chanak incident marked the beginning of a family quarrel within the British Empire, which weakened it. The mother country's children were no longer prepared to go to war simply because mother said so. In fact, Britain did not go to war over Chanak. In fact, also, it was the end for Lloyd George and the beginning of the end for the Liberal party as a potential British government. The Conservatives in Lloyd George's coalition rebelled against him (not only because of Chanak) and prevailed.

Hardly anyone in the West realized or understood at the time what was happening to the British Empire. Still less did the west understand what was happening in Russia. The Russian Revolution of 1917 appeared to be a victory for Communists who believed in world revolution and who were dedicated to work for it. The acknowledged leaders of the victorious Bolsheviks, Lenin and Trotsky, had maintained throughout publicly and sincerely their firm belief that revolution against capitalism could not succeed in one country only. For socialism to carry the day the workers in every country would have to band together to overthrow the capitalist system everywhere.

When the Bolsheviks took over power in October 1917, Russia was still at war with Germany. It was Lenin's belief that the German workers, inspired by the Russian workers' example, would revolt as well, overthrowing the German government and joining hands with the successful Russian revolutionaries. Instead, the German workers continued to obey the orders of their capitalist and military masters. They simply went on to defeat the Russian army.

The Treaty of Brest-Litovsk under which the Russian Bolsheviks acknowledged their country's defeat by Germany was a double disappointment to Lenin. His country had been beaten. His theory that the workers' revolt would inevitably spread from one country to another had been disproved.

The fact that the theory had been shown to be wrong did not, however, prevent the Bolshevik leaders and communist leaders in other countries from continuing to preach the doctrine of world revolution. Communists throughout the world went on assuring each other that the Red Dawn would come. Capitalist governments throughout the world continued to take this imagined threat seriously. In practice, the harsh difficulties of governing a backward continent combined with the effects of internal quarrels were obliging the Russian leaders to concentrate more and more upon their own internal problems. Russia, above most other European powers, had an interest in preserving peace. After the revolution of 1917, the Bolsheviks' main task was to modernize the remnants of Tsarist Russia.

Socially and economically the Tsars had left Russia in the eighteenth century. The man who brought it into the twentieth was Josef Stalin. Unlike Lenin and Trotsky, Stalin was not an intellectual or even a theorist. He was not even, strictly speaking, a Russian. Unlike Lenin he had spent the whole of World War I in Russia. Unlike Lenin and Trotsky he did not belong to the intellectual community of St Petersburg. He was a Georgian, the son of a cobbler, an underdog come to town. He seems to have taken no important part in the doctrinal quarrels which rent the Bolshevik leadership during the 1920's. Stalin, who had never been abroad, never seemed to have had much faith in the theories of Lenin (who had) about the inevitability of world revolution.

By 1928 Stalin had effectively gained supreme power in the Soviet Union. He seems to have made up his mind that the fomenting of world revolution was a waste of time, or at least that it was a less important task than that of transforming Russia from a backward, pastoral state into a modern industrial one. This was a formidable task. Stalin, who was not interested in democracy as such, performed it and completed it by using much the same methods as the Tsars would have used. At the same time he did not make it clear either to his followers or to the Western world that he thought the Leninist theory of world revolution was rubbish. What he was not doing – but what the West thought he was doing – was trying to spread subversion in other countries. The West saw Bolsheviks behind every bush when, in fact, the Russians were trying to perfect the caterpillar tractor. When the British trade unions called a general strike in support of the miners in 1926, the Government supposed that Bolshevism was around the corner for Britain. In fact, the unions were simply concerned that the pay of a day wage miner in, say, Durham should not be cut from 9s 3d to 6s 10d per shift.

The Western powers' suspicion that Bolshevism was imminent everywhere was an illusion which helped considerably to bring about World War II. The Western Governments believed not only that the Russians were plotting to overthrow the capitalist system in all countries but that because of its inherent inefficiency the Communist system as explained by Lenin must weaken Russia economically and not strengthen it. In fact, Stalin, convinced as he was that world revolution would not come and that Russia would have to go it alone, had begun to transform the Soviet Union into the second most important industrial power in the world.

His first Five Year Plan, introduced in 1928, was designed to make the Soviet Union independent of foreign industry and strong enough, if necessary, to resist any attack. A. J. P. Taylor has argued convincingly that the first plan and its successors ensured Germany's eventual defeat in World War II.[3] But the West's suspicions of Russia effectively prevented co-operation during the 1920's and 1930's between France and Britain and the one major continental power whose strength could have deterred Hitler.

In 1936, Stalin started a great purge of the Soviet Communist party. Almost all the heroes of the 1917 revolution were imprisoned, executed, or exiled to Siberia. Stalin probably feared that he was being plotted against. All dictators do from time to time. Stalin may well have been right. At all events the purge was sudden, complete and spectacular. A year later Stalin turned on the army, starting with the Chief of Staff, Marshal Tukhachevsky, who was shot. Only two of the thirteen army commanders survived. Most divisional commanders were also disposed of. Stalin decapitated his army.

To the West, Stalin's motives were and are an awesome mystery. But at the time the West drew one conclusion, a mistaken one. 'Nearly every Western observer', A. J. P. Taylor wrote, 'was convinced that Soviet Russia was useless as an ally: her ruler a savage and unscrupulous dictator, her armies in chaos, her political system likely to collapse at the first strain.'[4]

The conclusion was wrong, as the Red Army was to prove, but the Western observers cannot really be blamed for their mistake. Stalin never explained his motives. He simply killed his generals and left the world (and the Soviet peoples) to wonder why. The West's mistake was, however, a serious matter. It meant that in 1939 – when Russia and the Western Allies really did need each other's help – the Western Allies believed that Russian help was not worth having. What Stalin had done was to replace older generals by younger ones. Marshal Timoshenko became Defence Commissar and a Marshal at the age of forty-five. It is true that he was not promoted until his surviving elders had made a disastrous mess of a campaign against Finland in 1939. But the Red Army's new leaders were not generally incompetent and when the time came the army itself was not in chaos.

Suspicion of the Soviet Union and disbelief in its power continued even during the last-minute attempts by Britain to form an Anglo-Soviet alliance in the late summer of 1939. The Western powers believed the Soviet Union to be weak when it was actually strong. They believed that the Soviet Union was bent on world revolution when its real concern was self-defence and the improvement of the condition of the Russian peoples.

Hitler comes to Power

The new German regime, the Weimar Republic, began badly. It lacked popular roots. Unlike most other democracies the Weimar Republic, which came into being in 1919, following the Treaty of Versailles, was not the result of a popular revolt against autocracy. The Germans had not won their democratic freedom for themselves. They had had it imposed upon them, given to them, in effect, by the victorious allies, who – although they tolerated the continuance of a more or less unchanged German State – only insisted upon, or would only have insisted upon, the abdication of the German Emperor whose government had started World War I. The fragmented political parties of the Weimar Republic were the successors to the impotent parties which had existed before 1918. The Reichstag, as the new parliament continued to be called, was divided on almost every issue and became with time an object of derision. For all their good intentions the German statesmen of the immediate post-World War I period did not seem to the German people to know where they were going. Hitler, who did know where he wanted to go, attempted to seize power unconstitutionally in what came to be known as the Beer Hall Putsch in 1923. The attempt failed. Hitler was sent to prison for nine months which he used to write *Mein Kampf*, the political programme on which he came to power. The failure of the Beer Hall Putsch was a lesson which Hitler took to heart. He decided then and there that he would achieve power by legitimate means even if this meant that he would have to wait for it.

He waited ten years. By 1933 the world economic situation had gone from bad to worse. The German inflation and the monetary muddles of the early 1920's had been succeeded by a general world depression in trade. It was a period during which governments assumed that the resumption of business as usual also meant the resumption of unemployment as usual. Workers were seen as a commodity like any other. A surplus of coal or coffee meant that the price of coal or coffee would come down. A surplus of labour – unemployment in other words – meant that the cost of labour would come down. Even in the 1920's this was seen as a natural economic law, unchangeable by man.

The accepted economic wisdom of the day was that if trade declined and business was bad the only remedy was to economise in every direction. The consequence for the capitalist societies of the West was to make a bad situation worse. The arguments between the Allies and the argument between the Allies and Germany about reparations were made irrelevant by the great depression which overtook the world's markets in October 1929. The value of shares on the American stock market dwindled at a terrifying rate. Apprehension spread like the plague from market to market. Within days the Western world's investors had been impoverished by forces they did not understand.

Most governments reacted according to the received wisdom of the day. This was to reduce public spending instead of expanding it and to cling to the concept of a currency backed by an equivalent amount of gold. In Britain Ramsay MacDonald's Labour Government disintegrated in uncertainty and was replaced by a National Coalition Government also led by MacDonald. The entire British public service was ordered to take a cut in salaries and accepted almost without demur. The only serious objectors were the sailors of the British home fleet and King George V The Fleet mutinied half-heartedly at Invergordon where it was assembled· The King did better. He told his ministers that he was prepared to take a cut in the money that the Government allowed him but that he was not prepared to take the full cut proposed. He threatened to disband the beefeaters, the traditional wardens of the Tower of London, and to sell his horses which were essential to the Royal ceremonials of those days.[5] The King won. The sailors lost.

The nation as a whole experienced further retrenchment, more unemployment and more misery. Most other capitalist countries shared the British experience. Only in the United States did President Roosevelt boldly question the accepted economic doctrine that the answer to depression was to restrict public spending. Roosevelt's New Deal expanded public spending, public works and public enterprise in ways which the orthodox economists of that time had never conceived to be possible. John Maynard Keynes of Cambridge University, England, was one of the few economists – the leading prophet among them – who contended that retrenchment in public spending was likely to make a depression worse not better. The Europeans did not listen to Keynes. Roosevelt went ahead with his Tennessee Valley Project and with a major public works programme. The European governments behaved as MacDonald's behaved. Retrenchment was the fashionable remedy. Rising unemployment was the result throughout Europe. And it was worst in Germany.

This was Hitler's chance. At successive general elections during the late 1920's Hitler had promised full employment without really knowing how to attain it. At successive general elections the popular support for his National Socialist (Nazi) party grew until, following the election of September 1930, it became the second strongest party in the Reichstag.

Hitler's chance to become Germany's dictator came when a number of European banks failed following the closure of the Austrian Credit-Anstalt in May 1931. The general world depression spread throughout Europe. In Germany between 1930 and 1932 the average rate of unemployment was 33%. Hitler, who had consistently preached that unemployment was unnecessary, was in a strong political position. In the 1930 election he increased his Nazi party's parliamentary representation from 12 to 107. By 1932 the Nazi party had won 230 seats and was the biggest in the Reichstag. On 30 January 1933 President Hindenburg – an ageing hero of World War I – offered the Chancellorship of Germany to Hitler. From this date onwards, Hitler being the man he was, World War II became likely though not yet inevitable.

Hitler had used the constitutional processes of the Weimar Republic to gain power, but he did not intend to allow the same processes to hold him back in the future. His party activists, the para-military Sturm-abteilungen or S.A., treated non-Nazis, and Jews in particular, at first roughly and then, with growing confidence, violently. Hitler supported the S.A. publicly. He even sent a telegram of sympathy and support to two Nazis who had kicked to death a Communist, in the presence of his mother. Soon after he became Chancellor Hitler persuaded the Reichstag to grant him what amounted to supreme power to run Germany. When Hindenburg died in 1934, Hitler made himself President as well as Chancellor, effectively took command of all the German armed forces, and called himself 'Führer', or leader of the German people.

Mussolini and the Rome–Berlin Axis

Hitler had used apparently constitutional means. His Italian counterpart Benito Mussolini had seized power for himself. His Italian Fascist party had probably used more force and intimidation on the streets than Hitler's S.A. From 1919 until 1922, aided like Hitler by the general fear of Bolshevism, the Italian Fascists extended their political and physical power. In October 1922 they 'marched' on Rome and threatened in effect to start a civil war unless the king appointed them to govern Italy.

King Victor Emmanuel gave in. Mussolini consolidated his position quickly and skilfully. His 'corporate state' absorbed the trade unions into organizations which were virtually controlled by the Fascist party. Fascists took control of the Civil Service. Mussolini imprisoned any politician or trade unionist whom he suspected might resist. In 1924, the Italian Socialist Giacomo Matteotti was simply slain. Mussolini even sent assassins to France to kill two brothers, Carlo and Nello Rosselli, after Carlo had escaped from imprisonment on a Mediterranean island.

Mussolini was a tyrant and a dictator who did Italy a great deal of harm. At first, however, he gave the Italians at least some of the things that they wanted and needed. He restored order, which was not very difficult because the disorders which had preceded his march on Rome had been caused largely by his own followers. He also started a much needed public works programme. Part of it consisted of grandiose public buildings which Italy could not really afford, but it also included a quite large effort to restore prosperity to the poorer, southern parts of Italy which had been neglected by the central government. Grateful British tourists said that he had made the trains run on time.

Mussolini, like Hitler, was an opportunist. Like Hitler he preferred easy victories to difficult ones. Unlike Hitler, however, he did not pretend that the Italians were a master race. His philosophy did not tell him that he was destined to dominate Europe or anywhere else in particular. In foreign affairs Mussolini's chief motive was greed.

When Hitler came to power in 1933, and to absolute power in 1934, Mussolini was at first mistrustful of his intentions. Italy had been one of the victorious powers in 1918 and had signed the Treaty of Versailles. Mussolini was perhaps the first European statesman to comprehend that Hitler's immediate aim was to change the Versailles settlement in Germany's favour. In June 1933, when Hitler was Chancellor but not yet Führer, Mussolini tried to persuade France, Great Britain and Germany to agree that these four powers alone could alter the provisions of the Treaty. Formally they could only be changed by the League of Nations. Nothing much came of these negotiations. But nearly two years later, in April 1935 at Stresa, Italy, France and Britain undertook to resist jointly 'any unilateral repudiation of treaties, which may endanger the peace of Europe'. The so-called Stresa front was actually a sham. On 16 April 1935, two days after the Stresa conference ended, Hitler repudiated the Versailles Treaty by reintroducing conscription and launching a rearmament programme.

It is not clear whether Mussolini really wanted to restrain Hitler although at the time of the Stresa meeting he was certainly worried lest Hitler should annex Austria, and with reason. In any case Mussolini was planning transgressions of his own. He had his eyes on Ethiopia. In 1935 Ethiopia, governed by the Emperor Haile Selassie, was the only large independent African State. It was the only piece of Africa left for Europeans to colonize. It had a common frontier with Italian Somaliland. Mussolini picked quarrels with Ethiopia with the intention of causing 'incidents' which could lead to war and conquest. But he feared, needlessly, that the League would stop him.

On 3 October 1935, after a ritual quarrel about a well, Italian troops invaded Ethiopia. The Ethiopians resisted valiantly. On 7 October the

Ethiopian delegate to the League Council asked that Italy's conduct should be condemned as aggression under Article 12 of the League covenant. On 11 October the Ethiopian complaint won the support of 50 of the League's 54 members. Only Italy, Albania, Austria and Hungary voted against. The question of sanctions, joint measures by all members of the League to deter Italy, was referred to a co-ordinating committee. The committee rejected the only sanction that would have been effective, the closure of the Suez Canal, then controlled by Britain, because it was likely to lead to war. Probably in France and certainly in Britain public opinion was on Ethiopia's side. The 'peace ballot', a referendum organised by the League of Nations Union and other organizations which supported the League and its principles, had just shown that at least 6·7 million British citizens favoured military sanctions by the League against aggressors and that 10 million favoured economic sanctions. The League of Nations Union and the 'peace ballot' enjoyed at least nominal support from all political parties in Britain. The Conservatives, returned to power in the general election of 14 November 1935 with a very large majority of 247 (in a House of Commons of rather more than 600 members), decided that Prime Minister Stanley Baldwin's new government ought to take account of this expression of popular feeling.

What the government did in collusion with the French was to attempt to carve up Ethiopia behind the Emperor's back. In December the then British Foreign Secretary, Sir Samuel Hoare, and the French one, Pierre Laval, meeting secretly in Paris (while Hoare was supposed to be skating in Switzerland), agreed that they would offer Mussolini very large parts of Ethiopia in return for his promise to stop the war. If Mussolini agreed they would put the same points to the Emperor. If the Emperor disagreed he would be seen – or could be made to appear – as the warmonger, the national leader who refused peace when it was offered to him. By this betrayal of the Ethiopians, Hoare and Laval hoped to assuage public opinion in their countries. In fact their plan had the opposite result.

Hoare had scarcely got his skates on in Switzerland before the news of the Hoare-Laval pact as it was called was leaked to the newspapers, perhaps by the French Foreign Office – perhaps by the British one. There was public outcry in both countries. On 18 December Baldwin had to sack Hoare. In Paris the Government itself barely survived. Hoare was replaced by Sir Anthony Eden (later Lord Avon), a known supporter of the League and its principle of collective security. Diplomatically Mussolini had lost out. Militarily, he was not doing well either. The Italians had expected a walk-over. In fact they did not reach the Ethiopian

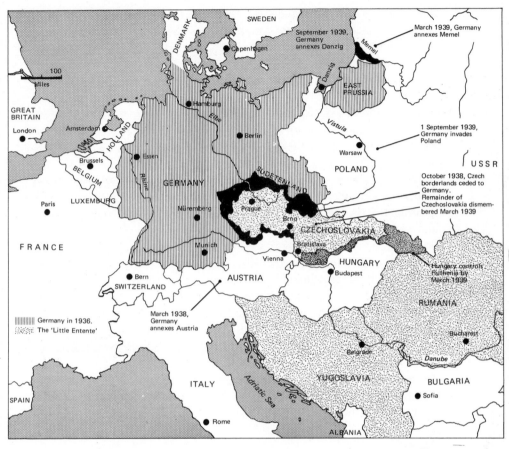

Europe 1936–9

capital, Addis Ababa, until May 1936; but no one except the Ethiopians themselves had tried to stop them.

In Ethiopia the League's collective resolve had foundered because its militarily effective members – Britain and France – had shrunk from risking war when the risk was small. From then on – as Hitler and Mussolini provoked one new crisis after another – the risk of war increased until, in September 1939, it became a certainty.

Hitler had stated his intentions almost as soon as he came to power. He became Chancellor on 30 January 1933. On 3 February he told the army Chief of Staff, General von Hammerstein, and the other responsible military leaders, that he intended to restore German might and to use it to conquer new living space in the East which could be 'Germanized'

15

regardless of the consequences. To make this possible the youth of Germany must be converted to the belief that only battle could save their country. The 'cancer' of democracy must be abolished. Rearmament was the essential pre-requisite for the achievement of these goals because without military power Germany could not exercise political power.

In August 1934, following Hindenburg's death, Hitler made all German servicemen swear an oath of personal loyalty to him as Führer. In the spring of 1935 he reintroduced conscription and started to re-arm in earnest. A year later, while Mussolini was still trying to conquer Ethiopia, Hitler re-occupied the Rhineland which had been de-militarized under the Versailles Treaty. This was another direct breach of the Treaty. Neither Britain nor France lifted a finger to stop him. Rightly, perhaps, the two Governments surmised that public opinion in their countries would not endorse or support a war fought to keep German soldiers out of German territory. Italy, the third member of the now-hopeless Stresa front, was busy elsewhere. Later in the year – and after Mussolini had finally conquered Ethiopia – Hitler established the Rome–Berlin axis of Fascist States. In November he signed a similar pact – the Anti-Comintern Pact – with Japan. On paper, at any rate, the German–Italian–Japanese Alliance was in existence, already formidable, already preparing hard for war, the Aggressors' International. When the time came for war itself, Mussolini turned out to be a grave embarrassment to Hitler. Germany never helped Japan. Japan never helped Germany. But from 25 November 1936, the Alliance existed for all to see, and for all to judge.

Rearmament

Hitler's re-occupation of the Rhineland, like Mussolini's invasion of Ethiopia, had shown that the League of Nations – for all its popular support in many countries – did not command the loyalty of the two Governments, those of France and Britain, which would have been necessary to make sanctions work. Each Government was in a dilemma, or believed that it was in one.

The French army, though strong and numerous, was organized mainly, perhaps only, for the defence of France; the French Government and the French Chief of Staff shrank from any more daring enterprise. The British armed forces had been instructed by the Government to organize and plan their requirements and operational developments on the assumption that there would be no major war for the next ten years. It is true that in 1935 the British Government cancelled this assumption and stated in a White Paper that Britain would re-arm because war might come soon. But rearmament did not begin effectively at once, partly because Baldwin had taken fright at the outcome of the peace ballot (which he may have misinterpreted to mean that the British were not prepared to fight for any cause) but partly also for technical reasons. The kind of rearmament that Britain needed to undertake in 1935 was more sophisticated than ever before. The weapons needed were aircraft like the Spitfire, the high-performance fighter which was to win the Battle of Britain, and which could not be produced over-night. A design programme had to precede production. It was no longer possible, as it had been before World War I, simply to order a new battleship, pay for it and get it.

British rearmament began in 1936 but in an unco-ordinated way. When Hitler reoccupied the Rhineland, Baldwin, yielding to parliamentary pressure, had appointed a minister, Sir Thomas Inskip, to co-ordinate the three defence services. Sir Thomas had no department and not much power except a seat in the Cabinet. In the event he was able only to preside over meetings of the service Chiefs of Staff, and to endorse the outcome of their debates. This resulted to begin with in more money for the air force and the navy and in not much more for the army. The navy and the air force were able to justify their need for modern equipment to counter the modern equipment that Germany was building. The army could only say that it must enlarge itself hugely if it was to be required to fight a major continental war. But a large army was something the Cabinet did not want to know about. Even in the mid-1930's when Hitler was urgently building tanks the notion horrified British ministers. The result was that in money terms the army came off badly.

In 1938, just twenty months before the outbreak of war, Inskip reported to the Cabinet that the two British divisions earmarked for war on the Continent had no infantry tanks, were 90% deficient in new machine guns, and 85% deficient in mortar ammunition. The British Expeditionary Force, as the two divisions were called, was also '100% deficient' in infantry tanks. Inskip said that the Chiefs of Staff had said that an expeditionary force of two divisions was 'the maximum force which could be mobilized as a complete force for service overseas'.[6] Three months after the outbreak of war, the Chiefs of Staff predicted, a cavalry light tank regiment might have become available as well. By that time too, the 'tank brigade' would have been equipped with tanks which would nevertheless be 'obsolete', and twelve territorial army battalions would be available but would be under strength and would have no modern equipment.

The Chiefs of Staff estimated that if war came Germany could put 39 divisions into the field immediately and would have 79 under arms within a week. The corresponding figures for France were 16 and 33; for Belgium 1 and 15. Britain, the Chiefs of Staff said, would be able to field two divisions but not until between twenty and thirty days after the outbreak of war. In spite of this gloomy assessment of Britain's military capabilities on land the Cabinet decided not to increase the army allocations. At what seems to have been the decisive Cabinet meeting (on 16 February 1938) Sir Thomas appears not to have supported the Chiefs of Staffs' request for more money for the army. The Prime Minister (by then Neville Chamberlain, Baldwin having resigned in May 1937) said that the Government was in a dilemma. If it accepted the advice of the defence departments there would be an 'unbearable strain on financial resources'. If the Government reduced the defence departments' demands 'we run into the possibility of the danger of war'. Chamberlain said that in two years' time the financial situation might be even worse than it was then, and higher taxation would be very difficult and unpleasant. He said that he agreed with Sir Thomas to postpone an increase in arms expenditure because of his 'hope for some improvement on the international scene'.

By 1938 the international scene had been further complicated by the Spanish Civil War which had broken out in 1936. This was a conflict between the political left and the political right. General Franco, a Fascist of the Mussolini type, had attempted a revolution against the newly elected Popular Front Government of Spain. It was to have been a military *coup d'état* on the familiar South American pattern. But the Government resisted, and found many friends. So did Franco. Hitler and Mussolini sent soldiers and air force units to help him. The Russians sent aid to the Government. Many British volunteers also fought for the Government. The Spanish Civil War and its outcome became a burning political issue in Britain.

The Spanish question became, in its tragic way, a distraction. The British Government, having failed to do anything to deter Mussolini in Ethiopia or Hitler from entering the Rhineland, preached non-intervention in Spain. The Labour party urged the opposite, accusing Baldwin of favouring a Fascist dictator. During the quarrel the most important military lesson of the Spanish war was ignored in Britain. Hitler was using it as an experimental battle ground, a war-game. German weapons and German tactics, later to be used in World War II, were first tried out in Spain. The Stuka single-engined dive bomber designed as a mobile substitute for army artillery was used first in Spain and scored its first successes there.

The Spanish Civil War divided Britain but not Germany. Anthony Eden, who had succeeded Hoare as Foreign Secretary, resigned in February 1938 after a dispute with the rest of the Cabinet about whether or not to speak sharply to Mussolini about his behaviour in Ethiopia and Spain. He was replaced by Lord Halifax. The German Government, on the other hand, had no hesitations about Spain.

On 5 November 1937 Hitler once more summoned his generals to hear his basic, strategic aims. According to the minutes of this important meeting,[7] Hitler said that the object of German policy must be the security, preservation and expansion of the German race. This would entail conquest. The German race, Hitler is quoted as saying, comprised more than 85 million people representing a 'racial nucleus' which had a better right than any other to 'living space'. The only solution to the German problem, Hitler is further quoted as saying, was force. Germany's first objective must be to subject (*niederzuwerfen*) Austria and Czechoslovakia in order to obviate any possible threat to Germany's flanks if an attack towards the West should become necessary. The British Government knew nothing of this and suspected nothing.

Chamberlain

Much of the blame for the outbreak of World War II has been attributed to the 'appeasers' in the British Government during the late 1930's. The man in charge was Neville Chamberlain who succeeded Baldwin in May 1937. His principal adviser was his eventual Foreign Secretary, Lord Halifax. These two statesmen were mainly responsible for British foreign policy during the two and a half years which preceded the outbreak of war in September 1939. It is proper, therefore, that they should share what blame there is to be shared. Chamberlain's biographer, the late Iain Macleod, defends him.[8] Others accuse him. Chamberlain certainly did appease Hitler. He certainly did persuade the Czechs to accept the Munich Agreement which was unjust. But he was not a coward. He was a very strong Prime Minister indeed.

One reason for Chamberlain's mistakes in his dealings with Hitler – and mistakes they were – was that he lived and worked in a cocoon of yes-men. A meticulous study of his long premiership by Ian Colvin[9] shows that in two and a half years Chamberlain never once changed his mind because of what had been said in Cabinet meetings. For most of the critical thirty months which preceded the outbreak of World War II, Chamberlain decided his own policy either alone or with the help of three like-minded politicians – Lord Halifax, Sir Samuel Hoare and Sir John Simon. These three took turns, as it were, at the Foreign Office. None of them disagreed with Chamberlain's basic philosophy. This was that Hitler was a statesman like any other, nurturing national ambitions but open to reason like any head of Government, and therefore fundamentally 'appeasable'.

However, Hitler was none of these things. Other British politicians, notably Anthony Eden and Winston Churchill, knew this. So did Sir Robert Vansittart, a senior member of the British diplomatic service who suspected Hitler's motives from the beginning and who never ceased to warn his political masters that Germany, under Hitler, was bent on war.

Chamberlain knew that these intelligent men disagreed with his policies. Prime Ministers are no more obliged than anyone else to accept advice they dislike. But Chamberlain went further. He refused to listen to it. Churchill, Eden and Vansittart were banished from his counsels. He listened instead to people who agreed with him on the fundamental principle that Hitler was 'appeasable'. These were Halifax, Hoare, Simon, Sir Nevile Henderson (the British Ambassador in Berlin) and Sir Horace Wilson, a special adviser from the Ministry of Labour whose views and intelligence Chamberlain prized highly. Chamberlain isolated himself, to the public danger, from advice that he did not want to hear. He surrounded himself, perhaps unconsciously, with yes-men. The advice he got was not really advice at all. His colleagues urged him to do what he himself had wanted to do in the first place. The reasoned alternative was missing.

A Prime Minister who does this is in peril. Mr Colvin explains why: 'Chamberlain was a shy autocrat and made his own policy in silence before he made it Cabinet policy. If appeasement began as a common Cabinet policy, it was he who gave it such emphasis as to add a pejorative sense to the word. I can find, moreover, no example in two and a half years of Cabinet meetings in which the discussions in Cabinet altered his mind on a subject, though he was known to alter it between Cabinets. . . . We must accept that his vision may have been distorted in a field where every error is grave and that his timing was probably wrong. . . . The three broad issues upon which the Chamberlain Cabinet stands at the bar of history are that with a large Parliamentary majority it failed to rearm in time; that it surrendered over Czechoslovakia in 1938, when it need not so have done; and that it failed in 1939 to achieve an alliance with Russia, thus entering war with less effective Allies than could have been found in 1938. . . .'

Colvin argues that Chamberlain's Cabinet was allowed to discuss but not to choose. After Chamberlain had promised to meet Hitler in Berchtesgaden to discuss the fate of Czechoslovakia, he simply told the Cabinet that he was on his way.[10] His colleagues had no option but to let him go. He did not want to hear about alternative courses of action. So he arranged not to hear about them.

Chamberlain was honest about the way he treated his colleagues and the principle, such as it is, of Cabinet Government. 'I saw that the moment had come', Chamberlain said, 'and must be taken if I was not to be too late. So I sent the fateful telegram and told the Cabinet next morning what I had done.'[11] He need not have worried. He was surrounded already by yes-men. Only Duff Cooper, First Lord of the Admiralty, objected and subsequently resigned.

Appeasement

On 12 March 1938 Hitler sent his armies into Austria. Two days later the country had been overrun and Austria was proclaimed a part of the German Reich. Hitler's preparations for this (his first) enlargement of Germany, had been brief and brutal. He demanded of the Austrian Chancellor Schuschnigg, a Social Democrat, a number of key posts in his administration for Austrian Nazis. Schuschnigg refused and proposed instead that the Austrians should be asked whether they wanted to join Germany or to stay independent. Hitler objected to a referendum. Schuschnigg complied. Thereafter, and with no shred of a popular mandate to justify his actions, Hitler simply appointed from Berlin his own Austrian Nazi nominee, Dr Seyss-Inquart to be Chancellor of Austria. Seyss-Inquart invited the German army in. Both Italy and Britain were indifferent. Lord Halifax had already assured Hitler that Britain would not intervene. He was as good as his word. Hitler's first conquest was easy.

His next acquisition, that of Czechoslovakia, was harder – but not much. The British Cabinet papers for 1938 show plainly that in the quarrel that Hitler then picked with Czechoslovakia Britain took Hitler's side, secretly but effectively. Initially the quarrel was about the Sudetenland, a border area inhabited largely by people of German origin which had been transferred to Czechoslovakia in 1918. Throughout the early part of 1938 Hitler was fomenting trouble in Czechoslovakia through his agent there, Konrad Henlein. 'I wonder sometimes', said the British Ambassador in Berlin, Sir Nevile Henderson, in a secret despatch to Halifax, 'whether we are backing Henlein enough in London.'

Sir Nevile need not have worried. Chamberlain was determined from the beginning to help Hitler to dismember Czechoslovakia. But he did not want to be seen doing this. He was frightened of the House of Commons. He was still to some extent frightened of what his own Cabinet colleagues – or some of them – might say. On the other hand he did not want simply to stand aside as he had stood aside when Hitler invaded Austria. He wanted the Czechs to give in without a fight lest there should be a 'major disturbance', as Halifax had put it. He was determined to put pressure on the Czechs to accept Hitler's demands but he was equally determined that no one at home should know what he was doing.

The leader of the Labour opposition in the British House of Commons, Clement Attlee, was suspicious. He asked the Government to publish a White Paper setting out the facts about its negotiations with Czechoslovakia. By 27 September 1938 Chamberlain felt obliged to grant Attlee's request. But the document was censored. Chamberlain decided 'to print the White Paper as in proof, subject to the excision of the message sent by the Czech Government accepting the Franco-British proposals'. This document would have to be omitted since it referred to 'the strong and continuous pressure' put upon the Czech Government by French and British representatives. If this was printed it would lead to a demand for the telegrams to the French and British ministers in Prague urging them to apply pressure.

While the British Embassy in Prague and Chamberlain's special envoy there, Lord Runciman, were 'applying strong and continuous pressure' on the Czech Premier, Dr Benes, Chamberlain himself was conferring with Hitler. He was secretive about this too. Having decided to visit Hitler he did not want to give his Cabinet colleagues a chance to dissuade him. The plan for his visit – 'Plan Z' – was prepared by Chamberlain and his three closest friends, Sir John Simon, Sir Samuel Hoare and Lord Halifax. Other members of the Cabinet only got to hear of Plan Z on the eve of Chamberlain's first visit to Hitler at Berchtesgaden in Bavaria, on 15 September. Chamberlain told them that he thought that it might be agreeable to Hitler's vanity if a British Prime Minister were to take the unprecedented step of visiting him in person. The Cabinet records report Chamberlain as saying that he would have to make it clear to Hitler that he could not speak for Dr Benes, but that he would undertake to put all the pressure he could on Dr Benes to give in. In fact he was doing this already.

The Cabinet's response to Plan Z was enthusiastic. The Lord Chancellor, Lord Maugham, said it was a 'magnificent proposal'. Simon, Chancellor of the Exchequer, called it 'brilliant'. Inskip said that Britain could not protect Czechoslovakia and that that country, once overrun, would never be reconstituted in its existing form. The only minister who remained unimpressed was the First Lord of the Admiralty, Duff Cooper. He said that the only choice open to Britain was 'war now or war later'. Next morning Chamberlain flew to Berchtesgaden.

When he got back Chamberlain told his colleagues that Hitler was excited but not mad. Hitler's objectives, Chamberlain said, seemed strictly limited. However, Hitler had said that any serious incident would release the 'spring' of the German military machine and the pincers would close on Czechoslovakia. Once the machine had been put in motion nothing could stop it, Hitler had said to Chamberlain. Chamberlain had offered to try to separate the Sudetenland from the rest of Czechoslovakia. But, Chamberlain said, any discussion of this offer in the British Parliament would wreck the negotiations. So Parliament would hear about the Government's decisions after they had been taken. Once again Duff Cooper was the only objector. He said he did not believe that the Sudetenland was Hitler's last aim. After all, Duff Cooper said, Hitler had promised not to attack Austria and had broken his promise. 'There was no chance of peace in Europe as long as there was a Nazi regime in Germany', Duff Cooper said.

Duff Cooper was almost alone. Inskip said that a war to deter Hitler might produce changes which would be satisfactory to no one except the Bolsheviks. Lord Runciman, still on his mission to Czechoslovakia, said that Benes was widely mistrusted whereas Henlein was 'genial and good tempered'. Runciman said that Czechoslovakia could not continue to exist as she was and something would have to be done, 'even if it amounted to no more than cutting off certain fingers'.

On 22 September Chamberlain flew to Germany to meet Hitler again, this time at Bad Godesberg near Bonn. Reporting on this second meeting he told the Cabinet that he thought he 'had established some degree of personal influence over Herr Hitler'. He said he thought that Hitler trusted him and was willing to work with him and that it would be a great tragedy if we lost this opportunity of understanding with Germany. Duff Cooper said he did not believe Hitler's promises; Hitler would not stop at any frontier which might result from any Czechoslovakian settlement.

B

The same day, Sir Horace Wilson flew to Berlin to follow up Chamberlain's conversations. Sir Horace saw Hitler, and reported: 'Herr Hitler had said that he had given sufficient assurances that this [the Sudetenland] was the last of his territorial aims in Europe. He had pledged his word to the Prime Minister and he had made the statement publicly. In Herr Hitler's view there were two alternatives. Either we [the British] persuaded Dr Benes to accept Hitler's memorandum demanding the occupation of the Sudetenland or there would be smash.' Sir Horace strongly advised the Government to send a telegram to Benes urging him to accept the occupation of the Sudetenland by the German Army. On 27 September the Government acted on Sir Horace's advice and sent the telegram. The next day Chamberlain told Parliament that he hoped to meet Hitler and Mussolini in Munich to settle the Czech crisis once and for all. Hitler (though Chamberlain did not say this) had refused even to allow Benes to attend the meeting at which his country was to be dismembered by Britain, Germany and Italy.

This was duly done at Munich on 29 and 30 September 1938. Chamberlain returned feeling triumphant on 30 September. He was welcomed at the airport by the Editor of *The Times*, Geoffrey Dawson, an ardent supporter of appeasement. At Buckingham Palace he was received by the King. Sir John Simon expressed his profound admiration for the Prime Minister's unparalleled efforts. Chamberlain said that he had done his best for Czechoslovakia and that the Munich meeting had been a triumph for diplomacy. Duff Cooper resigned from the Government immediately. Britain could not have stopped the German invasion of the Sudetenland which then immediately ensued; but Britain need not have acquiesced in the occupation or have helped it on its way.

War is declared

The summer of 1939 offered Chamberlain his last chance of averting a war with Germany by forming an alliance with Russia. On 15 March 1939, Hitler had finally dismembered Czechoslovakia, thus tearing up the Munich agreement which Chamberlain had just concluded. This convinced Lord Halifax, the Foreign Secretary, that if Hitler was to be stopped, Britain would need an ally in Eastern Europe. But, by what must now seem an extraordinary misjudgment, Halifax believed that Poland would prove to be a stronger ally than Russia. On 27 March 1939 Halifax told the British Cabinet's Foreign Policy Committee that

'If we had to make a choice between Poland and Soviet Russia, it seemed clear that Poland would give the greater value'.

The Minister of Defence, Admiral of the Fleet Lord Chatfield, supported Halifax. 'Russia', he reported on 25 April (in an assessment of the military strengths of the East European powers), 'although a Great Power for other purposes, was only a power of medium rank for military purposes. On the other hand the Chiefs of Staff could not deny that Russia's assistance in war would be of considerable, though not of great military value and the side with which she participated in war would undoubtedly fight better for her help'. The Parliamentary Secretary for Overseas Trade, R. S. Hudson, who had been on a trade mission to Moscow, was of the same opinion. At the end of March, Chamberlain told the Cabinet that 'Mr Hudson had informed him that while he had been treated in a friendly way by everyone in Russia, he had formed an impression that Russia would be of little or no assistance except for defensive purposes'. For himself, Chamberlain said that he had 'very considerable distrust of Russia, and had no confidence that we should obtain active and constant support from that country.'

At no time, apparently, did Halifax, Chatfield, Chamberlain or Hudson concede that perhaps the Russians knew more about Hitler than they did. The Russian Foreign Secretary, then Maxim Litvinov, had told Hudson in March 1939 that 'France was practically done for'. That country, Litvinov said, was full of German agents, disaffected and disunited. Litvinov foresaw that Europe would soon become entirely German from the Bay of Biscay to the Soviet frontier. Litvinov predicted further that even this would not satisfy Hitler's ambition. But the attack that he would then make would 'not be directed to the East'. Litvinov was wrong about the attack not being directed to the East. But in all other particulars he and the Russian foreign service were correct in their predictions. In May the Soviet Ambassador in London, Maisky, told Halifax that '. . . although Russia could win any war of defence, single-handed, they could not single-handed prevent war in general. She was therefore ready to collaborate with other powers for this purpose.' A. J. P. Taylor has delivered the written judgment that the diplomatic incompetence of the British Government during the rest of the summer of 1939, 'seems to have had no equal since Lord North lost the American colonies.'[12]

In March the Cabinet had realized for the first time, and with what seems to have been a sort of diplomatic shiver of dismay, that some sort of defensive agreement with the Bolsheviks might have to be considered. But the idea was distasteful. Chamberlain said that 'the impression left on his mind as to the probable attitude of both Poland and Russia was somewhat disagreeable. But of the two alternatives an arrangement with Poland seemed the lesser of the two evils.' Halifax said 'the essential point is to manage matters so as to secure the support of Poland'. He would also, however, take what steps he could to 'keep in with Russia'. The Cabinet agreed that it would be better if ministers would 'abstain from personal attacks on Herr Hitler and Signor Mussolini'. Halifax promised to try to see Maisky more often 'so as to avoid any suspicion that we are cold-shouldering the Russians.' The Cabinet's collective view seems to have been that Soviet help would be welcome if Hitler attacked Poland but that Britain ought not to commit herself to help the Soviet Union if the Soviet Union were attacked by Hitler. This, at any rate, was Chamberlain's view and no one seems to have disagreed with him. In effect the proposal was for a mutual assistance pact which would only work one way – in Britain's favour. Not unnaturally the Russians refused to accept this. Not unnaturally, they became suspicious.

In spite of his distaste for negotiations with the Russians, Chamberlain allowed them to continue fitfully. One reason he did not abandon the talks altogether seems to have been his justified fear that the House of Commons would want to know the reason why. The Cabinet papers for 1939 show clearly that the Government was particularly worried about parliamentary questions being asked by four M.P.s – Lloyd George, Winston Churchill, Attlee and Arthur Greenwood, Attlee's deputy. Meanwhile, the Russians were doing their mysterious best to explain to the British that unless they could conclude a mutual assistance pact with the Western Allies, and particularly with Britain, they might have to come to terms with Hitler. On 8 May, after hesitant negotiations had been going on for six weeks, the new Russian Foreign Secretary, Mr Molotov, told the British Ambassador in Moscow, Sir William Seeds that in his (Molotov's) opinion the British Government did not seem to be eager for agreement. Molotov went on to say that Soviet policy was liable to be altered if the other States (Britain and France) changed theirs.

As events were to show, this was a serious warning. It is not clear, even from the Cabinet papers, whether Halifax understood it properly. He may have done. At any rate on 5 June he suggested sending the head of the Foreign Office central department, William Strang, to reinforce Sir William in the talks that were going on in Moscow. Halifax did not want to send a minister because it would be 'undesirable to give the impression that we were running after the Russians'. A week later Maisky in London invited Halifax himself to join the talks in Moscow. Halifax refused.

The real difficulty was the one-sidedness of the British proposal. Britain wanted Russia's help if an attack on Poland led to a German attack on Britain and France but was not prepared to help Russia in the event of a German attack on the Soviet Union. The situation was further confused and complicated by the British Government's persistent delusions about Soviet Russia. Chamberlain and his ministers still thought of the Soviet Union as a country bent on promoting Communist revolutions all over the world. But Stalin's motives were not those inscribed in the tablets of the Bolshevik bible. By 1939 Stalin's chief concern was to defend his country by all means at his own disposal and, if other countries offered help and the offers seemed genuine, to accept them. The British offer did not seem genuine.

Strang reported from Moscow on 20 July: 'Their [the Russians'] distrust and suspicion of us has not diminished during the negotiations, nor, I think, has their respect for us increased. The fact that we have raised difficulty after difficulty on points which seem to them inessential, has created an impression that we may not be seriously seeking an agreement'.[10] At this stage the Russians had been asking the British Government to send a military mission to Moscow to discuss precise details of defence co-operation. After much hesitation, the British Government agreed, but not wholeheartedly. Halifax told his Cabinet colleagues that military talks would drag on until 'ultimately each side would accept a general undertaking from the other. In this way we should have gained time and made the best of a situation from which we could not now escape.' The situation from which he was wanting to escape was, in fact, the situation which he ought to have been trying to achieve – a firm undertaking that Britain and Russia would assist each other, if either was attacked by Hitler.

The man chosen to go to Moscow to gain time was Admiral Sir Reginald Ranfurly-Plunkett-Ernle-Erle-Drax, the King's principal naval aide-de-camp, and Commander-in-Chief at the Nore. He set off for Russia in an Ellerman Line steamer called the *City of Exeter*. Lord Chatfield could not spare a cruiser, had no suitable aircraft, hesitated to send the mission by train through Germany, and wanted to save money. Chartering the *City of Exeter* was the cheapest way as well as the slowest way of getting the mission to Moscow.

Sir Reginald found himself face to face with Marshal of the Soviet Union and Commander-in-Chief of the Red Army, Klementij Efremovich Voroshilov, the man responsible for the entire defence of the Soviet Union. The talks began on 12 August. Two days later Voroshilov asked the only question that mattered to him. 'Can the Red Army move across

Northern Poland . . . and across Galicia in order to make contact with the enemy?"[10] The Admiral did not know the answer. Halifax could not help him. The British Government did not want to offend the Poles. The Cabinet decided to leave the question unanswered and to wait and see what happened.

The question was, however, vital to the Russians. When it became clear that the British were not prepared to persuade the Poles to allow Russian troops to cross Polish territory to get at the Germans, Molotov and Stalin decided that they would have to change sides, and come to terms with Hitler. On 23 August, nine days after Sir Reginald had found himself without instructions and tongue-tied, the Russians signed a non-aggression pact with Germany.

The Russians were candid about their motives. As they saw it – and as Molotov had said on 8 May – Britain did not seem eager for a real agreement on mutual defence against Hitler. On 22 August Molotov explained to the British Ambassador Seeds why his Government had signed a non-aggression pact with Hitler. 'The height of [British] insincerity had been reached when the military missions arrived in Moscow empty-handed and, above all, quite unprepared to deal with fundamental points on which the whole question of reciprocal assistance depended, namely the passage of Soviet troops through Polish and Rumanian territory.'[10]

In making this request the Russians were being more punctilious than the Western Allies. They were seeking permission to do to the Poles and the Rumanians what the Allied Commander-in-Chief in the West, General Gamelin, intended to do to the Belgians whether the Belgians liked it or not. Both Voroshilov and Gamelin wanted to be free to move their armies forward to meet the German enemy on his own soil or, if not, on the soil of an intervening country. Seeds may not have known this, but Gamelin certainly would not have thought Voroshilov's request unreasonable.

Molotov went on to tell Seeds that the Soviet Government now had no option but to accept the proposed treaty with Germany, a proposal which caught the British Cabinet and the entire British diplomatic service unawares. Sir Reginald came home. There was nothing more to discuss.

Molotov and Hitler's Foreign Minister, von Ribbentrop, signed the Nazi-Soviet Pact on 23 August. Both Governments seem to have assumed that the Pact would deter the Western powers from coming to the assistance of Poland which could be safely dismembered and partitioned between them. But they were wrong. The British Government, which had consistently under-estimated Russia's military importance, felt rebuffed but decided also that the rebuff did not matter militarily. The French Government did nothing. The House of Commons reacted more strongly. Those Conservatives who had considered Hitler to be Europe's safeguard against Bolshevism were disillusioned and dismayed. Labour Members were dismayed that the Russians could have come to terms with Fascism. Chamberlain probably had no option but to do what the House of Commons wanted – which was to support the Poles. The day after the signing of the Nazi-Soviet Pact, Parliament gave Chamberlain full emergency powers. The next day, 25 August, the British Government signed a Treaty of Mutual Assistance with Poland. Hitler, who had intended to march that day on Poland, hesitated, but only for a week. Between 25 and 31 August he tried to persuade the Poles to give up territory without war. But they refused.

Hitler himself refused a last-minute British demand that he should withdraw his troops. After lunch on 2 September the British Cabinet decided to send an ultimatum to Hitler but did not actually do so. This time, again, the House of Commons took charge. That evening Chamberlain spoke from the Treasury bench about negotiations. He held out the hope of a further conference. But meanwhile Warsaw was being bombed. Britain's new ally was under attack. The House would listen no longer to Chamberlain's vague talk of peace. Members on both sides were angry and, in a way, ashamed. Arthur Greenwood, the Acting Leader of the Opposition, was urged by the Conservatives to 'speak for England'. He said that every minute's delay would imperil the very foundations of Britain's national honour. War must be declared at once.

The session was disorderly but the message was clear. If the Government could not pluck up the courage to declare war on Hitler in support of Poland, the Commons would rebel. The Cabinet knew this when it met again at 11 p.m. on 2 September. Once more the Cabinet decided to send an ultimatum and this time it was actually sent. It expired at 9 a.m. on 3 September. A French ultimatum expired at 5 p.m. the same day. Two of the self-governing dominions, Australia and New Zealand, followed suit. The South African Government wanted to stay neutral but was defeated in Parliament and the new Prime Minister, Smuts, declared war on Germany on 6 September. The Canadians followed suit on 10 September. Ireland, which still was a dominion, decided to stay neutral. World War II had begun, but for the time being the only military activity on land was in Eastern Europe. Hitler was not yet ready to attack anyone more formidable than the Poles. For the British at home this, the phoney war, began with a flurry of precautions against air-raids which did not come, and were not to come for another nine months.

Chapter 2

The Phoney War

To the British at home – where nearly all of them still were – the events of the winter of 1939–40 became known as 'the phoney war'. This is not to say that nothing happened in Britain to distinguish a state of war from a state of peace.

Rationing began. Children were evacuated from the cities to avoid bombs which did not fall. Britain was blacked out at night to deprive German pilots of navigational information they did not need.

At sea things were different. German submarines began to attack British merchant shipping. But the submarines were still few in number and did not then have the advantage in range and endurance which they were to enjoy when the Germans captured the Atlantic ports of France.

On the Western front in Europe the French army and the British Expeditionary Force contemplated but did not attack an inferior German army which, for most of the winter, had not a single tank. A friend of mine, eager to do his bit, joined the British army and was sent to Aldershot to learn to ride a horse.

This period of the war may have seemed phoney to the British; but it was real, horrifying and bitter for the Poles, the Esthonians, the Lithuanians, the Latvians, the Finns, the Danes, and the Norwegians. During the winter and spring of 1939–40 all these nations suffered invasion or defeat, or both.

Hitler began by attacking Poland, as he had said he would. Because of the Treaty of Versailles, Poland had access to the Baltic Sea at Gdynia through the so-called 'Polish Corridor' which divided East Prussia from the rest of Germany. In July 1939 Hitler sent strong forces by sea to East Prussia. He also assembled on the Polish borders what amounted to the entire striking force of the German army including all its best tank formations. Having already occupied Czechoslovakia he was able to threaten Poland not only from the north through East Prussia and from the west,

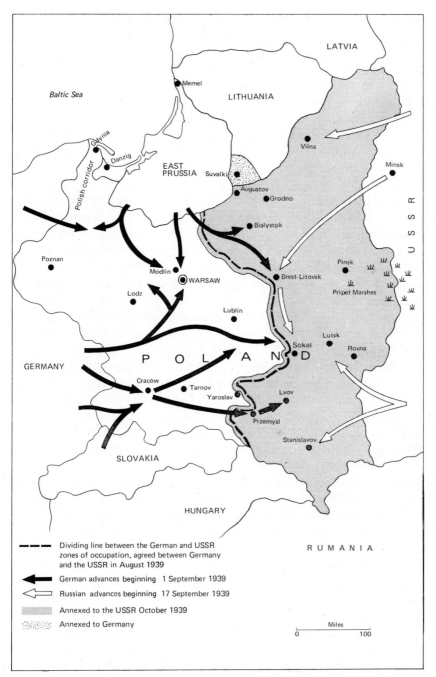

LATVIA

Baltic Sea

Memel

LITHUANIA

Gdynia

Danzig

Polish corridor

EAST PRUSSIA

Suvalki

Augustov

Grodno

Vilna

Minsk

USSR

Poznan

Modlin

WARSAW

Bialystok

Brest-Litovsk

Pinsk

Pripet Marshes

Lodz

Lublin

Lutsk

Rovna

Sokal

P O L A N D

GERMANY

Cracow

Tarnov

Yaroslav

Lvov

Przemysl

Stanislavov

SLOVAKIA

HUNGARY

RUMANIA

— — — Dividing line between the German and USSR
zones of occupation, agreed between Germany
and the USSR in August 1939

⬤ German advances beginning 1 September 1939

⬅ Russian advances beginning 17 September 1939

Annexed to the USSR October 1939

Annexed to Germany

Miles

0   100

The Invasion of Poland, 1939

but also from the south. But he could not move against Poland until he was sure that the Russians would not move against him.

The moment when his armies were cleared to go came on 23 August 1939, with the signing of the Nazi-Soviet Pact in Moscow. It was not only a non-aggression treaty, it also contained secret protocols which divided eastern Europe into German and Soviet spheres of influence. Most of Poland was to be German, the rest was to be Russian. Finland, Esthonia and Latvia were to be dominated by Russia. Lithuania was to be German, although – as a result of a subsequent German-Russian bargain – Lithuania's destiny was afterwards re-allocated to the Soviet Union.

Two days later on 25 August the British Government proclaimed the sanctity of Britain's alliance with Poland. It made no difference. Three days earlier, at Obersalzberg, Hitler had already given his generals their orders.[1] These were to destroy Poland in the shortest possible time. There were 35 million Poles. The Polish army was numerous but ill-equipped and the Polish air force was largely obsolete. The plan was for the German 4th Army to strike eastwards from Pomerania while the 3rd German Army struck westward from East Prussia to cut the Polish Corridor. The 8th, 10th and 14th German Armies were to strike north-eastwards from Slovakia and Silesia.

Almost everything went according to plan. The Luftwaffe began the attack early on 1 September destroying at one stroke almost the whole of the Polish air force. The Polish High Command, perhaps mistakenly, had decided to defend Poland's national territory in its entirety. The task was impossible. The Polish Government left Warsaw on 6 September. By 19 September the last major Polish unit, the Poznan army, surrendered.

Two days earlier the Russians had moved in to take their share. Two Russian army groups advanced into eastern Poland, one to the south and the other to the north of the impassable Pripet Marshes. The Russians took more than 200,000 Polish prisoners some of whom later made their way back to resume the fight against the Germans from bases in Britain and the Mediterranean. But at this time the Russians were showing no mercy to the Poles.

On 25 September they signed an agreement with Germany which abolished Poland as a State. There was to be no Polish Government, not even a puppet one. The country was to be divided between its two conquerors and to be allowed to survive, but not much more. In an order on 17 October Hitler instructed his prospective Governor General (it was to be Hans Frank, a senior SS man) that he was to keep the standard of living in Poland low, that he was to eliminate Polish intellectuals, and that Germany needed Poland as a source of workers.[2] However, Hitler also said in a secret discussion with his army Chief of Staff, General Halder, that Poland was of military significance to Germany as an advanced outpost which could be used as a place in which to muster an expedition. The roads, railways, and communications must be kept in working order for use by the German armed forces. The second German-Soviet treaty was only three weeks old. Hitler was already making preparations to betray and attack his new Russian ally.

The Russians invade Finland

By this time the Soviet Union had almost absorbed the Baltic States of Esthonia and Latvia having bullied them into granting rights of occupation to the Russian armies. On 2 October also, Russia had begun to negotiate threateningly with Finland. Russia made three main demands. She wanted to lease for thirty years a base on the island of Hangö on the north side of the entrance to the Gulf of Finland which lies some seventy miles west of Helsinki, the Finnish capital. Russia also wanted the western part of the Rybachi Peninsula which extends northwards from the (then) Finnish port of Petsamo into the Barents Sea. Finally, the Russians wanted territory in the Karelian Isthmus which separates the Gulf of Finland from Lake Ladoga. The isthmus, about fifty miles wide, links Leningrad with Viipuri, the main city of south-east Finland.

The Russians' motives were not the same as Hitler's. They wanted the Baltic States and they wanted Finnish territory mainly so as to be better able to defend themselves against a feared attack from the west. Hitler, on the other hand, conquered his part of Poland because he wanted to enlarge the Reich, or at least to add subject territory to it. The Russians' main motive in 1940 was defensive.

This was only dimly understood in the West at the time. The misunderstanding was to persist and to influence Western policy for thirty years to come. Soviet imperialism, as it came to be called, never was simply a matter of aggrandisement, as Hitler's was, and as Britain's had been in the nineteenth century.

But the fact that the Russians were trying to defend themselves – even if it had been clear at the time – would have been no solace to the Esthonians, the Latvians, the Lithuanians, and to the Finns, and would have been no excuse in any case for what the Russians did. The Finns refused to lease Hangö or to give up territory on the Karelian Isthmus.

The Russians immediately staged an incident on the isthmus on 26 November and attacked Finland four days later.

When the Finnish war began the Russians deployed about one million men, the Finns about 175,000. For most of the war the Russians were outwitted, out-manoeuvered, and militarily humiliated by the skilled and resolute Finns whose Commander, Field Marshal Mannerheim, quickly proved himself to be the best winter general in the business.

He had to defend, first of all, the Karelian Isthmus which was the Russians' easiest invasion route. In addition there was a 600-mile stretch of forest and tundra extending from north of Lake Ladoga to the Arctic seas. Mannerheim stationed two divisions on the isthmus and entrusted the defence of the northern frontier to the skill, mobility, hardihood, and intelligence of his few remaining forces. The Russians, with their million men, thought it would be easy simply to march west across Finland to the Gulf of Bothnia. In fact they never got there. Quite quickly they gave up trying.

The Finns defended their own forests, and – as it were, born on skis – held the line valiantly. In two separate engagements two Finnish colonels, Paavo Talvela and Hjalmar Siilasvuo, encircled and destroyed four Soviet divisions. At no time did either colonel have under his command more than two regiments of men.

In the end, however, Russian might had to prevail. Defeated in the north, the Russians simply added more weight to their attack on the Karelian Isthmus. The Finns were holding the Mannerheim Line, a fortification that was less formidable than the Russians made it out to be. But in March, when the ice was thick enough, the Russians were able to cross the bay to Viipuri and to outflank the Finns. The war ended on 12 March. The Treaty of Moscow gave Russia all her original territorial demands and Viipuri as well.

The Russians were quick to learn their lesson. Even before the Finnish war had ended they were teaching their soldiers to fight the Finnish way. Neither Hitler nor the Western powers seemed to have appreciated at the time that the Russians, for all the other military deficiencies which plagued them at the time, were apt pupils and quick learners.

The plight of the Finns and their gallant resistance aroused much sympathy in the West. The British (although otherwise engaged) and the Americans in particular volunteered to help to defend Finland against Russia. The Western powers had been able to do nothing to help to defend Poland. Perhaps, at least, there was something that could be done to help to defend Finland, which was also being bullied by another totalitarian power. The French, with less emotion but no more realism, saw in Finland

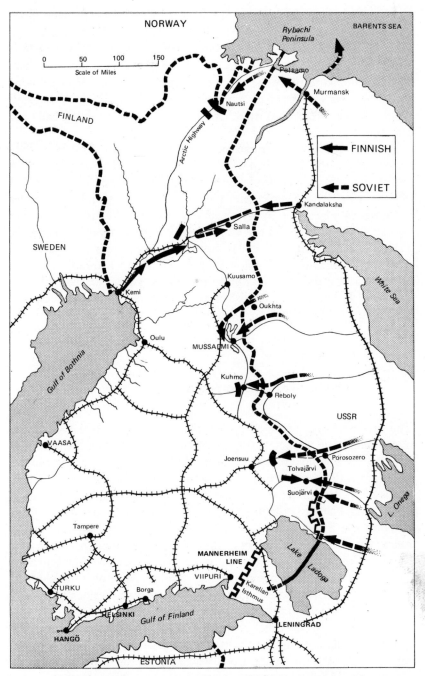

Rybachi
Peninsula

BARENTS SEA

Petsamo

Murmansk

0   50   100   150
Scale of Miles

FINLAND

Nautsi

Arctic Highway

FINNISH

SOVIET

Kandalaksha

Salla

SWEDEN

Kuusamo

White Sea

Kemi

Oukhta

Oulu

MUSSALMI

Kuhmo

Reboly

USSR

VAASA

Joensuu

Porosozero

Gulf of Bothnia

Tolvajärvi

Suojärvi

L. Onega

Tampere

MANNERHEIM
LINE

Lake Ladoga

TURKU

Borga

VIIPURI

Karelian
Isthmus

HELSINKI

Gulf of Finland

LENINGRAD

HANGÖ

ESTONIA

The Russian Invasion of Finland, November 1939–March 1940

the place where French arms could be used offensively. The main thesis of French defence policy was to fortify France with concrete in the hope that this would prevent the invasion of France. But this did not exclude the possibility of expeditions to other parts of Europe, remote from French national territory. There were French staff plans for expeditions to various parts of Europe. A possible French expedition to Lapland (which is where the troops would probably have had to operate) had been foreseen.

In practice, however, Britain and France were in no position to help the Finns directly. The expeditions were not ready and lacked the training and the equipment they would have needed if they were to be a help and not a hindrance to Mannerheim's adroit and hardy soldiers. Moreover there was no direct way by which they could get to Finland. One of the Russians' few successes in the Finnish war had been to capture Petsamo, Finland's only Arctic port, at the beginning of December and to advance from there south-westwards down the Arctic highway towards the Gulf of Bothnia. It is true that the Finns drove the Russians back but although the Finnish army had established positions close to Petsamo by the beginning of March the port never was safe enough to allow Allied landings.

The Norwegian Campaign

The strategic consequence of this was that the Western Allies' only route into Finland lay through northern Norway. If a Franco-British expeditionary force wanted to reach Finland at all it would have to land in the first place at the Norwegian port of Narvik. But Norway was neutral and, at this stage, determined to stay that way. Narvik was important for other reasons too. Narvik is the western terminal of an isolated railway which connects the Swedish iron ore mines at Kiruna with two harbours – Lulea at the head of the Gulf of Bothnia which is icebound in winter, and Narvik on the Atlantic coast which is ice free. Kiruna was the source of the main part of Germany's supplies of iron ore. Most of it was shipped from Narvik. Britain and France had other reasons, besides the plight of the Finns, for wanting to occupy Narvik.

The Commander-in-Chief of the German navy, Admiral Raeder, also coveted Narvik, not only for the sake of the iron ore but also in order to obtain more Atlantic bases from which to threaten Britain's trans-Atlantic supply lines. During the winter of 1939–40 Raeder and a singular and lonely (there were hardly any others) Norwegian Fascist, Vidkun Quisling, sought to persuade Hitler to invade Norway.

The man who eventually did persuade him was Captain Philip Vian, Royal Navy, the Commanding Officer of the destroyer *Cossack*. On 16 February 1940 Vian requested and obtained permission to pursue into Norwegian waters the German supply-ship *Altmark*, a large, fast tanker whose task had been to supply the pocket battleship *Admiral Graf Spee*. The Admiralty was sure that the *Altmark* was carrying some 300 British prisoners, taken from captured and sunk British merchantmen, back to prison in Germany. The Norwegian navy had intercepted the *Altmark*, had searched her, and had found no prisoners. Vian disagreed. On 17 February the German naval attaché in Oslo reported that at 10 p.m. the night before a British destroyer had pursued the *Altmark* into the Jössingfjord (a difficult inlet in which the German ship had sought refuge), that British sailors had boarded the *Altmark*, and that there had been firing. The 'English Captain' had told the Norwegian navy that his mission was to rescue 'several hundred' British seamen and that he would be obliged to complete his mission.

In fact the *Altmark* carried 299 British prisoners who had been hidden in store rooms and oil tanks to escape detection by the Norwegians. Vian brought them home.

He also shocked Hitler into action. On the 19th, two days after his Oslo attaché's message, Hitler ordered the High Command to complete plans and preparations for the invasion of the whole of Norway. Soon afterwards it became evident that Denmark, which was geographically in the way, would have to be invaded as well. Britain, France, and now Germany were all planning to invade Norway, a country which did not belong to them, which had done them no harm, which did not even contain the iron ore which Germany coveted, but which simply happened to own the port from which the ore was shipped.

Unbeknown to each other, both sides decided to make the first move on the night of 8 April, probably for the same mainly meteorological reasons. Britain planned to lay mines in the 'leads', the channels within Norwegian territorial waters which separate the off-shore islands from the Norwegian mainland. The Admiralty assumed that this would prevent the iron ore traffic from Narvik to Germany from continuing in territorial waters where the Royal Navy could not interrupt it. The Germans, on the other hand, planned a full-scale invasion with simultaneous landings early on 9 April at Oslo, at Kristiansand on the north shore of the Skagerrak, at Stavanger and Bergen, the principal ports of west Norway, at Trondheim, 200 miles further north and Norway's third city, and at

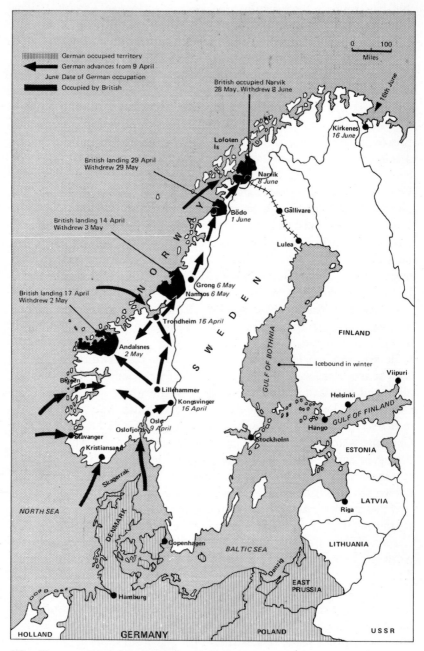

The German Invasion of Norway, 1940

1. 1 September 1939: Adolf Hitler declares war on Poland in the Reichstag in Berlin. Behind Hitler sits Hermann Goering

2. Chamberlain, Daladier, Hitler, Mussolini and Ciano during the Munich Peace Conference, 1938

3. Hitler greets Hindenburg following the former's appointment as Chancellor in January 1933. Goering is in attendance

4. Molotov, with Stalin behind, signs the Nazi–Soviet non-aggression pact, 23 August 1939

5. German troops cross the Rhine

6. Hitler leads a motorcade into the Chancellery in Berlin following the capitulation of France in June 1940

7. General Bor-Komorowski surrenders to SS General von dem Bach-Zelewski following the collapse of the Polish Resistance in Warsaw, October 1944

Narvik in the Arctic. They also wanted Denmark, though only as a stepping stone, and took it in a day.

The Germans were ready. The British and the French were not. The Allies, as it were, pursued the Germans into Norway, but this time at the Norwegian Government's request. The Allies landed at Namsos some 80 miles north of Trondheim on 14 April but were driven out on 3 May by German troops advancing from Trondheim. The British landed at Andalsnes on 17 April but were driven out on 2 May by German troops advancing from Lillehammer. The Norwegians achieved an initial success in the Oslofjord where the guns of the Oscarsborg fortress sank the German heavy cruiser *Blücher*, the lead ship in the German force that had been sent to capture Oslo.

This gave the Norwegian Government time to collect its thoughts, which were unanimous and defiant. The Government and the King refused to surrender. They retreated in anger to the mountains. The other Allied success, which cost the Germans many ships, took place at Narvik, at the other distant, Arctic end of Norway.

The German Defeats at Narvik

In their attack on Norway the Germans used virtually the whole of their surface fleet. The Royal Navy's two attacks on the German naval forces at Narvik, attacks by British submarines in the Kattegat, and attacks by aircraft of the Fleet Air arm failed to prevent the invasion of Norway but succeeded in reducing the strength of the German surface fleet to a level which was too low to allow the German navy to be confident of being able to protect an amphibious landing in Britain in the months that were to come.

In the Norwegian campaign the German navy lost one heavy cruiser, two light cruisers, and ten destroyers – all of them sunk. One of their pocket-battleships was put out of commission for a year and two other battleships were damaged. The naval balance of the Norwegian campaign came out decisively in the Allies' favour, mainly because of the two sea-fights at Narvik.

The first battle of Narvik happened, and was won, because the leader of a British destroyer flotilla, Captain Warburton-Lee, ignored the woolly intelligence that was reaching him and obeyed the simple Nelsonic precept that when in doubt the best thing to do is to seek the enemy out and destroy him.

As far as the Admiralty could comprehend them the German Navy's intentions during the night of 8 to 9 April were to mount a major sweep into the North Atlantic by battleships, or at least by heavy cruisers. This was what the Commander-in-Chief, the Home Fleet, Admiral Forbes, also assumed when the RAF told him that major German units had sailed from their home bases. In fact the Germans were planning to invade Norway immediately and the Allies were planning to invade within a fortnight. All the German landings took place on time and came as a surprise.

The British Home Fleet was at sea but it was mainly concerned to prevent the breakout into the Atlantic which the Germans were not intending to make. In the far north, however, Vice-Admiral Whitworth, flying his flag in the battle cruiser *Renown*, had been operating close to shore where his destroyers had orders to lay mines in the leads. One of his destroyers, The *Glow Worm*, which had lost company in bad weather, intercepted the German heavy cruiser *Hipper* which was covering the German landing at Trondheim. Heavily outgunned, his ship sinking under him, the Captain of the *Glow Worm* rammed the *Hipper* in the desperate hope of sinking her. The *Hipper* was damaged but did not sink. Further north, and in even worse weather, the *Renown* fought an inconclusive action against the German battle cruisers *Scharnhorst* and *Gneisenau* which had been covering the landing at Narvik – a landing that Whitworth did not then know about.

The landing had taken place already. Before dawn on 9 April ten large German destroyers carrying 2,000 mountain troops arrived at Narvik in a snowstorm. They quickly sank two Norwegian warships which were lying in the harbour and the troops were free to land. The destroyers, however, were for the time being trapped in Narvik because they had used up nearly all their fuel during the long voyage from Germany. One of the two tankers which had been assigned to meet them had not arrived. This uncovenanted delay was to lead to Germany's first considerable naval defeat of the war. On 9 April Captain Warburton-Lee decided to investigate an unconfirmed report which simply said that one German vessel had arrived in a north Norwegian port and had landed troops. Narvik lies at the head of a long, narrow fjord. Captain Warburton-Lee decided to be there at dawn on 10 April. He had five destroyers – his own, the *Hardy*, the *Hunter*, the *Havock*, the *Hotspur* and the *Hostile*. They were armed with 4·7-inch guns. The German destroyers were armed with five-inch guns.

During the afternoon of 9 April Captain Warburton-Lee had asked[3] the Norwegian pilots waiting at the pilot station at the entrance to the fjord leading to Narvik to tell him what ships they had seen. The pilots said that as far as they knew six German warships and one submarine had entered the fjord. Before dawn next morning Warburton-Lee followed them.

One German destroyer was on patrol, acting as sentry for the rest. But her captain left his station half an hour before Warburton-Lee arrived. Warburton-Lee found some German destroyers and attacked them, but he did not find them all. Of the ten German destroyers two were sunk and four were seriously damaged in the first British attack. But two groups of German destroyers had been berthed for the night in side fjords. Joining the battle belatedly they inflicted serious damage on the British ships – just as Warburton-Lee was turning for a second attack.

A five-inch shell hit the *Hardy's* bridge killing Warburton-Lee and every other man there except the captain's secretary, Paymaster-Lieutenant Stanning, who then took charge. But *Hardy* was seriously damaged already, had lost power, and had to be beached. The *Hunter* sank. The three surviving British destroyers made their way out to sea sinking a German supply ship on the way.

But three days later the British came back. Vice-Admiral Whitworth, by now embarked in the battleship *Warspite*, led into Narvik a force of four large destroyers, the *Bedouin*, the *Cossack*, the *Eskimo*, and the *Punjabi*, and five smaller ones, the *Hero*, the *Icarus*, the *Kimberley*, the *Forester*, and the *Foxhound*. This time the Germans were outgunned and this time they did not prevail. Even the *Warspite's* reconnaissance aircraft went into action. Its pilot, Petty Officer Price, bombed and sank a submarine – on his way to work, as it were.

The Allied landing which followed was successful too. The 2,000 German soldiers fled into the mountains. But the operation took time. It was not until the middle of May that the Allied troops were able to dominate the Narvik area. And by then the Germans were pouring their tanks into France. The Allies withdrew from Narvik between 4 and 8 June, bringing the surviving members of the *Hardy's* crew with them. The Norwegian army surrendered on 9 June.

On the previous day the navy had lost the aircraft carrier *Glorious*, intercepted on her way home from Norway carrying a load of land-based fighter planes on deck. She was sunk by the *Scharnhorst*, making her second expedition to cover the Norwegian coast.

The Norwegian campaign seriously weakened the German surface fleet. But it did not achieve its first purpose – the interruption of the supply of iron ore from Narvik to Germany. Nor did it save Norway, although the Norwegians, enraged and resourceful, harassed the German garrison throughout the war. Hitler was obliged to keep 300,000 soldiers in Norway, partly for fear of an invasion there, partly to counter the Norwegian resistance movement.

In one way the most important result of the Norwegian campaign was that it led to the fall of Neville Chamberlain. The Norway debate in the House of Commons which lasted from 7 May to the evening of 8 May 1940 marked the end of the phoney war for Britain as surely as Hitler's invasion of the Netherlands on 10 May marked the end of the phoney war for the Low Countries and for France. Chamberlain was brought down by his own party, the Conservatives. Leo Amery quoted Cromwell. 'Depart, I say, and let us have done. In the name of God, go.' The Labour Opposition said they would divide the House. Forty-one Government supporters voted with the Opposition. Sixty abstained. Chamberlain's majority fell from 240 to 81. It was a stunning moral defeat.

The mood of the House, and probably the mood of the country, favoured a coalition Government. Coalition was, after all, Britain's traditional response to the threat of a national emergency. To most Conservatives the obvious alternative to Chamberlain was Halifax. Churchill, who got the job in the end, was at first a reluctant candidate. But he agreed that, if asked, he would refuse to serve under Halifax and this was the first decisive political move. On 9 May Chamberlain asked Churchill whether he would support Halifax as Prime Minister. Churchill said nothing – for two minutes. The National Executive Committee of the Labour Party took the second decisive decision. Chamberlain had asked Attlee and Greenwood whether the Labour Party would join his Government. They had said that they must consult their party Executive, then meeting at Bournemouth. The Executive said 'no'. Later the Executive said that Labour would serve under 'another Prime Minister'. By this time the 'other Prime Minister' had to be Churchill. There was no alternative. For once the Labour Party Executive had itself sealed, confirmed and made final an important political decision. Churchill was to lead and direct the British to victory, but it was still a long way off. If anyone else could have done this great service his name has never been mentioned.

Chapter 3

The Fall of France

An immense French army and a much smaller British one spent the first winter of the war in Europe entrenched and motionless along the eastern frontiers of France. The French General Staff had overall command. Like other Frenchmen, the generals were determined first to protect French soil. France had suffered hideously in World War I. The French army understood its task to be not so much to defeat the enemy as to prevent another invasion.

The Commander-in-Chief, General Gamelin, did not doubt that the Germans would attempt one. He expected, rightly, that the Germans would attack through Belgium whether that country was neutral or not. He expected, rightly, that the Germans would not attack Alsace or Lorraine because these two French provinces were protected by the Maginot Line, a costly fixed fortification which was probably impregnable – though no one ever tested it. Gamelin's plan was to advance into Belgium from the west as soon as the Germans invaded that country from the east. From the French point of view this plan had the advantage that the industrial areas of north-east France would be spared and that there would be no fighting on French soil.

Gamelin foresaw – and here again he was correct – that the Germans' first instinct would be to do what they had done before – advance west through Belgium, then south into France. This was the so-called Schlieffen plan which had been used first in 1914. The Schlieffen plan called for a main German thrust into Belgium just north of Liége. To meet this expected thrust Gamelin proposed to advance with his best and strongest force, the mechanized 1st French Army under General Blanchard, from the Franco-Belgian frontier to Gembloux just north of Namur – a distance of some forty miles. The British Expeditionary Force, ten divisions under General Gort, was to support Blanchard's left by holding the line of the river Dyle east of Brussels. The French 9th Army under

General Corap was to support Blanchard's right, and to hold the line of the Meuse river from Namur to Sedan on the western edge of the forest of the Ardennes. The 9th Army was less well equipped than the 1st and it had a longer sector to defend. But Gamelin expected that it would be protected from any major attack by the supposedly impenetrable woods and hills of the Ardennes.

Gamelin also hoped that the Belgian army would be able to delay the German advance along the line of the Meuse between Namur and Liége and of the Albert Canal from Liége to Antwerp. The key to this defensive system was Fort Eben Emael on the German-Belgian frontier near Liége. This fortress was supposed to be the strongest in the world.

Gamelin's plan depended for its success on the Germans doing what he expected them to do. To begin with, and ironically, Gamelin's expectations were right. The German High Command's first plan for the invasion of France in 1940 was something very like the Schlieffen plan. One of the many things that went wrong for Gamelin was that the Germans changed their mind.

Gamelin was not just guessing. In January 1940 a German air force courier plane lost its way over Belgium and made a forced landing. The courier carried orders for a massive air operation in support of exactly the kind of ground attack that Gamelin expected. It was the Schlieffen plan all over again. And it was not a plant. The orders were genuine. The attack was scheduled for 17 January. What Gamelin did not know was that the Germans were privately having second thoughts.

Two German generals who were then relatively junior, Manstein and Guderian, had already raised objections against repeating the Schlieffen plan. There was an argument in high places. The High Command thought they could settle it by appointing Manstein to an insignificant command. But Manstein and Guderian were not to be silenced. And in any case Gamelin already knew of the German plans. 'An aeroplane accident', Guderian records, 'compelled our masters to abandon the Schlieffen plan. It had to be assumed that the Belgians and probably also the French and British, knew all about our proposed operation.'[1]

The argument about what to do instead lasted till the spring. Guderian wanted to attack through the Ardennes, to cross the Meuse at Sedan, and to advance from there due west to Amiens and on to the Channel coast. He said that the Ardennes were not impenetrable. He said that his tanks could cross the Meuse without too much difficulty. He said that the French would not know what to do to contain a concentrated tank attack. All three contentions were correct.

Two professional soldiers had long since foreseen precisely what would happen to France. One was Guderian, the man who effectively did the deed which brought France to her knees. The other was Colonel Charles de Gaulle of the French army. Neither of these two talented soldiers behaved secretively. Both published well in advance their assessment of what was to come. Guderian's book *Achtung Panzer* contained a description of what he rightly believed a concerted armoured attack could do to an enemy unprepared for this new form of warfare. De Gaulle's *Vers l'Armée de Metier*, was equally frank. Both these eminent soldiers diagnosed correctly the weakness of France.

'Public opinion', de Gaulle wrote, 'did not care for offensives.' The job of the mechanized army, he said, would be to break through the enemy's static defences and then 'deploy fanwise to exploit its gains.' 'Then will lie open the road to great victories, to those victories which, by their deep and rapidly extended effects, lead to a general collapse among the enemy, as the smashing of a pillar sometimes brings down a cathedral. . . . We shall see fast troops range far and wide in the enemy's rear, strike at his vital points, throw his dispositions into confusion. . . . Thus will be restored that strategic extension of tactical results which once used to constitute the supreme end, as it were, the nobility of the art. . . .'[2]

De Gaulle was right and so was Guderian. But in Germany Guderian was preaching to the semi-converted. In France de Gaulle was preaching to the deaf. In 1939 the French General Chauvineau published a book called *Is an Invasion still Possible?* The General's answer was 'No!' Marshal Pétain wrote the preface. He said that tanks and aircraft, however developed, did not modify the basic factors of warfare and that the main element of French security was the continuous front – fortified. De Gaulle was fighting a losing political battle. Almost the only French politician who supported him, Paul Reynaud, challenged the French General Staff's concept of the right way to defend French national territory. The Minister for War, General Maurin, told the National Assembly: 'When we have devoted so many efforts to building up a fortified barrier [the Maginot Line] is it conceivable that we would be mad enough to go ahead of this barrier into I know not what adventure?'[3]

The French army's distaste for adventure was endemic. It was also obvious. When Hitler re-occupied the Rhineland in 1936 the French did nothing. De Gaulle who was watching commented: 'Because we were only ready to hold our frontier and had imposed on ourselves a self-denying ordinance against crossing it in any case, there was no riposte to be expected from France. The Führer was sure of this. The whole world took note of the fact. The Reich, instead of finding itself compelled to withdraw the troops it had adventured, established them without a blow in the whole of the Rhinelands territory, in direct contact with France and Belgium.'[4]

Hitler had occupied the Rhineland in March. In October de Gaulle was summoned by the then French Prime Minister, Léon Blum. Blum wanted to know what de Gaulle thought would happen if war broke out. De Gaulle replied: 'Peering between the battlements of our fortifications, we shall watch the enslavement of Europe.'

This was, almost literally, what happened. While the French sat in their Maginot bunkers (and the British in their trenches) Hitler occupied or conquered Czechoslovakia, part of Poland, and the whole of Denmark and Norway. Russia occupied or tried to conquer part of Poland, Esthonia Lithuania and Finland. By the beginning of May 1940 the Netherlands, Belgium and France were due for the same treatment.

The German High Command had eventually agreed to allow Guderian to attack through the Ardennes. In addition, however, the Germans had laid plans to lure Gamelin into Belgium. He would have gone into Belgium anyway. But the Germans wanted to ensure that as many Allied troops as possible would be trapped in north-east France or on Belgian soil by the time that Guderian reached the sea and could cut them off.

With this in mind they attacked not just Belgium but the Netherlands as well, thereby luring a part of the French 7th Army under General Giraud as far as Breda in south-west Holland.

The Germans attacked from the sky before dawn on 10 May. For the first time parachutists won a decisive victory more or less unaided. By daylight on 10 May German parachute troops had captured bridges round the Hague and Rotterdam that were vital to the Dutch defence plans and had also captured airfields to permit their own reinforcement by transport plane. By the end of the day, too, the Dutch air force had been destroyed. The Dutch army was almost powerless. The German 18th Army struck west across the southern part of the Netherlands, turning the Dutch defence line along the river Meuse (the Maas as it is called in the Netherlands). The Dutch, surprised and shaken, were unable to resist for long. Queen Wilhelmina and her Government left for England. On the fourth day of the battle the Germans threatened to destroy Rotterdam from the air if resistance continued. It was an ultimatum of a new sort. It ended with what seemed to be a new refinement of treachery. Two hours before the ultimatum expired the Germans bombed Rotterdam anyway, killing 980 civilians and wounding 29,000 more. The treachery may or may not have been deliberate. There were reports that the Germans had tried to recall the bombers. But the attack was delivered and the people died.

The attack on Belgium was virtually simultaneous with the attack on the Netherlands. On 10 May General von Reichenau's 6th Army attacked the Belgian defences along the Meuse and the Albert Canal. By the next day German gliders landed within the perimeter of Fort Eben Emael, forcing the Belgian garrison to surrender. The Belgian army retreated to the line of the River Dyle. By 15 May, having conquered the Netherlands, the German 18th Army was able to swing south to help the 6th. By now, too, the attack through the Ardennes was well under way. Two days earlier on 13 May, General Rommel's 7th Panzer Division had crossed the Meuse in fog near Dinant. Later the same day Guderian had crossed the Meuse near Sedan. The Germans had arrived in France.

The Germans' next aim was to cut the Allied armies in two. They planned to do this from their new bridgeheads across the Meuse at Sedan and Dinant. This was to be their main thrust. Forty-five divisions had been allocated to the thrust through the Ardennes. Only 30 divisions had invaded Belgium and Holland and a mere 19 divisions were keeping an eye on the two hundred miles of the Maginot Line. 'So far as the French were concerned', Guderian wrote, 'the German leadership could safely rely on the defence of France being systematically based on fortifications.'[5]

The attempt to cut the Allied armies in two succeeded brilliantly and rapidly. British and French troops were still advancing, fatally, into Belgium to meet the German threat to Brussels as Guderian and Rommel, leading the van of a much stronger force, were cutting them off from the main French armies in the south. Once they were across the Meuse the Germans were able to accelerate. South of Sedan General Huntziger, commanding the 2nd French army, had stationed his best troops in the northern-most sector of the Maginot Line leaving his less experienced men to guard the southern part of the Ardennes sector. North of Sedan General Corap's 9th French army was in any case weak and ill equipped. Gamelin, who supposed the Ardennes to be impenetrable, had not wanted to waste his best equipment and his best troops by having them guard a gate that he thought could never be opened.

By 13 May the Germans were building up their strength on the western bank of the Meuse and were soon able to move forward. Using Stuka dive bombers instead of artillery (which could not keep up) they advanced at a speed which amazed the French. By the 16th they were moving forward against opposition at the rate of forty miles per day. Guderian told his commanders to keep moving until they had used up their last drop of petrol. By 20 May the German tanks had reached the sea.

Early on 19 May Gamelin ordered co-ordinated attacks from north and

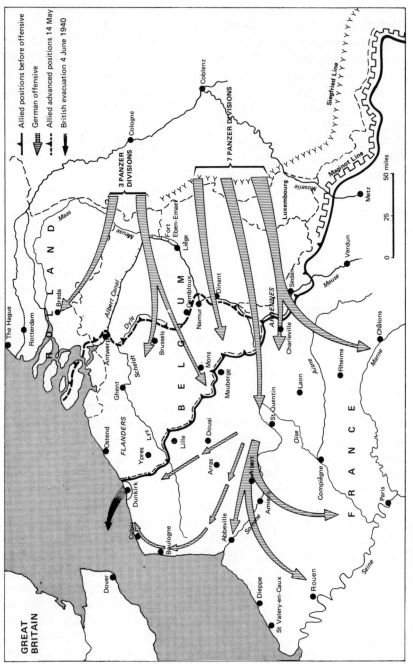

The German Campaign in N. W. Europe, 1940

Legend:
- Allied positions before offensive
- German offensive
- Allied advanced positions 14 May
- British evacuation 4 June 1940

GREAT BRITAIN

HOLLAND
The Hague
Rotterdam
Breda
Maas
Meuse
Albert Canal

BELGIUM
Antwerp
Ghent
Scheldt
Brussels
Dyle
Gembloux
Namur
Mons
Maubeurge
FLANDERS
Ostend
Ypres
Lys
Lille
Douai
Arras
3 PANZER DIVISIONS
Fort Eben-Emael
Liège
Dinant
ARDENNES
Charleville

Dover
Dunkirk
Calais
Boulogne
Abbeville
Somme
St Quentin
Oise
Aisne
Laon
Compiègne
Amiens
Dieppe
St Valery-en-Caux
Rouen
Seine

FRANCE
Paris
Rheims
Marne
Châlons
Verdun
Meuse

7 PANZER DIVISIONS
Cologne
Coblenz
Luxembourg
Moselle
Sedan
Siegfried Line
Maginot Line
Metz

0   25   50 miles

south on the German columns. He intended to re-unite his armies and to isolate the head of the German column. A co-ordinated attack would probably not have succeeded if only because the Germans had command of the air and were using their Stukas to hamper or prevent movement on the roads. In any case Gamelin's co-ordinated attack never happened. Later on the 19th the French Prime Minister, Reynaud, sacked and replaced him. Gamelin was sixty-eight years old. His sucessor, Weygand, was seventy-two.

Weygand ordered a postponement of the co-ordinated attack while he took stock of the position. He had only just returned to France after a year in Syria. He found, among other deficiencies, that the French army was virtually without reserves of soldiers. There were only eight infantry divisions. But they were in Lorraine and had already been cut off. Weygand could not reinforce the weak points in the French line because there were no men with which to do so.

As Guderian romped westwards across north-eastern France the French High Command sent for de Gaulle, promised to provide him with the scattered elements of an armoured division, and asked him – in effect – to halt Guderian by attacking the Germans' left flank in the neighbourhood of Laon. General Georges, Weygand's immediate subordinate, said to de Gaulle: 'For you who have so long held the ideas which the enemy is putting into practice, here is the chance to act.'

It was a slim chance. De Gaulle's division was improvised indeed. There was no radio. There were no dive-bombers at his command to emulate the work of the German Stukas. He had hardly any artillery. He had almost no infantry. Nevertheless, de Gaulle and his men tried hard. They probably inflicted upon Guderian the most important annoyance that he had suffered. But it was no more than annoyance.

While de Gaulle and other divisional commanders were doing their best along the fractured French line the strategic battle for France was being lost in the sky, on the ground, and on the plains of Flanders. Commenting afterwards on the failure of the plan to attack the German drive on both its flanks de Gaulle wrote: 'Theoretically the plan was logical. But for it to be carried out it would have been necessary for the High Command still to have hope and the will to win. The crumbling of the whole system of doctrines and organization, to which our leaders had attached themselves, deprived them of their motive force. A sort of moral inhibition made them suddenly doubtful of everything, and especially of themselves. From then on the centrifugal forces were to show themselves rapidly. The King of the Belgians was not slow to contemplate surrender; Lord Gort, re-embarkation; General Weygand, the armistice.'[6]

There was in any case, a genuine command muddle. The British commander, General Gort, obeyed the orders Gamelin had issued on the 19th, not having heard of the postponement subsequently ordered by Weygand. Gort's solitary attack failed. By the time Weygand had reinstated the plan for a co-ordinated attack it was too late. When the German tanks reached Abbeville, they had not only gained a very important tactical advantage by cutting the Allied armies in two, they had also created a situation which was bound to cause confusion among the Allied generals. This helped considerably to ensure and accelerate the German victory in France. When the vanguard of von Rundstedt's Army Group A, led by Guderian, reached the Channel coast on 20 May they were at the end of a German-held corridor which was only fifty miles wide. Theoretically, as de Gaulle said, the French armies to the south of the corridor, numerous but bewildered, might have been able to cut Guderian off. To the north of the corridor the British, the French, and now the Belgians were in a worse state. They were being hard pressed by the German Army Group B under von Bock who was already forcing them out of Belgium. Hindsight suggests that it is unlikely that the Northern Armies could have done much to pinch off the German-occupied pocket that ran west from the Meuse to the sea. Nevertheless Gamelin's proposal for simultaneous flank attacks on the Germans, belatedly endorsed by Weygand, was worth trying. In any case, there was little else that the Allies could do if they wanted to save France.

One difficulty was that Weygand, like Gamelin before him, was unable to gain a clear picture of the difference between what was militarily possible and what was not. Gamelin had established his supreme headquarters in the Chateau of Vincennes outside Paris. It was an imposing building but it had no radio. The information that reached Vincennes was either inadequate or wrong. Weygand, an abler, though older man than Gamelin, did his best. But communication failures, added to reports from the field which were more hopeful than accurate, led him to order the impossible.

There was nothing he could do, for example, to deploy usefully the eight reserve infantry divisions. Gamelin had stationed them in a position from which they could not be extricated. They were east and south of the German bridgeheads on the Meuse. They might as well have been German prisoners of war already.

Nor could the armies in the north be expected to do very much to re-establish contact with the main French forces in the south. The forces in the north consisted of the British Expeditionary Force under General Gort, General Blanchard's 1st Army, the remnants of the French 7th

Army whose commander, General Giraud, had been captured, and the remnants of the Belgian army. Their operations were being 'co-ordinated' though not commanded by the French General Billotte. These forces, hard pressed already by von Bock's armies, were in no position to do more than make supporting gestures in a southerly direction. Churchill, honourably determined to help the French and misled (though alarmed) by what he was told during a series of visits to Paris, urged and indeed ordered Gort to march the whole British Expeditionary Force south to Amiens and make contact with the main body of the French army.

When Gort received this order on the morning of 20 May, seven of his nine divisions were holding with difficulty the line of the Scheldt river against strong German pressure. Gort said that obedience to the order would be 'impracticable'. He had, however, already arranged for two of his divisions along with two French divisions to attack southwards the next day to secure Arras which, being an important junction, was an obvious target for the Germans. In the event the French infantry was unable to take part. The British under General Franklyn and the French cavalry under General Prioux attacked strongly. The British tank expert, General Martel, led the attack although he only had sixteen Mark II tanks, the one British type which proved effective. Attacking without air cover the Allies captured 400 prisoners and convinced the Germans that they were facing five Allied divisions.

There had been no corresponding attack from the south. Weygand was still wondering whether to order one. His orders went out – which did not mean that they all arrived – on the 22nd. But by then the field commanders no longer had the troops or the means with which to do what Weygand wanted. The divisions to whom he addressed his commands were either non-existent, short of ammunition, too exhausted to move, or no longer in the places where the French General Staff thought they were. Churchill, who had flown to Paris to talk to Weygand on the 22nd and who returned impressed, ordered Gort and Blanchard – the surviving commanders in the north – to attack south-westwards on the 23rd using eight divisions of their own and a screen of Belgian cavalry on their right flank.

Dunkirk

Weygand and Churchill had lost touch with reality. Gort and Blanchard did not have eight divisions. The Belgian cavalry had ceased to exist as a formed unit. The orders that Gort and Blanchard were receiving from on high were nonsense.[7] Wishful thinking and false reports made the situation worse. On the 23rd someone told Weygand that the French Army had begun its northward attack and had captured Amiens and Albert. Weygand told Churchill. Churchill, who had been on the point of telling Gort to withdraw his forces to the coast, changed his mind. Gort, independently and with better information, was already coming to the conclusion himself that the only reasonable thing to do would be to retreat to the coast and evacuate the British Expeditionary Force to Britain. It had not proved possible to hold on to Arras. The Allies in the north were surrounded in a corridor stretching some seventy miles inland and about twenty-five miles broad. And they were being hard pressed on all sides.

On the evening of 26 May the British Cabinet authorized Lord Gort to evacuate the British Expeditionary Force from France to England. The next day, 27 May, he began to withdraw his Force into a perimeter around Dunkirk. Twenty-four miles away across the Straits of Dover Vice-Admiral Bertram Ramsay, the Vice-Admiral, Dover, and his Chief-of-Staff, Captain Day, had been laying their plans to get the soldiers home. Unlike many a fussier Admiral, Ramsay believed firmly in the principle that the best way for a naval authority to get things done at sea was to appoint a good seaman to command each ship and to leave him alone to make his own decisions. Ramsay and Day were ultimately responsible for evacuating 338,226 men from Dunkirk to Britain. No one had expected more than 45,000.

The guiding principle of Operation Dynamo, as the evacuation of Dunkirk was called, was that the business of the naval staff at Dover was to ensure that all ships – however small – could get stores, fuel, provisions and charts. The rest was up to the captains, whether they were Royal Navy officers, merchant seamen, fishermen or yachtsmen. They knew where to go. They knew what to do. The navy would help them as best it could and so would the air force.

The miracle of Dunkirk did not consist so much in the fact that Ramsay's captains made the passage there and back time and again. The miracle, if there was one, was the weather. On 27 May Dynamo fared badly. On this, the first day of the evacuation, only 7,669 men were taken off. But on the 28th the weather was bad for flying and the flow of men from France to Kent increased. On the 29th, however, the Luftwaffe was able to concentrate its attacks on the beaches and five ships were sunk. On the 30th, although the weather was again good for flying, the RAF was able to keep the German pilots in check and 60,000 men were evacuated. On 1 June Ramsay lost three destroyers and many small craft, but the evacuation continued. From then on, however, it was only possible to continue the work at night. By 4 June the Germans were pressing hard against the dwindling Dunkirk perimeter and the evacuation ended.

Dynamo was a remarkable operation and it left the Germans bewildered. British destroyers, tied up alongside the quays at Boulogne (whence they were evacuating men of the Welsh Guards), halted the German armour with four-inch shells. It was probably the first effective anti-tank artillery that the Germans had met so far. But what astonished them most was that the men were evacuated at all. Perhaps the German High Command had overestimated the abilities of the Luftwaffe. Perhaps the German generals were simply at a loss, not knowing what to do next. Perhaps they thought that evacuation was impossible anyway, that they had plenty of time to mop up the British and the remaining French. At all events on 23 May in one of the most controversial decisions of the war, von Rundstedt ordered his armour to halt.

There could have been good reasons for this. The area round Dunkirk is bad for tanks. The ground is marshy and there are many canals. Moreover, the German armour had been driving hard for weeks. Only about half the tanks were serviceable.

On 24 May there was a consultation between Hitler and von Rundstedt at the latter's headquarters at Charleville. Hitler confirmed von Rundstedt's order on the grounds that the Germans had occupied a 'favourable defensive line' against which the enemy was to be allowed to exhaust himself. This may not have been Hitler's only reason. It certainly does not seem, with hindsight, to have been a good one. What is known about this crucial – for Britain – meeting at Charleville is that Hitler was at least temporarily annoyed with the High Command.

The day before, the German army Chiefs of Staff, Generals Halder and von Brauchitsch, had marginally reorganized the army command structure in Flanders without telling Hitler. He appears to have been irritated, to say the least, when he met his generals at Charleville. Perhaps Hitler was cross. Perhaps he did not really know what he was doing. But Ramsay did. While von Rundstedt and Hitler were dithering Ramsay was recruiting captains. By the time the evacuation was properly under way he had 848 working for him and he did not let them stop until the job was done.

Dynamo was only one of many evacuations that followed the fall of France. In the first days of June the navy and the merchant navy were less successful in an attempt to rescue the 51st (Highland) Division and a large contingent of French troops from St Valery-En-Caux where they had been cut off. Largely because of fog only about 3,300 soldiers could be rescued and most of the Highland Division was taken prisoner. Further west, from Le Havre and Cherbourg, British, Polish and other Allied ships evacuated some 30,000 soldiers who had been sent to France in a belated attempt to save the battle there. Others were evacuated during the latter part of June from the French west-coast ports of Brest, St Nazaire, and La Pallice, and eventually from Bordeaux, Bayonne, and St Jean de Luz. About half a million men in all were evacuated from France during the month which ended on 26 June. About two-thirds were British. The rest were French, Polish, Czech, Canadian and Belgian. In spite of the German tanks, in spite of the Luftwaffe, all these men escaped to fight another day.

Churchill takes over

There is no knowing what would have happened if Chamberlain and Halifax had been the undisputed masters of the Cabinet at the end of May 1940 as they had been for so many years before. They were then still in the Cabinet but no longer in control of it. Halifax was still Foreign Secretary but Winston Churchill was now Prime Minister.

Hitler's overwhelmingly rapid conquest of the Netherlands and of Belgium and his invasion of France had convinced Chamberlain and Halifax that Britain ought to sue for peace there and then. Their proposals were not revealed at the time. They were not even revealed after the war to the British official historians. But the plans were nevertheless precise and involved offering Malta and other British colonies to Mussolini in May 1940, in return for his interceding with Hitler to obtain acceptable peace terms for Britain. The Chamberlain-Halifax proposals were first published with the Cabinet papers for 1940 on 1 January 1971. The Cabinet's secretary's confidential file on war Cabinet conclusions for 28 May 1940 records that 'the Foreign Secretary [Halifax] said that we must not ignore the fact that we might get better terms before France went out of the war and our aircraft factories were bombed than we might get in three months time'.[8] He was commending a proposal that Britain and France should offer Mussolini 'concessions in the Mediterranean' in return for Mussolini's promise that Italy would stay neutral and that he would intercede with Hitler to grant peace terms which would not affect Britain's independence. Halifax had already discussed the matter with the Italian Ambassador in London, Signor Bastianini, on

25 May. The Foreign Office records for 1940, also released for the first time in 1971, show that the Foreign Office had already discovered Mussolini's asking price. From Britain he wanted Malta and Cyprus. From France he wanted Nice, Savoy, Corsica, and Tunis. He wanted Gibraltar to be internationalized. He wanted to establish Italian protectorates over Egypt, Syria and Iraq and he wanted the Sudan to be governed as an Italo-Egyptian protectorate. All this information had reached the Foreign Office through diplomatic channels before Halifax urged the Cabinet to authorize him to approach Mussolini and ask him to negotiate peace terms with Germany in return for 'certain concessions that we were prepared to make to Italy.'[9] The Cabinet records show that Chamberlain alone supported Halifax.

Halifax, again supported by Chamberlain, tried once more. His proposals having been rejected by the War Cabinet on 27 May, he put forward an essentially similar plan next day. But Churchill's War Cabinet was not the same as Chamberlain's had been. The appeasers were no longer in the majority. The new Cabinet of 5 included, besides Churchill himself, two Labour members – Clement Attlee (Lord Privy Seal) and Arthur Greenwood (Minister without Portfolio).

According to the Cabinet records Attlee spoke first and scathingly. He is reported as having said that the approach suggested by Halifax must lead to Britain's asking Mussolini to intercede to obtain peace terms and that the approach would be very damaging. Greenwood is reported as having said that if it got out that Britain had been sueing for terms at the cost of ceding British territory the consequences would be 'terrible'. Churchill is reported to have described the approach as 'futile' and to have said 'let us not be dragged down with France'. Greenwood described Halifax's proposal as a step towards 'ultimate capitulation'.[10]

Nobody knew anything about this at the time. Attlee and Greenwood refused to have anything to do with the Halifax initiative. Chamberlain's support for it was inevitable. He and Halifax had, after all, seen eye to eye throughout the appeasement years. Now, for the first time, they faced opposition in the British Cabinet.

There is no point in seeking to diagnose meticulously and in a prying way the reactions of dead statesmen in moments of appalling stress. Chamberlain, who had directed the affairs of the British nation for many years up to this particular moment of anxiety, seems at any rate to have repented of his support for Halifax's proposal to ask Mussolini to intercede with Hitler for the sake of a negotiated peace. Or perhaps Chamberlain forgot about it. At all events on 30 June he was saying in a BBC broadcast that 'anyone who lends himself to German propaganda

C

by listening to idle talk about disunion among us, or who imagines that any of us would consent to enter upon peace negotiations with the enemy, is just playing the Nazi game'. Chamberlain's biographer, the late Iain Macleod, says that the broadcast 'arose out of a story that Chamberlain and Halifax were intriguing to oust Churchill in order to negotiate peace terms with Hitler. It was of course a lie. . . .' 'W. C. [Churchill] was very pleased with my broadcast', Chamberlain wrote in his diary on 1 July.[11]

Chamberlain's character, his record, and their influence on history have been exhaustively and perhaps unfairly discussed. But the record shows, and must show, that even after his dismissal as a result of the debate on the Norwegian campaign he was still minded to appease to the extent of offering Mussolini important parts of the British Empire in return for Mussolini's good offices in the negotiation of a peace settlement.

As in 1939 when the war began, it was the House of Commons which had called the tune. Chamberlain resigned because Parliament, which was resolute, rejected him. But the British Parliament had a less difficult choice than other Parliaments. London was threatened but had not been occupied. Copenhagen, Oslo, the Hague, and Brussels had all been conquered and Paris was about to be conquered. In the event the Governments of Norway and the Netherlands went straight into exile with their parliaments' blessings and established themselves in London. With great difficulty the Belgian Government followed them, leaving their King behind. With the Germans at the gates, the French Government surrendered.

The French Armistice

De Gaulle had been right when he predicted the collapse of the French army. He did not predict the collapse of the French Government and, indeed, of France itself, though he feared that this would happen. The Third French Republic had for long been a leaderless community. A parliament fragmented by many parties had never succeeded for long in consenting to the survival of a strong Prime Minister.

When the Germans invaded, France, ironically, had for a change the strongest, most resolute Prime Minister to have held that office for many years. Paul Reynaud had not been Prime Minister for long before the German breakthrough. He was, however, the only first-rank French politician who had listened attentively to de Gaulle, who was deeply alarmed and discontented about the state of France, and who seems to have been determined throughout those difficult weeks of 1940 that he would insist as long as he had responsibility that the French should continue the war against Hitler from North Africa.

During the night of 5–6 June Reynaud appointed de Gaulle to be a member of his Government, the Under-Secretary of State for National Defence. De Gaulle, at this time still in command of his improvised armoured division, left at once for Paris. He urged Reynaud to prepare to move to North Africa. Reynaud was of the same opinion. But by then the French national will had been eroded. What was more the old, defeatist men had come back. Weygand was in command of the armies. Pétain was waiting to advocate surrender. The French, in their despair, had sent for their ancestors. But the ancestral voices were despairing too. On 8 June Weygand told de Gaulle 'when I've been beaten here England won't wait a week before negotiating with the Reich'.

Weygand and Pétain had done great deeds for France in the First World War. But they were old men now. Reynaud, desperate to reinforce his crumbling Government, invited Pétain to join it at the end of May. De Gaulle, who had no cause to welcome this news, foresaw what would happen. He knew that Pétain would want to surrender, that he would not want to carry on the struggle from the French overseas territories, and that he might not act decisively enough to deny the Germans the use of the French fleet. But de Gaulle was a generous man. 'In spite of everything', he wrote, 'I am convinced that in other times Marshal Pétain would not have consented to don the purple in the midst of national surrender . . . but, alas, under the outer shell, the years had gnawed at his character. Age was delivering him over to the manoeuvres of people who were clever at covering themselves with his majestic lassitude. Old age is a shipwreck. That we might be spared nothing, the old age of Marshal Pétain was to identify itself with the shipwreck of France'.[12]

During this anguished period for France, de Gaulle and Churchill were closer to each other in action and in mutual respect than at any other time. Churchill ached in his soul for France to survive. He was not just anxious that Britain should retain an ally. He was personally concerned for a nation that he knew and admired. De Gaulle understood this. At Reynaud's request Churchill paid repeated visits to France, conferring with the French Government three times in one week – on 11, 13 and 17 June. On the 13th de Gaulle was there as well. The immediate issues were the future of the French fleet and the validity of an Anglo-French agreement, signed in March 1940, under which each country undertook not to make a separate peace with the Germans. According to de Gaulle, Churchill spoke as follows on the 13th:

'We see plainly how things are with France. We understand how you feel cornered. Our friendship for you remains intact. In any case, be sure that England will not retire from the struggle. We shall fight to the end, no matter how, no matter where, even if you leave us alone'.[13]

The British Government made one more attempt to stiffen the French ministers' resolve. The Cabinet proposed an act of union between Britain and France. It was a grand and totally unconstitutional gesture. It was grand but it was also futile. Reynaud's wobbling Cabinet was about to disown him. Reynaud resigned. Pétain became Prime Minister. De Gaulle fled to Britain to rally the Free French in exile.

The French armistice was signed at Compiègne in the same railway carriage in the same forest in which the armistice of 1918 had been signed. Germany's revenge, as Hitler saw it, would have been incomplete in any other setting. Mussolini, like a self-important commissionaire, also elbowed his way into the act at the last moment. On 10 June, when the defeat of France was inevitable, he declared war on the Allies. Hitler allowed him to occupy Corsica, Savoy and parts of Provence. The Germans occupied the whole of eastern France, the north, the west, and the south-west, taking possession of the entire Atlantic and northern coastlines. Pétain retired to Vichy, a health resort north-east of Clermont-Ferrand, and set up there his puppet French Government.

For the next year and a half – until the Japanese attack on Pearl Harbor brought the Americans into the war on 7 December 1941 – Britain, Greece, the British Commonwealth, and the exiled forces of Britain's European Allies stood alone in the West. For Britain the fall of France was a disaster. But it was not quite as disastrous as it might have been. The French navy, to its honour, succeeded in repairing the battle-ships *Richelieu* and *Jean Bart* just in time to allow them to sail to North Africa. In fact, the Germans never did get their hands on these great French ships.

Chapter 4

The Battle of Britain

The Battle of Britain was an attempt by Hitler to destroy the fighters of the Royal Air Force so as to clear the way for an invasion of Britain in the autumn of 1940. The attempt failed. The failure was decisive. The Luftwaffe, operating from newly acquired bases in northern France, could not destroy the RAF fighters. Both the German army and the navy had assured Hitler, rightly, that invasion would be impossible unless the Luftwaffe had first established air superiority over the English Channel and south-east England. The Luftwaffe assured him, wrongly, that it would be able to eliminate Britain's Fighter Command.

Hitler's noisiest party comrade, Hermann Goering, was the head of the Luftwaffe and on this occasion he took personal charge of the operations. He believed that it would take four days to eliminate the RAF south of a line from Chelmsford to Gloucester. In the event it took the Luftwaffe a month – from 12 August to 15 September 1940 – to discover that it was incapable of doing what Hitler wanted. Fighter Command was still there and still fighting.

Hitler had conquered northern France in May and the whole of France by June. Throughout July he dithered. This was one of the periods during World War II when he supposed, wrongly, that he could persuade Britain to negotiate peace. In July 1940 he had a special reason for hoping that Britain would do this. His new Russian allies (whom he was, in any case, intending to attack) had adjusted their western frontier in their own favour in two places. Hitler became uneasy. He did not want to take on the Russians without first subduing Britain or negotiating her out of the way. He decided to explore negotiation first. He made a public speech in Berlin which was supposed to be conciliatory. Mussolini despatched devious peace-feelers through the diplomatic channels available to the Vatican. The British treated both offers with indifference. Hitler resolved to invade. But he had been wasting time. When he eventually

59

acknowledged that it would not be possible to talk Britain into sur-
rendering, the extremely benevolent summer of 1940 was well advanced.
Goering expected to be able to launch the initial attack on the RAF on
10 August. Hitler said that in that case the invasion itself should be
launched on 15 September.

In quality Fighter Command was reasonably prepared. In quantity the
margins were at best precarious. The Commander-in-Chief of Fighter
Command, Air Marshal Sir Hugh Dowding, had been striving for four
years to persuade the Air Ministry and the Government to allocate more
resources to Fighter Command. For most of this period the Government
had kept the RAF short of money – despite the assumption that 'the
bomber will always get through'. On 14 May 1940 Dowding became
seriously alarmed when the British Cabinet promised the French Government to send ten more British fighter squadrons to join the six that were
already stationed in France. Next day Dowding protested in person to
the Cabinet and the Cabinet changed its mind. On the 16th, however,
as the French position deteriorated fast, Churchill changed his mind and
again proposed sending six squadrons. Once more Dowding protested.
'If an adequate fighter force is kept in this country [Dowding wrote
to the chief of the air staff, Air Chief Marshal Sir Cyril Newall], if the
fleet remains in being and if the home forces are suitably organised to
meet invasion we should be able to carry on the war single handed for
some time, if not indefinitely. But if the home defence air force is drained
away in desperate attempts to remedy the situation in France, defeat in
France will involve the final, complete and irremedial defeat of this
country.'[1]

The Cabinet once again supported Dowding. Chester Wilmot, the
historian of the war in Europe, has described the Cabinet's decision to
keep the fighters in Britain as 'one of the gravest strategic decisions in
history'.[2]

Dowding's forces consisted of Hurricane and Spitfire single-engine
fighters armed with eight machine guns each. They were capable of the
remarkable (for those days) speed of 300 m.p.h. The Spitfire could turn
more tightly than its main German opponent, the Messerschmidt 109,
but was seriously deficient in firepower.

Besides developing his good aircraft Dowding had also developed a
good system for directing and controlling them. Pre-war radar, developed
by Sir Robert Watson-Watt, was far too ponderous to be fitted into
aircraft but was extremely efficient when used against them. By 1939
Britain had a chain of radar stations which could detect at long ranges
the approach of high-flying aircraft. To make the best use of this coastal

radar chain Dowding had also developed a sophisticated system of fighter direction and control. Radar and visual information would be fed into central control rooms. The controllers could then direct the British fighters to intercept the approaching enemy accurately and punctually. The system could locate an enemy formation more accurately and quickly than a fighter pilot looking around him in the sky. It also enabled the British to economize their efforts. Pilots were able to wait on the ground for instructions. They were able to stay airborne and to fight for longer because they did not have to waste fuel on patrol or searching for the enemy.

The Germans in 1940 had no comparable system. They possessed radar, but it was less efficient than the British. What they had not done, however, was to establish a system whereby the information obtained by radar could be properly exploited. In the Battle of Britain and for some time afterwards German fighter pilots flew unguided, if not blind. In addition – and during the summer of 1940 while Hitler was wondering whether Britain would surrender or not – Dowding began to improve his aircraft further by fitting them with better radio and with self-sealing petrol tanks. These greatly reduced the risk of fire by preventing petrol from leaking out of a tank which had been holed onto hot parts of the aircraft's engine, or into spaces where it would form an explosive mixture.

Up till the summer of 1940 the Luftwaffe had operated almost entirely in support of the German army. In Poland, Norway, Holland, Belgium and France the Luftwaffe Stuka short-range, single-engined dive bombers had been used mainly as a substitute for artillery. The German fighters had been used mainly to escort the Stukas. They had not, till 1940, been obliged to fight in the air against a competent, well-led air force. This is not to say that the German pilots were inadequate. Many of them had had long experience of combat flying in the Spanish Civil War. But the Battle of Britain was not the kind of combat to which they had become recently accustomed.

Nor had Goering. As a preliminary to his main assault on Fighter Command – scheduled for 10 August – he mounted a series of attacks on British convoys in the English Channel. His purpose was not merely to sink ships. He wanted if he could to lure Fighter Command out over the Channel where a pilot shot down might well be a pilot lost and where he could bring superior numbers of his comparatively short-range Messerschmidts into the battle comparatively easily. Dowding and the officer immediately responsible for the defence of south-east England, Air Vice-Marshal Park, commanding Number 11 Group of Fighter

Command, refused to be drawn. The Channel convoys were stopped. Dowding and Park husbanded their resources. By the time Goering had given up trying to tempt them the RAF had inflicted losses on the Luftwaffe which were twice as heavy as it had sustained itself.

As far as the Germans were concerned the real Battle of Britain began on 12 August, two days late. The Luftwaffe launched attacks on five coastal radar stations, three aerodromes in Kent, and on targets in London, Dover and Portsmouth. The next morning the Germans attacked Portsmouth and the Thames harbours in strength but were intercepted, the radar having been repaired during the night. In the afternoon the Germans attacked eleven airfields but not all of them were the right ones. Fighter Command suffered less than the Germans. On 15 August the Germans returned to attack south-east England with four waves of aircraft and north-east England with a force of bombers from Norway. The British lost 34 aircraft and the Germans 76. In further attacks on airfields on the 18th the Luftwaffe lost 71 aircraft. By 26 August the Luftwaffe had lost 602 fighters and bombers and Fighter Command had lost 259 fighters. For the next days, however, the RAF suffered more and the Luftwaffe less. Goering was at this stage concentrating his attacks on Fighter Command itself and on its airfields. In the first week of September the Luftwaffe came closest to success, destroying 185 British aircraft for the loss of 225 German ones. Dowding's reserves of pilots and aircraft were, at this stage, dangerously low.

At this point, however, Hitler intervened and relieved the pressure on Dowding's forces by ordering the Luftwaffe to switch its attacks to London. Hitler did this in what seems to have been a moderate rage caused by Bomber Command's having attacked Berlin during the night of 25 August. Hitler ordered reprisals and they began in daylight on 7 September. Goering sent nearly 400 bombers and more than 600 fighters in two waves to attack London's East End. For once many bombers got through. The damage was considerable and the fires that started were still burning that night when another wave of more than 200 bombers attacked after dark.

The Luftwaffe had been able to bomb London but it had not been able to defeat Fighter Command. Goering tried again on the 9th, mounting another attack on London which did not succeed. On 15 September Goering tried for the last time. He sent over two waves of heavily protected bombers. Each was broken up by Fighter Command in an extremely skilful action which finally convinced Hitler that Goering had not, and could not gain air superiority over south-east England. Two days later Hitler suspended his invasion plans. He never revived them. By itself remaining undefeated, Fighter Command had inflicted on the Germans their first defeat of the war.

Goering's (or Hitler's) decision to stop bombing the Fighter Command airfields and to bomb London instead was undoubtedly a turning point in the Battle of Britain. That is not to say that the battle would have been lost without the diversion. Fighter Command had already proved its resilience. It might well have been able to survive further attacks upon its aerodromes in south-east England. A German account[3] of the Battle of Britain by General Adolf Galland, one of Goering's most successful fighter pilots and wing commanders, has suggested that the attack was switched to London because neither Goering nor Hitler then knew how easily cities could recover from what was to be – in the light of subsequent events – a comparatively light attack. The attack on the East End of London, Galland says, was the very first occasion that the Luftwaffe or any other air force had been used in a purely strategic way. Nobody knew how many tons of bombs would be needed to destroy a big town. Galland, who was flying ME 109's out of France at the time, said that he did not then know why Goering had ordered the attack on London. Berlin was then beyond the effective range of the RAF. London was, or should have been, within the effective range of the Luftwaffe operating from northern France. Galland believed that this consideration tempted Hitler and Goering to switch the Luftwaffe's attacks from Fighter Command airfields to London. 'But', Galland continued, 'it is a matter of fact also that this switch to London from military targets, from air force bases, changed the situation for Great Britain and Fighter Command considerably. If we would have continued to attack the bases perhaps the situation would have been changed.' Galland has also said that the Luftwaffe was neither trained nor prepared to conduct an independent air war over England. The range of the German fighters was too short for them to operate successfully over London. 'Our range was very, very limited and we could only cover a small part of the British Isles including London. But over London, for example, we could only stay ten minutes if we wanted to get back to our bases. This limited range of our fighters acting as escorts was, perhaps, the main factor which prevented an effective air offensive against Britain.'

Robert Wright, a member of Dowding's staff, and his biographer, has said that throughout 7 September, a day on which the Government in London issued an invasion alert, things were remarkably quiet. 'All of us', Mr Wright has said, 'were beginning to wonder what the devil was going to happen next. Then late in the afternoon the Germans launched

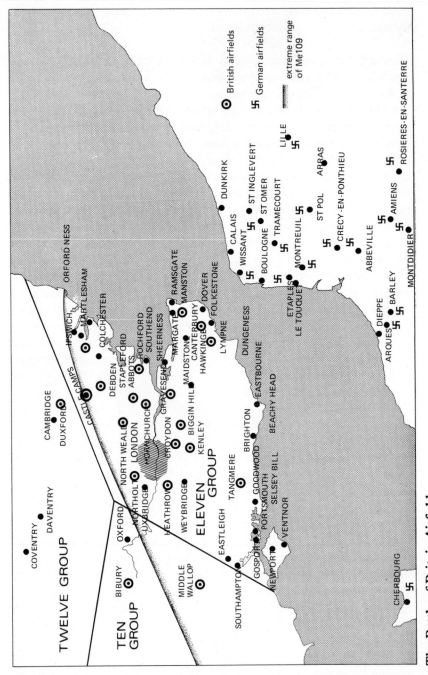

The Battle of Britain Airfields

Legend:
⊙ British airfields
卐 German airfields
extreme range of Me109

TEN GROUP

TWELVE GROUP

ELEVEN GROUP

COVENTRY
DAVENTRY
CAMBRIDGE
DUXFORD
OXFORD
CASTLE CAMPS
DEBDEN
STAPLEFORD
ABBOTS
HORNCHURCH
NORTHOLT
LONDON
UXBRIDGE
HEATHROW
WEYBRIDGE
CROYDON
KENLEY
BIGGIN HILL
GRAVESEND
MAIDSTONE
CANTERBURY
HAWKINGE
MARTLESHAM
IPSWICH
COLCHESTER
ORFORD NESS
ROCHFORD
SOUTHEND
SHEERNESS
MARGATE
MANSTON
RAMSGATE
DOVER
FOLKESTONE
LYMPNE
DUNGENESS
EASTBOURNE
BEACHY HEAD
BRIGHTON
GOODWOOD
TANGMERE
EASTLEIGH
SELSEY BILL
PORTSMOUTH
GOSPORT
NEWPORT
VENTNOR
SOUTHAMPTON
MIDDLE WALLOP
BIBURY

DUNKIRK
CALAIS
WISSANT
ST INGLEVERT
ST OMER
BOULOGNE
TRAMECOURT
MONTREUIL
ST POL
LILLE
ARRAS
CRECY-EN-PONTHIEU
ABBEVILLE
AMIENS
ROSIERES-EN-SANTERRE
MONTDIDIER
BARLEY
DIEPPE
ARQUES
ETAPLES
LE TOUQUET
CHERBOURG

what many of the pilots who were in the air . . . found out to be about the heaviest attack they had ever known. And then came what Dowding later described as the miracle. The attack didn't go to the airfields. It went to London. And the airfields were spared so they were able to pull themselves together, sort themselves out, repair things, and, most important of the lot, give the pilots more of a chance for a little rest.'[4]

Wright has said that the last week in August 1940 and the first week in September were the worst for Fighter Command because the Germans 'had been pounding the airfields mercilessly and 31 August was probably our worst day'.

The attack on London was one of two major mistakes that the Germans made during the Battle of Britain. The other was to believe their own pilots' estimates of British losses. On both sides in the Battle of Britain pilots reported in good faith that they had shot down enemy aircraft when they had not. On both sides the discrepancies between claims and the truth were wide. This difference between truth and fiction influenced the judgments of both British and German commanders but the influence it had on Goering was the more important of the two. Between 12 August and the end of September the Luftwaffe lost rather more than 1,100 aircraft whereas the British believed that the Luftwaffe's losses amounted to nearly 2,700 aircraft. But during the same period Fighter Command lost about 650 aircraft whereas the Germans believed that Fighter Command's losses exceeded 3,000. When the Battle of Britain began Goering knew fairly exactly the strength of Fighter Command. Believing his own figures he became more and more confident as the battle continued that Fighter Command had been broken. In fact it never was. But Goering's under-estimation of its remaining strength probably led him to launch operations which he would not otherwise have launched, and which failed. The Germans under-estimated Fighter Command throughout the Battle of Britain consistently, persistently and, from their point of view, fatally.

The band of men and women whom the Germans so badly under-estimated were an unusually talented fighting force. Fighter Command was in its way a typically British institution. It was an amalgam of amateurs and professionals who respected each other. Dowding was strong and decisive as a leader, but diffident and reserved in company. His pilots were mainly reservists who had set for themselves and had attained a high degree of skill. The Royal Air Force Volunteer Reserves had been for many years an extremely hard-working organization. By the time they were needed the reserve pilots were more than a match for

65

Goering's professionals. They were better able, also, to think for themselves. Pragmatic young men, trained for the learned professions, invented new tactics day by day. Flying with them was a large and valuable contingent of Poles. These were regulars from the Polish Air Force who had escaped to Britain. One Battle of Britain pilot in ten was a Pole. The Polish air force in exile proudly claimed to have shot down one German aircraft in every eight that were destroyed during the battle. The Polish regulars, smaller numbers of Czechoslovakian, British Commonwealth, and American volunteer pilots, the British volunteers, and the British regulars worked together more efficiently than the Germans did. Fighter Command squadrons thought for themselves in a way that the Germans did not. They wasted neither time nor ammunition. They were not daunted by being out-numbered. They saved Britain from invasion and, therefore, made it possible for the Western Allies to return in the end to Western Europe. Never, said Churchill, has so much been owed by so many to so few. Churchill, occasionally, used to exaggerate. But not this time.

Chapter 5

The Battle of the Atlantic

After losing the Battle of Britain in the autumn of 1940 the Germans tried to subdue their only surviving enemy in the West by starving her out. The Battle of the Atlantic was an attempt to force Britain to surrender for lack of food. The attempt very nearly succeeded.

One main reason why it failed was the extraordinary tenacity of British merchant seamen. More than 32,000 died at sea during World War II, all of them volunteers, out of a total of about 145,000. The overall casualty rate in the British Merchant Navy during World War II was higher than that in any of the armed services. It was comparable to the casualty rate suffered by the forces assigned to particularly desperate missions. For five and a half years British merchant seamen suffered roughly the same degree of casualties as General Wingate's Chindits, who penetrated behind the Japanese lines in Burma. British merchant seamen were never actually compelled to sign on for another voyage. Nor did they do it for the money. In 1939 the pay for an able seaman was £9.00 (then $36) per month plus 12½p per day danger money. These civilians went back to sea again time after time simply because they were sailors and thought they should.

The crews of tankers suffered most. If they escaped drowning they could still be burned to death by the cargo. Captain T. D. Finch, then Chief Officer of the *San Emiliano*, has described her sinking:

We left Trinidad on 6 August 1942 in convoy, bound for the Cape and eventually Suez, fully loaded with a cargo of high octane gasoline in all about 12,000 tons. In the evening of 9 August the convoy dispersed. Round about 6 in the evening as dusk fell I noticed a ship coming up from astern with full navigation lights blazing, indicating a neutral vessel. By 7 o'clock she was ½ a mile on our starboard beam and I noticed with the lights she was carrying that she was a hospital ship. By 8 p.m. when the 3rd officer relieved me of the watch she was well down on the horizon and disappearing. I've always had the idea that the U-boat must have been hanging around then, probably on the surface on that particular track and must have seen the hospital ship and more than likely saw us silhouetted against her lights. . . . At about 9 o'clock I decided to turn in for the night and was partially undressed when there was a terrific explosion from the starboard side which was immediately followed by another. I jumped out of the bunk, rushed to the cabin door, which came away in my hands, saw that the mess was ablaze, and started to run down the alley-way. I saw the apprentice running around and shouted to him 'Quick, this way . . . follow me'. We rushed back into my cabin, smacked the door back into position to prevent the fire entering, undid the thumb-screws to the port-hole, opened it up, and pushed the apprentice through it, and I followed him, landing on the shelter deck, down the ladder to the fore-deck and ran to the focs'lehead which I judged to be the safest place. By this time the ship was ablaze from bridge to stern, the whole sky being lit up by the flames which must have been hundreds of feet high. I saw the starboard life-boat had crashed into the sea but the port life-boat was still hanging in the davits, so I shouted to the apprentice 'Come-on . . . quick . . . we've got two minutes to get that boat away. If we don't, we're dead'. As we were running along the fore-deck towards the bridge, this boat also crashed into the sea. . . . We had to jump from the shelter deck to the falls about 6 feet and slide down them. Three other men threw themselves into the boat in desperation. At this time I had let go the after painter and noticed men running round the poop who were on fire, throwing themselves into the sea which was itself on fire.

We were about 40 ft. from the ship's side when the 3rd officer came running along the fore-deck from the focs'lehead shouting 'Wait for me, wait for me!' He dived over the side and we picked him up. At the same time there was another man on the focs'lehead shouting, but there was nothing we could do because out of the 5 or 6 who got away into the boat, only 3 were able to row. Slowly the ship drew ahead of us whilst we struggled to keep clear of burning sea. We heard some screams for help and rowed over and pulled out of the water a fireman who was terribly burned, so much so that when we pulled him into the boat, the skin from his body and arms came off in our hands like gloves, and he was in a very bad way indeed.

Eventually we heard two other cries for help and found in the water an able seaman who was clothed and not burned. Shortly after we picked up a pumpman in the same condition. We tried to pursue the ship, looking for survivors, but it was an impossible task because those in the boat were so gravely injured and collapsing, leaving only three to row against the wind and sea.

So we stopped rowing and found the first apprentice terribly burned, so much so that his hands had to be freed from the oars with scissors. The third officer and I attended to the wounded and were horrified at the extent of their injuries. There seemed no further signs of life anywhere so we hoisted sail and set course for Trinidad. This time, the fireman who had been in such agony all night, died, and within minutes the second steward who had suffered terrible abdominal wounds and burns also passed away. I went over to him and lifted the blanket covering him and noticed the whole of his stomach badly injured and exposed. He had been very patient during the night and the only thing he complained of was the cold. Both these men were committed to the deep. We had been sailing for an hour or two when the second mate called me. He had been badly burned and severely injured below the waist. He wanted water which I gave him, but even then I knew it was hopeless and a few minutes later he passed away, and as I covered him up with a blanket I noticed that the senior apprentice's life was also drawing to a close. About mid-day he died having been very badly burned all over his body and had been so very brave trying to keep up the morale of the rest of the men by singing. The most pathetic thing about the whole tragedy was the extreme youth of these lads, which was uppermost in my mind as I committed them to the deep.

We continued on our voyage, in utter despair and sadness. At about 1 o'clock in the afternoon we heard the hum of a plane. . . . He circled round several times, increasing height and then dropped a parachute, which held a cask of water but this broke on impact and so was wasted. I wasn't too concerned about water at that point as I reckoned I had enough to last us about 30 days. We proceeded and just before dark the plane returned.

He dropped the second parachute and this time it was a churn, rather like a milk churn. It was a good drop as it landed about 30 to 40 yards away from us. We picked it up and inside was a flask of iced water, cigarettes, chocolates and soup and a message saying 'steer south, coast within 110 miles'. I had had a rough idea that this was so, but steering south for me was against everything, e.g. current and the wind. However I decided to try so we turned round and headed south as far as we could judge. Dawn broke, we tidied the boat as far as we could and had a few rations. About ten o'clock the plane appeared again and dropped another parachute and this time it wasn't food but a message saying 'Help coming'.

About an hour after dusk we spotted a schooner sailing without lights. I grabbed a torch and signalled because I thought this was the help that had been sent, but as soon as he spotted the signal he turned away and went off into the night. About an hour and a half later the whole sky was lit up by flares, we heard a plane, and then the flares came down lighting up the whole ocean and we spotted our rescue ship which turned out to be the 'Admiral Jessop', U.S. Army Transport. He came along side and took the wounded off first, the rest climbed on board and then all were taken down to the sick bay and put under sedation. Before I was put under sedation the captain asked me what to do with the life-boat, and I told him to sink it as it had been such a boat load of misery, despair, and death, and I wanted no more to do with it. I learnt later that I could have sold it and with the cash I could have clothed the survivors.

Seven survived out of a crew of 48, but before the war was over I think another three of those saved at that time, lost their lives later. On this point I'm not quite sure but the senior wireless operator did die later. . . . I know that.

Those who got away in the boat were awarded one George Cross, two George Medals, one MBE, and three Lloyd's War Medals. Three were mentioned in despatches. The George Cross and two of the Lloyd's Medals were posthumous awards.

Almost as soon as the war in Europe began a German submarine already stationed in the Atlantic sank the British passenger liner *Athenia*, killing 112 people, 28 of them American citizens. In 1936 Germany had signed a convention which said that persons embarked in merchant ships must be safeguarded before these ships were sunk. In practice neither Hitler nor Admiral Doenitz, his submarine supreme commander, seem ever to have intended to abide by these rules. During September 1939 German submarines sank 26 British merchant ships without bothering overmuch or at all to ensure the safety of their crews.

They also sank the British aircraft carrier *Courageous* and, in October, the battleship *Royal Oak*. The sinking of the *Royal Oak*, moored in the supposedly safe waters of Scapa Flow, the northern fleet base in the Orkneys, was an impressive feat of arms by Lieutenant-Commander Guenther Prien, the commanding officer of the German submarine U47, and his crew.

When the war began, Admiral Doenitz had 26 submarines capable of operating in the North Atlantic. Only one-third of these could be kept on station at the same time. The rest were either on passage out or home

8. Allied soldiers waiting to be
evacuated from Dunkirk, May 1940

9. Survivors of the German battleship
Bismarck being rescued, 27 May 1941

10. Soldiers of the 5th Army advance under cover of smoke during the invasion of Italy

11. German soldiers during the attack on Arnhem in the Netherlands, September 1944

12. Gurkhas in action on the Tunisian front, March 1943

13. The Western Desert, December 1941: one of the crew of an Italian tank surrenders to a British soldier

14. Gracie Fields hands out tea after entertaining British troops, April 1940

15. Royal Fusiliers man an advanced post in France, January 1940

or refitting in Germany. On any one day about 2,500 British merchant ships were at sea and vulnerable to these submarines. The main British defence against the German submarines was to sail the merchant ships in convoys – large formations of up to 60 ships escorted by anti-submarine warship escorts. The convoy system had been adopted reluctantly by the Admiralty during World War I and had proved successful. Fewer ships were lost in convoy than if they had sailed independently.

The British had learnt this vital lesson in 1917 but had half-forgotten it by 1939. There were not enough escorts. Ships with speeds greater than 15 knots were encouraged to sail independently. The German submarines – only a handful of them at this time – concentrated on the ships that were not in convoy. By the end of 1939 they had sunk 102 ships sailing independently and only four ships in convoys.

For lack of escorts, and particularly for lack of long-range escorts, the Royal Navy was at first only able to maintain a convoy system in the North Atlantic from Britain to a line drawn about 100 miles west of Ireland. From this meridian – $12\frac{1}{2}°$ West longitude – the ships were expected to disperse and sail independently to North America. What the British did not realize – or if they did they could do nothing about it – was that although the range of the British escorting vessels had not increased much since 1918, the range of the German submarines was a great deal longer than it had been. Throughout the winter of 1939–1940 the Germans moved further out into the Atlantic and attacked the merchant ships after they had dispersed. In October 1940 the escort limit was extended to latitude 20° West. Once again the Germans moved further out and continued to attack the ships after the convoys had dispersed.

The British had yet to learn, also, the limitations of ASDIC, their underwater detection device. This consisted of an underwater directional sound transmitter and receiver. If the transmission encountered a submarine the sound would return as an echo. The British had much faith in ASDIC (named after the initials of the Allied Submarine Detection Investigation Committee) which was later known as SONAR. But the behaviour of sound waves in the sea, particularly in bad weather, is often wayward. Bubbles of air in water – caused by explosions, a ship's propellers, or simply by turbulence – can interrupt sound waves in the same way as rain interrupts light waves in the air. Variations in water temperature would also interfere with ASDIC beams. It was often useless in the Arctic. In any case the effective range of ASDIC was quite short. The operational use of ASDIC turned out to be much more of an art than a science.

ASDIC's most important limitation, however, was that it was unable to detect a submarine on the surface. The British had not, by and large, expected surface attacks by submarines. In World War I most German submarines had attacked from periscope depth – that is to say with virtually the whole of the submarine underwater. In World War II they attacked mainly at night and mainly when fully surfaced. This meant that ASDIC was useless at the very moment when it was most needed. For the first part of the war the British had no means other than their eyes of detecting a surfaced submarine at night, and even when fully surfaced a submarine is a very small target.

In the early part of the Battle of the Atlantic they also suffered from a lack of long-range aircraft. Later in the war aircraft equipped with radar were able to attack surfaced submarines at night with great accuracy and effect. But with or without radar, aircraft were always effective against submarines simply because they could keep them down.

The submarines of those days needed to remain on the surface for several hours each day for housekeeping purposes. When submerged they relied upon electric motors powered by immense batteries. When the power in the batteries ran low they had no option but to surface. Their main diesel engines needed air if they were to be used to recharge the batteries. Therefore submarine captains needed to spend some time by themselves on the surface recharging their batteries so as to be able to move under water. The threat of an air attack, by day or by night, real or imagined, would interrupt their recharging periods, and interfere perhaps seriously with their operational plans.

An already bad situation for the British changed substantially for the worse when the Germans conquered France and Norway in 1940. The fall of France left Britain to fight the war alone. It deprived the Royal Navy of the help of the French one, which was well versed in the use of ASDIC. Worst of all, however, the German conquest of France gave Doenitz better bases. France had fallen in June 1940. By July Doenitz had established his main submarine base at Lorient. This shortened the journey that German submarines were obliged to make from their bases to their operation areas by 450 miles. With the west coast of France in German hands Doenitz's captains could spend more time attacking convoys because they needed to spend less time and fuel travelling – as it were – to work. The effectiveness of the German submarine force had been multiplied at a stroke.

Britain's communications with North America, already threatened, were now hazardous. To make matters worse the Germans had exactly the type of long-range aircraft that Britain so badly needed. The Focke-Wulf 200 was a four-engined airliner with enough range to fly from France out across the North Atlantic and back to Norway. When they began operations in the late summer of 1940 the FW200's could locate virtually any British convoy, signal its position to the German submarines, and then bomb the ships.

An ocean convoy was a vast oblong of ships proceeding slowly sideways across the Atlantic. A 50-ship convoy would consist of 10 columns each of five ships in line ahead. This reduced the size of the target which the side of the convoy offered to a submarine. At the same time it was an awkward formation. Keeping station in a formation of 50 assorted merchant ships in bad weather is not an easy piece of seamanship, especially westbound against the prevailing wind and when most ships were empty or in ballast, and therefore high in the water. Moreover it was necessary to zigzag. Fifty ships in close company would have to alter course sharply together by the clock several times each hour. Sailing in convoy was a practice which ran counter to the basic instinct of an ocean-going master which is to keep well clear of other ships.

The FW200's were mastered in the end. The British introduced catapult ships into convoys. These could launch fighter aircraft to shoot the FW200's down or at least to chase them away. The fighters were deemed expendable. The pilots could not land on the catapult ships. All they could do was bale out into the sea in the hope of being rescued. Later the British introduced the escort aircraft carrier so that the fighters had a deck to land on. Reconnaisance by FW200's became ineffective. Doenitz used another tactic instead.

As soon as he had enough submarines to be able to keep fifteen or so operating in the Atlantic at any one time he ordered them to take up a series of patrol positions through which any convoy would have to pass. The submarines, stationed singly many miles apart, would simply wait until one of them saw the convoy's mastheads coming over the horizon. The submarine that had made the sighting would radio news of the find to Doenitz. Doenitz would order all the other available submarines to converge on the convoy. The following night they would all attack together. They would shadow the convoy during the day and attack again during the second night, and so on until their torpedoes were exhausted. Doenitz called it the 'wolf-pack technique'.

It was appallingly effective. Because the Royal Navy was still desperately short of escort vessels the convoys were very lightly guarded. In the early part of the Battle of the Atlantic the commanding officer of a single sloop or corvette could find himself responsible for the safety of 40 or 50

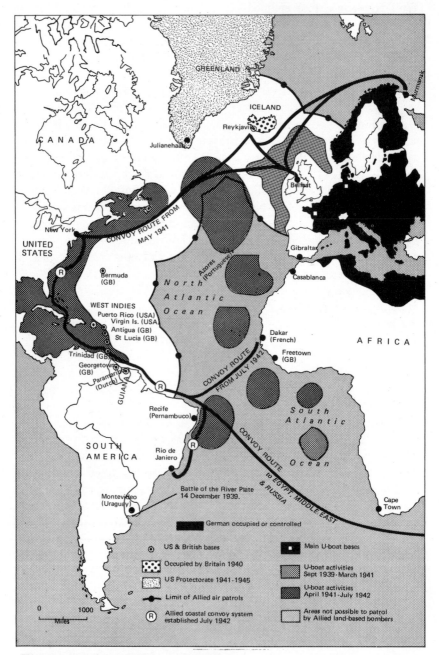

The Battle of the Atlantic, 1939–42

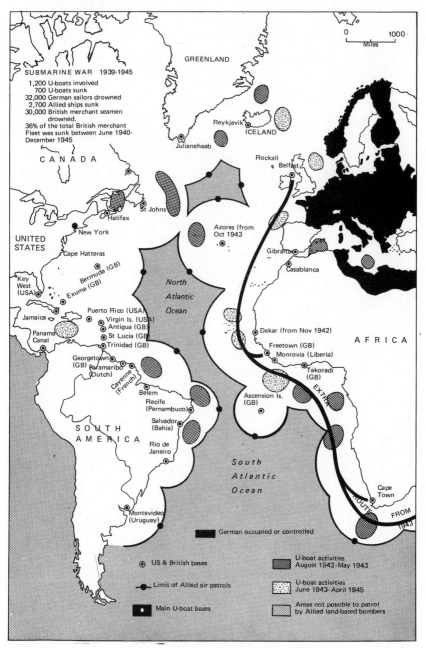

SUBMARINE WAR 1939-1945

1,200 U-boats involved
700 U-boats sunk
32,000 German sailors drowned
2,700 Allied ships sunk
30,000 British merchant seamen
 drowned.
36% of the total British merchant
Fleet was sunk between June 1940-
December 1945

GREENLAND

Reykjavik
Julianehaab   ICELAND

Rockall
Belfast

CANADA

St Johns
Halifax
New York

UNITED
STATES

Cape Hatteras

Azores (from
Oct 1943)

Gibraltar
Casablanca

Key
West
(USA)
Bermuda (GB)
Exuma (GB)

North
Atlantic
Ocean

Jamaica
Panama
Canal
Puerto Rico (USA)
Virgin Is. (USA)
Antigua (GB)
St Lucia (GB)
Trinidad (GB)

Dakar (from Nov 1942)
Freetown (GB)
Monrovia (Liberia)

AFRICA

Georgetown
(GB) Paramaribo
(Dutch)
Cayenne
(French)
Belem
Recife
(Pernambuco)

Takoradi
(GB)

SOUTH
AMERICA
Salvador
(Bahia)
Rio de
Janeiro

Ascension Is.
(GB)

EXTRA

South
Atlantic
Ocean

Cape
Town

Montevideo
(Uruguay)

German occupied or controlled

SOUTH

FROM
1943

US & British bases

Limit of Allied air patrols

Main U-boat bases

U-boat activities
August 1942-May 1943

U-boat activities
June 1943- April 1945

Areas not possible to patrol
by Allied land-based bombers

0   1000
        Miles

The Battle of the Atlantic, 1942–45

precious merchantmen. German coastal convoys in the Channel and the North Sea commonly employed twelve or more escorts for each merchantman. On one occasion British MTB's attacking a convoy near Boulogne encountered an escort of twenty-eight guarding one ship. For a long time, until the British escorts became more numerous, the German submarines had a comparatively easy time.

The art of the night surface torpedo attack is to recognise and interpret a dimly seen situation in seconds. It is an art that cannot be learnt on a simulator. In this specialized warfare skill comes with experience. Three of Doenitz's captains, Guenther Prien, who had sunk the *Royal Oak*, Otto Kretschmer, and Joachim Schepke, were conspicuously more successful than their colleagues. They had more experience. Therefore they sank more ships. Kretschmer in particular practised the deadly technique of penetrating between the columns of a convoy and attacking it from within. The Royal Navy scored an important success when, during two nights in March 1941, the escort of a westbound convoy south of Iceland sank the three submarines that they commanded. Kretschmer was captured by HMS *Walker*. The other two captains went down with their submarines.

This success, though important, was not enough. Doenitz had lost three of his best captains; but he was by now building new submarines more quickly. By September 1941, he had 150, although not all of them could operate at the same time. Simply because the submarines were plentiful and the escorts were still too sparse Doenitz's captains were able in April 1941 to sink a record number of Allied ships, most of them British. The rate at which ships were being sunk then far exceeded the rate at which they could be built. The tonnage of imports into Britain had been halved. In spite of everything that the Royal Navy and the RAF could do, Britain was being starved to death.

America joins the Battle

The most hopeful development for Britain during 1941 was that the United States, at first unofficially and then officially, became involved in the Battle of the Atlantic. America was not at war; but she helped. The fall of France and Hitler's occupation of nearly the whole of the West European mainland had alarmed the Americans badly. The United States had relied to a large extent upon Britain to maintain naval supremacy in the Atlantic. US naval strategy was based upon the expectation that America would be supreme in the Pacific while two more or less friendly powers – Britain and France – would help to dominate the Atlantic. When France fell this theory became untenable. The US Chief of Naval Operations, Admiral Stark, demanded and received at once a large appropriation for the expansion of the US Atlantic Fleet. This was America's first tacit commitment to the war against Hitler, which Britain was at that time fighting alone.

Throughout the rest of 1940, however, Britain imported the food and armaments she needed from the United States in her own ships on what was known as the 'cash and carry' basis. Britain paid for the imports with her dwindling stock of dollars and fetched them from across the Atlantic. The next step in America's involvement followed President Roosevelt's re-election to a third term of office. He was the only American President ever to have served a third term. His unprecedented victory in the November 1940 presidential election strengthened his domestic political position to the point at which he could afford to offer Britain open support without falling foul of America's hardcore isolationists. Roosevelt wasted no time. In December he abolished 'cash and carry' and replaced it by 'lend-lease'. Roosevelt told the American people that if your neighbour's house was on fire you would naturally lend him a hose pipe to put it out. Your neighbour would naturally return the hosepipe afterwards. 'The people of Europe who are defending themselves do not ask us to do their fighting', Roosevelt said, 'they ask us for the implements of war. . . . We must be the great arsenal of democracy'.[2]

Congress approved lend-lease. It did not, to begin with, approve the next stage in American involvement which was the actual protection by the US navy of lend-lease supplies. This protection began gradually and was seen, at least by Roosevelt, as a logical extension of the principle of lend-lease. Lending your neighbour a hose pipe was a useless gesture if the hose pipe was going to be stolen or destroyed on the way.

The American navy's first involvement in the war came about indirectly after the US marines had occupied bases in Iceland, relieving a British force which had been sent there following the occupation of Denmark, Iceland then being a Danish dependency. The British needed bases in Iceland in order to protect the Atlantic convoys. They needed also to deny Iceland to the Germans. In July 1941, by agreement, the US marines replaced the British garrison; the US navy therefore had a duty to escort convoys between the United States and Iceland; American and Icelandic ships were offered protection. So were 'ships of any nationality which may join'. In theory the US navy was simply safeguarding its own lines of communication. In practice it had begun to escort British convoys in the western part of the North Atlantic. American involvement became closer and more certain when a German submarine attacked the American destroyer *Greer* unsuccessfully south of Iceland in September 1941. In October a German submarine sank the USS *Kearney*. The US navy had been attacked and had suffered its first casualty. Roosevelt authorized the US navy to counter-attack. The Japanese attack on Pearl Harbor and Hitler's declaration of war on the United States were yet to come. But in the cold seas south of Iceland, America was at war already.

The state of the Battle of the Atlantic nevertheless remained critical and was to become more so. The American escorts between the United States and Iceland enabled the British to give better support to convoys in the eastern part of the Atlantic. But by then they had a new commitment. When Hitler attacked Russia in June 1941, Churchill at once offered all the aid and help that Britain could afford. This entailed the opening up of a new convoy route from Iceland to Murmansk in north Russia. It was the most perilous route of all, not so much because of submarines, but because much of it was within easy reach of German aircraft based in northern Norway. The north Russia convoys were also threatened by the presence of German surface ships in the northern Norwegian fjords. The first north Russia convoys managed to get through. But those that followed suffered hideously.

The transatlantic convoy route, however, was still Britain's main lifeline. Slow convoys, capable of a theoretical seven and a half knots, assembled at Sydney, Cape Breton, and so-called fast convoys, theoretically capable of nine or ten knots, assembled at Halifax, Nova Scotia. By now the German submarines were concentrating their attacks in the 'air-cover gap', the area south of Iceland and west of Cape Farewell, Greenland, which could not be surveyed by shore-based reconnaisance aircraft.

In December 1941, when Hitler declared war on the United States (following the Japanese attack on Pearl Harbor), Doenitz realized at once that although the British may have been ill-prepared to defend their convoys against submarines, the Americans were not prepared at all. Very large numbers of ships were at sea daily moving unescorted up and down the main coastal sea routes from the Saint Lawrence to New York, thence south again round Cape Hatteras to the Straits of Florida. From there they would head either into the Gulf of Mexico or south-eastwards between the Bahamas and Cuba to the Windward Passage, which separates Cuba from Haiti. The whole of this long lifeline was unprotected. There was no convoy system. Had there been one the escorts would have been lacking. The US navy had not yet had time to re-build its strength in the

Atlantic. Starting in January 1942, in the area of Atlantic City, the Virginia Capes, and Hatteras, German submarines had sunk 360 merchant ships in American coastal waters by the middle of July. By then the Americans had organized a convoy system covering the route from New York through the Windward Passage to the north-east coast of South America. From there convoys could proceed to the Red Sea and the Middle East round the Cape of Good Hope or to Freetown in West Africa. Doenitz simply extended his operational area. The German submarines moved to the neighbourhood of Freetown, to the Gulf of Mexico, and to the coastal waters of Brazil. The sinkings continued.

Centimetric Radar

The British and the Americans, now formal allies, still had not solved the basic problem which bedevilled the Battle of the Atlantic – how to detect a surfaced submarine and attack it effectively at night or in bad weather. They still needed more long-range aircraft for reconnaisance and to keep the submarines down. But they also needed a sure means by which aircraft and surface ships could detect a surfaced submarine at night and attack it.

The answer to this serious problem was centimetric radar, a decisive British discovery which changed the fortunes of war in the Allies' favour. It is improbable that they would have won the Battle of the Atlantic without it. Radar had been in existence since before the war. In principle it resembles ASDIC. You transmit a beam of electro-magnetic waves. When the beam hits a target it bounces back. By measuring the time elapsed between the transmission and the receipt of the echo you can measure the target's range. By observing the bearing you can determine the direction of the target from your own ship or aircraft. You have located the target. The principle was well understood before the war in Britain and a chain of radar stations had been established to give early warning of approaching aircraft. The navy had fitted radar to several warships and Admiral Cunningham, the Commander-in-Chief of the British Mediterranean fleet, had used it for the first time to good effect when he defeated the Italian fleet at the Battle of Matapan. However, the trouble with the early radar sets was that they were too bulky. Cunningham could accommodate radar because he had a battleship. What the Allies still needed in the Battle of the Atlantic and in many other struggles too was a radar small enough to be fitted into an aircraft or into a small warship. The

79

reason the sets were too bulky was that the wavelengths they used were too long. One absolute requirement for a useful radar beam is that it should be narrow because a wide beam will reveal range but not bearing.

If you wanted a narrow beam a long wavelength obliged you to use a very large 'mirror' to concentrate the beam. If you wanted to reduce the size of the mirror so that it would fit into an aircraft you had first to reduce the wavelength.

When the war began no one had yet managed to generate electro-magnetic waves at really short wavelengths, measured in centimetres. The answer (discovered during the winter of 1939–1940 by two British scientists, J. T. Randall and H. A. H. Boot, and embellished and developed by many others in Britain) was the cavity magnetron which could generate wavelengths of ten centimetres and shorter. In 1941 another British scientist, J. Sayers, found a cure for the frequency jumping from which some early magnetrons suffered by strapping their segments together.

Centimetric radar, as the Germans admitted, turned out to be the most decisive of the many new devices the Allies introduced. In May 1943, Doenitz went to see Hitler at Berchtesgaden to tell him that the Battle of the Atlantic would have to be broken off, at least for the time being. 'What is now decisive', Doenitz told Hitler, 'is that enemy aircraft have been equipped with a new location apparatus . . . which enables them to detect submarines and to attack them unexpectedly in low cloud, bad visibility, or at night. If the aircraft did not have this location device they would not be able, for example, to detect submarines in rough seas or at night. Much the largest number of submarines now being sunk are being sunk by aircraft'.

Doenitz went on to say that 'in the last month losses have risen from 14 submarines, that is about 13% of those at sea, to 36 submarines or perhaps 37, that is about 30% of the submarines at sea. These losses are too high. We must now husband our resources because, to do anything else, would simply be to play the enemy's game'.[3]

The tide had turned. March 1943 had been the worst month of the war for the Allies in the Atlantic with 43 ships sunk in the first 20 days of the month. But April and May 1943 were to be the worst months for Doenitz. Not a single Allied ship was lost to submarines in the Atlantic between 17 May and September 1943. Doenitz was never able to prevail again, although he tried. Hopefully, in an order of the day on 24 May 1943, he promised his men new devices and new weapons with which they would triumph. Meanwhile there would be a pause in the battle. But the new devices were not enough. The first was the homing torpedo. This was fitted with an acoustic device which steered it towards the sound of the target's propeller. Doenitz hoped that it would enable his captains to fire 'blind' at a convoy from a safe distance and from below the surface. The acoustic homing torpedo scored a brief success. The British and the Americans had foreseen this torpedo and were ready with a simple answer. The 'foxer', a device which could be towed astern of a ship and which made more noise than the ship's propellers, was ready and waiting. German acoustic torpedoes destroyed many 'foxers' but hardly any ships.

Doenitz also gave his captains the Schnorkel, to enable them to recharge their batteries without surfacing fully. The Schnorkel was a breathing tube for the submarine's diesel engines. Instead of surfacing and exposing the entire conning-tower to radar detection a captain could simply extend his Schnorkel until it broke surface. But neither the Schnorkel nor the acoustic homing torpedo enabled the German submarines to become an effective force again in the North Atlantic. The retreat of the U-boats was not temporary, as Doenitz had told Hitler at Berchtesgaden, it was permanent.

Doenitz's submarines were much the most effective naval force that Germany used during World War II. They sank 2,828 Allied merchant ships and 145 warships. Altogether the Germans built 1,162 submarines and lost 785 of them. But their investment in submarines, though heavy, was far more profitable than the men, money, and treasure which they invested in surface warships. German surface warships made several incursions into the Atlantic and none was worthwhile.

In 1939, when the war began, the German navy already had two 'pocket-battleships' stationed in the Atlantic. These were fast, heavily armoured, heavily armed, 12,000-ton vessels which could theoretically outgun and outstrip every British warship except the very largest and fastest. Nevertheless their operations were unproductive. In the North Atlantic the *Deutschland* found no target, fired no shot, and returned to Germany through the Arctic when her fuel began to run low. In the South Atlantic the *Admiral Graf Spee* sank a number of British merchant ships sailing to or from South American ports. On 26 September she was intercepted by the British South Atlantic squadron consisting of the cruiser *Exeter*, armed with 8-inch guns, the light cruiser *Ajax*, and the Royal New Zealand Navy cruiser *Achilles*. With her 11-inch guns the *Graf Spee* could outrange them all. But she lost the fight. The British Commander, Commodore Harwood, divided his forces to compel the *Graf Spee* to fire in two directions at once. The *Graf Spee*'s gunnery control system, like that of any other ship, worked best when it could concentrate on a single target. In a running fight lasting nearly two hours, dodging into and out of range, Harwood's ships inflicted more damage on the *Graf Spee* than the *Graf Spee* had been able to inflict upon them. The *Graf Spee* had retired into neutral waters at Montevideo, badly damaged, with 37 men dead, and 57 wounded. Her commanding officer, Captain Langsdorff, scuttled his ship in the River Plate and then committed suicide.

The 'Scharnhorst' and the 'Gneisenau'

The Germans sent two more heavy warships singly into the North Atlantic during 1939. The first was Germany's third pocket-battleship, the *Admiral Scheer*. She passed through the Denmark Strait which separates Iceland from Greenland in October and on 5 November sighted an eastbound British convoy escorted by the armed merchant cruiser, *Jervis Bay*. Her commanding officer, Captain E. S. F. Fegen, ordered the convoy to scatter and steered straight for the *Admiral Scheer*. The *Jervis Bay* was no more than an armed merchantman and no match for the *Admiral Scheer*. But by inviting the destruction of his own ship Captain Fegen gave his convoy time to scatter. The *Admiral Scheer* sank the *Jervis Bay* but only managed to sink five ships out of the convoy of 37. The *Admiral Scheer* sank another 11 merchant ships – all of them unescorted – before returning to Germany.

In December the heavy cruiser *Hipper* made another lonely foray into the Atlantic. She attacked one convoy on Christmas Day 1939, but was driven off, damaged, and forced to put into Brest for repairs. The *Hipper* did rather better in a second expedition from Brest in February 1940 sinking seven ships out of a convoy of 19. But she had not accomplished nearly as much as even a pair of submarines.

The Germans seem then to have decided that an expedition by a single ship would not produce worthwhile returns. The next surface mission was entrusted to two large, fast battle-cruisers, the *Scharnhorst* and the *Gneisenau*. They stayed together and they were indeed a formidable force. But they had no aircraft. Nor could they establish a line of scouts to locate convoys in the way that Doenitz's U-boats could. They were also effectively deterred from attacking the convoys that they happened to find by the sight of an ancient British battleship. While the *Scharnhorst* and the *Gneisenau* were at large the British Admiralty had added to the escort of as many convoys as possible one slow but well-armed battleship, some of them veterans of World War I. The deterrent worked. Whenever the *Scharnhorst* and the *Gneisenau* sighted one of these venerable ships they moved off in search of easier targets. In the end they sank 21 ships before retiring to Brest where they were at once subjected to constant air attacks by the RAF.

The Commander-in-Chief of the German Navy, Admiral Raeder, was probably the last living admiral who never understood the importance of air-power and who continued to suppose – even in the 1940's – that battleships were impregnable and all-powerful. Raeder's next plan was to bring together as a single large raiding squadron the *Scharnhorst*, the *Gneisenau*, the *Bismarck*, Germany's only battleship at that time, and the heavy cruiser *Prinz Eugen*. They were to assemble at Brest. The *Bismarck* and the *Prinz Eugen* were at Gdynia in the eastern Baltic. Raeder had hoped to send them into the Atlantic undetected. He was frustrated by a Royal Navy reconnaisance pilot who established during the fourth week of May 1941 that the two ships had sailed from a fjord near Bergen.

For the British Admiralty this was a direct challenge. Incursions into the Atlantic by single pocket-battleships or by pairs of battle-cruisers were one thing. An organised expedition by Germany's most powerful warship in conjunction – as it then seemed – with two battle-cruisers from Brest and a heavy cruiser was a more formidable threat altogether. The Commander-in-Chief of the British Home Fleet, Admiral Jack Tovey, mobilized his ships at once. So did Admiral Somerville, the Commander of Force 'H', at Gibraltar. The movements of these two powerful forces were co-ordinated by the Admiralty in London. Tovey ordered the Home Fleet to sail westward from Scapa Flow in the Orkneys and from the Clyde towards Iceland and the southern exit from the Denmark Strait.

The commander of the German squadron, Admiral Luetjens, had been at sea for two days and two nights when he was detected by one of Tovey's cruisers, HMS *Suffolk*, as he was heading south through the Denmark Strait. *Suffolk* and her consort *Norfolk* shadowed the German ships through the night of 23–24 May, keeping Tovey and his captains informed about the German squadron's position, course, and speed.

The vanguard of Tovey's force comprised the old but fast battle-cruiser, HMS *Hood*, and the new battleship, *Prince of Wales*, commanded by Vice-Admiral Holland. Guided by the *Suffolk* and the *Norfolk*, Admiral Holland intercepted the German squadron punctually as intended at dawn on 24 May. The British came off worst. The lightly armoured *Hood* was sunk when a shell from the *Bismarck* exploded in her after-magazine. The *Hood* blew up and sank in three minutes. Virtually all her crew went down with the ship. The *Prince of Wales* suffered serious damage, but so did the *Bismarck*. A shell from the

Prince of Wales flooded a compartment which contained the transfer valves for the *Bismarck*'s fuel supply. This meant that the *Bismarck* was short from then on of 1,000 tons of fuel. The *Norfolk*, the *Suffolk*, and the *Prince of Wales* continued to shadow her. Admiral Tovey, hurrying after them with the main body of the Home Fleet, decided to launch an air attack from the carrier *Victorious*. The attack was delivered in the evening of the 24th and scored one torpedo hit; but during the night, unhappily for the British, the *Bismarck* managed to give the shadowing *Suffolk* the slip.

In fact the *Bismarck* had altered course for Brest. Tovey, fearful of the damage the *Bismarck* could cause in the western Atlantic to unescorted ships, headed westwards, determined to prevent this, the worst eventuality. The *Bismarck*'s real course, however, was now taking her towards Admiral Somerville's force 'H' steaming north-westward from Gibraltar. This consisted of the old battle-cruiser *Renown* and the aircraft carrier *Ark Royal*.

By the morning of 26 May the Admiralty had again located the *Bismarck*. She had given her position away on the 25th by using radio. Early on the 26th she was spotted by a Catalina flying-boat of the RAF. The Admiralty then knew that she was certainly heading for Brest. Soon afterwards the *Bismarck* was spotted again by one of the *Ark Royal*'s scouting aircraft.

At 5.0 p.m. *Ark Royal* launched her second and successful strike of the afternoon. The *Bismarck* received two torpedo hits, one of which jammed her rudders and made her unsteerable. A flotilla of destroyers under Captain Vian kept contact with the now crippled *Bismarck* through the night. By the morning Admiral Tovey had arrived with the Home Fleet. The *Bismarck* was first disabled by the 16 and 14-inch guns of the *Rodney* and *King George V*. Then she was sunk by torpedoes from the cruiser *Dorsetshire*. Hitler's only battleship went down at twenty minutes to nine on the morning of 27 May 1941, taking most of her crew with her.

Prinz Eugen, however, had escaped. She had been detached from *Bismarck* two nights before with orders to head straight for Brest where she joined the *Scharnhorst* and the *Gneisenau*.

German breakthrough in the English Channel

The *Scharnhorst*, the *Gneisenau* and the *Prinz Eugen* rested uneasily in Brest from May 1941 until February 1942. On 12 February, in a bold operation which took the RAF and, to a lesser extent, the Royal Navy by surprise, the three ships steamed, at full speed and in daylight, up the English Channel, through the Straits of Dover, and home to Germany. The operation was ordered and planned by Hitler himself who had become impatient with his admirals. The big German ships had had little success raiding in the Atlantic. There was no point in sending them out again. At the same time Hitler feared an invasion of Norway. He wanted his big ships in Norwegian waters.

Hitler's admirals, notably Admiral Ciliax, who led the operation, did not believe that the Channel passage would be possible. Hitler had guessed correctly that the British would be confident that Bomber Command could easily sink the ships if they came through in daylight. Hitler did not believe that Bomber Command was capable of this; but he thought the British believed it, and he was right.

In February 1942 the Japanese air force had just sunk the British battleships *Repulse* and *Prince of Wales* off the Malayan coast in daylight. Most responsible British admirals and air marshals assumed that the RAF could do the same to the *Scharnhorst*, the *Gneisenau*, and the *Prinz Eugen*. The British assumed that the Germans would assume this too. If, therefore, the Germans decided to make a dash for home they would do so at night. Therefore the navy must be ready to attack them then.

Hitler's plan was for the ships to sail from Brest after dark on 11 February, for them then to sail at high speed up the Channel aiming to pass the Straits of Dover at about noon on 12 February when the tide would be strongly in their favour. Their passage was to be protected by a large number of fighter aircraft operating from northern France. They were to be given a heavy surface escort of destroyers and MTB's.

Hitler got his battleships home from Brest partly because his plan was bold and good but also because of several failures on the part of the British.[4] The Germans also had good luck. The big ships sailed late because of an air raid and because one of them had carelessly allowed a wire to foul her propeller. This meant that the British submarine *Sealion* had withdrawn from her station at the entrance to Brest when the ships finally left. An RAF aircraft fitted with radar which ought to have been watching the entrance to Brest had been obliged to return to base because its set had failed. By the time the aircraft was back on station the German squadron was out to sea and rounding Ushant. The Germans' luck continued. A second RAF radar patrol aircraft should have been covering the area from Ushant to Brehat Island near Roscoff. But this aircraft, too, had a defective radar set. By six o'clock on the morning of 12 February the German squadron was off Cherbourg and nobody had noticed. Worse still, no one in authority on the British side seems to have realized that the prescribed reconnaisance had not been carried out. The German ships had not been spotted but there was no reason why they should have been. The watchdog had failed to bark because the watchdog had not been there.

The German ships were first identified by a Spitfire pilot, Sergeant Beaumont of the RAF, at 10.35 a.m. on 12 February steaming north at high speed off Le Touquet. Almost one hour later staff officers of the RAF's Eleven Group were still hesitant to interrupt Air Vice-Marshal Leigh-Mallory with Sergeant Beaumont's news because Leigh-Mallory was taking a parade.

The Vice-Admiral, Dover, still then Sir Bertram Ramsay, had five operational MTB's available and a squadron of torpedo-carrying Swordfish aircraft. The MTB's had been at immediate notice for sea for a fortnight. But at dawn on 12 February the MTB's were de-alerted to four hours' notice. At 11.40 on the 12th – after Sergeant Beaumont and his chief, Squadron Leader Oxspring, had managed to persuade their superiors to listen – the Dover MTB's were ordered to sea and left at 11.55. At this stage the German squadron consisted of three big ships, *Scharnhorst*, *Gneisenau*, and *Prinz Eugen*, fifteen fast torpedo boats, ten large fleet destroyers, and three flotillas of E-boats, as the Germans called their MTB's. The five British MTB's from Dover were the resident remnant of a force of 36 which had been gathered there in anticipation of the German squadron's making a night passage. But the other 31 British MTB's had been dispersed back to their bases on 10 February because the Admiralty thought that the threat of a break-out had passed. Elaborate and quite sophisticated plans had been worked out for a night attack on the German squadron based on the assumption that Dover would get several hours' notice of its coming. In the event the notice was so short and the German squadron was steaming so fast that there was no time for sophistication. There was no darkness either. The Dover MTB's, which were two knots slower than the German squadron, could only attack immediately, or not at all. All five MTB's fired their torpedoes – a total of 10 – mostly at the *Prinz Eugen* through a gap in the smoke screen that had been laid around her. The *Prinz Eugen* saw the torpedoes coming and altered course to avoid them.

When the speed of a torpedo, in this case 35 knots, is not much higher than the target's speed through the water (in this case 29 knots) avoiding action by the target is usually effective, especially in daylight when the torpedoes' tracks can be seen. All the torpedoes missed.

The MTB's were saved from destruction by the Swordfish. There were perhaps 50 German fighter aircraft armed with cannon in the air at this time, but they were saving their ammunition for the Swordfish. The Swordfish, who had saved the MTB's, could not themselves be saved. Their leader, Lieutenant-Commander Esmonde, VC, was shot down almost at once and was killed. The German fighters flew with their landing gear extended to reduce their speed to match that of the 80-knot Swordfish without overcooling their engines. A part of the Swordfish squadron's intended escort of RAF Spitfires found the Swordfish and did its best to guard them. But ten Spitfires could not protect them against 50 of Germany's latest fighters, Focke-Wulf 190's capable of 300 knots. All the Swordfish were shot down. Only some of their crews were saved.

The weather thickened during the afternoon. As the German squadron hurried on into the North Sea, RAF bombers and torpedo bombers strove hard to find them through the overcast. Many Bomber and Coastal Command pilots died that afternoon in a series of unrehearsed attacks on the German ships. The 21st Destroyer Flotilla attacked with torpedoes off the Meuse Estuary but, once again, the torpedoes were seen running and the attack failed. *HMS Worcester* was badly damaged and suffered many casualties. The only serious damage suffered by the Germans was to *Gneisenau*, which struck a mine off the Dutch island of Terschelling during the evening. Later, while being repaired in dry dock, she was badly damaged by bombs and was not able to put to sea again.

This was no immediate consolation, however, to the RAF and the Royal Navy. For the first time since the arrival of the Spanish Armada in 1588 an enemy battle fleet had sailed the English Channel and, unlike the Armada, had got through. Besides the original reconnaisance failures there had been command muddles and a certain dreamlike incompetence. RAF pilots took off without having been told what to look for (the leader of Esmonde's escort had been told to intervene in a 'scuffle' between MTB's and E-boats) because the information was thought to be too secret. The rest of the Swordfish escort failed to find the battleships at all. But no one had told them to look for battleships. RAF torpedo bombers were flown from Scotland to Lincolnshire to load torpedoes which were not there. It took the RAF a long time to act upon Sergeant Beaumont's good and accurate report.

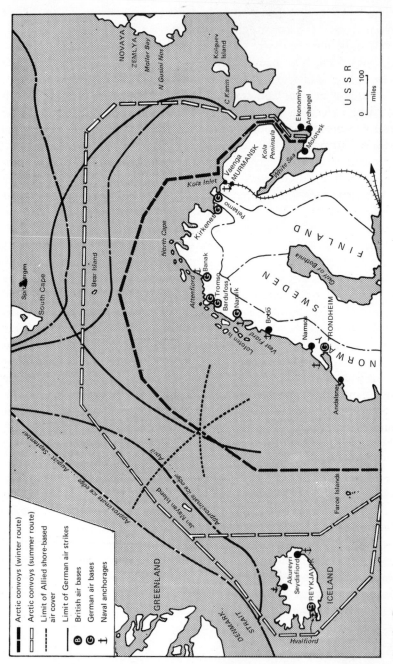

Arctic Convoys

Legend:
- Arctic convoys (winter route)
- Arctic convoys (summer route)
- Limit of Allied shore-based air cover
- Limit of German air strikes
- Ⓑ British air bases
- Ⓖ German air bases
- ✠ Naval anchorages

Map labels:

GREENLAND

DENMARK STRAIT

Jan Mayen Island

Approximate ice edge
August–September
Approximate ice edge
April–May

Spitzbergen
South Cape
Bear Island

NOVAYA ZEMLYA
Matter Bay
N. Gusini Nos
Kolguev Island
C. Kanin

North Cape
Alten fiord
Banak
Tromsø
Bardufoss
Narvik
Kirkenes
Petsamo
Kola Inlet
Vaenga
MURMANSK
Kola Peninsula
White Sea
Ekonomiya
Archangel
Molotvsk

Bjotö
Lofoten Is.
Vest Fiord
Namsos
TRONDHEIM
Andalsnes

NORWAY
SWEDEN
FINLAND
Gulf of Bothnia

USSR

0 ——— 100
miles

Faroe Islands

ICELAND
Akureyri
Seydisfiord
REYKJAVIK
Hvalfiord

By concentrating his heavy surface warships in Norway, Hitler did not in fact deter the Allies from invading that country – an undertaking which they never contemplated. On the other hand the presence of formidable German ships in Norwegian waters complicated the already hazardous business of running convoys to north Russia. Simply by sitting in north Norwegian fjords the German heavy ships obliged the Admiralty in London to take precautions and weighty decisions – some good, some bad – which it would not otherwise have had to take.

The British had begun to convoy supplies of war materials to the north Russian ports of Archangel and Murmansk as soon as possible after Hitler attacked Russia in June 1941. Churchill's immediate reaction to Hitler's attack had been to promise the Soviet Union whatever aid could be supplied. He promised more than Britain could manage. It never was possible to run a convoy to Russia once every ten days, as Churchill had hoped. German aircraft based in north Norway were one formidable hazard. The climate was another. A third which, in practice, was to remain no more than a grave threat, was the presence of German capital ships in north Norwegian waters. The *Tirpitz*, *Bismarck's* sistership, was based in the Altenfjord.

The equation of risk for the Arctic convoys was grim. During the winter the ice, extending southward, obliged them to pass between Bear Island and the North Cape of Norway and then to pass within two or three hundred miles of German-held territory on their way to the Kola inlet which itself was only thirty miles from the German-Russian front line. In summer they could go further north. Summer convoys, starting from Iceland, could pass north of Jan Mayen Island (which is normally iced in during the winter) and between Spitzbergen and Bear Island before turning south in Longitude 43° East for Cape Kanin which marks the eastern side of the entrance to Archangel. The summer route was further north and therefore further away from the German airfields; but the daylight was perpetual. The winter convoys had to pass dangerously close to German bases. The summer ones were exposed twenty-four hours a day to German air attack for at least one third of the voyage. The problem of transporting supplies to north Russia was complicated further by the fact that Archangel, further from the front and therefore safer, was frozen up during each winter.

The convoys to north Russia began sailing in September 1941, three months after Hitler's attack on Russia. The first twelve arrived safely.

But PQ13, as the thirteenth north Russia convoy was code-named, lost two ships out of nineteen. PQ15 lost three ships, and PQ16 lost seven. The north Russia convoys were obviously becoming increasingly risky and expensive. Churchill, nevertheless, was determined to do all he could to help the Russians. The thirty-six merchant ships of PQ17, a larger convoy than its predecessors, sailed for Archangel in June 1942. The Germans located PQ17 from the air on 1 July, and air attacks began on 4 July. The Admiralty believed, wrongly, that the *Tirpitz* had sailed to intercept PQ17 and to destroy it. In fact, the *Tirpitz* did not sail until the following day, 5 July, stayed at sea for only a few hours, and never got anywhere near the convoy. The *Tirpitz* had, nevertheless, sealed the fate of PQ17 simply by being where she was. Misled by false intelligence, the Admiralty ordered the escort of PQ17 to return westward and the convoy itself to scatter. The Admiralty had decided in advance that the comparatively heavy and powerful escorts which accompanied the north Russia convoys were more valuable than the convoys themselves. Obeying orders that could not be questioned the escort retired and the convoy was massacred by German aircraft. Twenty-four ships were sunk. Some of the others were beached on the west shore of Novaya Zemlya. A few struggled on to Archangel.

PQ17 had been a disaster. The next north Russia convoy did not sail until September but it was escorted by an aircraft carrier and lost only thirteen out of forty ships. The threat of the heavy German warships stationed in north Norway remained, nevertheless.

In September 1943 two out of six British midget submarines managed to penetrate the *Tirpitz's* protected anchorage in Kaafjord, a branch of Altenfjord. Submarines X6 and X7, commanded by Lieutenant-Commander Cameron and Lieutenant Place, succeeded in penetrating the defensive anti-torpedo nets which surrounded *Tirpitz*. Both midget submarines were able to place charges beneath the German ship which caused serious damage. *Tirpitz* was immobilized for seven months.

The End of the 'Scharnhorst' and the 'Tirpitz'

Just after Christmas 1943 the *Scharnhorst*, which had by then also been stationed in north Norway, sailed with destroyers to intercept two north Russia convoys, one eastbound, the other westbound. The *Scharnhorst* was then Hitler's only effective capital ship. The new Commander-in

Chief of the Home Fleet, Admiral Sir Bruce Fraser, embarked in the battleship *Duke of York*, suspected that the *Scharnhorst* might sail to intercept one or both convoys. His suspicions were confirmed when the German Admiral Bey, unsure whether to proceed or not in bad weather, sent a signal from sea asking for instructions. Fraser closed in from the west. Admiral Burnett, commanding a force of cruisers which were screening the two convoys, intercepted the *Scharnhorst* early on Boxing Day and at once attacked. A shell from *HMS Norfolk* destroyed one of *Scharnhorst's* radar sets. The weather was appalling. *Scharnhorst*, much the bigger ship, was able to maintain a higher speed than Burnett's cruisers and escaped them. By now Admiral Bey in the *Scharnhorst* had lost contact with his escorting destroyers. He was on his own and perhaps bewildered. He turned in search of the convoys. Burnett, correctly anticipating Bey's intention, intercepted him again. Bey's second encounter with Burnett's cruisers convinced him that his proper course was to retreat to Norway. He headed back for Altenfjord only to be intercepted again, this time by Fraser and the main force of the Home Fleet.

Fraser came up with Bey in the darkness of an early Arctic evening. In a night gunnery action lasting an hour the *Duke of York* inflicted so much damage on *Scharnhorst* that she lost power, stopped, and could no longer fire back. In the end the *Scharnhorst*, built to be unsinkable by gunfire, had to be sunk by torpedo. She received eleven hits before sinking.

The Battle of the North Cape, as this skilful and decisive night action came to be called, was a serious blow to the German navy. Only the damaged *Tirpitz* remained as a floating threat to the north Russia convoys. By March 1944 the damage done by the midget submarines had been repaired.

In April, acting this time on accurate intelligence that the *Tirpitz* was about to sail, the Admiralty ordered a concerted attack by carrier-borne aircraft on the *Tirpitz* in her northern anchorage. Damaged by fourteen direct hits, the *Tirpitz* was once again rendered useless as a warship. Later, immobilized at Tromsoe, she was sunk by the RAF. The *Tirpitz* was the last of the German navy's capital ships. When she went down off Tromsö she had never fired her main armament in anger against another warship. Yet, without firing a shot and simply because of her existence, the *Tirpitz* had ensured the destruction of a valuable convoy. PQ17 was lost because the Germans still had a fleet in being.

A main purpose of the Battle of the Atlantic was to keep the sea-lanes open so that the Allies could build up enough military strength in Britain to invade north-western Europe when the time came. As the Battle of the Atlantic continued the forces assembled.

Between 1940 and 1944 a considerable army gathered in Britain, but had no one to fight and nothing to do except train. Partly to try out landing techniques, partly for the sake of their own morale, the British set up Combined Operations Headquarters, to mount a series of raids on German occupied territory. Some were more successful than others. Two raids on the Lofoten Islands off the coast of Norway sank many ships, but the reprisals to which the Lofoten islanders were afterwards subjected by the Nazis were harsh and undeserved. Two more raids, carried out this time by airborne troops, were launched against a heavy-water plant – deemed essential to any German attempt to manufacture a nuclear weapon – in Telemark in south Norway. With the gallant and ingenious help of Norwegian resistance fighters, some of them landing from Britain, these two raids succeeded not only in interrupting production but also in providing the Allies with precise information about how far the Germans had advanced in their search for the bomb. They had not advanced very far.

Two larger raids were launched from Britain against St Nazaire on the west coast of France, and against Dieppe, a Channel port opposite Sussex. The purpose of the raid on St Nazaire was to destroy that port's important dry-dock facilities. The raid was a spectacular success. An old American destroyer, flying the white ensign as *HMS Campbeltown*, was loaded with explosives and rammed the gates of the lock. The operation was extremely hazardous, but it was carried out with great determination and skill. The St Nazaire dry-dock was useless for the rest of the war. The Germans could not use it to repair their heavy ships.

The raid on Dieppe was a disaster for the Allies. The full report on the operation was not published for thirty years.[5] It showed that out of 4,961 Canadians who took part 3,363 were killed, wounded, captured or went missing. At the time the British Cabinet and the British public were told that the raid had taught the Allies 'invaluable lessons'. The only real lesson learned from the Dieppe raid was that it should never have been launched. The Allies wanted to see if they could capture a defended port, but they were not prepared to risk the ships that would have been necessary to destroy the defences for the unfortunate Canadians who went ashore. Lord Mountbatten, the then Chief of Combined Operations, said that 'the lesson of greatest importance is the need for overwhelming fire support including close support, during the initial stages of the attack. Without such support, any assault on the enemy occupied coast of Europe is more and more likely to fail as the enemies' defences are extended and improved'. Yet the Allied navies only felt able to spare four small destroyers and a China River gunboat to bombard the Dieppe defences. Four of them, the report shows, were unable to communicate with their observation officers who were supposed to direct their fire. One ship ran out of ammunition.

Dieppe was a very well defended port indeed. The Germans had fortified not only the harbour but many commanding buildings in the town. There was a battery of heavy guns on high ground on each side of the entrance. Because four destroyers and one China River gunboat had not been able to quell the defences, the main Canadian assault was a general and bloody failure. The beach consisted of shingle and was backed by barbed wire and a wall three feet high. The plan was for engineers to blow holes in these defences so that tanks could advance through them into the town. But the undamaged fire power of the Germans made it impossible for the engineers to work on the beach. Only one hole was blown. For the most part the Canadians could do no more than land and die.

The official report[6] describes how the force commander, Major-General Roberts, uneasy about the strength of the German resistance, sent the floating reserve, the Fusiliers Mont-Royal, ashore.

The landing was successfully carried out at 07.04 hours shielded by smoke until the last moment. The enemy's fire, however, had not been subdued and the troops met the full force of it immediately on landing. Their Commanding Officer, Lt.-Col. D. Menard, was wounded, the casualties they at once began to suffer were very severe and they could accomplish very little. Some found momentary cover behind stranded tanks. Others, such as Lt. P. P. Loranger who remained in action though severely wounded at the moment of landing, endeavoured to engage the enemy from folds in the shingle. Two small parties, one commanded by Captain G. Van Delac the other under Sgt. P. Dubuc, penetrated into the town and reached the dock area. The first was subsequently captured on the beach, the second in the town. . . .

Sgt. Dubuc and his men landed opposite the western end of the Casino and succeeded, after a while, in subduing two pill boxes to their immediate front. The Sergeant and one man went back to a deserted tank left high and dry by the receding tide. This was the tank which had fallen off the damaged ramp of LCT 159 during the landing. They entered it and got its gun into action against the German defences on the western headland. Having fired off all its ammunition, Sgt. Dubuc left the tank and collecting a party of about eleven other ranks of the Fusiliers Mont-Royal led them into the town through the backyards of houses in the Rue Alexandre Dumas to the west of the Casino. Reaching the Rue de Cygogne he met Captain Van Delac of his regiment who with about twenty men was attacking from the rear houses situated on the Boulevard de Verdun. Sgt. Dubuc and his party then turned east and pushed on towards the harbour destroying on the way an enemy machine-gun nest at the corner of the Rue Claude Groulard. They reached the edge of the Bassin Duquesne and eventually the Bassin du Canada, being all the time under intermittent machine gun fire. They engaged and killed a number of Germans on two invasion barges in the Bassin du Canada and then moved south along the railway tracks on the west side of the Bassin until they encountered a patrol of Germans in superior numbers. By this time all their ammunition was exhausted and they surrendered. They were ordered to strip to their underwear and were then lined up with their faces against a wall. The Germans then departed leaving the Fusiliers in charge of a single guard. Sgt. Dubuc asked him to obtain some water for the prisoners. As he turned to do so they all set upon him, killed him and took to their heels, but became scattered passing through the town on the way back to 'White Beach'. Sgt. Dubuc reached the beach, reported to Lt.-Col. Menard his Commanding Officer, who was wounded, and eventually succeeded in getting him on board an LCP. Then, taking up a wounded NCO, he boarded another, transferred to an LCT and so reached England.

Sgt. Dubuc's story was one of the very few which had a happy (personal) ending. Only twelve out of a party of about 300 Fusiliers Mont-Royal, who landed west of Dieppe returned to Britain. The rest were killed, wounded or captured.

The raid on Dieppe helped to convince the Western Allies that the second front, when it came, would require more preparation than they had thought. If anyone still supposed in August 1942 that a second front could be opened in 1943 the Dieppe raid disabused them. Desperately though the Russians needed the second front, the Western Allies were in no position yet to open one.

Chapter 6

The War in the Desert

The war in North Africa began as a happening. The fighting started simply because soldiers were there. A British army reinforced by Australians and Indians was guarding the Suez Canal from bases in Egypt. An Italian army was guarding the Italian colonies in Libya, Cyrenaica, and Tripolitania. The two armies came to blows for the first time in June 1940 after Mussolini's belated declaration of war on Britain.

The opposing armies, British and Italian, were not interested in acquiring sand. They were interested in defeating each other. The crude aim of Generals Wavell and O'Connor on the British side and of Marshal Balbo on the Italian was to kill or capture as many enemy soldiers as possible.

The Loss of the French and Italian Fleets

As the war in the desert began, France surrendered, thereby altering the naval balance of power to Britain's extreme disadvantage. Before the fall of France the Allied navies, French and British, were supreme in the Mediterranean. Their fleets dominated that sea. The French, with bases at Oran, Mers-El-Kebir and Bizerta, controlled the western Mediterranean. The British, with bases at Alexandria, Malta and Gibraltar, were dominant everywhere else. Or so it seemed until France capitulated and Mussolini tardily followed his German master, Hitler, into war.

The British had first to deal with the new threat represented by France's unpredictable navy. Its revered Commander-in-Chief, Admiral Darlan, had not supported de Gaulle or made common cause with Britain. Seen from London by an anxious British Government, Darlan

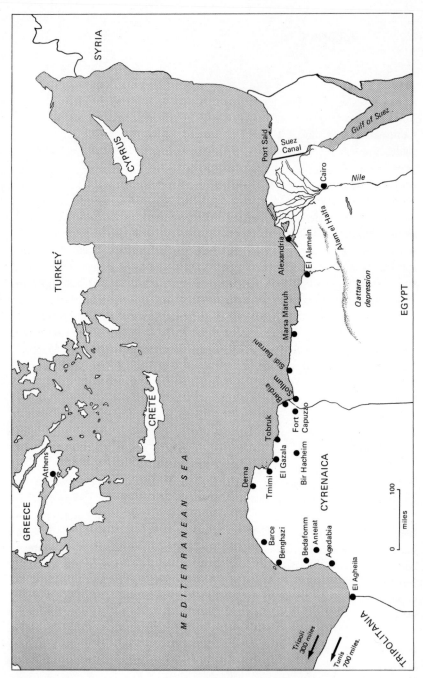

The Eastern Mediterranean

appeared at best to be a prevaricator. But the powerful French Mediterranean fleet was loyal to him – or so it seemed. Churchill was not prepared
to risk that these important ships should fall into German hands.

On 3 July 1940, within weeks of the fall of France, the Royal Navy
attacked French warships at Oran and Mers-El-Kebir after the French
Admiral there had refused to join with Britain. The next day the French
fleet at Alexandria in Egypt was neutralized peacefully. The British
Commander-in-Chief, Admiral Andrew B. Cunningham, was able to
make the French dependent upon him for supplies. Without money,
provisions, fuel or ammunition, the French ships in Alexandria could do
nothing without Cunningham's consent. No fleet has ever been captured
more economically.

On the other hand the attacks on Oran and Mers-El-Kebir, and
another on Dakar in French West Africa, killed French sailors and
embittered Anglo-French relations; but neither Churchill nor any of his
ministers or commanders could see an alternative.

Cunningham's British Mediterranean fleet had weighty problems in
any case. The Italian navy was an apparently formidable force. It included
some of the latest and fastest warships in the world. But these ships were
less effective than they looked. On 11 November 1940, Cunningham's
aircraft attacked the Italians at anchor in Taranto, their main south
Italian base. Cunningham's pilots managed, for the first time, to make
torpedoes dropped from aircraft effective in shallow water. The Royal
Navy lost two aircraft. The Italians lost about half their fleet. It was the
first time that carrier aircraft had been used in this decisive fashion. The
Commander-in-Chief of the Japanese navy, Admiral Yamamoto, was
deeply impressed. He studied Cunningham's tactics carefully. His attack
on Pearl Harbor in December 1941 owed much to the lessons he had
learnt from Cunningham.

On land the British Commander-in-Chief, General Wavell, and his
field commander, General O'Connor, took the offensive also. Their
battlefield, which was to be fought over again and again for the best
part of three years, was the 600 miles of desert between Alexandria in
Egypt and Benghazi in Cyrenaica – the point at which the North African
coast bends southwards to Bedafomm and El Agheila, before bending
west again to Tripoli in Libya.

Between Alexandria and Benghazi, and linked together by a coastal
road, lay the towns and settlements whose names the war was to make
famous – El Alamein, Mersa Matruh, Sidi Barrani, Sollum, Bardia,
Tobruk, Tmimi, and Derna. During September 1940 the Italians had

advanced about 60 miles from Cyrenaica into Egypt, and had stopped just east of Sidi Barrani. The British harassed them during their advance and the Italians lost about 3,000 men. Better still, from Wavell's point of view, the Italians had extended their supply lines to the limit. O'Connor moved against them in December. On 11 December after two days of fighting he had taken Sidi Barrani and had captured 38,000 prisoners. O'Connor was in Bardia on 4 January and had taken Tobruk by 22 January. From there, and with bold good judgment, he sent the Australian 6th Division in pursuit of the Italians along the coast road to Benghazi and the 7th Armoured Division straight across the desert to intercept the Italians at Bedafomm. The manoeuvre was a brilliant success.

Surrounded and beaten at Bedafomm, the Italian 10th Army surrendered. In two months the 30,000 men of O'Connor's 13th Corps had taken 130,000 prisoners and had captured about 400 tanks for the loss of 500 men killed. Italian resistance in North Africa was broken, the road to Tripoli was open. It was virtually certain that O'Connor could have cleared the enemy out of North Africa in the first half of 1941 had he been allowed to advance.

The Greek Campaign

What held O'Connor back was the British Government's decision to send help to Greece. Greece had been invaded in October 1940 by Italian troops from Albania. But in Greece as in Africa, the Italian army had proved incompetent. The Italians were losing. In February 1941, however, the Greek Government came to the conclusion that the Germans, who were about to invade Yugoslavia, would invade Greece as well. The Greeks deduced correctly that Hitler would not allow his Italian ally to be beaten. The Greek Government asked Britain for help. After some heart searching the British Government decided to respond and to send an army. Churchill was conscious that Britain, though unbeaten, was nowhere in contact with the German enemy on land. He was eager to have the British army fight the Germans wherever and whenever an opportunity offered. He was, in any case, convinced and was to remain convinced that Britain could hurt the Germans badly by striking at the 'soft under-belly of Europe'. The British Government was worried too about Turkey. The Government believed that a German success in Greece might tempt the Turks to join the war on Germany's side.

All these considerations weighed heavily with the Cabinet in London but they did not affect the bleak military fact that Britain did not have enough forces in the Middle East both to help Greece and to drive the Italians out of Africa. O'Connor had to stay where he was.

O'Connor, a modest and marvellously unembittered soldier, has since said: 'I'm quite certain that if we had advanced immediately we could have pushed them [the Italians] out. . . . But if we were required to go elsewhere, well that was too bad.' It was a question, O'Connor said, as to whether the British could 'do both Tripoli and Greece, but Tripoli immediately. If we could do Tripoli immediately – and it still left all the options open for doing Greece – I've no doubt we would have done it without any difficulty at all. . . .'[1] O'Connor's record confirms this and so does his own account of his battle:

> We started this campaign with what was intended to be only a five days' raid. Our resources were limited to two divisions, the 4th Indian Div, and the 7th Armd Div. But their morale and training were extremely high in contrast to the Italians, who had a vast numerical superiority of about 8 to one, but low morale and no enthusiasm for the War. It was nevertheless necessary to redress this balance by some surprise attack, which would prevent him using his vast superiority against our small numbers.
>
> His method of defence consisted of a number of strongly fortified camps, which were too far away to give support to each other if one was attacked, and could therefore be attacked and dealt with individually. To achieve surprise we decided to move the 4th Indian Div by night through the gap between two of these camps, moving right round and attacking one of them from the rear (the way their rations came). This proved completely successful, and we attacked and defeated each camp in turn without any interference.
>
> The day after the battle of Sidi Barrani the very unwelcome news arrived that the 4th Indian Div was to be withdrawn for service in East Africa, and that the 6th Aus. Div was to take its place. This Division proved to be first class, but unfortunately could not be ready for nearly a month.
>
> We then had to decide whether we would continue to push the enemy out of Benghazi, by just following him up, or drive right across the desert across his lines of communication and so cut him off from Tripoli. This was a considerable risk. But thanks to the splendid work of the 7th Armd Div, we successfully achieved it, and really liquidated the whole Italian 10th Army.[1]

But O'Connor was not allowed to exploit his success. General Harding, one of his wisest subordinates, has since said[2] that the decision to divert resources to Greece was 'disastrous'. 'It was a great strategic mistake. I think there was considerable misunderstanding between High Command in Cairo and the Government in London. . . . The opportunity that was lost was really that of holding Rommel in the early part of his advance, of preventing him from ever getting within striking distance of the [Nile] Delta.' Harding said that Wavell was 'over-pressurized from London into launching operations before he was fully ready for them', and that he was misled by bad intelligence into underestimating the capability of the Africa Korps which the Germans were, even then, preparing to send to Libya.

In the event Wavell loyally mustered a mixed British, Australian and New Zealand army of nearly 60,000 men and sent them to Greece on 5 April 1941. The Germans invaded Greece the next day as the Greeks had feared.

For the British, the Greek campaign was not a disaster but it was still a very serious reverse. It took the Germans, invading from the north, three weeks to capture Athens. Three days before Athens fell the British forces began to withdraw from the Greek mainland but they still held the island of Crete.

A mixed force of Greek, British and New Zealand troops amounting to about 14,000 men and commanded by General Freyberg, VC, the commander of the New Zealand division, was ordered to hold the island. Freyberg – one of the Allies' most resolute and thoughtful generals – did his best. But he was beaten.

What beat him was the first really large, sophisticated, and well co-ordinated airborne assault in history. It was directed by the German General Kurt Student, the man who invented and conceived this form of warfare. Crete was captured by the parachute.

Student had assembled in Greece about 500 transport aircraft and 70 gliders. He also had a sizeable force of bombers which he used first to soften up the Allied positions. After a week's bombing he sent in his first airborne troops. By the next day they had captured the Maleme airfield, the only useful one on Crete, and Student was able to reinforce at speed. By the end of May Freyberg's position was hopeless. So was the Royal Navy's. Student had command of the air. Because of this the navy suffered heavier losses than it could afford. Nine precious ships were sunk and seventeen damaged.

Freyberg was forced to withdraw. The last Allied soldier left Crete on 31 May. The Greek campaign had lasted fifty-six days and its main, obvious, and immediate achievement was a political gesture.

On 24 April, while Freyberg was still struggling to resist the German assaults on Greek territory in Crete, the Greek Government capitulated. Although casualties on both sides were high, especially in Crete, the Germans had shown themselves to be superior not just in equipment but principally in military technique. The British, the Australians, and the New Zealanders probably lost – killed, captured or missing – 12,000 men in the defence of Greece and 26,000 in the defence of Crete.

At the time the Greek adventure seemed to be a melancholy reverse, unredeemed by any compensating advantage to the Allied cause. It may, however, have helped to delay Hitler's attack on Russia. If the Yugoslavs had not been in revolt against a pro-German Government, if British forces had not landed in Greece, Hitler might have invaded the Soviet Union on 15 May 1941, the date originally fixed. In the event he invaded on 22 June. This meant that the Germans had five weeks fewer before the snow came to halt their advance into Russia. It meant that the Russian's chief ally in 1941 – the Russian winter – came to their aid sooner; there is no knowing where the Germans would have got to had they had an extra five weeks' campaigning weather in Russia in that year.

The campaigns in Yugoslavia, Greece, and Crete were not, however, the only reason why Hitler failed to invade the Soviet Union on 15 May. The weather was bad in Poland and would have imposed a delay probably until the second week in June. Chester Wilmot, the historian of the war in Europe, believes that it is impossible to say whether or not the British, the Australians, and the New Zealanders who died in Crete can be counted among the soldiers who helped to prevent the capture of Moscow in the winter of 1941. 'The decision to postpone', wrote Wilmot in *The Struggle for Europe*, 'had been made . . . without taking the weather into consideration, and it is impossible now to tell whether Hitler would have tried to start on 15 May, as originally planned, if he had not been drawn into Yugoslavia and Greece. The opinion of Blumentritt, then Chief of Staff of the Fourth Army in Poland, and of Halder, is that "the friction in the Balkans and the exceptional weather in 1941 caused the loss of four precious weeks". Those weeks were to be worth many months before the year ran out.'

Hitler let himself in for this, but the Balkan campaign was not a last-minute adventure. On 12 November 1940 Hitler had issued a directive to the army to be ready to invade Greece so that the Luftwaffe could attack air bases from which the RAF might attack the Rumanian oil-fields. By the time he sent the actual order for the attack on Greece and Yugoslavia – on 27 March 1941 – he had other motives too, including a need to guard his southern flank while he launched his great drive east-ward into Russia. But, for whatever compelling motives, Hitler invaded the Balkans at his peril. The Russian winter was waiting for him, and he was losing time.

The Desert Fox arrives

The Greek adventure was only one of four expeditions which Wavell was obliged to mount during the winter of 1940 to 1941 and during the first half of 1941 and which forced him to disperse his scarce resources. Responsible as he was for the protection of British interests throughout the Middle East, Wavell had to intervene in three other countries – Iraq, Syria and Ethiopia. Iraq was one of the Allies' major suppliers of oil which reached the Mediterranean and Wavell through a pipeline ending at Haifa in Palestine (as it then was). Early in April 1941, pro-German politicians seized power in Iraq. Wavell had to send troops that he could ill afford to spare to protect the pipeline and to reinstate a pro-British Government.

In June the non-Free French forces in Syria, a French dependency, began to show signs of pro-German activity. Again Wavell had to send troops. The campaign, which succeeded, lasted only six days.

In Ethiopia Wavell faced a bigger problem. Ethiopia had been Mussolini's first prey. When Italy joined the war, it contained a considerable Italian army commanded by the Duke of Aosta. Wavell was not prepared to leave the Duke in peace. Nor were the Ethiopians. They had been the first victims of Fascist aggression. They were also the first effective partisans. Inspired, organized, and instructed by Major Orde Wingate – whose subsequent operations behind the Japanese lines in Burma made him famous – the Ethiopian partisans took heart during the winter of 1940–41, and harrassed the lonely Italians severely. By February 1941 Wavell's regular forces were ready to move. Two Indian Divisions moved into northern Ethiopia from the Sudan. A mixed force of South African, British and African troops moved into southern Ethiopia from Kenya. An amphibious force from Aden landed at Berbera. The Italians did not resist very hard. Malaria turned out to be the Allies' most formidable enemy. The capital, Addis Ababa, fell on 6 April. The Duke of Aosta surrendered on 16 May. By the end of May, Wavell was able once again to concentrate his mind and his forces on the main struggle in the western desert.

For the Allies the situation in North Africa had changed radically and for the worse since O'Connor's spectacular success at Bedafomm in

16. Russian guerilla fighters in training

17. Paratroops in action with 3″ mortars

18. American soldiers in Belgium dig foxholes in the snow as enemy artillery opens up.

19. Action in the Burmese jungle

20. British infantry advance through the desert, November 1942

21. Soviet infantrymen heading towards the enemy's forward line in the winter of 1943

22. May 1944: Monte Cassino – Polish dead being removed from the battle-field

23. 5th Army Anzio offensive: British soldiers take cover in a German trench while waiting for reinforcements, May 1944

February. Even though Hitler was about to undertake the most hazardous adventure of his vivid and disastrous military career by invading Russia he was still determined to reverse and avenge the defeats suffered by his wayward Italian ally.

The Greeks had very nearly beaten Mussolini on their own soil. O'Connor had had the Italians at his mercy in North Africa. In spite of his planned invasion of Russia, Hitler hurried to Mussolini's aid in Greece. To Africa he sent Erwin Rommel, the tank commander who had made his name in France.

This remarkable soldier arrived in Tripoli on 12 February 1941 and at once took charge. The Afrika Korps, consisting at first of two German divisions, followed him. After O'Connor's victory at Bedafomm, the diversion to Greece had pared the Allied forces in the western desert to one division – the Australian 9th – and to parts of a British armoured division and of an Indian motorized brigade. Rommel attacked them at the end of March. He re-took Benghazi on 3 April, Bardia and Sollum on 11 April. In this extremely rapid advance General O'Connor was captured too. This gifted and gallant general was the Germans' most important prisoner to date. He escaped at his third attempt. But for the time being he was out of action.

With the Italians and now the Germans advancing fast towards Egypt and the Suez Canal, Wavell sought to delay and embarrass them by leaving a threat on their flank. He ordered the Australian 9th Division and other Australian units to fortify Tobruk and stay there.

The siege of Tobruk lasted from April until December 1941 when the British came back. The Australians did not defend Tobruk in vain. Mainly because of the threat to his flank, but partly also because of supply difficulties Rommel did not get much further. Sollum, some sixty miles further east towards Alexandria, was for the time being the effective limit of his advance.

In June Wavell mounted a counter-attack which failed. It was clear that the Allies would need to arm and organize themselves far more thoroughly in order to beat Rommel than they had had to do in order to beat the Italians. However, on 5 July 1941, after contending uncomplainingly and unfailingly with a host of political and military problems which did not recur, General Wavell was replaced by General Auchinleck. Churchill felt, unjustly, that Wavell was a loser. It fell to Auchinleck to organize the next offensive against Rommel.

Auchinleck was ready on 18 November. The Australians in Tobruk were relieved by the New Zealanders on 10 December. The Allies re-occupied Benghazi on Christmas Eve having gained 300 miles of territory.

A daring counter-attack by Rommel failed for lack of fuel and ammunition. By the end of December he had retired to El Agheila eighty miles along the road from Bedafomm to Tripoli. But he did not stay there long. At the end of January, resilient as ever, Rommel advanced again. When operations ended the Germans and Italians were occupying a line from El Gazala on the coast to Bir Hacheim. The Allies retained Tobruk. They had re-occupied Benghazi only to lose it again.

The line stayed where it was until the following May. By western desert standards Auchinleck's offensive had been comparatively costly. Allied casualties amounted to about 17,000 men, although the Germans and Italians probably lost more than twice as many. Allied losses in tanks were especially heavy. What made matters worse for Auchinleck was what had happened to Wavell before him. For reasons that had nothing to do with him some of his best troops were suddenly called away. On 7 December 1941 the Japanese had attacked Pearl Harbor. By the end of the month they were threatening New Guinea, and, with it, Australia's national territory. Two of Auchinleck's Australian divisions had to hurry home.

For the second time the desert generals saw the chance of victory receding. 'I was again very upset', said Harding, 'and felt frustrated and disappointed because I felt that an opportunity of doing something which was important in the Middle East theatre was lost for the sake of something which was very doubtful and unlikely to pay off in the Far East.'

Even so at this time the Allied forces still were using inferior equipment. Harding said, 'I can remember well being told by representatives from London that the two pounder anti-tank gun mounted in the Crusader tank was about the best weapon there was. But of course it wasn't because it couldn't really destroy a German tank at all.'[3]

There were other problems too. Hugh Daniel, a despatch rider with armoured formations, has spoken of the need not to get lost and of Cassiopeia as 'our favourite constellation'. (Cassiopeia is a chair-shaped group of stars on the opposite side of the Pole star to the Plough.) 'Your vehicle', Daniel said, 'was your life, quite literally. We loved our vehicles and we'd do anything to keep them going.

'There was a particularly nasty form of ending one's days if one is trapped in a tank and the tank blows up and is on fire. Nobody who's been involved in this will ever lose the awfulness or the horror of screams of men trying to get out of vehicles. If a tank was shot up and burning it didn't matter whose side it was on, the crew had to escape. Once they'd escaped from this tank I know of no occasion when they were ruthlessly shot down by machine guns. They had the elements to face, they had sand and thirst and hunger to face and the fact that they were out of their tank and couldn't make it back to their base was sufficient. If you could take them prisoner you would, but you wouldn't do anything out of hand.'[4]

Auchinleck had much to contend with. One of his main troubles, which he did not know about at the time, was that Rommel was receiving from the Italians – or by courtesy of the Italians – all the information that the American military attaché in Cairo (Colonel Bonner Frank Fellers), was sending to his headquarters in Washington.[5] Colonel Fellers was a competent and intelligent officer, extremely well informed about Auchinleck's intentions, and he was dutifully passing his information on to the Military Intelligence Division in Washington in a code which the Italians unfortunately had stolen from the US Embassy in Rome. The code – known as the 'Black Code' – had been stolen, copied, and returned to the Embassy in September 1941 by the Italian Military Intelligence Service, the Servizio Informazione Militare, the SIM. The SIM had a man in the US Embassy in Rome, an Italian citizen. Through him the SIM obtained a copy of the 'Black Code'. From then on everything that Colonel Fellers knew the Italians also knew. So did Rommel.

During Rommel's rapid advance in January and February 1942, he was receiving information almost daily about the state and positions of British armoured divisions, about forthcoming Commando operations, and about Auchinleck's intentions. In June 1942, Fellers told Washington intentionally and Rommel unintentionally of British plans to mount Commando raids on nine German aerodromes in North Africa. Rommel was waiting for them.

But later in June the British themselves broke the 'Black Code' and began to read Fellers's messages. There were consultations at the highest level. The British and the Americans decided that the code must have been broken by the Germans too. It was changed. Fellers was recalled. His messages are said to have provided Rommel with the broadest and clearest picture of enemy forces and intentions available to any Axis commander throughout the whole war.

There were two main reasons for Rommel's uncharacteristic four-month pause on the El Gazala–Bir Hacheim line. The first was the continued activity of the Royal Navy. The second, and probably the more important, was Malta. Having successfully attacked the Italian fleet in harbour at Taranto in November 1940, Admiral Cunningham attacked them successfully at sea at Cape Matapan four months later. In a skilful night action he sank three heavy Italian cruisers, the *Zara*, the *Pola* and the *Fiume*, and damaged the battleship *Vittorio Veneto*, besides sinking two large destroyers. The Italian battle fleet did not come out to meet Cunningham again.

The impotence of the apparently powerful Italian fleet was one reason for Rommel's shortage of supplies. Another reason was that Malta did not give in. The Royal Navy, the RAF, the US navy and the Allied merchant navies risked much to keep Malta supplied and suffered heavy losses in doing so. But the island stayed bombed but defiant.

In January 1942, Rommel returned to Germany to plead with Hitler for an attack on Malta which would eliminate the island's capacity to interfere with his supply routes. He complained with justification that ships and aircraft based on Malta were restricting his mobility and preventing him from attacking Egypt and threatening the Suez Canal. Although the German armies were even then hard-pressed on the Russian front, Hitler granted Rommel's request. A strong German air fleet was sent to Sicily with orders to bomb Malta in preparation for an airborne landing. The bombing took place and was devastating. But the landing never followed.

During the early months of 1942, Malta was holding out but some of Rommel's supply ships were still getting through. By the end of May 1942 Rommel thought he had enough in hand to move again.

His offensive began on 27 May. He sent his tanks round the southern end of the Allied line to threaten the British rear and Tobruk. British counter-attacks forced the Germans to form a defensive position within the British minefields. The Germans' position held, but Bir Hacheim, garrisoned by the Free French, could not hold out without armoured support. After sixteen days of heavy fighting the Allies, beaten, were in retreat. Auchinleck turned to fight at El Alamein.

El Alamein

As both generals knew, Alamein is virtually the only defensive line in the western desert whose southern, or inland, end cannot be outflanked. Forty miles south of the coast lies the Qattara depression, a salt marsh lying below sea level at the bottom of a line of cliffs. Tanks sink in salt marshes and cannot climb cliffs.

From July 1942 the two armies faced each other on a battlefield bounded on the north by the sea, and on the south by the Qattara depression. It was like a deadly boxing ring from which there was no escape.

Through the first half of July Auchinleck's forces held their line against Rommel's determined and ingenious attacks. Rommel spent his strength. His supplies replenished once, were exhausted again. At the end of August, however, Rommel received some fuel and was promised more. He resolved to try again.

In mid-August Churchill for the last time reshuffled his generals. General Alexander succeeded Auchinleck as Commander-in-Chief, Middle East. General Montgomery took command of the forces in the field, now known as the 8th Army. It then consisted of seven divisions, two of which were armoured. Rommel had four armoured divisions, two German, and two Italian, and six other divisions. Because of the Qattara depression Rommel could not do what he had done before – outflank the British lines at their landward end. All that he could try to do as an alternative was to concentrate superior strength at the southern end of the line in an attempt to break it. He might then have the opportunity to sweep north behind the British lines and take Montgomery's main forces in the rear.

The weakness of Rommel's plan was that it was the only one he could try. If he was going to attack at all he had no alternative. And Montgomery could see this as clearly as Rommel. Montgomery foresaw correctly that when Rommel's forces turned north they would need to take the Alam el Halfa Ridge which lies about halfway between the sea and the Qattara depression. Montgomery stationed his armoured divisions in defensive positions well dug in at Alam el Halfa. Rommel attacked on 31 August. By 2 September his armoured divisions had still made no impression on the Alam el Halfa defences. Five days later his troops were back where they had started from. The battle of Alam el Halfa was Rommel's last real offensive in the western desert. He counter-attacked skilfully thereafter. But a counter-attack is not the same as an offensive.

Despite his success at Alam el Halfa Montgomery was still not satisfied that the 8th Army was ready to advance. He was not sure that his men were yet familiar with the new and more powerful tanks they were receiving. He was not sure yet that the 8th Army was the well-trained and confident force that he knew it could be and would be. Throughout the autumn he trained, he lectured and above all he inspired. He convinced his men that they were invincible, that defeat was behind them. By October they did not just hope to win, they knew that they would.

The battle of El Alamein was won partly by the courage, skill and determination of the 8th Army but also by extremely delicate and sophisticated generalship. There was more to El Alamein than 'hitting them for six', as Montgomery cheerfully and rousingly described it to his troops.

It was not just a question of waiting until the 8th Army was stronger than Rommel's (which it was by October) and then attacking in the certainty that the big battalions would beat the small ones. Alamein could have been lost by bad decisions as easily as any other battle.

The German defences were extremely strong. The minefields and anti-tank batteries covered an area five miles deep. Montgomery's eventual aim was to clear passages through the minefields and the anti-tank defences so that his armour could pass through and operate in the enemy's rear. As part of his scheme Montgomery decided also to mount attacks first on the enemy's unarmoured formations, the troops which held the ground as distinct from the armoured divisions which were Rommel's main mobile attacking and counter-attacking forces. Montgomery foresaw that the enemy armour would come to the defence of the holding troops. He intended that his own armour, deployed on ground of his choosing, would then destroy the enemy armour. He calculated that the enemy armour's movements would be restricted by the enemy's own minefields.

Montgomery began his attack during the night of 23–24 October with an artillery bombardment. One thousand guns were brought to bear on the enemy batteries. In the north, where Montgomery planned to make his main attack, there were two minefields, one in front of the enemy's forward positions and one behind them. The initial attack, led by the New Zealand Division, cleared gaps through the first minefield, but failed to breach the second. The armoured divisions which were to pass through the gaps were in any case delayed by unexpected pockets of resistance. For the next two days the 'crumbling process' as Montgomery called it – the process of neutralizing the enemy's holding forces – continued as planned.

Day and night until 30 October progress was steady but slow. Montgomery exploited weakness where he found it, especially in the north, but he refrained from wasting resources where resistance was stubborn. He also succeeded in obliging Rommel to keep strong forces in the south although there was no plan to launch heavy attacks there. By the time Rommel did, in fact, move his 21st Panzer Division to the north of the line Montgomery was in a strong enough position to make a proper breakthrough into the open desert.

On 2 November the New Zealand Division, reinforced by two British infantry brigades, succeeded in driving a third corridor through the enemy defences. This breakthrough, quickly exploited by the New Zealanders and by the 7th Armoured Division, seems to have convinced Rommel that the battle was lost. On 3 November he began to retreat. His

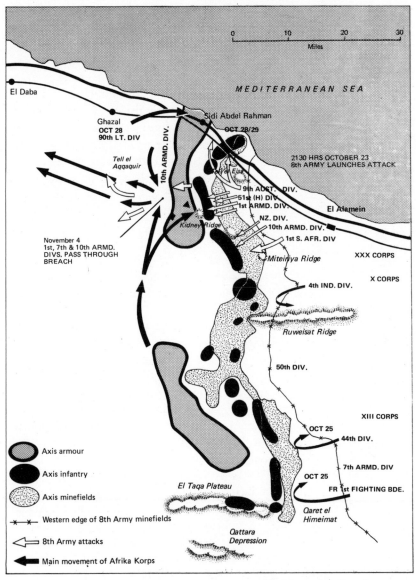

0   10   20   30
Miles

MEDITERRANEAN SEA

El Daba

Ghazal
OCT 28
90th LT. DIV

Sidi Abdel Rahman
OCT 28/29

Tell el
Aqqaquir

10th ARMD. DIV.

2130 HRS OCTOBER 23
8th ARMY LAUNCHES ATTACK

Tel el Eisa

9th AUST. DIV.
51st (H) DIV.
1st ARMD. DIV.
NZ. DIV.
10th ARMD. DIV.
1st S. AFR. DIV.

El Alamein

Kidney Ridge

November 4
1st, 7th & 10th ARMD.
DIVS. PASS THROUGH
BREACH

Miteiriya Ridge

XXX CORPS

X CORPS

4th IND. DIV.

Ruweisat Ridge

50th DIV.

XIII CORPS

OCT 25

44th DIV.

7th ARMD. DIV

OCT 25

FR 1st FIGHTING BDE.

El Taqa Plateau

Qaret el
Himeimat

Qattara
Depression

Axis armour

Axis infantry

Axis minefields

Western edge of 8th Army minefields

8th Army attacks

Main movement of Afrika Korps

El Alamein, October 1942

rearguard resisted stubbornly. But Freyberg's men were the real experts
in manoeuvres. Rommel was beaten.

El Alamein cost the Germans four divisions and the Italians eight. It
was a truly decisive victory and a thoughtful one. Looking back on
Alamein Montgomery wrote:

The battle had conformed to the pattern anticipated. The break-in, or battle for position, had given us the tactical advantage; the dog-fight which followed reduced the enemy's strength and resources to a degree which left him unable to withstand the final knockout blow. The dog-fight demanded rapid regrouping of forces to create reserves available for switching the axis of operations as the situation required; in this way the initiative was retained and the battle swung to its desired end. Tactical surprise was an important factor; the break-in operation achieved it completely, for the enemy had expected our main thrust in the south. In the final thrust again the enemy was deceived; he had prepared for it in the extreme north, and concentrated his German troops to meet it. It was delivered against the Italians, two miles south of the German flank.[6]

When the battle began Rommel had been on sick leave in Germany. He hurried back but there was nothing he could do. There had been nothing that he could have done. The German defeat was planned, certain, and inevitable.

Rommel's only stroke of luck was a rainstorm on 7 November which delayed supplies to the British 1st Armoured Division for 24 hours – an interval which allowed more Germans to escape than would otherwise have done so. But from then on the 8th Army pursued the enemy along a familiar road. Tobruk was taken on 13 November and Benghazi on 20 November. But this time the pursuit did not stop at Bedafomm and El Agheila. This time the 8th Army was bound for Tripoli, and beyond.

Montgomery's conduct of the Battle of El Alamein has been criticized on the grounds that he could have won more quickly, that he allowed Rommel to escape, and that – in general – he was over-cautious. He did, in fact, enjoy a large superiority in tanks when the battle began. It is true also that Rommel's main force was able to make its way westward more or less unimpeded to fight another day in Tunisia. These are important and serious criticisms; but they concern not what happened but what might have happened. Like most British generals Montgomery was more conscious than his American opposite numbers of the need to conserve manpower, and skilled manpower in particular. The New Zealand Division, for example, might have advanced faster and sooner if Montgomery had given permission, but would probably have suffered heavy casualties. But Montgomery needed the New Zealanders, who were some of his most experienced soldiers, and was to need them again not just in Africa but also in Italy.

By now the 8th Army was no longer alone with the enemy in North Africa. On 8 November, the day that Montgomery's pursuit gathered speed, a strong Anglo-American force under General Eisenhower landed in French North Africa. By 11 November the Allies had captured Casablanca on the Atlantic coast and Algiers and Oran on the Mediterranean shore. The same day the Vichy French Commander Admiral Darlan not only surrendered to the Allies but appealed to the French fleet at Toulon to join them.

The Tunisian Campaign

The German army at once occupied the whole of France, Toulon included, to find that the French had scuttled their fleet. Simultaneously, however, the Germans told the Vichy Government that they would use the Tunisian ports. Hitherto they had been using Tripoli to supply their armies in Africa. From now on they used Tunis and Bizerta as well. And it was from Tunis that eventually they left North Africa.

Some French units, mostly naval, resisted the Allied landings and at Bizerta some Vichy French units joined forces with the Germans who were hastening to reinforce Tunisia. But the Allies were still a long way from Tunis. General Anderson, who had taken command of the British 1st Army in Algiers, hurried to close the gap. On 11 November, only three days after the original landing, his troops occupied Bougie, 120 miles east of Algiers. Bône, 150 miles further on still, was occupied next day by British parachutists supported by Commandos landing from seaward. The important airfield at Souk-el-Arba was taken on the 16th. But on the 17th the 1st Army's advance units met the Germans at Tabarka about halfway between Bône and Tunis.

In one important respect the military balance in the Tunisian campaign, which was about to begin, had been reversed. At El Alamein, Montgomery's supply lines had been short and Rommel's had been long. In Tunisia Rommel's were short, and to begin with at any rate, Montgomery's were long. So were Anderson's. The Germans sent reinforcements by air. They even withdrew about 400 aircraft from the Russian front and sent them to Tunisia – bringing some relief to the Russian armies. The Germans were determined not to sell Tunisia cheaply. The weather also was on their side. Heavy rain made the roads and airfields soft and sometimes unusable. By Christmas 1942 the 1st Army had lost momentum. The assault on Tunis would have to wait.

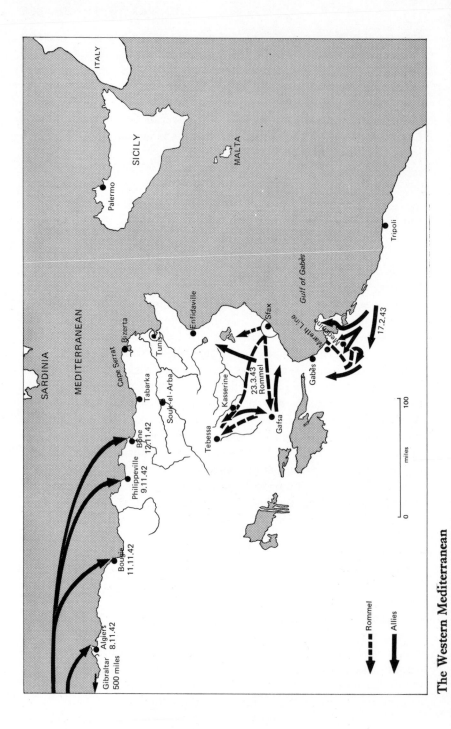

The Western Mediterranean

By February 1943, when it became possible to move again, the 1st Army had secured a line running inland from Cape Serrat, about halfway between Tabarka and Bizerta. The US Second Corps held the line further south passing through Faid and bending west towards Gafsa. The 8th Army, having chased Rommel all the way from El Alamein, had captured Tripoli in January and was approaching Mareth. The Germans with their remaining Italian Allies, were surrounded but by no means defeated.

On 14 February Rommel attacked the US 2nd Corps at Faid. He advanced quickly to the Kasserine Pass which crosses the range of hills lying south-east of Tebessa. By the 20th Rommel's advance units were through the pass and were threatening the Allies' advanced airfields. The 2nd Corps fought back strongly and by 3 March Rommel's men were back at their starting point. But within three days Rommel was on the attack again. This time he struck at the 8th Army, which, by this time, had reached Medenine some 20 miles south of Mareth on the Gulf of Gabès where Rommel had prepared a strong defence line. But in spite of four determined attacks the 8th Army was unmoved. Rommel, still a sick man, handed over his command to General von Arnim and left Africa for ever.

At the end of March Montgomery attacked the twenty-mile length of the Mareth line and, by switching his main attack from the seaward end to the landward he broke it and turned it, with the veteran General Freyberg leading his New Zealanders through the inland hills. By mid April the 8th Army had occupied Sfax and was in sight of Enfidaville. In the north and west the 1st Army and the US 2nd Corps attacked early in May. Tunis and Bizerta fell on 7 May. By 13 May von Arnim surrendered along with about 125,000 Germans and almost as many Italians. After nearly two years the Desert War was over. It had cost Germany and Italy almost one million soldiers killed or taken prisoner.

Chapter 7

The Campaign in Italy

The main reason for the invasion of Sicily and Italy in 1943 was that there was nothing else that the British and American forces in North Africa could then do to engage the enemy. At their Casablanca conference, Roosevelt, Churchill and General George Marshall had reluctantly agreed that it would not be possible to invade France from Britain until 1944. This left the Allied forces in North Africa – battle trained and eager – with three choices. They could either be kept idle, brought back to Britain, or sent into southern Europe. If they were to keep fighting they could strike at what Churchill had always believed to be Europe's 'soft under-belly'.

Marshall had doubts. He had contended from the beginning that the Allies should not disperse their forces in Europe. Marshall wanted to concentrate on one simple, massive blow at occupied Europe. He said that the place from which to launch this assault was Great Britain. But the need to divert German strength from the hard-pressed Russians was urgent. The British and Americans had to do something, and had to be seen to be doing something.

For a long time Churchill had had a hankering to invade through the Balkans. Perhaps, like Mussolini before him, he underestimated the difficulties. At all events Anglo-American military advice was solidly in favour of an invasion first of Sicily and then, if the outlook was favourable, of Italy itself. At a meeting in Algeria in May 1943, Churchill and Marshall agreed with Eisenhower, Alexander, Ismay, Tedder (the air commander) and Admiral Cunningham the Commander-in-Chief of Allied naval forces in the Mediterranean, to invade Sicily anyway. If things went well the Allied forces would then go on to Italy. If resistance was unexpectedly stubborn the Allies might strike at Sardinia and Corsica instead. Marshall insisted that this option should be kept open. The field commanders, however, believed that the conquest of Sicily would not take long and that they would soon be able to invade Italy itself.

The Invasion of Sicily

The invading forces were to be the British 8th Army under General Montgomery and the American 7th Army under General George Patton. Eisenhower was the supreme commander. The commander of the land forces was General Alexander. The commander of the naval forces was Cunningham. Tedder commanded in the air.

One reason for the success of the Allied invasion of Sicily – one reason among many, but probably an important one – was that the Royal Navy had led the Germans to believe that the invasion would take place in Greece. At 4.30 in the morning on 30 April HM submarine *Seraph* surfaced briefly in the middle of a fleet of Spanish fishing boats off Huelva and launched into the water the body of a man wearing a lifejacket and carrying papers. The papers said that he was a Major Martin of the Royal Marines. He also carried letters. There was one from his bank manager, another from his tailor, and a rather moving letter from his fiancée whose unassailably English name was Pam, who had a stiff upper lip, and whose people lived at the Manor House, Ogbourne St George, Marlborough. But Major Martin also carried letters from the Chief of the Imperial General Staff, General Nye, to General Alexander; from the Chief of Combined Operations, Lord Mountbatten, to Admiral Cunningham and to General Eisenhower. They referred, the first explicitly, the others by delicate implication, to the imminence of an Allied operation against Greece.

All the letters had been written by Lieutenant-Commander Ewen Montague[1] and others in Naval Intelligence in London. Major Martin was a literary masterpiece. He did not drift ashore in vain. The Spaniards found him. The Germans were told. The Germans were taken in. At least one complete Panzer division was sent from France to Greece to defend that country against the attack that never came. A large-scale mine-laying effort was ordered along the coasts of Greece. A flotilla of German warships was despatched from Sicily to southern Greece.

The invasion of Sicily, planned by Admiral Ramsay, took place in two sectors on 10 July. The 8th Army landed between Syracuse and the south-eastern tip of Sicily. The 7th landed in the Gulf of Gela between Licata in the west and Scoglitti in the east. Ramsay, who had organized the evacuation of Dunkirk, had laid his plans well. Alexander, the land forces commander, was given a good send-off.

For the first time specially-designed LST's (Landing Ships, Tank) and LCT's (Landing Craft, Tank) were used to put tanks as well as troops ashore in the assault wave. Eight divisions landed from a thousand ships. The front was 100 miles long. Despite indifferent weather the 8th Army had captured Syracuse by 11 July and Augusta on the 12th thereby securing two useful harbours. By the 15th, the 7th Army had captured the ports of Agrigento, and Porto Empedocle. The Allies were in Sicily to stay.

The objective of both armies was Messina at the north-eastern tip of the island. The Allies hoped to reach Messina in time to prevent the Germans – or as many of them as possible – from escaping to the Italian mainland, across the Messina Straits. Patton's 7th Army, driving west and north and then east again along the northern shore of Sicily, had farther to go. But Montgomery's route up the east coast, though shorter, was much harder.

From Augusta to the larger port of Catania the coastal lands are comparatively flat. But north of Catania the coast is high and rocky and the roads are few and easily defended. Mount Etna, a 10,000-foot volcano, lies just inland and to the north of Catania. Because of the narrowness of the gap between Etna and the sea Montgomery sent half his troops west of the mountain through Adrano and Randazzo. The other half struggled north along the shore against bitter German opposition. It took the 8th Army four weeks to reach Catania.

From the American beach-head at Gela, General Patton sent two divisions under General Bradley straight across the island to the northern coast. A third division struck north-west to Palermo and a fourth division drove west along the southern coast from Agrigento. By 22 July Palermo was in Allied hands and the drive eastward along the north shore began. Twice as they drove eastward Patton's troops called in the navy to make landings behind the German lines.

Both armies reached Messina on 17 August, Patton's men arriving a few hours before Montgomery's. Sicily had been captured but the German commander, Field Marshal Kesselring, had begun to evacuate his troops to the mainland while the Allies were fighting their way over the last difficult miles towards Messina. 39,000 German soldiers and 70,000 Italians were evacuated safely. And they took their equipment with them.

In another respect, however, the conquest of Sicily was no empty victory. It led quickly and directly to the downfall of Mussolini and soon afterwards to the Italian surrender.

The Invasion of the Mainland

When the Allies invaded Sicily, Italy was in a bad position to defend herself. She had already lost 200,000 soldiers, killed or captured, in North Africa. 217,000 Italians were fighting alongside the Germans on the Russian front. 580,000 Italians were fighting the Yugoslav and other partisans in the Balkans. And the Italian army was about to lose another 160,000 men, killed or captured, in Sicily. On 24 July, a fortnight after the Sicilian landings, Mussolini was summoned to attend a meeting of the Fascist Grand Council.

The Council was supposed to be the supreme policy-making body for the Fascist party and, therefore, for Italy itself. In practice Mussolini made his own policy. The Council had not met since the beginning of the war. This time, however, the Council was obstreperous. For once there was a vote of no confidence in Mussolini. King Victor Emmanuel was appointed to succeed Mussolini as Commander-in-Chief of the Italian armed forces. Next day the King sacked Mussolini, arrested him and sent him to prison in an ambulance. Marshal Badoglio became Prime Minister. The Allies under Alexander had dethroned their first dictator.

It is unlikely that any Italian Prime Minister could have carried on the war. Like many other Italians, Pietro Badoglio did not want to carry it on in any case. He hoped, correctly, that Italy would get better terms if he made a separate peace. But he foresaw, also correctly, that the Germans would resist the Allies on Italian soil and that, whatever he did, Italy would suffer the ravages of war.

His reasonable aim was to minimize the damage that the warring armies would do to his country. He tried to persuade the Allies to invade in the north, hoping to prevent the long and damaging campaign that would – and did – result from an invasion in the south. But the Allies were not to be persuaded.

After protracted negotiations in Lisbon between Badoglio's emissaries and Allied representatives, Italy signed a secret act of surrender on 3 September.

It was not clear whether the surrender was 'unconditional' as the Casablanca Conference had decided that it should be. But this did not matter. The day the surrender was signed, the Allies crossed the Straits of Messina and landed on the Italian mainland in Calabria. Five days later on 8 September, the news of the surrender was broadcast. The Germans occupied Rome, forestalling a planned Allied airborne attack. Badoglio and the King withdrew to Brindisi in southern Italy, which was soon to become Allied-occupied territory. However, as Badoglio had foreseen, the Germans stayed to fight in central Italy and to govern their part of Italy as best they could.

Mussolini, who had been imprisoned by the new Government in the Gran Sasso Mountains east of Rome, was rescued by an intrepid German airborne detachment, was taken first to Germany, and then re-installed as dictator of Italy, but this time as Hitler's puppet. For all practical purposes most of Italy remained a German-occupied country until the end of the war.

The Germans sold Italy dearly. Rome is 400 miles from Reggio where the first Allied landings took place and 200 from Salerno, where the second landing force went ashore. The Allies seriously had hoped to reach Rome by Christmas 1943. In fact, Rome did not fall until the following June. By then the main Allied invasion force was already about to sail from Britain to France.

The September landings in Calabria, the toe of Italy, went well. Resistance was light, although the Germans left ruined roads and bridges behind them as they retreated northward. In a fortnight, two divisions of the 8th Army had secured control of southern Italy as far north as Bari on the Adriatic coast.

The Allies' real trouble began at Salerno where they landed on 9 September. The Gulf of Salerno is a large bay thirty miles south-east of Naples. It is ringed by hills and the coastal plain is narrow. But southern Italy being the mountainous country that it is, Salerno was virtually the only place where the Allies could attempt a landing. The Germans were waiting for them, because there was nowhere else to wait.

For four days at Salerno the British 10th Corps and the American 6th were in serious danger. The Germans had sown the hills with artillery. On the first day, 9 September, the Allies progressed only on their left, or northern flank. In the centre and the south progress was slow against bitter opposition. Progress was still slow on 10 and 11 September and on the 12th the Germans mounted a strong counter-attack against the Allied centre. But with the help of a heavy naval bombardment and of numerous air attacks, the Germans were halted. By 14 September the Salerno beach-head was reasonably secure.

Kesselring made the Apennine Mountains his allies. They were the only ones he had. He knew he could not expect much help from home. In France, the German garrison was already preparing for an Allied invasion from Britain. On the eastern front, the German armies were already hard pressed by the Russians. Kesselring was on his own.

After Salerno, he knew that he could not push the Allied armies back into the Mediterranean. So he decided to make them pay the highest possible price for every inch of Italy.

He made his first stand on the Volturno River, which descends from the Apennines into the Gulf of Gaeta, north of Naples. But Kesselring did not try to hold the Volturno line for long. There was a better one behind it. This consisted of a number of fast rivers – the Sangro, the Rapido, the Garigliano, and the Liri. With the mountains on their right, with a boggy coastal plain on their left, and Kesselring's so-called 'winter line' ahead of them, the Allies faced a formidable tactical problem.

And there was yet another line beyond. Behind the winter line rose Monte Cassino, a Benedictine monastery of great antiquity built, as the name suggests, on the top of a mountain. It commanded the junction between the Rapido and Liri valleys. It dominated the road the Allies would have to take – Route Six, the road to Rome.

Kesselring made Monte Cassino into the vital and commanding link in his next defensive position – the Gustav Line. From where the Allies stood, the Gustav Line looked so formidable that Churchill, Alexander and General Mark Clark, commander of the 5th Army operating on the south-western side of Italy, decided that there should be a landing behind the German lines. The landing was to be at Anzio, a few miles south of Rome but nearly sixty miles from the Gustav Line.

This distance seemed to some Allied planners to be too great. They feared that the presence of Allied troops so far to his rear would not bother Kesselring overmuch. They feared that the landing force might not be able to break out and move south fast enough to make a difference. On the other hand, the hope was that the force landed at Anzio would be able to break out of its bridgehead and create havoc across Kesselring's supply lines and that it would be able to do this within weeks, if not days.

The fears were realized. The hopes were not. The Anzio landing did nothing to make any easier the Allied assault on the Gustav Line. The forces landed at Anzio, the British 1st Division and the American 3rd under the command of the American General Lucas, themselves ran into dire trouble. General Lucas landed his men punctually on 22 January. He then spent the next eight days consolidating his bridgehead.

For this General Lucas has been much criticized. Hindsight enables everyone to know better afterwards. But hindsight cannot reproduce the total flow of reports, correct or incorrect, which beset a commander at the time he must make his lonely decision. In his book *Total War* Calvocoressi says that Lucas 'on discovering that there were no Germans in his path behaved as though there were'.[2]

This certainly is what appears to have happened. By 30 January, when

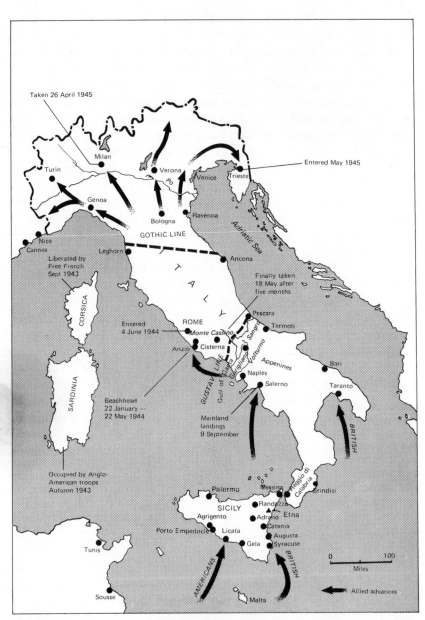

Taken 26 April 1945

Milan

Turin

Verona

Entered May 1945

Venice

Trieste

Po

Genoa

Bologna

Ravenna

Nice

Cannes

GOTHIC LINE

Adriatic Sea

Liberated by
Free French
Sept 1943

Leghorn

Ancona

I T A L Y

CORSICA

Finally taken
18 May after
five months

Pescara

ROME

Entered
4 June 1944

Monte Cassino

Termoli

SARDINIA

Anzio

Cisterna

Sangro

Voturno

Apennines

Naples

Bari

GUSTAV LINE

Gulf of Gaeta

Garigliano

Beachhead
22 January —
22 May 1944

Salerno

Taranto

Mainland
landings
9 September

BRITISH

Occupied by Anglo-
American troops
Autumn 1943

Reggio di
Calabria

Palermo

Messina

Brindisi

SICILY

Randazzo

Agrigento

Adrano

Etna

Catania

Porto Empedocle

Licata

Augusta

Tunis

Gela

Syracuse

BRITISH

0   100

Miles

AMERICANS

Sousse

Malta

Allied advances

The Italian Campaign, July 1943–May 1945

the bridgehead had been established to General Lucas's satisfaction, Kesselring organized a counter-attack. It very nearly succeeded. Lucas could make no headway towards his main objective, the Alban Hills south of Rome. The best that he could do in the face of the German counter-attack was to hold on to what he had.

In a renewed counter-attack, starting on 16 February, Kesselring very nearly threw the landing force back into the sea. The attack having been repelled, Lucas was relieved by General Truscott, the commander of the American 3rd Division. The Anzio beach-head remained but its garrison was powerless – at least for several months – to help the main Allied armies. Kesselring taught the Allies a fearsome lesson. In an early attempt to capture the town of Cisterna at the foot of the Alban Hills only six out of a force of 767 US rangers avoided death or capture.

In the hope that the landing at Anzio would help him, General Clark had prepared a series of attacks on the Rapido River line and on Monte Cassino. To sustain these attacks he received reinforcements from the British 8th Army which still was on the north-east side of the Apennines and making slow progress. On 12 January, ten days before the Anzio landing, General Juin's Free French Expeditionary Corps launched an attack inland of Monte Cassino towards St Elia. In three days the Free French had reached their objective. The same day, 15 January 1944, the Allies advanced to the Rapido River and five days later they crossed the Garigliano. But for the time being this was as far as they could get.

They held their bridgehead across the Garigliano, but that was all they could do. An attempt to cross the Rapido failed. On the west, the south and the east the German defences of Monte Cassino appeared impregnable.

Monte Cassino to the Po

The late Fred Majdalany, a writer whose distinction at that time was to be a Lancashire Fusilier (then part of the 78th Division), has written that all who fought at Cassino must remember as long as they live how the Benedictine monastery 'dominated and overshadowed their bodies and their minds during the winter of 1944'.[3]

'It took half a dozen months of bitter, bloody fighting before these defences were finally broken. By the time the monastery fell, soldiers of Britain, Canada, New Zealand, America, India and Poland had all bought at a high price the right to include in their battle honours "Cassino".'[4]

The battle of Cassino was mountain warfare at its harshest. The opposing lines were sometimes only yards apart. It was impossible for soldiers to dig themselves in with spades. This piece of Italy, as the German local commander, General von Senger und Etterlin, has pointed out, was not a land of oranges and sunshine.

The acoustically magnified noise of bombarding guns [he wrote] is the first unpleasantness. In the plains it was still possible to hold a conversation in the intervals between the single detonations, but in the mountains it became almost impossible because of the lingering peals and echoes. The broken stones greatly increased the splinter effect. Unlike the lowlands, the rocks absorbed nothing of the detonation, but provided a means of ricochet firing, whose effect resembles that of firing with time fuses. Anyone suddenly overtaken by artillery fire while on a mountain track had no possibility of evading it by moving away into open country.[5]

Because of the mountains, and because the other side nearly always possessed a mountain which could overlook yours, it was impossible for men to show themselves by day. The opposing troops had to supply themselves by night. The supplies had to be brought up by mules, and after that on the backs of soldiers. Nearly all the machines that were supposed to make warfare mobile, quick and easy had to be left behind in the plains. Only the soldiers' basic tools – guns, mortars, machine guns and hand grenades – were still at hand.

In this hideous place the monastery, as Majdalany noted, dominated everything. The German army had not, in fact, driven the monks out or replaced them. The German fortifications were outside the monastery walls – but only just. Von Senger und Etterlin said that the monastery itself was unsuitable as an observation post 'since we could expect it to be put out of action by heavy fire very soon after the big battle had started. It was the German practice,' he said, 'to place the artillery observers half way up the hills in a concealed position with a camouflaged background'.[6]

The Allies, who were not to know this, bombed the monastery all the same at the request of the New Zealand Corps commander, General Freyberg. Freyberg's motive was the simple and compelling one that men matter more than monasteries. He could not be sure, and nor could his soldiers, that the Germans were not actually safe and sound inside the monastery. In every good military formation, and the New Zealand division, which had been picked to lead the first attack, was one of the best – loyalty is a motive force which works in both directions – down-

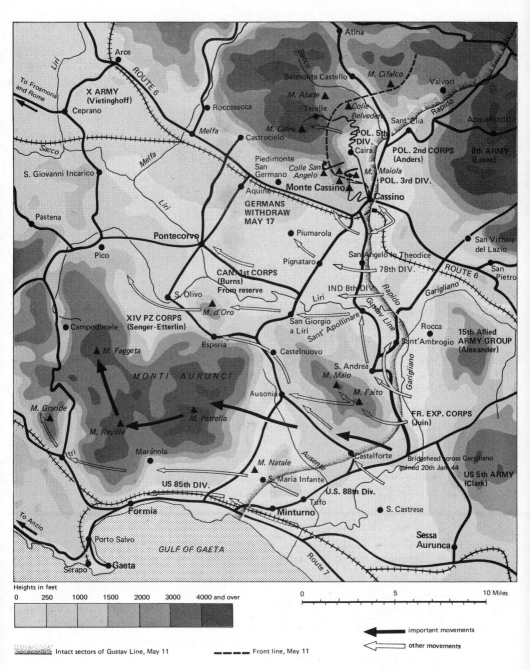

Monte Cassino, May 1944

Heights in feet

| 0 | 250 | 1000 | 1500 | 2000 | 3000 | 4000 and over |

Intact sectors of Gustav Line, May 11   — — — Front line, May 11

important movements

other movements

wards as well as upwards. The question which politicians and others who have not fought battles seldom ask themselves is the one which haunts every field commander – 'what do I say in my letter to the next-of-kin of the man who has just been killed under my command?' Freyberg had to ensure that before he sent his men into a battle that was bound to be desperate their chances of survival and success were as good as he could make them. Freyberg had another responsibility as well. The New Zealand division was, in effect, the whole of that section of the New Zealand nation which was of military age, Maoris and white men together.

The monastery was duly destroyed by the Allied air forces on 15 February 1944. This was, and remains, a controversial attack. The monastery was the birthplace of the Benedictine Order. It had been there since the sixth century and, although four times sacked (by the Lombards, the Saracens, the Germans and the French) it remained a building of impressive beauty and replete with history. General Mark Clark later regretted having allowed it to be bombed.

One military reason for regret was that the monastery was extremely strong. The enormous weight of bombs dropped upon it by the Allied air forces did not, in fact, destroy the arched cellars. Von Senger und Etterlin took advantage. 'The bombing', he said, 'had the opposite effect to what was intended. Now we could occupy the abbey without scruple, especially as ruins are better for defence than intact buildings. In time of war one must be prepared to demolish buildings which are required for defence.'[7]

The bombing of the monastery seemed to make no difference to the German defences. But Freyberg was not to know this. In the event, Clark sent first the 34th American Division and then Freyberg's New Zealanders round to the north side of Cassino to try to take it from there. The New Zealanders made gallant progress, but failed to prevail. They lost many men. They had gained some ground and some bloodstained buildings. But Monte Cassino, and with it the Gustav Line, remained unimpaired, an apparently insuperable obstacle on the road to Rome.

Alexander regrouped his forces. He moved a large part of the British 8th Army across the Apennines to take over the front opposite Cassino itself and the Liri Valley. By 11 May 1944, he was ready. On that day two divisions of the 8th Army crossed the Rapido, the Polish Corps (newly formed from Poles who had made their way from Eastern Europe and Russia to the Middle East), assaulted Cassino from the north. Alexander had moved the Free French – notably two divisions of Moroccans from the Atlas Mountains – from St Elia to the already secured bridgehead across the Garigliano from which they were to break out.

Their commander, General Juin, newly arrived from Africa, contended that the weak point in the German defensive line was an appalling mountain, the Petrella Peak, which was opposite his troops' positions. The High Command on either side considered it to be unscalable and therefore impregnable. Juin and his Moroccans thought otherwise. In the event they beat the rocks and the Germans too. The Poles, with equal gallantry and suffering sad casualties, eventually captured the monastery itself on 18 May. Victory at Cassino was signalled by the French flag on Petrella and the Polish one on the monastery. These were the signals. The fighting, however, had been shared by all. The British advanced slowly but steadily against heavy opposition through the Liri Valley. The Americans advanced along the coastal plain. On 23 May Kesselring gave up the Gustav Line and headed back for positions north-west of Rome. The same day the Anzio garrison, reinforced to six divisions, advanced out of its beach-head. By 4 June the Allies had taken Rome.

Once again Kesselring withdrew his forces to a weak defensive line only to withdraw again later to a stronger one. His next line ran from north of Rome across Italy to Pescara. The one behind it – the so-called Gothic Line – followed, roughly, the course of the Arno River just north of Leghorn and ended on the Adriatic coast near Ancona. At the end of September Kesselring retired again to a third line north of Florence and north of Rimini.

Here the armies stayed throughout the winter of 1944–45. The mountains and the weather were again on Kesselring's side. In accordance with the agreed strategy for the invasion of France, Alexander had had to give up seven of his divisions for Operation Anvil, the landings between Cannes and Nice in the south of France which took place on 15 August 1944. Throughout the winter the reduced Allied forces faced the Germans in the mountains north of Florence.

In April 1945 Alexander renewed the attack. His aim was to force the Germans out of the hills, into the Po Valley, and across the river towards Austria. By 20 April the advance was accelerating. The 8th Army under its new commander General McCreery led the attack with General Truscott, by now commander of the 5th Army, attacking further west. The Allies, now outnumbered because of the diversion of seven divisions to France, nevertheless pushed the Germans across the Po. By this time, Germany itself was collapsing. Kesselring had by now been summoned home to take command of the Western front in Germany. His successor, General Vietinghoff, was short of everything – especially air support. By the end of April the Germans in Italy could fight no longer.

It had taken the Allies nearly one year and ten months to conquer Sicily and Italy. The Italian campaign helped the Allies towards final victory in three ways. It occupied up to twenty-six German divisions, which might otherwise have fought on the Russian front or have been sent to France to resist the invasion from Britain. It provided the Allies with aerodromes from which to bomb the Balkans, central Europe and southern France – areas which would otherwise have been out of reach of Allied aircraft. Finally, the campaign eliminated the Italian armed forces from the war, not just in Italy, but also progressively in the Balkans and on the Russian front. It is not clear, even now, whether these gains were worth the price paid for them.

Chapter 8

Victory in the USSR

Three months before his attack on the Soviet Union Hitler had told his generals that this was to be a war of destruction.[1] There could be no question of soldierly comradeship with the Russians because the Russians were sub-human.

It was in this spirit that Hitler sent three million Germans – about half the total strength of his armed forces – into attack on 22 June 1941. They were supported, then or soon afterwards, by eighteen Finnish divisions, three Italian ones, some Croatians, sixteen divisions of Rumanians, three Hungarian brigades and three divisions of Slovakians.

As usual the Germans opened fire without warning and before dawn. Hitler described the operation, probably rightly, as the largest military assault in history. There were three Army Groups supported by most of the Luftwaffe. Army Group North under Field Marshal von Leeb drove north-eastwards from East Prussia towards Leningrad. Army Group Centre under Field Marshal von Bock headed for Moscow, skirting the impassable Pripet Marshes to the south and aiming to capture the important cities of Minsk and Smolensk on the way. Army Group South under Field Marshal von Rundstedt headed south-eastwards from German-occupied Poland towards the Crimean Peninsula, the Ukranian wheatfields, the Don Basin, and – hopefully – the Caucasian oilfields on which the Soviet armies depended for liquid fuel. The Russians had been warned, but were nevertheless taken by surprise because Stalin disbelieved the warnings.

When Hitler attacked, the Russians had stationed 170 divisions in advanced positions close to their new western frontiers. But their communications were still disorganized. Partly because of the Stalin purges of the 1930's their commanders were inexperienced. In any case the army and the air force both happened to be re-equipping. Most of the weapons they had were obsolete or were nearing the end of their useful

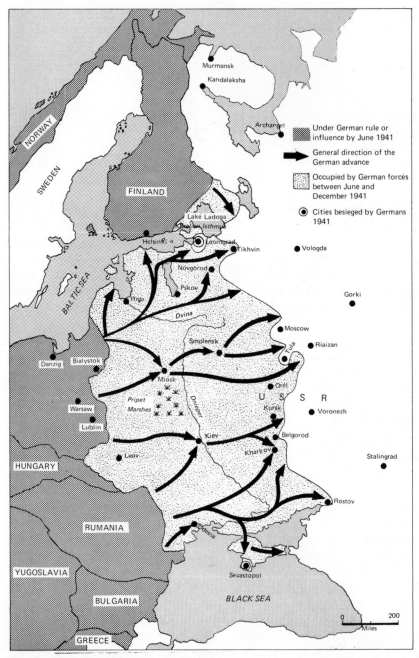

The German Invasion of Russia, 1941

Legend:

Under German rule or influence by June 1941

General direction of the German advance

Occupied by German forces between June and December 1941

Cities besieged by Germans 1941

Map labels:

NORWAY, SWEDEN, FINLAND, Murmansk, Kandalaksha, Archangel, Vologda, Gorki, Lake Ladoga, Karelian Isthmus, Helsinki, Leningrad, Tikhvin, Novgorod, Pskov, Riga, Dvina, BALTIC SEA, Moscow, Smolensk, Tula, Riaizan, Danzig, Bialystok, Minsk, Dnieper, Orel, Voronezh, Kursk, U S S R, Warsaw, Pripet Marshes, Lublin, Kiev, Belgorod, Lvov, Kharkov, Stalingrad, HUNGARY, Rostov, RUMANIA, Odessa, YUGOSLAVIA, Sevastopol, BULGARIA, BLACK SEA, GREECE

0 200 Miles

life. This had a negative merit. The equipment that they lost in the early days of the war was equipment that they could afford to lose. But in the short run this did not help.

The German armies advanced about fifty miles a day, sometimes faster. Army Group Centre reached the neighbourhood of Minsk within a fortnight and had by then surrounded 290,000 Russian soldiers. Army Group North was through the Baltic States and into Russia. By 17 July Army Group South was threatening Kiev. On 10 July the Finnish army, taking revenge for the Russian attack of the previous winter, had advanced down the Karelian Isthmus to threaten Leningrad from the north-west.

In the beginning the attack on Russia appeared to be yet another glorious joyride for the German army. Hitler said he hoped to conquer the Caucasus before the end of 1941. The supporting evidence existed. On 10 July Army Group Centre had completed the encirclement of 323,898 Russian soldiers in two separate operations near Minsk and Bialystok. On 5 August the same Army Group had virtually eliminated resistance at Smolensk. On 19 August Army Group South captured 650,000 Russian soldiers at Kiev and, a week later, had broken the Russian army's resistance east of that town and of the Dnieper River and seemed free to sweep forward to Kursk, Belgorod, and Kharkov on the Donets River. Army Group North had established an advance unit on the River Neva ten miles from Leningrad by 31 August and nine days later had captured Schlusselburg on Lake Ladoga, thereby severing Leningrad's land communications with the rest of Russia. The Finns had advanced towards Leningrad down the Karelian Isthmus but had not cut Leningrad off from access to Lake Ladoga itself. Six weeks after the campaign had begun the Russian position was grave, though less grave than it appeared.

On 11 August General Halder, the army Chief of Staff, wrote in his diary that the High Command was even then concerned to prevent the German army from becoming bogged down in a war of position. Halder said that it was becoming ever clearer, overall, that 'the Russian colossus ... has been under-estimated by us'. He said that the main reason for concluding that Germany had under-estimated Russia was the Russians' 'straightforward military capability' which, Halder said, was unexpected. 'When the war began', according to Halder, 'we had expected 200 enemy divisions. Now we have already counted 360. These divisions are certainly not properly armed and equipped as we would see it and they are often lacking in tactical leadership. But they are there. And whenever a dozen of these divisions are destroyed the Russians replace them with another dozen. The Russians have time to do this because they are close to their sources of supply whereas we are moving further and further from ours.'[2]

Six weeks' campaigning had caused the perceptive Halder to change his mind. As lately as 3 July he had been confident that his armies could defeat the Russians west of the Dvina in the north and of the Dnieper in the south within weeks if not months and that thereafter the war would be over. The Russians would have been finally defeated. Army Groups North and Centre had, indeed, advanced well beyond the Dvina by 17 July and Army Group South was on the banks of the Dnieper on 1 September. But the war had not been won. The Russians were not defeated and even Hitler – more given to wishful thinking than his generals – did not then pretend that they were, even to himself.

During the latter part of August the German offensive slowed down, and parts of it ran out of steam. There was also a command muddle, or at least a military dither in high German places. On 5 August Army Group Centre withdrew its tanks from the front for refitting. Army Group South was about to cross the Dnieper but was still a long way from the Caucasus. Even with the help of the Finns, Army Group North had not succeeded in subduing Leningrad. The Germans paused to reflect. There ensued the first of several debates between Hitler and his generals, debates in which Hitler nearly always got his way. Now the generals to a man were in favour of an all-out assault on Moscow. Hitler wanted to renew the pressure on the flanks.

Hitler decided, in effect, first to have his own way and then, when it was too late, to follow the generals' advice. On 21 August he decided that Army Group North should press on to capture Leningrad and that Army Group South should press on towards the Crimea and the Caucasus and that the assault on Moscow could wait. The Second German Army and the Second Panzer Group were diverted southward by Army Group Centre to help Army Group South. Passing eastward of the Pripet Marshes they joined Army Group South's forward elements east of Kiev on 16 September. Army Group North got no closer to capturing Leningrad partly because Hitler deprived the group of its armour, partly because he had decided against a full-scale assault on that city, but mainly because of the total stubbornness and self-sacrifice of Leningrad's defenders. Though he may not have realized this at the time, Hitler had already encountered at Leningrad the true quality of Russian defiance – the utter refusal of the Soviet nations to acknowledge that Germans had any right on Soviet soil or that surrender was an option.

In any case, on 6 September Hitler had changed his mind a second time. The attack on Moscow was to get priority after all. Army Group

Centre was to be reinforced once more. Moscow would fall by Christmas.

Reinforced and with its tanks repaired, Army Group Centre was ready to go by 2 October. But it was too late in the year. Von Bock's divisions moved fast but could not move fast enough. By the third week in October they had encircled three vast pockets of Russian soldiers, one near Viazma opposite Moscow towards the northern end of their front and two more near Bryansk. They had taken some 650,000 prisoners. But for the time being that was all they could do.

In mid-October it began to rain. The rain continued into early November turning the Russian country roads into lanes of mud in which the German vehicles stuck, or sank, or had to be abandoned. The German generals prayed, mistakenly, for the frost to come to harden the roads so that their troops could move again.

When the frost came to Russia in mid-November 1941 it was harder and colder than the Germans had expected. But to begin with, at least, their tanks and their vehicles could move. At this stage the German generals were in some doubt as to whether to go on or not. Field Marshal von Bock, commanding Army Group Centre, was in favour of continuing. His was to be the main attack on Moscow. He was on the spot. His view prevailed. Army Group Centre began to advance on 15 November. Von Bock's plan was to encircle and envelop Moscow by despatching an armoured thrust from each end of his front. General Guderian was to break through the Russian lines south of Tula and then turn north towards the Russian capital. General Reinhardt was to break through the lines north of the Moskva River and then turn south.

It was a classical German plan identical with many that had succeeded before. What turned this one into a disaster was the weather. When the ground froze on 15 November Guderian's and Reinhardt's tanks were able to move again over the frozen mud. What they had not foreseen and what stopped them in the end was that the temperature continued to fall. Before the end of November it was snowing hard, the temperature was down to minus 20° centigrade, and the cold was stopping their machines. It was also stopping their men. But it was not stopping the Russians.

The German army did not have winter clothing nearly thick enough for the Russian weather. The generals blamed Hitler. He had said he would finish the Russians before the winter. Therefore winter clothing would not be necessary. Either way, this grave administrative failure affected both Army Group North and Army Group Centre. Early in December Army Group North reported, for example, that the Twelfth Panzer Division had lost 63 men killed by the enemy and 325 through frostbite. On 5 December from their positions north and south of Moscow both Reinhardt and Guderian said that they could make no progress and were hard pressed. Von Bock records in his diary that Guderian reported a temperature of minus 30° centigrade which virtually prevented any movement of the exhausted troops. The German tanks, von Bock said, would not run whereas the Russian ones were running well. Further north the temperature was minus 38° centigrade. What was worse for the Germans was that the Russians, better clad and better equipped, did not seem to notice.

There is the additional fact that if you touch a gun with your bare hands in temperatures the Germans were then experiencing for the first time your fingers will stick to the metal and if you try to pull your hand away you will lose the skin off your fingers. But there are some things which have to be done to machine guns which cannot be done in gloves.

This was one discovery that the Germans made as they lay in the snow in front of Moscow. Another was that ordinary lubricating oil is useless if it gets too cold. In all important ways the Germans were unprepared for temperatures that the Russians could live with because they were normal in Russia. A German officer, Lieutenant Maurer, remembers the time before Moscow with dreadful clarity:

We had no gloves. We had no winter shoes. We had no equipment whatsoever to fight or withstand the cold. I think this became a very, very big problem right away. We lost a considerable part of our equipment, guns, heavy and light equipment in general. Due to the cold we lost a lot of people who got frost-bitten, and we had not even the necessary amount of ointments, or the most simple and primitive things to fight it. We cut strips off our overcoats to wrap them around our hands instead of wearing gloves. As it became colder towards the end of November and early December most of our artillery had become completely unusable. Guns didn't fire anymore. Even our wireless equipment didn't work properly anymore because the batteries were frozen hard. So there was no way of communicating even between the advancing lines and the artillery batteries in the background. It was of course a very, very bad thing if you got wounded. We could hardly take care of our own wounded, not to speak about the enemy. We were afraid to become wounded and to become just the prey of a very bad winter climate or the prey of the enemy. And we had seen enough of the enemy to know that in cases like that prisoners were hardly taken. A good number, when it came to a decisive moment, tried not to stick their heads out as much as they might have done otherwise. . . .

The Russian soldier was a very robust and hardy soldier, well used to those climatic conditions. They did not seem to harm him very much. Sometimes we got terribly angry and really mad at everybody and everything because if we had to leave behind our arms – machine guns or what have you – because they didn't work anymore, the Russians just grabbed them; we sometimes saw them put some winter oil on and turn them on us.[3]

The Germans were forced to retreat as best they could, leaving many soldiers frozen to death behind them. They did not retreat far at first. But the Russians did not relax their pressure and before long the Germans were in serious trouble, locally at least. The cold continued. The Germans were short of fuel and supplies. They were not sure whether they could hold the positions to which they were retreating. Hitler, meanwhile, was ordering the impossible – that the army should not retreat one step. On 16 December von Bock reported:

> The reason why it is doubtful whether the units can hold a new, unprepared defensive line is clear – because of the shortage of fuel and because of the icy roads I am not getting my motorized units back; I am not even getting my horse-drawn artillery back because the horses cannot manage the weather. Today, for example, the 267th Division had to leave its artillery behind. There is therefore a grave danger that as we retreat we may reach new positions, but without artillery. On the other hand an order to stand and fight would induce in me the fear lest the soldiers would, somewhere or other retreat without orders.

Von Bock, in other words, feared mutiny.

This was the Germans' general dilemma in front of Moscow in December 1941. If the forward units were ordered to retreat they would have to leave their equipment behind because of the weather. If they were ordered to stand and fight they might disobey the order. At this awkward moment the Russians amazed the Germans by mounting a counter-offensive.

Considering the Soviet losses to date in men (probably about four million), in territory, in productive capacity (two-thirds of their coal and three-quarters of their iron production) and considering above all the weather, the Russian offensive of 6 December 1941 was an heroic achievement. The main attack was delivered on the Moscow front by an army group commanded by General Zhukov. To the north, troops manning the Kalinin front under General Konev joined in. So, on the south, did the right flank of the south-west front armies commanded by Marshal Timoshenko.

Hitler had ordered his troops to stay where they were. But obedience to this order was impossible. The Russians fell upon the Germans like wolves from the woods.

By the end of December the Russians had opened two gaps in the German line at the northern and southern end of Army Group Centre's sector. The northern gap was 160 miles wide. The Germans' position was serious, if not desperate. They probably only managed to avoid encirclement because on 15 January 1942 Hitler changed his mind and ordered a retreat. The Germans had been retreating anyway, but from then on they had definite orders – orders which, this time, made sense – to retire to a line some 90 miles west of Moscow and to hold it. This proved possible. Army Group Centre was able to stabilize a front at Rzhev.

Stalin, unlike Hitler, had never doubted for a moment that the battle for Moscow would be the one that mattered. Although the Russians resisted fiercely on the northern and southern fronts their main effort during the winter of 1941–42 was concentrated in the centre in order to save their capital.

Two factors helped mightily. The Germans were unprepared for the weather. This was largely the fault of Hitler's arrogance. He had boasted that he would capture Moscow before the winter. He refused to retract his boast. Requests for winter clothing were turned down. The other factor was the Russians' December offensive. This was a brilliant campaign which owed its success partly to Zhukov's generalship, partly to the hardiness and fortitude of Russian soldiers fighting in the cold, and partly to the arrival of reinforcements from Siberia.

Before Hitler launched his attack the Russians had been engaged in a sporadic but sometimes fierce defensive war against the Japanese in Mongolia. On the fringes of their vast attempt to conquer China the Japanese had also been engaged against Russian forces sometimes successfully, sometimes (when General Zhukov was in command) disastrously. But the threat had persisted. In the spring of 1941 Stalin had no option but to be ready for a continuing war in the east as well as a possible war in the west. His salvation from this dilemma was his good spy in Tokyo. Richard Sorge, a German Communist and the Tokyo correspondent of the *Frankfurter Zeitung*, was on the best of terms with both the German and Soviet ambassadors in Tokyo but his allegiance was to the Soviet one. He was Karl Marx's secretary's grandson and was perhaps the most important and effective spy in World War II. On 20 May 1941 Sorge was able to assure the Soviet Ambassador that the Germans would attack Russia on 22 June. Churchill and Roosevelt had

24. A Focke-Wulf 200 reconnaissance bomber

25. A B.17, Mark 3, USAAF, raiding Berlin in 1944

26. RAF pilots scramble to their Hurricanes at Vassincourt, France, 1940

27. The Liberator, a widely used US heavy bomber

28. A Hurricane squadron on patrol

29. A Catalina aircraft

30. Wellington bombers, Mark I

31. A Junkers 87

32. Superfortress B29 bombing a Japanese airbase in Burma

33. A Focke-Wulf 190A-5 abandoned on a Belgian airfield

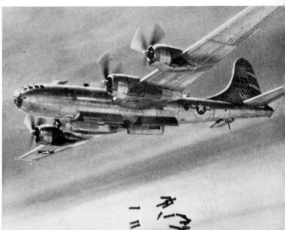

34. The *Admiral Graf Spee* scuttled at Montevideo, 17 December 1939

35. Blindfolded *Scharnhorst* survivors being landed at a British port. The *Scharnhorst* was sunk on 26 December 1943

given Stalin the same warning, though in more general terms, and he had not believed them. But he half-believed Sorge. He also, in the end, believed Sorge's further information that the Japanese had decided finally and irrevocably to attack the United States and to leave the Soviet Union alone. Sorge was correct on both counts.

For some months Stalin still hesitated to believe Sorge's information about the Japanese. But when the Mongolian campaigning season ended he took a chance and acted. In the autumn of 1941 he began to move his Siberian armies west. By November they were on the Moscow front under Zhukov's command. Their unexpected presence added to the Germans' alarm. They had no need to acclimatize. To men who had come from Siberia even the Moscow front seemed warm. Their arrival added to the German soldiers' apprehensions. Another German officer, Lieutenant Elble, was one of the first to meet the 'Siberians'.

'We saw them after taking this small village. My soldiers came to me with prisoners of war and we were very surprised to see people, very, very big men with very good winter clothes, all new winter clothes. My first question was what division – because we knew very well all division numbers, Russian division numbers we had already had to fight with. But now for the first time we had met the first Siberian divisions and then my feeling was a very bad one, because this was the sign that the Russian people, the Russian Government was able to take troops from the far east and to transport them to the front at Moscow and that now we would have to fight against very new divisions, against very hard divisions.'[5]

'We were very much impressed', said the German General Hinrichs. 'We were attacked by a Soviet company in the early morning at approximately 35° below zero. This company attack was repulsed, the Soviet soldiers remained almost motionless about eight hours lying in the snow. And in the evening they again attacked with the same spirit.'[6]

The Russian winter offensive of 1941, besides gaining ground, restored the Allies' morale as nothing else could have done. It was a time when good news was scarce. The Japanese, apparently invincible, had destroyed most of the US Pacific Fleet at Pearl Harbor and were sweeping through South-East Asia. Only the Russians seemed to be prevailing. The Permanent Secretary of the British Foreign Office, Sir Alexander Cadogan, met Timoshenko in Moscow on 20 December and found him 'very blatantly confident about German loss of morale'.[7] Stalin, Cadogan said, was also confident 'but in a quiet way'. In a dark hour the Russians' confidence spread comfortingly to the other Allies.

But Hitler was confident too. By the spring of 1942 he had convinced himself that the failure of his attack on Moscow had been due not so much to the fact that the Russians were stronger and were better winter fighters, as to a failure of leadership by the German generals. This was a mistake that Hitler was to repeat. Like other dictators before him, he decided that all would be well if he himself took personal command. He sacked von Brauchitsch. Halder became, in effect, Hitler's aide-de-camp. Hitler established his own personal supreme headquarters at Rastenburg in East Prussia, and gave it the code-name of 'the Wolf's lair'.

In a directive on 5 April 1942, Hitler told his generals that he intended to launch that summer a major offensive south-eastwards towards the Caucasus. On the northern and central fronts the German armies would remain 'active' but would not attempt major offensive operations. He added, almost as an afterthought, that Leningrad would have to be captured – a proposition that was never to be realized.

Hitler's main declared objective was south-east Russia. His plan was to possess himself of the Don Basin and, above all, of the Caucasian oilfields. He would thus deprive Russia of her vital fuel supplies and, on his way to the Caucasus, would destroy Russia's remaining reserves of military manpower. To accomplish all this Army Group South – divided now into Army Groups A and B – would first conquer the Crimea and eliminate those Russian forces still in possession of a quite large area west of the Donets River and just south of Kharkov. After that there was to be a three-pronged concerted attack on Voronezh by two forces of assault troops moving east from the neighbourhood of Orel and Kursk. Having occupied the Crimea, the Germans were to advance eastwards, cross the Straits of Kerch, which connect the Black Sea with the Sea of Azov, and invade the north-west Caucasus. Having captured Voronezh, the German armies were to converge from there and from a point east of Dnepropetrovsk upon Stalingrad on the River Volga. By this time, Hitler calculated, the way would be open to the Caucasus. Once established in the Caucasus Hitler would have the Russian oil for himself. And beyond the Caucasus lay the Middle East with more oil still and which provided an overland route to the Suez Canal. To Hitler, peering south-eastward in the spring of 1942, the horizon seemed boundless and every prize attainable.

The march of events did not conform, however, to Hitler's plan. The Russians upset his timetable in two ways. Their first intervention, an abortive attempt to recapture Kharkov, worked to Hitler's advantage. The other Russian surprise was more serious. Russian resistance in the Crimea was unexpectedly stubborn. It took the Germans eight months instead of six to capture besieged Sebastopol in the Crimea.

In 1942 as in 1941, the Germans were late in starting, and lived to regret their tardiness. The Russians under Timoshenko began their attempt to retake Kharkov on 12 May. Timoshenko's plan was to cross the Donets – which then separated the German and Russian armies – north of Kharkov and at the same time to strike north from the Izyum bridgehead south of Kharkov which the Russians still held. Timoshenko hoped thus to surround Kharkov and capture the Germans who were holding that city. After that Timoshenko intended to drive towards Dnepropetrovsk, one hundred miles south-west on the Dnieper River.

Unfortunately for Timoshenko, the Germans were even then preparing to eliminate the Izyum bridgehead in accordance with the first phase of Hitler's plan. The forces which were preparing to do this had already taken up their positions when Timoshenko struck. German resistance turned out to be much stronger than the Russians had expected. Within days it became apparent that at this point on the front at least the Germans were not only strong enough to defend themselves but to attack as well. Stalin, like Hitler before him, forebade retreat. Like Hitler he was wrong. He changed his mind, but he changed it too late. By 27 May, a fortnight after Timoshenko's offensive started, the Germans had surrounded his force and had taken about one quarter of a million prisoners.

The German offensive towards Voronezh and the River Don began a month later on 28 June. The Germans took Voronezh on 6 July and thence moved south eastward along the bank of the Don. During the early part of July, as the German troops who had captured Voronezh and the others who had struck east from Kharkov moved south-eastward towards Stalingrad, Hitler modified his grand design. He decided that he would not, for the moment, bother to clear all the Russians out from the wide territories between the Donets and the eastward bend of the Don and that he would move troops south immediately to capture Rostov, the major Russian city at the head of the Sea of Azov and the main gateway to the Caucasus. The Germans captured Rostov on 23 July without much trouble, but without taking many prisoners either. The Russians had learnt, or had begun to learn, the vital strategic lesson that if you have a big empty country, men matter more than territory.

At this time, nevertheless, the Russians' position could scarcely have been worse. The Caucasus, and with it Russia's oil, appeared to be at Hitler's mercy. The German Army Group A, reinforced by the Fourth Panzer Army, occupied Rostov. The Caucasian mountains lay ahead of them and separated them from the oilfields and were formidable indeed. But their chances of capturing Baku and Tiflis by the autumn still seemed good.

But July 1942 turned out to be another of those baffling moments in the history of the war when Hitler made the wrong decision by not making a decision at all. In 1940 he had changed the course of history by deciding wrongly that the attack on Britain could wait. In 1942 he probably changed the course of history by deciding, in effect, to postpone the attack on the Caucasus by weakening the forces which were due to mount it.

After Army Group A and the Fourth Panzer Army had captured Rostov, he ordered the Fourth Panzer Army to turn about, proceed north-east, and help the Sixth German Army to capture Stalingrad nearly 300 miles away. Simultaneously he ordered Army Group A to send a substantial part of its artillery as well as other units to Leningrad to reinforce Army Group North.

Even in the light of Hitler's own plan for the 1942 summer offensive, these were extraordinary decisions. Their effect was to disperse the overwhelming strength which the Germans then possessed in Rostov and which, probably, would have enabled them to achieve Hitler's prime objective for 1942 – the capture of the Caucasus and its oilfields. In the event the German thrust was, comparatively, no more than a feeble shove. Army Group A captured the nearest oilfield at Maikop to find that it had been destroyed. An armoured thrust towards Grozny stopped before it got there for lack of fuel and ammunition.

Army Group A was already a long way from home. By diverting a major part of the Group's resources and supplies to belated and, in the event, futile attacks on Stalingrad and Leningrad, Hitler effectively deprived it of any real chance of success. Its commander, Field Marshal List, was expected to conquer the Caucasian mountains with inadequate supplies of fuel and ammunition. His failure to do this – a failure which was crucial to Hitler's entire campaign in 1942 – was inevitable.

Stalingrad

Hitler had not only dispersed his forces, he had also lengthened his front. Stalingrad seems to have obsessed him, even then. It lay more than 200 miles to the east of the direct route from occupied Poland to the Caucasus. It is true that it was, and still is, a main centre of Russian industrial strength and that it lies on the Volga. The Volga was, and is, one of Russia's main communication arteries. Hitler seems to have feared (rightly) that the Russians would defend Stalingrad at all costs and to the death. He also seems to have supposed (wrongly) that the Russians would be able to use Stalingrad as a base from which to launch attacks upon the flanks of his line of communication from occupied Poland to the Caucasus.

Here Hitler's logic was faulty. Had he occupied the Caucasus, thereby depriving the Russian armies of their fuel, it is, to say the least, unlikely that they could have mounted a major campaign from Stalingrad or from anywhere else which could have threatened the German lines of communication. Had the Germans captured the Caucasus it would have been open to them, in the last resort, to do without land communications altogether. The Black Sea was waiting to be used. The Germans could have supplied their Caucasian armies with food and ammunition and themselves with oil simply by using ships. Perhaps Hitler never thought of this.

Stalingrad in those days was a long, thin city twenty-five miles long and between two and three miles broad, strung out along the west bank of the river Volga. It was and is a major manufacturing centre and commands the main communications network of southern Russia. Hitler was determined to conquer it, perhaps even to level it to the ground. He moved his own headquarters south from East Prussia to Vinnitsa in the Ukraine the better to direct the detailed battle. To the same end he sacked a number of generals mainly, it seems, because they were telling him things about Stalingrad that he did not want to hear.

They told him, for example, that the German line was dangerously extended because of the drive towards Stalingrad. They said that communications between the 6th Army facing Stalingrad and the depleted Army Group A in the Caucasus were impossibly thin.

Hitler did not want to hear this sort of news. Field Marshal List was sacked first. Halder followed him at the end of September. By this time the German 6th Army under General von Paulus had driven the Russians back into the city of Stalingrad itself where the Russian 62nd Army under General Chuikov held on grimly to nine miles of the river bank, sometimes to no more than a street or two of the city.

The 62nd Army was immovable. With the river behind them the Russians clung to every building, they defended the ruins of every factory, they regained by night the territory that the Germans, with their superior fire power, had gained during the day.

They were also well led. In the Russian army Chuikov was something of a rarity – a general who did not hestitate to disagree with his superiors if he thought they were wrong. He had been demoted early in the war to become second-in-command of the 64th Army. When Stalingrad was threatened Krushchev, the political commissar responsible for the district, promoted him again and gave him command of the beleaguered 62nd Army. It was one of the best and most important appointments of the war. Chuikov loved his men. The men loved him. He fought with them in the ruins, he ate with them, drank with them, laughed with them and never left them. There was a rough gaiety about Chuikov which inspired the 62nd Army to perform heroic feats.

Chuikov's men received hardly any reinforcements. His men had no room to manoeuvre. And, quite soon, the Germans had brought up 22 divisions to destroy them. The Germans destroyed the city but they did not destroy the men.

Chuikov, for one, was indestructible; and intelligent as well. Against the Germans as against the Finns, the Russian generals were good learners. Chuikov knew what he was doing.

The enemy stuck to the same pattern in his tactics. His infantry went into an attack wholeheartedly only when tanks had already reached the target. The tanks, however, normally went into an attack only when the Luftwaffe was already over the heads of our troops. One had only to break this sequence for an enemy attack to stop and his units to turn back. . . . The Germans could not stand close fighting; they opened up with their automatic weapons from well over half a mile away, when their bullets could not cover half the distance. They fired simply to keep up their morale. They could not bear us to come close to them when we counter-attacked. Some threw themselves to the ground, and often retreated.

Their communications between infantry, tanks and aeroplanes were good, especially through the use of rockets. They met their aeroplanes with dozens, hundreds of rockets, pinpointing their positions. Our troops and commanders worked out this signalling system and began to make use of it, frequently leading the enemy to make mistakes.[8]

Chuikov decided that the best way to fight the Stalingrad battle would be closely, and to continue fighting night and day in different ways and particularly at night. 'We should get as close to the enemy as possible, so that his air force could not bomb our forward units or trenches. Every German soldier must be made to feel that he was living under the muzzle of a Russian gun.'[9]

After Chuikov had crossed the Volga by ferry to take up his new command, no one at first could direct him to army headquarters. At length he found it with the help of an intelligent sapper. It was dark. Army headquarters contained two people only, the Chief of Staff and acting commander, General Krylov, and the duty telephonist, Elena Bakarevich, described by Chuikov as a blue-eyed girl of about eighteen. When Chuikov walked in, both of them were on the telephone. Chuikov looked about him at his new headquarters.

> Krylov's dug-out, strictly speaking, is not a dug-out at all, but a broad trench with a bench made of packed earth along one side, a bed made of earth on the other, and a table made of earth at the end of the bed. The roof is made of brushwood, with bits of straw sticking through it and on top of the straw a layer of soil about 12 to 15 inches thick. Shells and mortar are exploding nearby. The explosions make the dug-out shake and soil runs down through the ceiling onto the spread out maps and onto the heads of the people inside.
>
> I listen to Krylov and at the same time study his working map, the marks and arrows on it, trying to feel my way into the events taking place. I realize that he has no time to give me a report on the situation in peace and quiet. I have to trust Krylov; I do not disturb his operations or alter his plans for tomorrow, because in any case, necessary or not, there is nothing I am capable of changing.[10]

What Chuikov did change, before he had finished with von Paulus, was the legend of Germany's invincibility.

As the autumn nights lengthened von Paulus sent for reinforcements. He concentrated all his German troops in Stalingrad itself, leaving his flanks to be defended by Rumanians and Hungarians. This was imprudent but he probably had no choice.

Stalin had sent General Zhukov, the man who had saved Moscow, to take overall command of the Stalingrad operation. The reason that the hard-pressed Chuikov was not getting many reinforcements was that on the other side of the Volga Zhukov was preparing not just to relieve Stalingrad but to encircle and capture the besieging Germans. During five weeks in October and November Zhukov collected a mighty force of twelve armies for the counter-attack.

On 19 November when the ground had frozen and the tanks could move, the Russians attacked the Rumanians north of the city and defeated them within the day. On the 20th the Russians attacked to the south of the city and broke through the Rumanian lines there as well. By the 22nd the two Russian striking forces – the northern one commanded by General Rokossovski and the southern one by General Yeremenko, had reached the Don and had joined forces near Kalach. Von Paulus and about a quarter of a million men were surrounded.

Hitler told him not to surrender. Goering promised that the Luftwaffe would supply the 6th Army by air. Neither Hitler's order nor Goering's promise could be carried out. In mid-December Manstein, by then in command of Army Group B, tried to relieve von Paulus by attacking the encircling Russians from the west hoping that von Paulus would simultaneously try to fight his way out from the east. But von Paulus had orders to stay where he was. Nothing happened. The plan failed. Von Paulus remained encircled.

The German position was now hopeless. Goering's promised airlift was a farce. Rations had to be reduced. Ammunition was running low. In January the Russians called on von Paulus to surrender. Hitler ordered him to refuse, and made him a Field Marshal. By February von Paulus's forces had been divided into two parts by a Russian thrust. On 2 February von Paulus surrendered. By then 70,000 Germans had died in Stalingrad. The Russians took 91,000 prisoners including twenty-four German generals. They had already taken a great many more during the siege.

The German defeat at Stalingrad was a catastrophe that could not be measured simply in terms of casualties or of the number taken prisoner. Stalingrad proved for the first time that the Germans could be beaten in the field. It was not as if they had tried and failed to achieve some daring success which proved to be just that much too hard for them – like their attempt to capture Moscow the previous winter. At Stalingrad the Germans were beaten at their own game. The Russians had encircled a German army just as the Germans, in earlier campaigns, had encircled other armies. The Germans, supposedly the masters of the art of war on land, had been outgeneraled. The people whom Hitler called 'sub-human' had proved that they were cleverer than he was.

Long before Stalingrad surrendered, the Germans were in trouble elsewhere in the south. In mid-December the Russians began a drive towards Rostov to threaten Army Group A, which was still in the Caucasus. Rostov was the gate through which Army Group A would have to withdraw, if it could. A second Russian drive threatened Army Group B. The Russians exploited to the full the dangerous openness of the German front between Stalingrad and the Caspian Sea.

Kursk

In the south, though not in Stalingrad, Hitler was at last persuaded to allow retreat. At the end of January, he withdrew the first Panzer Army from the Caucasus through Rostov. The rest of Army Group A retreated into the Taman peninsula on the eastern side of the Straits of Kerch. In March they had to be rescued, mainly by air. Harried by bold and rapid Russian thrusts during February, the Germans retreated in something approaching confusion to the line from which they had started the previous summer and even, in some places, beyond it. They were saved by Manstein. By concentrating his remaining tanks into effective striking forces, by shortening the line, and by counter-attacking the Russians when they were running out of fuel and ammunition, he managed to contain the attack. The Russians captured Kharkov only to lose it again. By the spring, when the thaw turned the frozen country into mud, the opposing armies were facing each other once again along the line of the River Donets. Further north Zhukov had retaken Voronezh, and the Russians were occupying a large salient – a hundred miles deep and a hundred and fifty miles wide – centred on the town of Kursk, the starting point of the German offensive of the year before.

The Kursk salient tempted Hitler into risking and sustaining a further defeat which was as serious as his defeat at Stalingrad had been. The Russians did not actually lay a trap for him. They occupied the Kursk salient simply because they had conquered that territory. But, as the Russians knew, a salient is a great temptation to a German general. Or it was in those days. The German General Staff's classic reaction to an enemy promontory, an enemy-held outpost stretching beyond the general run of the front line, had always been to pinch the promontory off by attacking each of its flanks simultaneously. This is what Hitler resolved to do at Kursk, just as the Russians had expected.

On 15 April 1943 Hitler issued a secret directive ordering the elimination of the Kursk salient. 'The victory at Kursk', Hitler said, 'must shine like a beacon to the world.'[11] Operation 'Citadel', as the attack was to be called, would have a special importance. It would be a sign that Germany was still invincible. It would be the first and most important offensive that the German armies would undertake that year. The ultimate aim would be to open the road from Orel, at the north-eastern corner of the salient, to Moscow.

Orel at this time was in German hands, but only just. Hitler wanted to secure it absolutely, having first destroyed the Russian forces within the salient and any others who came to their aid. To make this possible Hitler planned to have General von Kluge attack the salient from the north, while von Manstein struck from the south.

The attack on the Kursk salient was scheduled to begin in May. For once Hitler and all the generals concerned were in agreement. The attack would throw the Russians off balance and interrupt, interfere with or prevent any plans they might have for a summer offensive in 1943. The attack was to begin as soon as the ground had hardened again after the spring thaw.

The Russians would probably have won at Kursk anyway. What made their victory certain was a joint decision by Hitler and General Model, the commander who was to lead the tank assault from the northern side of the salient, that it would be better to wait for the vast (for those days) new 'Ferdinand' Porsche tank. This carried an 88 mm gun, its armour plating was 120 mm thick at the front and 82 mm thick at the side, and the whole machine weighed 73 tons. In many ways it was a good and formidable tank. But it had never yet been tested properly in battle. Its drawback, discovered at Kursk, was that it was vulnerable to courageous Russian infantry men. 'Ferdinand' had no machine gun to protect itself against the (by now) skilled Russian soldiers who quickly learned how to drop incendiaries into the engine air intakes.

The earlier Panther tank, the German Mark V, was vulnerable for the same reasons. Nor was it in all respects a match for the now proven T34. The Panther's armour was heavier than the T34's but the Panther was slower, ran on petrol instead of diesel oil, and had a smaller radius of action (although the range of its gun was greater than the range of the T34's). What Hitler and Model did not know was that while they were waiting for their new tanks the Russians tank men had trumped their ace.

For the first time at Kursk the Russians produced and used two new vehicles each of which outclassed both the German tanks – the Panther and the Ferdinand. The Russians had succeeded where the Germans had failed in mounting a really heavy gun on a comparatively light basic vehicle. The new Russian SU 122 mounted a 122 mm gun on a T34 chassis and weighed only 30 tons. The SU 152, which also made its first appearance in battle at Kursk, mounted a 152 mm gun and weighed 40 tons. Apart from anything else that went on at Kursk the Russian armaments industry had outclassed the German one.

The attack began during the afternoon of 4 July. The Germans found the Russian defences unexpectedly strong. They had difficulty in clearing a path through the minefields. And no wonder; the Russians had been waiting for them, landmine-laying since May.

On 5 July when the German tanks began to move, seventeen German armoured divisions drove into the salient from Belgorod in the south and from the neighbourhood of Orel in the north. By the 9th the northern divisions, commanded by Model, had advanced about twenty-five miles. Again they met unexpectedly harsh resistance. For the next four days they could make no progress. Meanwhile, on the 12th, the Russians, under Zhukov's direction, had launched a heavy attack on the German positions around Orel whence the German tanks had set out. The southern German expedition, commanded by General Hoth, was at this time in rather better shape than the northern group, but Hoth like Model had his difficulties.

At virtually every point the Germans had done what Zhukov had expected them to do and had wanted them to do. Zhukov knew that he could probably beat the Germans anyway because he had prepared the ground well for defence and because he had collected large forces for the counter-attack. Zhukov knew also that he could defeat the Germans more certainly and more decisively if he could allow them to use up fuel and ammunition and generally exhaust themselves before he was obliged to commit his own fresh troops and machines. When Zhukov struck his first, main blow the Germans had been fighting for a week and the Russians were only just beginning. Even so, the Germans had only managed to narrow the gap between their two spearheads to about fifty miles. For once Hitler acted quickly and decisively. To prevent a rout he ordered a retreat. Once again the Germans, who had invented and perfected mobile tank warfare, had been beaten at their own game.

The battle of Kursk was another occasion on which Hitler made things worse for himself by delaying the planned start of an operation. It is almost certain that he would have been beaten at Kursk in any case, because the Russians had correctly anticipated what he would do. But it is certain, too, that his defeat would have been less serious if he had not waited until he had gathered together a great mass of tanks, many of them new. He did this because throughout the Russian campaign the Germans had been more and more dismayed to find that the Russian T34 tank (which was just coming into service during the winter of 1941) was invulnerable to any gun smaller than the Germans' high-velocity 88 mm anti-tank and anti-aircraft weapon which, like the T34, was not yet in general use. Later, the Russians introduced heavier and better tanks still and the Germans replied with even heavier tanks of their own. These new machines, the Germans hoped, would once again make German armour invincible. They were prepared to wait for them. But they waited too long.

After the battle of Kursk not even Hitler seems to have continued to believe that Germany could win in the east. Announcing to his generals his decisions to abandon Operation Citadel he said that the Anglo-American landings in Sicily (which had taken place three days before) had made it necessary to withdraw troops from the eastern front and send them to Italy where, he was sure, the Italians would give up. Hitler was right about the Italians. But the reason he gave for abandoning the Kursk offensive was less than candid. Perhaps he wanted to excuse himself in front of his generals. He had been telling them since the Russian campaign began that the German army must on no account yield an inch of Russian soil. Nevertheless his real reason for abandoning the Kursk attack was that the Russians were threatening to annihilate seventeen out of the nineteen armoured divisions which Germany then had deployed on the eastern front.

The Sicilian landings did, of course, make a difference. Hitler was indeed obliged to withdraw troops from Russia to reinforce this new front in Sicily and Italy. The British and the Americans were, at last, beginning to relieve the pressure on the Russians. But for the Germans the decisive military factor in July 1943 was not the invasion of Sicily. It was total defeat at Kursk, followed by serious reverses elsewhere.

After two fearsome years of war the Russians were at last in a position to begin to repel the invader and to avenge their dead.

The 20,000,000 Russians who died – most of them between 1941 and 1943 – must command the respect and understanding of the rest of the world. Some of them died horribly. Atrocity stories, generally speaking, are doubtful evidence. But this does not mean that all of them are false. General Chuikov, who having defended Stalingrad went on to capture Berlin, whose 62nd Army (later renamed the 8th Guards Army) seems to have been in a real way a band of brothers, speaks for one of his sergeants, Yukhim Remenyuk.

Remenyuk had fought bravely at Stalingrad and had taken part in many actions. Off duty, or during halts on the march, he used to say to his friends, 'Now when we get close to our frontier, I'll invite you in as my guests. I've got a wife called Yarinka and a daughter called Oksana, and my old father and mother live with us. It's a good spot where we live: there are the woods, there's a clearing where the beehives stand; plenty of elbow room.' And it so fell out that Sergeant Remenyuk's unit really did come to Yukhim's home, and his company went into action for his village. . . . He was the first man into the village and rushed to his own place. But it was not there: the cottage had gone – only ruins left. The orchard was burned. Only one old apple tree still standing, and on it his father hung, and under it his mother lay dead. Yarinka and Oksana the Germans had taken away.[12]

What impressed Chuikov was that even after his dreadful homecoming Sergeant Remenyuk continued to take prisoners. Sergeant

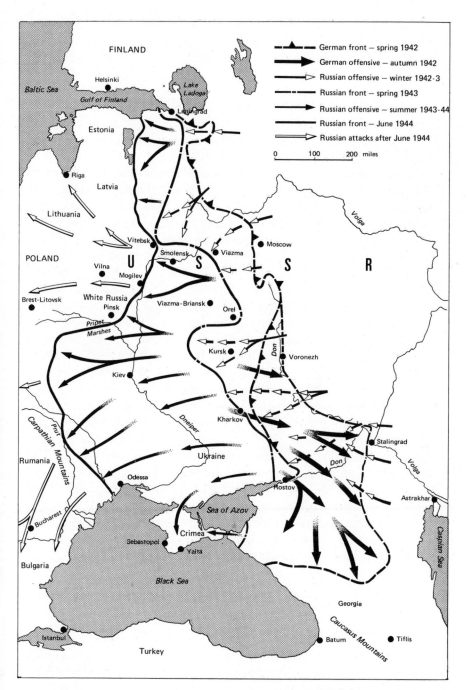

FINLAND

Baltic Sea

Helsinki

Gulf of Finland

Lake Ladoga

Leningrad

German front — spring 1942
German offensive — autumn 1942
Russian offensive — winter 1942-3
Russian front — spring 1943
Russian offensive — summer 1943-44
Russian front — June 1944
Russian attacks after June 1944

0   100   200   miles

Estonia

Riga

Latvia

Lithuania

POLAND

Vilna

Vitebsk

Smolensk

Viazma

Moscow

Volga

U   S   S   R

Mogilev

White Russia

Viazma-Briansk

Orel

Brest-Litovsk

Pinsk

Pripet Marshes

Don

Kursk

Voronezh

Kiev

Dnieper

Kharkov

Stalingrad

Carpathian Mountains

Ukraine

Don

Volga

Rumania

Prut

Odessa

Rostov

Astrakhan

Bucharest

Crimea

Sea of Azov

Bulgaria

Sebastopol

Yalta

Caspian Sea

Black Sea

Georgia

Istanbul

Turkey

Batum

Caucasus Mountains

Tiflis

Russian Movements, 1942–4

Remenyuk may or may not have been an exception. But it is probable, to say the least, that a soldier who comes home to find his father hanging from an apple tree is less likely to be merciful than other soldiers.

For the rest of the summer of 1943 the Russian armies in the south launched a series of bold, fast attacks on the German lines which had driven the Germans back to the Dnieper River by the autumn. The Russians recaptured Orel almost before the battle of Kursk was over. Soon afterwards they re-took Bryansk. By the end of August they had retaken Kharkov, following a bold attack on Belgorod. The whole German front in southern Russia was in danger. Neither Hitler nor his generals had any option but to retreat to the Dnieper, which is theoretically a defensible line. In practice, and here and there, the Russians got to the Dnieper first and established bridgeheads west of the river. In September the Russians advanced on the central front as well, re-taking Smolensk. By the autumn in the south the Russians had pushed the Germans back about 150 miles towards Poland. The Germans still held the Crimea, Hitler having insisted that the Allies should not be allowed to use Crimean airfields to bomb the Rumanian oilfields. But the Germans had evacuated their useless Caucasian bridgehead in the Taman Peninsula. On the mainland they had lost the richest territory that they had gained in Russia. Behind their new, shorter lines the Germans awaited uneasily the next Russian offensive, which would be a winter one.

Their uneasiness was justified. By 14 October, as the Germans may or may not have known at the time, they were out-numbered by the Russians by more than two to one. The Russians had 5,512,000 soldiers, the Germans 2,468,500. The Russians had 8,400 tanks, the Germans 2,304. The Russians had 20,770 field guns, the Germans 8,037.

These figures (collected and compared by the *Documentensammlung Jacobsen* of Darmstadt, Germany) may not be meticulously accurate down to the last man and the last gun. But the disparity was overwhelming. On the eastern front by the autumn of 1943 the Germans were beaten strategically, tactically and numerically.

The Siege of Leningrad

When the war in the east began Leningrad was a city of three million inhabitants. It was besieged by the Germans for 890 days from September 1941 until January 1944. By then about 200,000 of the city's inhabitants had been killed by German shells. About 630,000 had died of cold or starvation. The defence of Leningrad by its own people as well as by the Russian army was a feat of unexampled valour and endurance.

The defence might have failed had it not been for what was almost certainly an act of forbearance by the Finns. When Hitler advanced into Russia Marshal Mannerheim re-occupied the territory in the Karelian Isthmus which the Russians had taken from Finland in 1939. But the Finns either could not or more probably would not go further. They did not advance beyond their original frontier with Russia.

This was crucial to the defence of Leningrad because it left the south-western shore of Lake Ladoga in Russian hands. As the Germans closed in on the city from the west, the south, and the east, the besieged Russians lost control of their land link between Leningrad and the rest of the country. They were compelled to use the lake, as their only remaining supply route. When winter came and the lake froze, they built two roads across the ice. For most of the siege Leningrad was close to total starvation. People collapsed in the street from hunger or from cold or both. A water shortage made matters worse. But at the end of 890 days the people of Leningrad were still there.

Their city was still there too, but cruelly battered. During the first week of the siege Stalin sent Zhukov to organize Leningrad's defences. He converted Leningrad into a fortress. Its garrison was all its people. Hitler is said to have hated Leningrad, the birth-place of Bolshevism, more than any other Russian city. At first, in 1941, he seems to have been determined to capture it and to destroy it utterly. It is not certain that the Germans could have done this even then, but later Hitler changed his mind and decided to surround the city and starve it out. This decision was probably forced upon him – or would have been forced upon him because of events elsewhere.

As the war continued he repeatedly weakened Army Group North, which was besieging Leningrad, in order to reinforce his other, harder-pressed armies further south. By the end of 1943 the besieging German army was weak, but it was still there. Hitler had also abandoned altogether another strategically important operation in the north. A German expedition had set out from Narvik in German-occupied Norway, to cut the railway which links Murmansk on Russia's Arctic coast with Moscow. This railway carried virtually all the British and American equipment which was reaching Russia by the northern route. It was the landward extension of the Arctic convoys against which the Germans were launching continuous and bitter attacks. Perhaps Hitler thought he could interrupt the supplies more easily by attacking the ships at sea. Perhaps the terrain of north Finland was too harsh for the Germans. At all events the advance was cancelled. The railway kept running throughout the war.

The winter of 1943–1944 was different from the others that the Germans had experienced in Russia because it was warm. But this, too, worked to the Russians' advantage. They were not dismayed by mud any more than they had been dismayed by snow. Their tanks had broader tracks than the German tanks. Their lorries rode higher off the ground. In any case by now they had more men. And it was not their practice to stop fighting simply because of the weather.

On Christmas Eve 1943 the Russians began a series of offensives in the south one of which nearly succeeded in February in surrounding a large German force at Krivoi Rog. At Cherkassy Zhukov captured about 30,000 Germans, and about 30,000 others only escaped after the German Army Group South had sent almost all its tanks to the rescue. By the spring the Germans had been forced back to a line which ran between the rivers Dnieper and Bug. The Russians, by this time, had plenty of strength in reserve. By 1944 they no longer needed to pause and rest in the spring.

In March the Russians advanced again. There were three main thrusts. One was aimed at the German line south of Krivoi Rog, another at Uman, and a third was directed towards Shepetovka. In six weeks the Russians advanced about 160 miles. They had also nearly re-conquered the Crimea and were to do so completely by 9 May. In the north an offensive starting in January had relieved the siege of Leningrad. By March the Germans had retreated to the so-called Panther Line, a prepared fortification, which was part of the 'East Wall', a line which Hitler was then proposing to hold and to treat as the unalterable eastern frontier of his Fortress Europe.

Hitler's first and (irrelevant) response to the Russian advance in the Ukraine had been to sack the two Army Group commanders Manstein and Kleist. Manstein and Kleist did not matter. The Russians were now planning to attack in the centre. At the end of June Zhukov launched a strong attack near Borbruisk and captured or destroyed twenty-five divisions in a fortnight. By the end of July the Russians had reached the sea at Riga thereby isolating Army Group North which had to be rescued later by sea from the Courland peninsula.

Further south the Russians had advanced by way of Brest–Litovsk and Lublin to the suburbs of Warsaw. At the end of August another Russian attack encircled important German forces near Kishinev. By 31 August the Russians had captured the Ploesti oil fields in Rumania as well as Bucharest, the capital. Ten days later they were in Bulgaria and both Bulgaria and Rumania had surrendered. By 20 October they were in Belgrade. By the New Year they had captured Budapest.

The Warsaw Rising

On 1 August, while the Russians were sweeping through the Balkans, though remaining stationary outside Warsaw, the Polish Home Army, on instructions from the exiled Polish Government in London, had risen in revolt against the Germans within the city. The Home Army's Commander, General Tadeusz Bor-Komorowski, had been biding his time, probably wisely. The political purpose of the rising was to assert the Polish people's sovereignty in the face of a double invasion. In London, the Polish Government in exile wanted to demonstrate to the Russians as well as to the Germans that the Polish nation lived.

The Warsaw rising was gallant to the point of suicide, but it failed. For two months the Home Army attacked the German garrison with ferocity, capturing about half Warsaw. But the Poles could not prevail. About 20,000 resistance fighters were involved at one time or another. About 10,000 of them were killed. Nearly all the rest were wounded. Flying from bases in Italy the Free Polish Air Force dropped supplies to the Home Army and so did some British and American pilots. But the missions were extremely hazardous and the supplies, in any case, were insufficient. When the fighting in Warsaw ended on 2 October the Germans revenged themselves cruelly on the Warsaw population. The city itself was largely destroyed.

Russian indifference to the Warsaw uprising was deliberate. The Russians wanted the Polish Home Army dead. The best that can be said in their defence is that the senior Russian soldier on the spot, the Front Commander, Marshal Rokossovski, was much concerned at this time with the new problem of defeating a German army which had shortened its front radically, which was therefore able to station more soldiers per kilometre, and which was also facing up for the first time in the war to the task of defending Germany itself. In 1944 the German army, unlike all other continental European ones, had never yet been forced to defend its own homelands. Rokossovski may have been more apprehensive than necessary. But his apprehension was understandable, particularly at the end of a long, rapid advance.

When the Russians reached the Vistula they had very nearly outrun their supplies. Looking forward to a difficult campaign on German

F

territory, they decided to consolidate, to amass fuel, stores, and ammunition and to look before they leaped. General Chuikov, a man not given to over-estimating the problems that lay before him, has said why the Soviet command was in no hurry to begin the decisive advance towards Berlin.

'There was a mass of construction work to be done or redone in improved form, on highways, non-metalled roads, and on railways. There were tens of thousands of tons of fuel to be brought up, millions of mortar bombs and shells and hundreds of millions of cartridges, and all the equipment and provisions needed to keep us in the field. And all these colossal quantities of stores had to be brought up as close as possible to the front line, to give us the necessary conditions for a breakthrough in depth and the gaining of broad scope for manoeuvre.'[13]

The Russian commanders had immediate tactical worries too. On 3 August, two days after the Warsaw rising began, Rokossovski received reports from his Intelligence Section that no less than four German Panzer divisions were operating on the east bank of the Vistula. His intelligence was wrong. But had it been right the Russians would have been in a particularly awkward situation. They were already establishing bridgeheads across the river on the western bank against stubborn opposition. Chuikov, who had established the most important one at Magnuszew about thirty miles upstream from Warsaw was ordered to divert three divisions to positions about twenty miles north of his bridgehead and on the eastern side of the river. 'This order', said Chuikov, who was never averse to speaking his mind, 'robbed the [8th Guards] army of all strength on the bridgehead it had seized.'[14] In fact Chuikov disbelieved the report about the four Panzer divisions and he was right.

Chuikov was also right, however, in his prediction that German resistance on the west bank of the Vistula would be stubborn and that his army, which had advanced all the way from Stalingrad, would need reinforcement and replenishment before it could make much impression. The 8th Guards Army had advanced about 150 miles in less than a month. Four German divisions were attacking the Magnuszew bridgehead west of the Vistula. And the 8th Guards Army was a long way from home. Chuikov's first reinforcements did not arrive until 10 September, nearly six weeks after the Polish Home Army had begun its gallant attack on the German garrison in Warsaw.

At this politically controversial time the Russian commanders obviously were mainly interested in defeating the German invaders of their country without having to sacrifice too many men. Their interest in helping the Poles was non-existent.

The political priorities are another matter. The date on which Stalin became aware of the Warsaw rising is not known. But on 13 September the Russians did themselves begin to drop supplies to the Polish Home Army fighting in the city. The supplies came too late and – like those dropped by the Western Allies, were insufficient. The Polish Home Army in Warsaw bled to death. But whatever may have been the rights and wrongs of Rokossovski's military decisions Stalin did not mind. He had been resolved since 1939 that Poland must be subservient to Russia. Neither the Polish Government in exile in London nor the Home Army had shown credible signs of subservience to either of Poland's invaders – Germany or Russia. In March 1944 Stalin effectively decapitated the surviving non-communist leadership of the Polish Home Army. Rokossovski and Chuikov may have left the Home Army in Warsaw to its fate for good military reasons, or may not even have known what was happening. Stalin had political reasons for wanting the uprising to fail, as it tragically did.

The Russians had other military reasons for concentrating on the Balkans instead of Warsaw in the autumn of 1944. When they were ready to assault Germany itself they did not want to leave their southern flank vulnerable to German counter-attack. When they drove south and west into the Balkans in the late summer of 1944 they did so partly to exploit an obvious and immediate advantage. Everywhere south of the Carpathian Mountains the Germans and their wobbly Balkan allies were collapsing. The Russians would have been silly not to have exploited this demoralization. But it would have been imprudent also for them to have left large German forces unmolested in south-eastern Europe. Their main purpose was to capture Berlin. They expected a resolute German defence. They did not want to be disturbed by attacks on their southern flank.

By January 1945 the Russians were ready to move west again. In the middle of the month two Russian army groups attacked East Prussia. By the end of the month they had established positions on the Baltic east of Danzig and had cut off the German forces north-east of there. Two other Russian army groups advanced westwards from the south of Warsaw. By early February 1945, they had both reached the River Oder and had established several bridgeheads west of the river. By the beginning of March the Russians had occupied the whole of Silesia and had reached the River Neisse. On 16 April the three Russian army groups threatening Germany attacked together. The southern group, commanded by Marshal Konev, made rapid progress from the start.

The rest of the European war did not take long. The central Russian army group broke out of its bridgehead over the Oder at Kustrin after two days hard fighting and was soon on its way to Berlin. In the north the Russians started an encircling movement which had enveloped Berlin by 24 April. Hitler, alive but mad, continued to issue orders from his air-raid shelter which either did not reach their destinations or, if they did, could not be obeyed. Negotiations began between the German General Krebs, nominal Chief of Staff of the 56th Panzer Corps, and the Russians. Krebs told them that Hitler – having sprung his last surprise by producing a mistress – had killed himself (and her) and that there was a plan to form a substitute German Government.

Krebs was not, however, a serious intermediary. A Soviet major was shot while attending a parley to which he had been summoned. The Russians decided that the Berlin garrison, such as it still was, was divided in its councils. Krebs tried to make a separate bargain with the Russians, leaving the Western Allies out. But the Russians did not believe either in the bargain or in Krebs's authority.

In any case the man he was up against was Chuikov. 'Between the soldiers of the anti-Hitler coalition there were no contradictions. We had one common aim, one common enemy, and did our best to finish that enemy as quickly as possible. The closer contact became between Soviet soldiers and those of the Allies, the stronger their union grew, and the more their mutual respect for one another increased. This was not understood, and not reckoned with, by the leaders of the Third Reich, and by some people in the West.'[15]

No one would suggest now that the union between the Allies continued to grow stronger. But it was the truth as Chuikov saw it at the time, when the Germans came to dicker with him about the surrender of Berlin.

In fact there never was an ordered surrender. Some Germans kept firing after others had stopped. The Russians had no option but to weed them all out. The record says that the last resistance of all came from a bunker in the Tiergarten and was extinguished by a Captain N. I. Kruchinin of the 79th Russian Guards Division.[16] Hitler's grand assault on Russia ended, shorn of glory, in an air raid shelter in a zoo.

Chapter 9

The Struggle for the Pacific

The Pacific war was one of two wars either of which would have happened even if the other had not. The conflict in Europe and the conflict in the Pacific had separate causes. They became entangled partly, though not solely, because of one of Hitler's biggest mistakes.

When the Japanese attacked the American Pacific Fleet in Pearl Harbor in December 1941, Hitler declared war on America. He need not have done this. The Japanese did not need his help. In any case he had none to offer. Although Roosevelt was already committed to the fight against Hitler, Congress was not. American strategists had always feared a two-ocean war. Some of them would have been content in 1941 to forget about Hitler and to concentrate on Japan. But Hitler did not want to be forgotten. George Ball, later a senior presidential adviser and then a lawyer in Chicago, has said that 'if Hitler had not made this decision and if he had simply done nothing, there would have been an enormous sentiment in the United States . . . that the Pacific war now was our war and the European war was for the Europeans and we should concentrate all our efforts on the Japanese.'[1]

The consequence of Hitler's rash gesture was to ensure what would not otherwise have been certain – that America and Russia, the world's two greatest military and industrial powers, became united against him in an alliance as improbable as it was formidable.

The main cause of the Pacific war was Japan's decision to acquire an empire. Japan is an island dependent like Britain on raw materials from overseas. In the 1920's the Japanese resolved to try to accomplish in the twentieth century what Britain and France had accomplished in the eighteenth and nineteenth centuries by conquering their own markets and raw materials. Since the 1930's Japan had been invading China, laboriously and cruelly, partly in search of glory, but mainly to secure wealth and customers for Japanese industry. When Germany and Britain went to war in 1939 Japan's ambitions grew.

The wealth she coveted belonged in those days to European colonial powers with possessions in the Far East. French Indo-China, as Vietnam used to be called, was rich in rice. The Federated Malay States and Burma, which then belonged to Britain were rich in tin, oil, and rubber. The Netherlands East Indies were rich in oil.

In the autumn of 1941 all these territories were easy prey. France and the Netherlands had been occupied. Britain was at bay, totally committed to the war against Germany. The European owners of the rich far eastern territories were in no state to defend them.

The remaining obstacle to Japan's new imperial ambition was the Philippine Republic. The Philippines had recently become independent of the United States, but their armed forces were still under American command in the person of General Douglas MacArthur, a tenacious and indomitable man, whose seniority in the US Army was so mightily exalted that hardly anyone in Washington could order him about.

Throughout the summer and autumn of 1941 the Japanese Government tried to persuade the United States to allow Japan a free hand to expand southwards into the rich archipelagos of the East Indies. The United States saw this demand as a challenge to American influence not only in the Philippines but also in China and throughout the Pacific and resisted it.

In December 1940, six months after the fall of France, the United States had imposed a ban on the sale of raw materials and scrap-iron to Japan. Roosevelt wanted to help his Chinese ally, Chiang Kai-shek, for whom the continuing war in China was going badly. The American embargo hurt. Japan began to run short of oil. In the spring of 1941 the Japanese opened negotiations with the United States in the hope of persuading the Americans to lift the embargo and to stop helping China.

In July, the negotiations notwithstanding, the Japanese moved fresh troops deep into French Indo-China. They did not just want rice. They also wanted the good harbour of Camranh Bay whence they would be able to mount assaults on the Netherlands East Indies and the Malay peninsula. The Americans froze all Japanese assets under their control and Britain did likewise.

Pearl Harbor

The negotiations – which were being conducted in Washington by the Japanese Ambassador Admiral Nomura and Secretary of State Cordell

Hull – became embittered. On 16 October the moderate (in Japanese terms) Prime Minister Prince Fumimaro Konoye resigned. His successor was the tougher, more militarist General Hideki Tojo. Tojo's government decided to send what amounted to an ultimatum. America was asked to meet virtually all Japan's demands by 29 November. The task force of Japanese aircraft carriers that was to attack Pearl Harbor, lurking in its cold and secret rendezvous at Tankan Bay in the Kurile Islands, had orders to sail on 26 November.

There can be very little doubt that at this stage already the Japanese intended treachery. What they did not know was that their treachery was suspected. American code breakers were reading their diplomatic radio messages to Nomura in Washington as easily as he could read them himself. Quietly, with numbers, American mathematicians were making Nomura the biggest fool in all diplomacy. The US navy's Bainbridge Island intercept station in Puget Sound read the coded radio traffic. In Washington the cryptographers decoded it. As often as not their decodes were ready before the Japanese embassy's.

The first clouded warning of war reached Ambassador Nomura on 20 November 1941. 'There are reasons beyond your ability to guess', Tokyo said 'why we wanted to settle Japanese–American relations by the 25th. . . .' The telegram went on to say that Japan had decided nevertheless to give the Americans four more days, until the 29th. But, Tokyo said, 'This time we mean it; the deadline absolutely cannot be changed. After that things are automatically going to happen.'[2]

What automatically happened was the attack on Pearl Harbor. The next significant message from Tokyo to Nomura instructed him to be ready to tell the Americans that negotiations were at an end. He was told to be ready to give 'our reply' to America at short notice. At 1.28 a.m. on 7 December Tokyo told Nomura: 'Will the Ambassador please submit to the United States Government (if possible to the Secretary of State) our reply to the United States at 1 p.m. on the 7th, your time.'[3]

The man who read this first was Lieutenant-Commander Alwin D. Kramer, the duty Japanese-language expert at the Navy Department in Washington. It was a Sunday morning. Kramer ran, he didn't walk, eight blocks along Constitution Avenue to the State Department. Like the tidings from Marathon, the first news of the Pacific war was brought by a running man.

The Americans knew when but they did not know where. They knew that they were about to be attacked. They did not know the one piece of intelligence they badly needed – the position of the Japanese navy's carrier groups I and II. These groups included Japan's most formidable ships, the ones which represented the main threat to the US Pacific Fleet and, as events turned out, to the fleet's main base at Pearl Harbor on the island of Oahu in Hawaii.

During November and early December the Americans had monitored an unusual amount of radio traffic from Japanese naval ships. These appeared to be moving south towards Hong Kong, Indo-China, and Malaysia. From this traffic the Americans deduced, correctly, that the Japanese were planning to invade South-East Asia, or at least to be in a position to do this. What was missing, however, from the Japanese traffic was any signal at all, to or from, carrier groups I and II. Japan's six large, fast carriers – the *Akagi*, the *Kaga*, the *Hiryu*, the *Soryu*, the *Shokaku* and the *Zuikaka* were silent.

The big carriers had gone silent before. Earlier in 1941 there had been an interval of three weeks during which they had transmitted no signal. It became clear later that the carriers had been silent because they had been in home waters. When they went silent again the Americans assumed, this time incorrectly, that the carriers had gone home.

On 1 December the Commander-in-Chief of the US Pacific Fleet, Admiral Kimmel, asked his Fleet Intelligence Officer whether he knew where the two carrier divisions were. Fleet Intelligence Officer Layton recalls having given this reply: 'No Sir, I do not. I think they are in home waters, but I do not know where they are.'[4] On that same 1 December, the six carriers accompanied by twenty-four escorting warships, were already one day out on their voyage from Tankan Bay to Pearl Harbor.

The Fleet Commander was Vice-Admiral Nagumo. The architect of the operation was Japan's supreme naval commander Admiral Yamamoto. Nagumo's big ships sailed east into bad weather and an empty sea for another six days before launching the first strike. They had not broken radio silence since they left Japan. The only people in Hawaii who saw them coming were two American privates on watch at an experimental US army radar station. Nobody listens to privates.

Pearl Harbor is a deep inlet shaped like a ragged clover leaf with its entrance on the south side of Oahu Island. The army radar was on the northern tip of Oahu. At 7 a.m. on 7 December the watch-keeping soldiers saw radar echoes corresponding to a large number of aircraft, 139 miles north of the island and approaching it. The men who saw this were Privates Elliot and Lockhart, US army. Private Elliot's account is clear:

We were scheduled to operate from 4 a.m. to 7 a.m. It was just training, picking up flights and turning them in to our information centre. Since I had learned the plotting end of the radar operation I did not know definitely how to operate the scope for picking up the enemy targets and that was why we had pre-arranged permission to operate beyond the 7 a.m. period. And of course it was just shortly after 7 a.m. that we picked up this large flight of planes and Lockhart at that moment thought that the machine was out of kilter because of the large blip that we were receiving 139 miles out. After verifying the equipment and information shown, we decided it was a flight of planes coming in. I suggested to Lockhart that we sent it in to our information centre. He didn't seem to think at the time that it was necessary because our problem was over, but in any event we did send the information in to Private McDonald who was the switchboard operator at the information centre and, of course, it being after seven, everybody had left, the problem being over. I left word with McDonald to see if he could find somebody who would know what to do, and to call us back. A little later, why, this Lieutenant Tyler called back and Lockhart answered the phone and in essence was told to forget it. And that was the beginning of Pearl Harbor.

In defence of the man that said to forget it he had only been in the information centre on the officers orientation tour one time previous to his assignment that morning.[5]

Nobody acted on this first radar contact with Nagumo's strike force. The army seems to have assumed that the planes belonged to the navy, or that they were an expected flight of B17's, or perhaps that they did not matter anyway. The alarm was not given. It was the first inter-service communications failure of the Pacific war, and the worst.

When the Japanese planes appeared on the army radar they had already flown about 100 miles from their parent carriers. It took them another half hour to reach Pearl Harbor. Flying in from the north, the first wave of 183 aircraft approached from three directions. One section flew round Oahu to the west and came in to approach the harbor from seaward. Another section approached from the west. A third crossed the island and attacked from landward.

A second wave of planes attacked from the east and also from seaward. The raid was spread over two hours. Whereas Admiral Cunningham, with meagre resources and economic by nature, had used twenty-three aircraft in his raid on the Italian fleet in Taranto, Yamamoto used 353. His losses were twenty-nine aircraft and fifty-five officers and ratings. The Americans lost 349 aircraft, most of them destroyed on the ground, nearly 3,700 sailors, soldiers, marines and civilians, and eighteen warships lost or damaged.

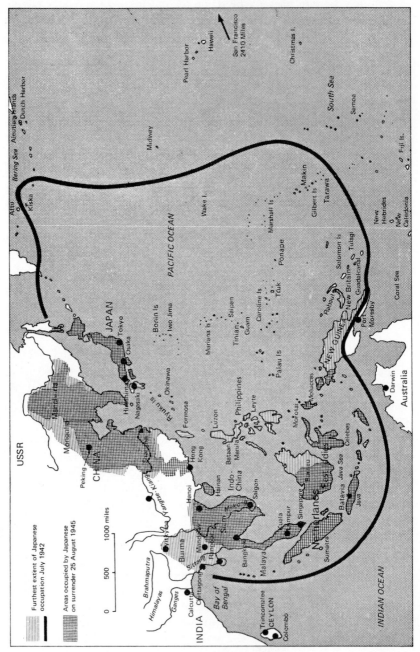

The Pacific

Furthest extent of Japanese
occupation July 1942

Areas occupied by Japanese
on surrender 25 August 1945

0   500   1000 miles

The attack began in earnest at 8.00 a.m. By 8.30 the battleship *Arizona* had blown up, the *West Virginia* had sunk and the *Oklahoma* had capsized. Four other battleships, the *California, Tennessee, Nevada, Maryland* and *Pennsylvania*, had been damaged. The only thing that went right for the Americans that dreadful morning was the failure of a Japanese submarine attack on Pearl Harbor. Five, perhaps six Japanese submarines were detected and lost in an operation which produced no result.

But the destruction wrought by Nagumo's aircraft was hideous, the more so because of the surprise. Marine Fiske of the battleship *West Virginia* remember seeing the *Arizona* blow up – 'she just rained sailors'. He remembers watching a Japanese pilot who 'kind of smiled'.[6] A sailor on Admiral Kimmel's staff who was standing next to him remembers seeing the Admiral tear off his four-star epaulettes. Kimmel was right about the epaulettes. His successor was Admiral Chester W. Nimitz, one of those very few Allied commanders who understood from the outset the changed nature of war in the twentieth century.

The attack on Pearl Harbor, fearsome though it was for the Americans, was not the only Japanese assault on 7 December. That same day (which was 8 December on the western side of the international date line) the Japanese attacked Hong Kong, Malaysia, and three American-held islands in the Pacific. Midway Island, which is effectively the north-western tip of the Hawaiian archipelago, was shelled by warships. Wake Island, about a thousand miles south-west of Midway, was attacked from the air. Fifteen hundred miles further west again, Guam Island, the only American foothold in the Japanese Mariana archipelago, was also attacked.

On the Asian mainland, Hong Kong was attacked from the air and by assault from the sea. There were air raids on Singapore and the Malaysian airfields. The Japanese army landed in southern Thailand and northern Malaysia. In the Philippines the main American air base, Clark Field, was also attacked. The Netherlands East Indies were spared, but only for a month.

The political consequences of these attacks – especially the attack on Pearl Harbor – were as formidable as the military ones. Roosevelt knew that America had been betrayed. He could not say this without giving away the precious secret of America's codebreaking ability. He was able nevertheless to convey his sense of outrage to a Congress which was itself shocked, furious, and humiliated by an air raid which had apparently destroyed at one stroke America's capacity to dominate a hemisphere. 7 December, said Roosevelt, was 'a date which will go down in infamy'. Congress agreed at once to declare war on Japan. Hitler declared war on the United States. America was at war in two oceans.

In Washington the war began with an inquest into Pearl Harbor. How had Admiral Kimmel come to be surprised? The warning which had reached Roosevelt and Cordell Hull had been sent to him but had arrived too late. The army radar warning had been ignored. There were many questions to be asked. America asked them all.

But the angry Americans did not then pause to reflect that the Japanese, too, had made an error. It was a big one. In the end it helped mightily towards their defeat. In their attack on Pearl Harbor, Yamamoto and Nagumo had won a spectacular victory. But they had sunk the wrong ships. All four American aircraft carriers in the Pacific escaped. All four were away from Pearl Harbor on 7 December.

The Japanese came to regret bitterly the survival of these formidable ships. Although the United States navy was reluctant to admit it at the time, the battleship was already on its way to becoming an encumbrance. The ships that would matter carried planes. For the rest of the war in the Pacific the decisive formation was the fast carrier task force. The Americans knew how to use it just as Yamamoto did. But they had more pilots than the Japanese and the pilots were more skilful.

Most of the war in the Pacific was about the possession of islands. To protect their new possessions the Japanese planned to seize, fortify and hold a ring of bases which would keep the Americans at a safe distance from the Philippines, South-East Asia and the East Indies. This plan – to transform the western Pacific into a defended, Japanese lake – was not so ludicrous as it sounds. Unlike the Atlantic, the Pacific Ocean is punctuated with archipelagos and island chains. The Japanese proposed to establish a defensive line which would include Wake Island. the Marshall Islands and the Bismarck Archipelago.

The Fall of Singapore

The Japanese intended that everywhere west and north of Wake and the Marshalls should be their sea forever. In the open water between Japan itself in the north, New Guinea in the south, and the Philippines to the west, Japan would own and occupy two main archipelagos – the Carolines stretching in a ragged line from Palau in the west to Truk and Ponape in the east, and the Marianas which lie in a curve further north with Guam at their southern extremity. Another string of islands within Japan's own piece of sea runs south from Tokyo Bay to the Bonins and Iwo Jima. Yet another chain, the Ryukus, links south Japan with Okinawa and Taiwan – or Formosa as the West then knew it.

In the three months which followed the attack on Pearl Harbor, the Japanese war effort had two purposes. The first was actually to capture the rich and coveted lands of South-East Asia and the Netherlands East Indies. The second was to secure and fortify their outer defensive line and to extend it southward so as to threaten communications between the United States and Australia.

The Japanese achieved their first purpose with frightening speed. Pearl Harbor was bombed on 7 December 1941. By 10 December the Japanese had captured Guam. On 23 December they captured Wake. On Christmas Day they captured Hong Kong. On 8 February 1942 they captured Rangoon, the capital of Burma. On 15 February they captured Singapore. By 19 February they were bombing Darwin in Australia. By 2 March they had captured Batavia (as the Dutch called Djakarta), the capital of the Netherlands East Indies. On 9 April 1942 they were bombing Ceylon from aircraft carriers which had penetrated into the Indian Ocean. On 6 May they captured the Philippines.

In effect, the Japanese fought five separate campaigns. They struck at the outlying islands like Wake and Guam. They besieged Hong Kong. They landed in the Philippines. They invaded Malaysia and captured Singapore. And, step by step, they conquered the Netherlands East Indies.

In Hong Kong the British garrison staved off defeat for longer than anyone had expected. Isolated at the south-eastern tip of China, Hong Kong had always been regarded as expendable. But the Japanese success in Malaysia was another matter. First in the Malaysian jungle and then in Singapore they inflicted a humiliating defeat on the British who had supposed that the jungle was impenetrable and Singapore impregnable.

In London, no one felt the loss of Singapore more cruelly than Winston Churchill. In 1940, as First Lord of the Admiralty, he had been responsible for the Singapore defences and had circulated a paper to his Cabinet colleagues which said:

Singapore is a fortress armed with five 15-inch guns and garrisonned by nearly 20,000 men. It could only be taken after a siege by an army of at least 50,000 men . . . as Singapore is as far from Japan as Southampton is from New York, the operation of moving a Japanese army with all its troop ships and maintaining it with men and munitions during a siege would be forlorn. Moreover such a siege, which should last at least four or five months, would be liable to be interrupted if at any time Britain chose to send a superior fleet to the scene. In this case, the besieging army would become prisoners of war . . . it is not

163

considered possible that the Japanese, who are a prudent people and reserve their strength for the command of the Yellow Sea and China, in which they are fully occupied, would embark on such a mad enterprise.[7]

In the event, the Japanese used bicycles instead of troop ships. They bombed and sank the superior fleet which Churchill had despatched – the battleship *Prince of Wales* and the battle-cruiser *Repulse* – within two days of Pearl Harbor. They captured Malaysia and Singapore with an army whose strength was not 50,000 but 35,000 men. 130,000 Allied troops had been captured by the time Singapore fell on 15 February 1942.

The chief lesson the Japanese taught the Allies in Malaysia was that jungles are neutral – to quote the title of a book by a British officer, Colonel Spencer-Chapman, who stayed behind in the jungle after Singapore fell.

The jungle, which had been expected to defend Singapore from the landward side, did not impede the Japanese. They did not ride in trucks. They walked. They bicycled. They did not need roads. Within weeks, not months, they had reached the north shore of the strait which divides Singapore Island from the Malaysian mainland. Some (but not all) of Singapore's 15-inch guns pointed only to seaward. The defence was stubborn, but hopeless. In the end the garrison, reinforced at a late stage, surrendered, largely for lack of water.

Reflecting afterwards on this serious British defeat, Churchill wrote: 'I ought to have known. My advisers ought to have known and I ought to have been told, and I ought to have asked. The reason I had not asked about this matter, amid the thousands of questions I put, was that the possibility of Singapore having no landward defences no more entered into my mind than that of a battleship being launched without a bottom.'[8]

By capturing Singapore the Japanese had not only possessed themselves of the riches of Malaysia, but had gained command of the Straits of Malacca – the main sea-lane connecting the Pacific and Indian Oceans.

The Japanese navy quickly took advantage of this gain to mount its first and last major raid into the Indian Ocean. A force of five carriers commanded by Admiral Nagumo, the man who had attacked Pearl Harbor, sailed towards the British naval and air bases in Ceylon. The Japanese force was superior to the British commanded by Admiral Somerville. In the engagements which followed the Royal Navy lost two cruisers and the aircraft carrier *Hermes*. But the Japanese aircraft did not succeed in doing to Colombo what they had done to Pearl Harbor. Nor did they succeed in eliminating, as they could have done, Admiral Somerville's main force of battleships.

Somerville offered Nagumo a difficult choice – either to pursue the British ships into the middle of the Indian Ocean if he wanted to bring them to action; or to stay within reasonable reach of what was, by then, the Japanese base of Singapore. In the event Nagumo simply hung around. He damaged Somerville's force but not decisively. He bombed Ceylon, but not disastrously. Afterwards he went home and did not return.

The RAF and the Royal Navy had inflicted more damage on Nagumo's force than the British realized at the time. This was the Japanese navy's elite striking force, manned by the heroes of Pearl Harbor. It seems likely now, though it was not evident then, that this precious force was irreplaceable and that it never fully recovered from the resistance offered in the seas off Ceylon.

Nagumo had also discovered the limits of the Japanese navy's radius of action. Somerville had forced the Japanese to use up their supplies of ammunition, fuel and stores in a part of the ocean which was a long way from Japan. (They never learned from the Americans the technique by which aircraft carriers can be supplied continuously at sea from a train of supply ships.) Although the Allies could not have known this at the time, the Japanese navy discovered off Colombo that it was not all-powerful and could not afford to range too far.

The Japanese conquer Burma

The Japanese conquest of Burma took longer than their conquest of Malaysia. But the secret of their success was the same. They did not allow the jungle to hinder them. When they came to a roadblock they took to the woods and outflanked it. The Burmese forces, raised by the British, were unable to stop them. The Japanese forces' first objective was Rangoon, Burma's only port, and they reached it early in March 1942.

Essentially Burma is a huge valley containing two rivers, the Irrawaddy and the Sitang. Crossing this valley from east to west some 600 miles north of Rangoon was the Burma road – the only remaining land link between China and India. The Americans, wrongly, believed that China could and would contribute mightily to the defeat of Japan. To them it seemed essential to keep China supplied. Therefore the Burma road was an essential link in Allied strategy.

The Japanese captured the Burmese end of the road, the town of Lashio on 29 April 1942. They had not only gained for themselves the rubber and oil which they coveted in Burma but had succeeded also in cutting China's land communications with her Western Allies. Chinese troops, inspired by the American General Stilwell, had sought to prevent this in alliance with the British and the Burmese. But the Japanese prevailed. The Allied forces retreated northward and westward into India. Allied resistance ended, effectively, with the capture first of Lashio and then of Mandalay on 30 April.

Burma was to remain in Japanese hands for another three years. The Allies did not recapture Rangoon until 3 May 1945, when the war was nearly over.

The Japanese attack on the Netherlands East Indies, as Indonesia was then called, began in mid-January 1942. By then Japanese forces in Malaysia were threatening Singapore. Further east across the South China Sea, they were fighting hard against General MacArthur's American–Philippine forces in Luzon, the main Philippine island.

A joint American–British–Dutch–Australian command under General Wavell had just been formed and was responsible for the defence of the Netherlands East Indies. The main part of the area to be defended consisted of the curving chain of islands which begins in the north-west with Sumatra. The chain continues eastwards and southwards through Java, Bali, Flores, and Timor – which lies some 400 miles west-north-west of Darwin in Australia.

Already in December the Japanese had successfully attacked the then British possessions and protectorates in North Borneo – Sarawak and Brunei. The Japanese launched their main attacks on the Netherlands East Indies from Camranh Bay in what is now South Vietnam. The invasion convoys steamed south between the existing areas of conflict in Malaysia and the Philippines.

When Wavell arrived in Batavia to take command on 10 January, the outlook was bleak. The Dutch forces were scattered in small garrisons throughout the islands. Air support was meagre. The Allied naval forces – Dutch, American, British and Australian – did not include an aircraft carrier.

The Japanese aimed their first serious blow at the Netherlands East Indies proper on 13 February 1942, when 700 parachutists attacked the airfield at Palembang in southern Sumatra. With Singapore in Japanese hands the threat to Java was both imminent and overwhelming. On 18 February a convoy that included fifty-six transports sailed from Camranh Bay for Java. The situation appeared hopeless. Wavell, on direct

36. July 1943: tanks and transport are rushed ashore during the invasion of Sicily

37. An American infantry column advances towards Mandalay in Burma

38. Two child victims of Belsen. The photograph was taken on 17 April 1945, by which time the British had taken over control

39. Another Belsen scene, also dated 17 April 1945

40. The ovens at Lublin in which the Germans burned the bodies of prisoners

41. A crowd of Polish workers about to leave for forced labour in Germany

42. German troops cross the River Meuse in a rubber boat, May 1940

43. Fighting in the streets of Stalingrad

orders from Churchill, left by air for India. Admiral Helfrich of the Royal Netherlands Navy remained. With him and his own Dutch forces were three Australian battalions, a squadron of British tanks and five squadrons of the Royal Air Force.

On 26 February, as the invasion force approached, the Dutch Rear-Admiral Doorman set forth from Sourabaya at the eastern end of Java to intercept and destroy. He flew his flag in the cruiser *De Ruyter*. The rest of his fleet consisted of HMS *Exeter*, USS *Houston*, HMAS *Perth*, the Dutch light cruiser *Java*, and nine destroyers – three British, four American and two Dutch. It was the first time that these ships had worked together. Doorman made two sorties into the Java Sea – one on the night of the 26th–27th and another the following night. The main action took place during the second sortie. The battle of the Java Sea, as it came to be called, was gallant. But the Japanese were not to be stopped. Both Dutch cruisers were sunk, Rear-Admiral Doorman going down with his ship. *Perth*, *Houston* and *Exeter* were all sunk in subsequent engagements. By the time the Japanese invaders arrived, the Allied naval forces in Java had ceased to exist.

Resistance on land was not prolonged. Without air cover or naval support the scattered Dutch garrisons were overwhelmed one by one. The Japanese at all times secured air cover for themselves before advancing. Admiral Helfrich surrendered on 8 March.

The Collapse of the Philippines

The longest and most arduous of the campaigns of conquest that the Japanese fought was the one in the Philippines. The Philippines were not rich like Malaysia and the Netherlands East Indies, but the Japanese had to conquer them because they represented a threat to all Japanese plans. The Philippines were a strong American outpost in the middle of what the Japanese wished to regard as their own part of the Pacific Ocean. The not inconsiderable Philippine army was even then being re-organized and trained by MacArthur. At Clark Field, just north of the capital, Manila, on the main island of Luzon the US Army Air Force had stationed a squadron of B-17 bombers. The Japanese went for the B-17s first.

Clark Field, unlike Pearl Harbor, was on the alert. Early on 8 December the B-17s took off so as not to be caught on the ground by the expected Japanese attack. Later that morning, however, they landed to refuel in preparation for a raid on Formosa. That was when the Japanese struck. The attack destroyed 18 B-17s – about half the force available – and 80 other aircraft. From that moment the Philippines were without air defences.

The main Japanese sea-borne landing took place in northern Luzon on 22 December. The Japanese committed the whole of their 14th Army. It hardly sufficed. After a fortnight's hard fighting the American and Filipino troops had been forced back into the Bataan Peninsula on the west side of Manila Bay. By occupying and defending Bataan MacArthur managed to deny the Japanese the use of Manila as a port. The peninsula was well fortified, but horribly overcrowded. One hundred and six thousand servicemen and civilian refugees were crowded together for the three months of this famous and bitter siege. As often happens in a siege sickness and malnutrition caused more casualties than the enemy.

The attempt to retain a foothold in the Philippines was gallant but it was doomed. In February 1942, Roosevelt and Marshall ordered MacArthur to leave. He was needed to take command of the defence of the now-threatened lines of communication between Australia and the United States. He left the Philippines reluctantly in a motor torpedo boat during the night of 12 March.

Bataan and Corregidor

His successor in Bataan, General Wainwright, soon had to face a rein-forced Japanese army. Having sent for more men the Japanese General Homma renewed the assault on Bataan on 3 April. By 8 April the defenders starving and exhausted, surrendered Bataan. For four more weeks until 6 May, Wainwright held out on the fortified island of Corregidor in Manila Bay. Even then resistance continued for a while in the southern Philippine islands of Panay, Cebu and Mindanao. But this had virtually ceased by mid-summer 1942.

The fall of Bataan had been inevitable. The garrison was cut off, short of ammunition, and desperately hungry. Rations were halved in January and were halved again in March. By the time the Bataan garrison sur-rendered on 8 April it was an army of starving men. The Japanese did nothing to make their plight any better and a good deal to make it worse. General Homma made them march the 65 miles north to what was to be their prison at camp O'Donnell. Homma's soldiers showed neither mercy nor respect. Nor did they offer much in the way of food and water. About 25,000 Americans and Filipinos died either in the last hours of the fighting on Bataan or – most of them – during the march to Camp O'Donnell. About 22,000 others died in the camp within two months. It was one of the worst examples of Japanese brutality towards prisoners of war. General Homma was not the only Japanese who disregarded the customs of war and the dictates of humanity. But he was probably the cruellest and certainly the most blatant. 'The Imperial Japanese Army', he said in the flush of his Bataan victory, 'are not barbarians.'[9] Wars breed lies as dirt breeds lice. In a war which produced many falsehoods General Homma's claim was one of the most infamous of all. The treatment of the Bataan survivors gave the Americans and the world the measure of their Pacific enemy. For the rest of the war no American forgot Bataan.

The surrender of Bataan marked the end of any real, organized resistance on land to Japanese conquest of their new domains. In four months, from Pearl Harbor on 7 December 1941, to the surrender of Bataan on 8 April 1942, they had acquired the empire they wanted.

The Battle of the Coral Sea

In April the Japanese raised their sights. They decided to extend their defensive perimeter to include not simply the Marshall Islands and Wake but other archipelagos as well. Encouraged by their easy four-month ride, they resolved to take into their possession Midway, the Gilbert Islands, the Ellice Islands, the New Hebrides, Fiji, New Caledonia, the Solomons, Papua (the south-eastern extremity of New Guinea), and Port Moresby in New Guinea itself. Japan's attempt to extend its defences in this way posed a direct threat to Australia, as well as to Australia's communications with the United States.

In deciding to extend their perimeter the Japanese may not have reckoned with Australian tenacity. They may not have understood the strength, even then, of Australia's links with America. Be that as it may, in extending their defences southward, they helped to accelerate their own defeat. By trying to occupy Papua and the southern Solomons the Japanese overreached themselves for the first time.

Their immediate objectives were the small island of Tulagi in the south-eastern Solomons and Port Moresby. The immediate consequence was the battle of the Coral Sea. This was the first battle in which naval air fleets fought each other, in which neither Admiral ever saw the other's flagship, and in which all the fighting was done by the pilots of the planes. The Japanese lost.

The Coral Sea is bounded on the south-west by the Great Barrier Reef which protects Australia, on the north by Papua and the Louisiade Archipelago, and on the east and south by the Solomons and New Caledonia.

The main Allied striking force consisted of the American carriers *Lexington* and *Yorktown* commanded by Rear-Admiral Fletcher. The Japanese striking force consisted of two veterans of the attack on Pearl Harbor, the carriers *Zuikaku* and *Shokaku* with their experienced pilots embarked. Their task was to cover the passage of the invasion force which was to take Port Moresby. Fletcher's aircraft intercepted the invasion force, north of the Louisiades and sank its escort carrier, the *Shoho*. This was America's first success in the Pacific. The invasion force turned back. Fletcher began to seek out the Japanese covering force.

Fletcher now faced for the first time the new naval problem of ensuring that – if the worst came to the worst, and the Japanese reconnaisance was better than his – his carriers might not be caught with their aircraft refuelling on deck. Hide and seek continued. The Japanese were lucky, to the extent that the weather was bad over their carriers. Nevertheless American pilots severely damaged the *Shokaku*, which had to return to Japan for repairs. They also shot down at least 43 Japanese aircraft for the loss of 33 of their own. *Lexington* was damaged but was still able to steam after the action was over, although an internal explosion an hour afterwards made her unmanageable and she had to be sunk. But her precious pilots and her crew were saved.

Assessed with hindsight, the outcome of the battle of the Coral Sea was a clear gain for the Allies. One Japanese carrier had been sunk; the invasion of Port Moresby had been cancelled; and another Japanese carrier, along with many of its experienced pilots, was out of action.

Midway

The battle of the Coral Sea was the Japanese navy's first defeat of the war. The battle of Midway was its first nearly-decisive defeat. Yamamoto planned to capture Midway on 3 June 1942, and, having done so to attack and destroy the US Pacific Fleet. He was rightly convinced that the fleet's new commander, Admiral Nimitz, would not tolerate the capture of the western-most island of the Hawaian archipelago and that the diminished American fleet would come out to challenge the Japanese. Weakened by the attack on Pearl Harbor, the US Fleet was, on paper, no longer a match for the Japanese. Yamamoto had eleven battleships and five aircraft carriers. Nimitz had no battleship and three carriers, and one of these – the *Yorktown* – had been damaged in the Coral Sea encounter. But what Nimitz did have and Yamamoto did not, was the key to his adversary's cypher.

On 20 May 1942, Yamamoto broadcast a long, involved operation order to his fleet. Because of an administrative hang-up he had to use a cypher which had been in use for three months already so that the Americans were familiar with it. It ought to have been changed, but Japanese bureaucracy was on Nimitz's side. The old code was like an open book.

By 27 May Nimitz's codebreakers were able to tell him that Yamamoto intended to carry out a major attack probably on 3 June and a feint attack on the Aleutians on 2 June. They suspected that the main attack would be on Midway. But they could not be sure. Yamamoto was using a letter-code to identify place names.

The code group for the place which was to be attacked was 'A.F.'. Nimitz's chief codebreaker, Lt.-Commander Joseph J. Rochefort, needed to know for certain where A.F. was. He ordered the Midway garrison to send a signal in a code that he knew the Japanese had broken saying that the island's water distillation plant was giving trouble. Having baited the hook, Rochefort waited for the fish. Within two days he had a bite. Yamamoto sent a signal to his ships saying that A.F. was short of water.

Nimitz now knew exactly where he was going. He had already gathered his three remaining carriers – *Yorktown*, *Enterprise* and *Hornet* – at Pearl Harbor and had ordered immediate repairs to *Yorktown*. The engineers said the repairs would take three weeks. Nimitz said they must take not more than three days. On the third day *Yorktown* was back at sea.

Nimitz stationed his carriers where Yamamoto did not expect them to be – to the north and east of his main striking force. Air attacks on Midway launched from Yamamoto's carriers began on schedule. There were four Japanese carriers, *Akagi*, *Kaga*, *Hiryu* and *Soryu* – all of them Pearl Harbor veterans. In command was the Pearl Harbor commander Admiral Nagumo. Yamamoto himself was in overall command.

Early on 4 June, after changing his mind more than once, Nagumo ordered his aircraft (which had been armed to defend the fleet against seaborne attack) to be re-armed ready for a second strike at shore targets on Midway. Torpedo-carrying planes from *Hornet*, *Enterprise* and *Yorktown* attacked first and scored no hit. The next wave of American aircraft –

dive bombers from *Enterprise* – fared better. They sank the *Akagi* and the *Kaga*. Dive bombers from *Yorktown* disabled *Soryu* and a combined attack on *Hiryu* was also successful. By the end of the day Yamamoto had lost all his carriers. The Americans had lost only *Yorktown*. The smaller force had defeated the bigger one. Yamamoto turned back to Japan. Midway was saved. It was a bigger victory than Nimitz could have known at the time. The Japanese carriers were never again to be a match for the Americans.

A Japanese cameraman, Teichi Makishima survived the sinking of the *Akagi*:

> The final attack was undertaken by dive bombers. They first con-
> centrated on the *Kaga* and scored direct hits on the *Kaga*. I saw the
> bombs exploding and I also took pictures of the *Kaga* being hit. Then,
> after the *Kaga*, they concentrated on the *Akagi*. The first one missed,
> the second one managed to drop a bomb amidship, and the third one
> hit the rear end of the *Akagi* – or so we thought. The reason why we
> thought the third bomb had hit the ship was because the rear part of
> the flight deck was torn all up but it was actually torn up because of
> the blast from the explosion. I did not actually see the *Soryu* being hit.
> But after the planes stopped their attack on *Kaga*, I looked towards
> the *Soryu* and saw that it was all in flames. At the beginning we didn't
> think it was very serious but all the planes on the *Kaga* were below
> decks. Their fuel tanks were full and all were carrying torpedoes and
> bombs. At first one of the planes took fire and that set off a torpedo.
> That torpedo blast created an explosion on the next plane and in this
> way, one plane after another exploded until all the under deck was a
> mass of fire. There must have been about fifty bombs and torpedoes
> had exploded altogether.[10]

Defeat at Midway did not discourage the Japanese from pressing on with their operations in the Solomons and New Guinea. Having been prevented by Admiral Fletcher from rounding Papua to take Port Moresby from the sea, they began to mount an assault overland from the north side of the peninsula. And they had already established a base at Tulagi.

The Tulagi base and the assault on Moresby together constituted a serious threat to communication between Australia and the United States.

The Solomons archipelago is a double chain of islands stretching 600 miles north-westward from Tulagi and Guadalcanal to New Britain, where the Japanese had already established a strong base at Rabaul.

Papua runs parallel with the Solomons. The Australian base at Moresby on the south-west shore of the Papua peninsula lies only 300 miles from the northernmost tip of the Australian continent. The Owen Stanley mountains rising to 13,000 feet run down the middle of the Papuan peninsula and divide Salamaua where the Japanese were entrenched from Moresby and the Australian side of the range. The Allies decided that they must drive the Japanese not only out of Papua but out of the Solomons as well. General MacArthur was to lead the mainly Australian assault on Papua. Vice-Admiral Ghormley, USN, later to be relieved by Vice-Admiral Halsey, commanded the operation in the Solomons.

Guadalcanal

The Solomons campaign began on 7 August 1942, when the first US Marine division established bridgeheads against light opposition at Tulagi and on Guadalcanal. Within forty-eight hours, however, Japanese warships from Rabaul had forced the American covering force to retire leaving the Marines without air cover, and without naval support. But by 17 August the Marines had constructed their own airstrip, Henderson Field, within a defended perimeter in time – but only just in time – to be ready for a long, fierce series of Japanese counter-attacks.

The conquest of Guadalcanal was the first of a long catalogue of American amphibious assaults on Pacific islands. The Japanese spurned surrender. They fought tenaciously and bravely. They welcomed jungle conditions; and, to begin with at any rate, they often had superiority in the air. Each American assault, from Guadalcanal at the beginning to Okinawa at the bitter end, met ferocious resistance. The experience of the US Marines and of the army on Guadalcanal was repeated time and again as the war continued.

General Collins (of the US army) remembers having to 'annihilate' a Japanese force because its commander would not surrender.

It was jungle fighting, but not entirely so. Guadalcanal is a rough, volcanic island. The streams that lead down to the sea are filled with heavy jungle but the ridges in between were covered with tall grass that grew to a height of eight to ten feet. In the earlier fighting of the Marines and the American Division this grass was burned off, leaving the ridges bare, but the stream valleys still filled with jungle. We surrounded the Japanese in the valleys by seizing the ridges. It was

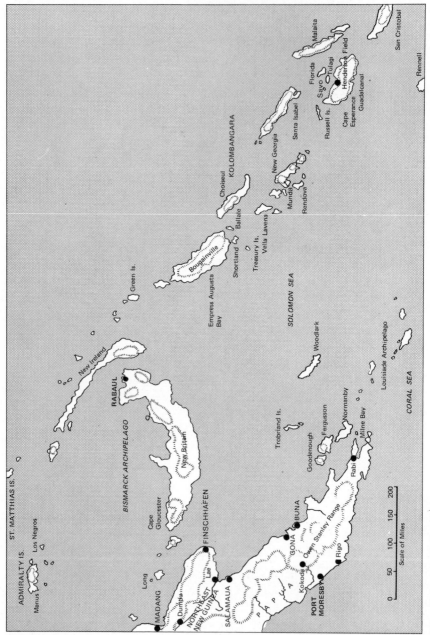

The Solomon Islands

tough fighting because these ridges were quite narrow and the Japanese were tough fighters. They would never give up. We isolated the remnant of a Japanese regiment in the Gifu strong point. After we had surrounded this strong point we used loud speakers and tried to persuade the Japanese soldiers to surrender. But they kept fighting, and we had to go down into the valleys and annihilate them. They would not surrender.[11]

They very seldom did. On island after island, as they made their way north towards Japan, American soldiers and marines found themselves fighting a ferocious enemy who would recognize no finality except the finality of death. The war of the Pacific islands was as bloody and as hard-fought as anything that befell soldiers in the whole of World War II.

Moving their troops by night down the channel which runs through the middle of the Solomons, the Japanese brought reinforcements from Rabaul to make repeated assaults on Guadalcanal. A small one was repulsed on 21 August. A larger one was intercepted by the navy on 24 August. But in early September the Japanese were able to move 6,000 soldiers into Guadalcanal from the north-west. In late October they began a major assault but did not prevail. In November they sent an even bigger contingent – 10,000 soldiers – but the convoy was successfully intercepted and only 4,000 soldiers managed to land whereas two American battleships, the *Washington* and *South Dakota*, had sunk an escorting Japanese battleship and had played havoc with the convoy. Early in 1943 the Japanese retreat from Guadalcanal began. They evacuated 13,000 troops in January and the early part of February. The Allies were established in the Solomons.

In Papua the battle was in the mountains. In July 1942 the Japanese occupied a base at Buna on the north-east shore of the peninsula and opposite to Moresby on the south-west shore. From Buna they advanced into the jungle and up the hills.

At first the 11,000 Japanese made good progress through appalling country. But the Allies – MacArthur's Australians and Americans – still retained a measure of air cover. And the Australians, most of them veterans from the western desert, learned fast to live with jungles and were undismayed. In September the Allies began to overcome the Japanese and to push them back to Buna. Buna was besieged from November until the end of January 1943 when Japanese resistance finally collapsed.

With most of Papua in their hands and with an established base at

Guadalcanal the Allies' next major objective was the strong Japanese base at Rabaul. Without it Japan would no longer be able to maintain even a presence in the Solomons or in the south-west Pacific. But neither MacArthur nor Halsey separately or together had the forces at this time to take Rabaul immediately. They resolved first of all to eliminate one by one the minor Japanese bases in the Solomons and in New Britain. But while they were preparing their assault on the Japanese bases in Bougainville and the other Solomon islands, in New Britain, and in the eastern tip of New Guinea, the opportunity for yet another 'victory of intelligence' came their way.

On 13 April 1943, the commander of the 8th Japanese Fleet broadcast details of a tour of inspection by Admiral Yamamoto. It said that on 18 April Admiral Yamamoto would leave Rabaul at 6 a.m. in a medium attack bomber escorted by six fighters to inspect the Japanese bases at Ballale and Shortland close to the south-eastern extremity of Bougainville island. It was an inspection that never happened. Eighteen P.38s of the US Army Air Force from Henderson Field intercepted Yamamoto's plane thirty-five miles north of Ballale. Captain T. G. Lanphier, US Army Air Force, had been detailed to shoot him down.

'I fired a long steady burst across the bomber's course of flight from approximately right angles. The bomber's right engine, then its right wing, burst into flame. . . . As I moved into range of Yamamoto's bomber and its cannon, the bomber's wing tore off. The bomber plunged into the jungle.'[12]

Before breakfast, over Bougainville, a laconic American captain had eliminated Japan's most revered, most intelligent, and most determined war lord. Yamamoto was irreplaceable. The Japanese mourned him deeply and were – in most important ways – lost without him.

On 30 June 1943, Halsey and MacArthur made their next major move. Halsey's men landed in New Georgia, MacArthur's at Nassau Bay in New Guinea. Halsey's objective was to prepare to capture Bougainville. MacArthur's was to prepare for the capture of Salamaua and Lae and to drive the Japanese out of New Guinea altogether. An Australian force had already fought its way to Wau, inland from Lae. Supplied by air, the Australians advanced slowly through terrible country towards Lae and Salamaua. On 4 September the Australian 9th Division landed at Lae and took the town. The next day 1,700 paratroopers landed inland to cut off the Japanese retreat. By mid-September the Allies had taken both Lae and Salamaua. Finschhafen was attacked on 22 September and the Australians had captured it by early October. For all practical purposes the Japanese were out of Papua.

In the Solomons Halsey's immediate objective was the Japanese air base at Munda, in New Georgia. After many privations the Americans captured Munda on 5 August. Halsey in the Solomons and MacArthur in New Guinea were ready now to besiege Rabaul. Halsey's men landed on Bougainville on 1 November 1943 and on the Green Islands on 15 February 1944. By then they were 100 miles from Rabaul and with American air power at his disposal, Halsey was able to dominate Japan's only important southerly base. Meanwhile MacArthur moved into the western end of New Britain and the Australians advanced north-west-wards through New Guinea.

By the autumn of 1943 the United States navy had got its breath back and its strength. The losses sustained at Pearl Harbor, twenty months before, had been made good. There were men, planes, and ships to spare for another offensive to complement MacArthur's drive in New Guinea and Halsey's in the Solomons. The Americans decided to start recapturing the islands on the Japanese defensive perimeter. They would work their way, as it were, from island to island towards Japan itself.

It was a controversial decision. The Americans were to lose many soldiers and marines. The Japanese had fortified their new possessions well. They fought desparately and skilfully to hold them. On the other hand the Americans were eager to possess themselves of bases from which their new Superfortress bombers, the B.29s, could strike at Japan. Rightly or wrongly they were ready to risk the lives of many men for the sake of a single runway.

They began with the Gilbert Islands, south-west of the Marshalls. In November 1943 they assaulted Makin and Tarawa Islands capturing Makin easily but losing 1,000 men in the assault on Tarawa. In February 1944, using air support from Tarawa, they landed on Kwajalein in the Marshalls. Again the fighting was bitter but by 22 February the Americans had taken not only Kwajalein but three other islands in the archipelago – Engebi, Eniwetok, and Parry.

With the Marshalls in American hands the navy turned its attention to the important Japanese base 1,200 miles to the westward at Truk in the Carolines. The Americans did to Truk what the Japanese had tried but narrowly failed to do to Pearl Harbor – they destroyed it by air strikes launched from carriers. In two days, 17 and 18 February, a carrier task force commanded by Rear-Admiral Marc Mitscher dropped and launched thirty times as much high explosive on Truk as the Japanese had dropped on Pearl Harbor. Truk was then unusable.

So, by this time, was Rabaul. Japan's two major bases in the south-west Pacific had been rendered harmless. The Americans were free to bypass them. MacArthur moved to Hollandia in Dutch New Guinea. Nimitz turned his attention to the Marianas.

On 15 June two divisions of US Marines began an assault on Saipan, in the southern Marianas. Four days later a Japanese carrier task force intervened and Japanese naval pilots suffered one of their worst defeats of the war. Mitscher's pilots shot down 300 Japanese aircraft for the loss of thirty of their own. American submarines sank two of the Japanese carriers. The next day Mitscher's pilots seriously damaged another. In the end this carrier sank also. The battle of the Philippine Sea was another encounter which was more nearly decisive than it seemed at the time. After it was over the Japanese task force had left only thirty-five operational naval strike aircraft.

On Saipan, the Japanese resisted bitterly. By July when the fighting ended they had lost almost 24,000 men. Two other islands in the Marianas, Guam and Tinian were in American hands by August. And Tinian was the base that launched the B.29 which dropped the atomic bomb on Hiroshima.

Leyte

With the Marianas and the Carolines in American hands MacArthur and Halsey decided to go straight for the Philippines. By September 1944 MacArthur's forces controlled New Guinea. He and Halsey decided to strike north for the southern Philippine Islands of Mindanao and Leyte and to leave the Japanese forces – still in control of the Netherlands East Indies, the Celebes, and Borneo – to their own devices. Lesser commanders might have hesitated before making so bold a leap.

On the way, however, they needed three bases – Pelelio in the Palau archipelago which possessed a needed airfield, another air base, Morotai, and a fleet anchorage at Ulithi in the Carolines. There was fierce Japanese resistance on Peleliu but the other two bases were taken more easily. MacArthur was now ready to return – as he had promised – to the Philippines whence he had come.

The first consequence of the landings on Leyte was a major naval engagement which, although this was not known at the time, virtually eliminated the Japanese fleet as an offensive force. The Japanese had divided their naval forces into three groups. Their main carrier task force, its striking power reduced by the recent loss of many experienced pilots, was stationed to cruise north-east of the Philippine archipelago, in the hope that the American carrier task forces would be tempted to divert their attention and their aircraft from two other Japanese task forces which

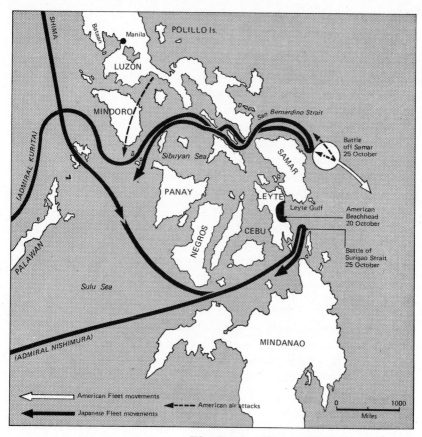

The Battle of Leyte Gulf, October 1944

were to destroy the landing force. One force, under Admiral Nishimura, had orders to penetrate to Leyte Gulf itself by way of the Surigao Strait. This force was virtually destroyed by an American squadron commanded by Rear-Admiral Oldendorf in the first and last battle of the Pacific war to be fought by surface war ships and in the classical manner.

Like many another Admiral before him Oldendorf prevailed by 'crossing the enemy's tee'. Nishimura was advancing through the strait with his ships in line ahead. Oldendorf led his force across Nishimura's line of advance. Every American gun in the fleet could be brought to bear on the Japanese but the Japanese ships at the rear of the line were unable to reply. One Japanese cruiser and one destroyer survived.

Oldendorf ensured success by arranging for a number of torpedo attacks on the enemy force as it approached the head of Surigao Strait. He disposed several units of motor torpedo boats towards the southern entrance of the Strait. On each side of the Strait itself he had positioned destroyers. At the head of the Strait he kept four lines of heavier ships – six battleships, three heavy cruisers, and two units of light cruisers including one Australian cruiser – on the move but ready. When his main force, moving like a line of sentries from one side of the Strait to the other, eventually opened fire at ranges of between eight and ten nautical miles, the spectacle and the consequences were memorable. Captain Roland Smoot, commanding a destroyer division, reported that 'the arched line of tracers in the darkness looked like a continual stream of lighted railroad cars going over a hill. No target could be observed at first. Then shortly there would be fires and explosions and another ship would be accounted for.'[13]

The third Japanese task force, under Admiral Kurita, also had orders to head for Leyte Gulf and to attack MacArthur's transports. American submarines sank three of Kurita's heavy cruisers and pilots from Mitscher's task force 58 sank a battleship in the Sibuyan sea. Halsey believed wrongly that Kurita had been beaten. The landings proceeded. Halsey, unwilling to let the Japanese carrier task force escape unharmed, sent his main carrier groups north in pursuit. But Kurita, with four battleships and six heavy cruisers left, was steaming eastwards through the night. By midnight on 24 October he had passed through the narrow Strait of San Bernadino and was heading south towards Leyte Gulf and MacArthur's still-precarious bridgehead. There was a command muddle. Halsey still thought Kurita was finished. MacArthur thought Halsey would deal with Kurita. In the event six light American escort carriers under Admiral Sprague met Kurita east of Samar island early on 25 October.

Admiral Sprague's escort carriers were converted merchant ships designed to carry a maximum of thirty aircraft whose main duty was to fly reconnaisance missions for the protection of convoys. The escort carriers had been developed for use against submarines in the Battle of the Atlantic. They did not have the capacity to mount the air strikes which were the main offensive and defensive weapon of the far bigger fast, fleet carriers. Moreover, the ships themselves were slow. At the start of the battle of Samar Island Admiral Sprague's main force of escort carriers had a 14-knot speed disadvantage. In the event, he was able to take advantage of rain. He also used artificial smoke, the traditional ally of every out-gunned admiral. His comparatively few planes did their best, refuelling meanwhile on the only Philippine airfield that was usable, thereby sparing Sprague from the necessity to keep his ships heading into the wind so that the aircraft could land on the small carriers during a period when this obligatory heading would have been fatal. It is likely, however, that the actions of Sprague's destroyers decided the issue. Half an hour after the battle began Sprague reported that the enemy was closing his force 'with disconcerting rapidity and the volume and accuracy of fire was increasing'. The screening destroyer closest to the enemy was the USS *Johnston*.

The *Johnston* had been in commission for two days short of one year when the battle was joined. Her captain, Commander Ernest E. Evans, was a Cherokee Indian who had taken to the sea and was determined that Japan should not prevail. On 27 October 1943, he told his new crew: 'This is going to be a fighting ship. I intend to go in harm's way. Anyone who doesn't want to go along had better get off right now'.[14]

The Japanese force, as identified aboard *Johnston*, consisted of four battleships, seven cruisers, and twelve or more destroyers. For twenty minutes Commander Evans experienced the warship captain's supreme nightmare – that of being within range of the enemy's guns without being able to hit back. He made smoke to protect the escort carriers. He 'steered for the last burst' – the outranged captain's traditional method of upsetting the calculations of the gunnery officer of the ship which is firing at him.

At sea the normal calculations for aiming artillery are complicated by the fact that both the gun which is fired and the target at which it is to be fired are moving. The gunnery officer of the firing ship must calculate the course and speed of his target and must also take into account the course and speed of his own ship, the time of flight of the shells, and the speed and direction of the wind. If he observes from the splashes made by his shells that he is firing short he will increase the range. If he sees that his shots are falling ahead of the target he will increase his estimate of the target's speed. The practice of 'steering for the last burst' is calculated to make the gunnery officer's first calculations correct and his recalculations incorrect. The art of 'steering for the last burst' – which is more sophisticated than it may sound – is to persuade the man who is firing at you to overcorrect his initial mistakes. If his first salvo misses astern he will conclude that you were going faster than he thought. The correct response is not to go faster still, but to go slower. Steering for the last burst is a well-tried technique which, with variants, continued to delude intelligent gunnery officers throughout World War II. But it is an art which requires steady nerves. Commander Evans had to practice it for twenty minutes – which is a very long time in a destroyer action. As soon as the enemy was within range of his 5 inch guns, he fired 200 rounds and 10 torpedoes, most of them at the Japanese cruiser *Kumano*, which later sank. However the *Johnston* received three hits herself which knocked out one engine, power for the steering gear, power for three of the ships 5-inch gun turrets and the gyro compass. After an encounter with a Japanese battleship, the *Johnston* engaged a Japanese cruiser which was firing at the escort carrier *Gambier Bay*.

Evans' object was to draw fire away from the carrier and then to engage a Japanese destroyer flotilla which was approaching the carriers. With no torpedoes left, with only one engine working, with the ship under hand steering, and with the bridge on fire, *Johnston* finally lost all power on her gun turrets and her second engine also failed. Japanese destroyers finished her off at about quarter past ten in the morning. She had been in action for nearly three hours. Commander Evans and 185 of his crew of 327 were lost.

Two other American destroyers, the *Hoel*, and the *Samuel B. Roberts* were lost in the same gallant action after similar deeds. It had been one of the most desperate destroyer actions of the Pacific war but it had succeeded. The crews of the USS *Johnston*, *Hoel*, and *Samuel B. Roberts* were first among those who made MacArthur's return to the Philippines not only possible but secure.

Admiral Sprague had lost five ships. Two escort carriers, *Saint Lo*, and *Gambier Bay*, were sunk despite the efforts of the destroyers to protect them. (*Saint Lo* was sunk by one of the first Kamikaze suicide attacks by Japanese naval airmen.) Sprague's opponent, Admiral Kurita, nevertheless decided that he had been beaten. During the afternoon he headed back for the San Bernadino Strait and later for the East Pass intending to return to Brunei in Borneo.

The Battle of Samar Island was a close-run thing. The Americans stood to lose many ships. Neither of the admirals immediately concerned – Sprague and Oldendorf – for Halsey was then committed to pursuit of the main Japanese carrier task force – could be certain at the time as to whether or not the force that had come through San Bernadino was or was not Japan's main effort against the Leyte Gulf landing. Oldendorf, who had already won his precise, mathematical, rule-book victory in the Surigao Strait and who had his fleet intact, decided rightly to stay where he was in close support of MacArthur. His fleet was strong on battleships, short on carriers and he could not have got there in time. Sprague was on his own. Samar Island was a sea fight conducted by the US navy in the highest traditions of John Paul Jones. An inferior force refused to give in to a superior one.

MacArthur was able to consolidate his position in Leyte but only in spite of dreadful difficulties. In barges and destroyers, Japanese reinforcements crowded onto Leyte from the other Japanese-occupied Philippine islands. For the first time the surprised Americans had to contend with the Kamikaze pilots who flew planes loaded with explosives and stayed with them until they hit their targets. The Americans were not prepared for this strange and deadly practice.

MacArthur's men made slow progress on Leyte. Halsey's carriers, providing air cover, suffered considerably. MacArthur's forces did not secure full control of the Philippines or of its main island Luzon until early in 1945. MacArthur saw his next task as the invasion of Japan. The Philippines were to become the main base from which in November 1945 an army of five million men would invade Japan.

But all these preparations were unnecessary. The Battle of Leyte Gulf had been a much more important victory than the Americans realized. They knew they had defeated the major Japanese naval force in the Philippines. What they did not know was that this had been the only major naval force that the Japanese still possessed.

Hindsight can be a cruel messenger. Had the Americans known after Leyte that they were already supreme at sea they might have fought the rest of the war in a different way and many lives might have been spared. As it was, however, they thought that they needed yet more islands.

Iwo Jima and Okinawa

The two that they wanted were Iwo Jima which lies at the southern end of the chain of islands stretching south from Tokyo Bay through the Bonins and on into the central Pacific, and Okinawa, a fortified island in the Ryukyu chain which links south Japan with Formosa. The Americans wanted an airfield on each mainly to enable American fighters to support the B.29s on their raids over Japan.

To make this possible 6,000 Americans died on Iwo Jima and 12,500 on and around Okinawa. 21,000 Japanese died on Iwo Jima, about 100,000 on Okinawa. Iwo Jima is bleak, volcanic and small. Its surface area is eight square miles. The Americans had expected to take it in four days. In fact the fighting lasted five weeks. Three divisions of Marines struggled upwards through the lava to find the Japanese entrenched, concealed, and determined in positions dug into the sides of Iwo Jima's volcano, Mount Suribachi.

Okinawa was even more heavily fortified, and it lay within range of Japanese airfields in Formosa and Kyushu. The Americans, two army corps, had to deal not only with determined defenders dug into the hills but also with Kamikaze attacks launched from land bases. Task Force 58, covering the Okinawa landings, also suffered from the Kamikazes. On

G

7 April 1945, a week after the first landing, the Japanese Admiralty sent its biggest and only remaining effective battleship, the *Yamato*, to join the Okinawa battle. *Yamato* was sunk long before she could get there by pilots from Task Force 58. She could never have survived anyway. The Japanese naval staff had sent her to sea with enough fuel to reach Okinawa but not enough to get back. *Yamato* was the biggest Kamikaze of them all.

Okinawa fell to the Americans on 21 June 1945. On 26 July President Truman, Churchill and Chiang Kai-shek jointly called upon Japan to surrender. The alternative they said was 'prompt and utter destruction'. The Japanese did not surrender. Destruction followed on 6 August 1945.

Three B.29s took off from Tinian and headed for Hiroshima, the eighth largest city in Japan. One B.29, the Enola Gay, carried an atomic bomb. The other two rode shot-gun, took pictures and made readings of temperatures, pressures and radioactivity. The mission commander was Colonel Tibbetts, aged thirty, and a pilot of wide experience. Colonel Tibbetts has described the mission that started the nuclear age:

Up to this point it was common practice in any theatre of war to fly straight ahead, fly level, drop your bombs, and keep right on going, because you could bomb several thousands of feet in the air and you could cross the top of the place that you had bombed with no concern whatsoever. But it was determined by the scientists that, in order to escape and maintain the integrity of the aircraft and the crew, that this aeroplane could not fly forward after it had dropped the bomb. It had to turn around and get away from that bomb as fast as it could. If you placed this aeroplane in a very steep angle of bank to make this turn, if you turned 158 degrees from the direction that you were going, you would then begin to place distance between yourself and that point of explosion as quickly as possible. You had to get away from the shock wave that would be coming back from the ground in the form of an ever expanding circle as it came upwards. It's necessary to make this turn to get yourself as far as possible from an expanding ring and 158 degrees happened to be the turn for that particular circle. It was difficult. It was something that was not done with a big bomber aeroplane. You didn't make this kind of a steep turn – you might almost call it an acrobatic manoeuvre – and the big aircraft didn't do these things. However, we refined it, we learned how to do it. It had been decided earlier that there was a possibility that an accident could occur on take-off, and so therefore we would not arm this weapon until we had left the runway and were out to sea. This of course meant that had there been an accident there would have been an explosion from normal powder charges but there would not have been a nuclear explosion. As I said this worried more people than it worried me because I had plenty of faith in my aeroplane. I knew my engines were good. We started our take-off on time which was somewhere about 2.45 I think, and the aeroplane went on down the runway. It was loaded quite heavily but it responded exactly like I had anticipated it would. I had flown this aeroplane the same way before and there was no problem and there was nothing different this night in the way we went. We arrived over the initial point and started in on the bomb run which had about eleven minutes to go, rather a long type of run for a bomb run but on the other hand we felt we needed this extra time in straight and level flight to stabilize the air speed of the aeroplane, to get everything right down to the last minute detail. As I indicated earlier the problem after the release of the bomb is not to proceed forward but to turn away. As soon as the weight had left the aeroplane I immediately went into this steep turn and we tried then to place distance between ourselves and the point of impact. In this particular case that bomb took fifty-three seconds from the time it left the aeroplane until it exploded and this gave us adequate time of course to make the turn. We had just made the turn and rolled out on level flight when it seemed like somebody had grabbed a hold of my aeroplane and gave it a real hard shaking because this was the shock wave that had come up. Now after we had been hit by a second shock wave not quite so strong as the first one I decided we'll turn around and go back and take a look. The day was clear when we dropped that bomb, it was a clear sun-shiny day and the visibility was unrestricted. As we came back around again facing the direction of Hiroshima we saw this cloud coming up. The cloud by this time, now two minutes old, was up at our altitude. We were thirty-three thousand feet at this time and the cloud was up there and continuing to go right up on in a boiling fashion, as if it was rolling and boiling. The surface was nothing but a black boiling, like a barrel of tar. Where before there had been a city with distinctive houses, buildings and everything that you could see from our altitude, now you couldn't see anything except a black boiling debris down below.[15]

Three days later a second bomb was dropped on Nagasaki. The following morning, 10 August, the Japanese said they would surrender and stopped fighting. On 2 September they signed the surrender instrument on the quarterdeck of the USS *Missouri* anchored in Tokyo Bay. General MacArthur became the not un-benevolent ruler of Japan.

Chapter 10

Burma Regained

The effective Japanese occupation of Burma lasted from 29 April 1942 when they captured Lashio, thereby cutting the road between India and China – the so-called Burma Road – to 3 May 1945, when the British re-occupied Rangoon, Burma's only port. During this long occupation of a rich and for the time being supine country, the Japanese were mainly content to stay where they were. At the time, anyway, they do not seem to have been ambitious enough to attack India as the British feared they would. Burma and India are separated by difficult, mountainous country and the Japanese were already hard pressed elsewhere in China and the south Pacific. They did not build up their forces in Burma to a point at which an offensive into India would have been feasible or sensible. In any case they had achieved an important military objective simply by being where they were.

By occupying Lashio and cutting the Burma Road, they were depriving Generalissimo Chiang Kai-shek of the supplies he had been getting from the United States. After Japan had invaded China in the early 1930s and had later occupied the Chinese ports, the Burma Road was the only land link by which America could reinforce Chiang Kai-shek's armies. The Japanese cut it in 1942 by occupying Burma.

The Burma Road always seemed more important to the Americans than it did to the British. For historic and sometimes haphazard reasons the Americans had more faith in Chiang Kai-shek than he may have deserved. They certainly had more faith in him than the British had. Certainly also some Americans doubted deeply Chiang Kai-shek's ability and determination to fight the Japanese. He was suspected, probably rightly, of a deeper concern to defeat his Communist rival, Mao Tse-tung. The British were probably right in thinking that Chiang Kai-shek would not devote all his resources to throwing the Japanese out of China. The Americans were probably wrong in hoping that he would.

In any event the importance which the Allies attached to the Burma Road, and hence to the bloody and difficult campaign which they waged in 1944 and 1945 to re-open it, had been largely determined by events in China in the 1930's. The first was an incident staged by the Japanese in Manchuria on 18 September 1931. A bomb destroyed a part of the south Manchurian Railway, a Chinese facility under Japanese protection and control. The Japanese at once pretended to be outraged and sent their army to occupy all Manchuria. China appealed to the League of Nations. The League simply 'urged' Japan to desist and to negotiate directly with China. The League also appointed a commission under Lord Lytton, to investigate the problem. The Japanese, like Mussolini after them, paid no attention. They occupied Manchuria, set up a puppet Government, and ran the country themselves. They also seized Shanghai but, in the initial stages, agreed to withdraw under pressure from the League. But this was the League's only real success in the Far East.

The Lytton Commission reported that Japanese forces ought to evacuate Manchuria where they had no right to be. There was a long debate in the League of Nations Assembly about what to do. In February 1933 – seventeen months after the original explosion – the League resolved to call on the Japanese to withdraw and said that it would refuse to recognize the puppet Manchurian State (now known as Manchukuo). Again the Japanese paid no attention. No major member of the League seemed inclined to act in its support. The high hopes of 1918 on which the League had been founded remained unrealized. The nations remained nations. National governments remained national. A determined aggressor had been able to show in Manchuria that the world's new peace-keeping system did not work.

The United States, which was not a member of the League, turned out to be more concerned. America was closer to Japan than the League's main European members. Next to America Japan was the second most important power in the Pacific. The United States was concerned when Japan showed signs of aggressive tendencies. America had been born in revolution against the imperialism of King George III. Anti-imperialism was then – and to some extent still is – a part of America's conscious destiny as this was understood by most Americans. China had been rapaciously exploited by the main Western powers – Britain, France, Germany (before the First World War) – but not by the United States or not, at least, in the same way. China's European exploiters had extracted trade concessions, treaty ports (in which they enjoyed special privileges) and the control of the Chinese customs. The United States, though present in China, had taken pride in being more tactful. For reasons which were partly sentimental and certainly insufficient, the Americans felt a kinship for the Chinese which the European powers did not share.

On 7 January 1932 the United States – perturbed about Manchuria and anxious about the balance of power in the Pacific – formally told the Japanese Government that America would not recognize Japan's sovereignty over territory which Japan had taken from other countries by force. The Japanese paid no more attention to America than they had paid to the League of Nations. They ignored the American note (incorporating the so-called Stimson Doctrine named after the then Secretary of State) and in doing so committed one of their first major imprudent acts of diplomacy in the Pacific. From January 1932 onwards the United States was suspicious of Japan, and with reason.

Having consolidated their position in Manchuria, the Japanese announced in April 1934 that any attempt by an outside country to bring help to China would be opposed by the Japanese army. In 1936 the Japanese Government declared in effect that – like Hitler – the Japanese Emperor felt destined to be the leader of the master-race of South-East Asia. In November 1936 Japan signed the Anti-Comintern pact with Hitler. In July 1937, following another incident (probably staged) near Peking the Japanese invaded China proper. The Chinese, numerous, determined, but disorganized, were unable to prevent the Japanese from occupying Peking, the lower part of the Yangtze River Valley, and large parts of southern China. By early 1939 the Japanese army had captured China's rich eastern coastal strip, but they had not conquered China or the Chinese and never did. Instead the Japanese success in eastern China alarmed and alerted not only the Western powers and the United States but Russia as well. There had been serious border fighting between Japanese and Russian troops in north Manchuria, and there was more to come. The Russians were on their guard against Japan. Britain and the United States were concerned about China. Both countries began seriously to organize military support for Chiang Kai-shek. The Americans with their superior resources sent more than the British. But from then on the Burma Road became what appeared to be a necessity for the curbing of Japan.

The Japanese were unable to conquer China partly because it was too big, but partly also because of strong resistance by the Chinese. When the Pacific war began in December 1941, thirteen out of Japan's forty-three army divisions were tied down in Manchuria and twenty-five in China. Chiang Kai-shek had moved his capital and his headquarters to Chunking in China's south-western mountains. The Communists had a free hand in the north. When the Pacific war began there were already virtually two Chinas, with rival governments. They were both fighting the Japanese and occasionally also each other. But the Japanese made slow progress. In June 1940, the month in which France fell to the Germans, and Britain seemed doomed, Japan insisted that Britain should close the Burma Road. Britain, hard-pressed at home, had no option but to agree temporarily. For the time being, Chiang Kai-shek was on his own.

In October 1940 Chiang Kai-shek asked President Roosevelt for an air force of 500 aircraft to be flown by American pilots in his service. He did not get 500 but he got some. Their commander was Colonel Claire Chennault, a brilliant pilot and a recently retired officer of the US Army Air Force. Chennault founded his Chinese air force, the American Volunteer Group (or AVG) later to become famous as the 'Flying Tigers', with 100 fighters and pilots released from the US navy and army. The AVG mustered in Burma in November 1941. By then the Lend-Lease Act of March 1941 had enabled Roosevelt to begin to send aid to China in sizeable quantities. Barbara Tuchman, in her detailed history of American-Chinese relations, suggests that this was the point in time at which America's involvement with Chiang Kai-shek's China began to change in character from friendly help into an eventually embarrassing entanglement.

Thereafter the flow of aid became an investment, and the need to protect the investment increased the flow until it became a silver cord attaching America to the Nationalist [Chiang Kai-shek's] Government. There is no more entangling alliance than aid to indigent friends. . . . The programme was not philanthropy but intended as a means of enabling the Chinese to keep the Japanese occupied. Through all changing circumstances and conditions in the coming period, this remained the purpose of American aid and it retained the original flaw; the American purpose was not the Chinese purpose. China's primary interest was not to keep the Japanese actively occupied burning and terrorizing in China in order to keep them off American backs. The Nationalist Government wanted American money and arms mainly in order to strengthen itself. Unlike Britain, which had only a foreign foe, Chunking [Chiang Kai-shek's capital] could always hear at its back the internal enemy hurrying near.[1]

The internal enemy was the Chinese Communist party and its armies. At the time, the man who suspected most deeply that Chiang Kai-shek would be more interested in using his new arms against the Communists than against the Japanese was General (Vinegar Joe) Stilwell, who had served long years on the staff of the US embassy in China. Early in 1942, along with his supplies and aid, Chiang Kai-shek got Stilwell. He was appointed Chiang's American military adviser and his orders from Washington were to equip and train the Chinese armies to fight the Japanese more fiercely.

Stilwell arrived at a bad time. The Burma Road had been closed decisively since April 1942 when the Japanese invaded Burma from the south, driving the British out into India. American pilots were flying Chiang Kai-shek's supplies into him across the 'hump' from aerodromes in Assam across the eastern Himalayas and into China. The 'hump' was held by pilots to be the worst air route in the world.

Stilwell and the British Commander-in-Chief in India, Sir Archibald Wavell (who had taken up this post when Churchill dismissed him from the Middle East Command), resolved to recapture as soon as they could northern and central Burma and to build a new road from Ledo through Myitkyina and Bhamo, so as to re-establish a land route to Kunming, Chiang Kai-shek's railhead in China. At the same time Stilwell set himself the task of re-equipping as many Chinese divisions as possible and of training three of them in India. Wavell resolved to recapture Akyab on the west coast of the Arakan peninsula. His first plan had been to combine an attack from the north with an amphibious attack from the sea. But the landing craft he needed were being used to land troops in Madagascar where the French garrison remained loyal to the Vichy Government. The Madagascar operation took longer than expected. Without amphibious support the attack on Akyab failed and by May 1943 Wavell's forces were back where they had started.

Wavell's main effort, however, was the reorganization of the Indian Army in preparation for an assault in north and central Burma. He formed a long-range penetration group, General Wingate's famous Chindits, to harass the Japanese in the forests. The Chindits' first expedition behind the enemy lines began in February 1943, and cost them dearly. About 3,000 men crossed into or were flown into enemy-held territory in gliders, but only about 2,200 returned. The Chindits were behind the enemy lines for nearly four months and harassed the Japanese severely besides proving to themselves and to the rest of the Allied armies that it was possible for troops to survive while being supplied by air. But they also proved, to the Japanese, that the Chindwin River could be crossed by determined men. Sir Robert Thompson, at that time a Flight Lieutenant, was one of them:

At the end of 1942 the British and Indian armies all over South-East Asia had been defeated. One of the main reasons for that defeat was that in these vast spaces of South-East Asia they had been confined to roads where they existed. I think Wingate provided the answer. He saw the troops had to operate in this enormous space and that there were two factors that we were not making sufficient use of. The first was wireless. After all, with a good wireless set you can talk back to base, you can talk to nearby units and, above all, you can talk to aircraft. The air was the second factor. The real question is what do you do with that air superiority when you've got it, and here Wingate provided the answer: the air force could help the army to get forward on the ground and to operate in these vast spaces by air supply, by closer support and, above all, by helping you evacuate wounded.

This air supply became so efficient that the troops relied on it completely. You could run yourself down to one day's rations or less, you could go a day almost without rations and know perfectly well that if you demanded a supply drop at 10.00 p.m. one night in a particular area of jungle or in a paddy field alongside you knew you were going to get it. . . .

Another important aspect – I would almost put it as the most important aspect of air support when one is operating in the vast spaces of jungles and valleys – was what do you do with your wounded? Because, above all, any units operating in those circumstances have to be mobile all the time and wounded of course immediately bring you to a halt. Well, fortunately, Wingate was able to abtain assistance from the United States and we were given a remarkable aircraft called an L1, which was a very short take-off and landing aircraft and could get into any little valley or bit of paddy and field and evacuate our wounded for us. I think the most remarkable effort that I remember was when it was very close to the Monsoon period and the only area we could find to land this L1 was on the banks of a lake and the lake was fairly low, it still being the dry season, and this sloping bank ran for about 150 yards. Well, it was very marshy at the bottom point but we got some coconut matting so that there was this 150 yards strip and the aircraft came in over the lake and landed up the strip. This L1 had a bench that you could put down from the back of the pilot's head over the back seat. On that bench we could put two lying wounded. In the seat underneath one walking wounded, and we could even put another man right at the top of the bench with his feet in the pilot's lap. Now that meant four men. That's roughly eight hundred pounds of extra weight. This aircraft then had to take off downhill into the lake and we realised that it probably wouldn't get off. The only way that we could ensure it got off was to put a line of sand bags along the bottom edge of the strip about six inches high so that when the aircraft hit those sand bags it jumped about ten feet into the air and that was just enough for it then to stagger across the lake. Well, I remember that this particular American pilot, starting before dawn one day and continuing until after dark, did 18 trips in a day and took out 72 wounded. He didn't get overtime for it but he got a Distinguished Flying Cross. . . .

Of course this type of operation meant that the troops had to learn to be mobile in the jungle and to live on fairly tight rations. I certainly think that the two things from my point of view that I felt the need of most were hot sweet tea and rice. I got very used to rice as the bulk food. You could make that up into something more palatable even if you were only adding curry powder to it or chocolate or melted cheese or something to make a hot evening meal. We could never have done those type of operations on what I would call normal rations. One, you couldn't have carried them. Secondly, I don't think that troops in those sort of circumstances need them. If you are fit before you go in and well fed then you can manage two or three months on very light rations. You know you're going to be well fed again when you come out and you have, I think, a better stamina if you go in a bit too well fed. I always used to think that one didn't go into a thing like this like a Derby winner. You went into it with quite a bit of fat left on you because that's part of what you were living on while you were in there.[2]

In 1943 the Japanese seemed disinclined to make any move against India from Burma. They held good defensive positions in the Arakan peninsula and along the river systems of Burma. But by crossing the Chindwin the Chindits had shown that these defences were less strong than the Japanese seemed to think. During the winter of 1943–44 the Japanese, like Wavell, prepared to take the offensive. The objective was to cut the Assam–Bengal Railway, which connected Calcutta with the Indian railhead for the 'hump' airlift at Ledo, which lies in the foothills of the Himalayas.

The Japanese were ready first. They forestalled the Allies but did not in fact seriously disrupt their plans. By now, all Allied forces in South-East Asia were under the command of Admiral Lord Louis Mountbatten, whose deputy was Stilwell. Their joint plan for 1944 envisaged combined attacks by Chinese forces under Stilwell's command towards Myitkyina;

by the British–Indian 14th Army towards Indaw; and by Chiang Kai-shek's forces westward from China across the Salween River. There was also to be a second attempt to capture Akyab, on which the 14th Army had just embarked when the Japanese began their offensive.

In theory, the Allies' position was then perilous. Chiang Kai-shek had changed his mind about an offensive west across the Salween. At all events it did not move fast or far. At first, too, the Japanese offensive prospered. They advanced quickly through the Arakan Hills outflanking the forward elements of the 14th army. The army commander, General (later Field Marshal) Sir William Slim, was well and calmly prepared. He did not try to fight the Japanese on their own ground which was the jungle and the mountains. Instead, he withdrew his forces to the plains around the two first, main, obvious objectives of the Japanese drive, the towns of Imphal and Kohima. In bitter fighting the 14th Army held both towns. Slim could reinforce his troops by air. The Japanese could not. Surrounded and cut off from each other Imphal and Kohima withstood a siege which lasted through April 1944. Slim kept the garrisons supplied. He reinforced the equally important communications centre of Dimapur further north. He waited for the reinforcements from India which he knew were on their way. By June the two sieges had been lifted and the Japanese were on the retreat back into Burma. It was the Japanese army's first major defeat in the field, a defeat from which the army in Burma never recovered.

Imphal was a defensive battle which assured the success of a subsequent offensive one. It was won mainly by the skill, determination, and training of the British, Indian and Nepalese troops who fought it, but also largely by the foresight, calmness and confidence of General Slim. He and his field commanders, from General Scoones and Stopford at Imphal and Kohima downwards, at all times knew what they were about. Slim, a modest man with very little to be modest about, attributes part of his success to the stupidity of his opponent, the Japanese General Sato. He was, according to Slim, 'without exception, the most unenterprising of all the Japanese generals I encountered. He had been ordered to take Kohima and dig in. His bullet head was filled with one idea only – to take Kohima. It never struck him that he could inflict terrible damage on us without taking Kohima at all'.[3]

Slim in his modesty may be right. But another theory suggests that for lack of supplies Sato simply could not have done what Slim feared he would do. It is possible, even likely, that the Japanese had under-estimated the 14th Army so badly that they had prepared themselves for nothing more serious than a walk over. In fact their attempts to take

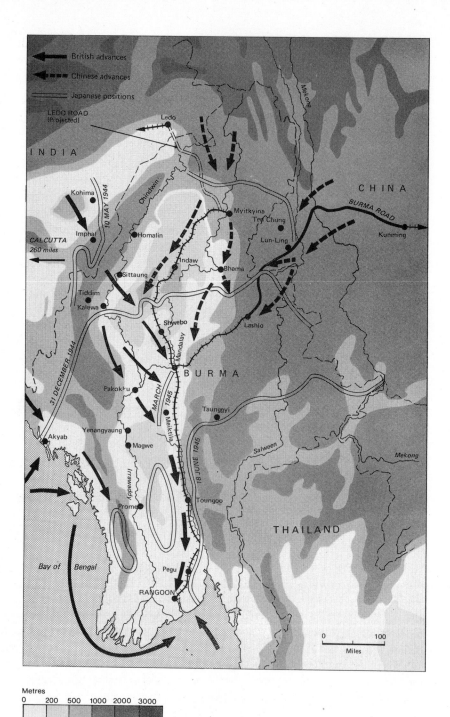

British advances
Chinese advances
Japanese positions

LEDO ROAD
(Projected)
Ledo

I N D I A

Kohima

10 MAY 1944

Chindwin

Myitkyina
Teng-Chung

C H I N A

BURMA ROAD

Imphal

Homalin

Lun-Ling

Kunming

CALCUTTA
260 miles

Indaw

Bhamo

Sittaung

Tiddim

Kalewa

Shwebo

Lashio

Mandalay

31 DECEMBER 1944

B U R M A

Pakokku

MARCH 1945

Taunggyi

Akyab

Yenangyaung

Magwe

Meiktila

Salween

Mekong

18 JUNE 1945

THAILAND

Irrawaddy

Prome

Toungoo

Bay of Bengal

Pegu

RANGOON

0   100
Miles

Mekong

Metres
0   200   500   1000 2000 3000

The Burma Campaign, 1944-5

Imphal and Kohima cost them 53,000 men whereas the 14th Army lost 16,700.

While Slim was making the Japanese look silly at Imphal, Stilwell and General Merrill, Wingate's American counterpart (the commander of 'Merrill's Marauders'), were making good but laborious progress in northern Burma. They faced two impediments – the determination of the Japanese and the hesitations of Chiang Kai-shek. Starting from Ledo, Stilwell's objective was Myitkyina. He began his advance from Ledo in January. Chiang Kai-shek's men did not begin to move west across the Salween River until April and only then, apparently in response to a threat by the United States, to cut off all aid to China unless the soldiers moved. They moved too late to help Stilwell who, with Merrill and the Chinese and American forces under their command were the real and final captors of Myitkyina.

This town was vital because from it a pilot could fly into China without having to climb to cross the Himalayas. He needed to carry less fuel and could therefore carry a bigger pay load. By capturing Myitkyina, the Allies would outflank the mountains. After many setbacks Stilwell's and Merrill's soldiers did this on 3 August 1944.

In southern Burma, meanwhile, the 14th Army had gone over to the offensive despite the monsoon – the climatic catastrophe which afflicts South-East Asia for many months of the year. The Japanese had been beaten in Arakan. They were for the first time retreating fast on land. By December 1944, the 14th Army had established several bridgeheads across the Irrawaddy River, on both sides of Mandalay. The 14th Army had already recaptured Akyab on the west coast of the Arakan peninsula. By March 1945 it was set to capture the whole of southern Burma. In the same month Slim's forces captured Meiktila. Soon afterwards the Japanese garrison in Mandalay itself was threatened. The Japanese tried, angrily but in vain, to regain Meiktila which was a vital communications centre. They were out of Mandalay by April. By 3 May the Allies had recaptured Rangoon.

The fighting in Burma was bitter, hazardous and awful. Indian, British, Nepalese, and Chinese soldiers as well as Americans suffered grim privations in order to expel the Japanese from the Burmese territories they had conquered. Wingate's Chindits and Merrill's Marauders ventured daringly and suffered grievously in order to recapture Burma. But was Burma worth it?

India was, in fact, safe from invasion. Hindsight, cruel as ever, suggests strongly that the Burma Road was not worth the blood that was spilt for it.

The battle for Burma was one of the nastiest and most adventurous campaigns of the whole war. The 14th Army felt forgotten by everyone except the Japanese. One of Slim's sergeants, Sgt Tomkins, has said that the worst moment was the first – the encounter not with the Japanese but with the jungle.

I'd seen a forest but I hadn't seen a jungle. There were all sorts of animal noises we'd never heard before. We had come out from England and gone into this jungle which we'd never seen. We got in there and couldn't see a thing. There were all these noises and it really put the wind up us more than the Japanese. After many weeks we got used to this noise and all these funny sounds and we realized that for the Japanese it must have been exactly the same. . . . We were all on tenterhooks and thorns expecting the enemy to come round the corner any minute or to come straight at us from the jungle. But then we realized that they couldn't move in it any more than we could without making a noise. Then we got acclimatized to it and fashioned ourselves round the jungle. When we had done this, this one of our main battles was over – getting acclimatized to the jungle and to the jungle sounds and noises and conditions. . . .

There weren't any roads as such. We could walk along little animal tracks. You just couldn't wander off into the jungle anywhere you liked. You had to go down these animal tracks the same as the Japanese had to go down them. If you met each other you had a battle.[4]

Chapter 11

The Politics of War

The alliance that won the war was an improbable group of nations. Communist Russia, capitalist America, and imperialist Britain were not natural friends. Only Hitler could have brought them together. Their two other main allies – de Gaulle's Free France and Chiang Kai-shek's Nationalist China – generated diplomatic complications for everyone. The Allies won the war together, but they suspected each other from start to finish although in public they pretended otherwise.

The anti-imperialist Americans suspected the British, wrongly in the event, of an intention to extend and consolidate their Empire. The Russians suspected capitalism and all capitalists and, to their cost, refused to believe almost everything that Churchill and Roosevelt told them about Hitler's plans. The British suspected the Russians, eventually but rightly, of the intention to substitute communist dictatorship for democratic and other forms of government in eastern Europe. Chiang Kai-shek suspected, rightly, that the British did not really want to help him. De Gaulle was suspicious of everyone. Yet the alliance worked. Germany and Japan were defeated by a group of quarrelling and dissimilar nations whose sole common resolve was not to be pushed around.

The British and the Americans began to confer seriously about the war as soon as Churchill became Prime Minister in May 1940. Churchill had been exchanging messages with President Roosevelt before, while he was still First Lord of the Admiralty. When he replaced Chamberlain the flow of messages increased in volume and in candour. Churchill confided in Roosevelt directly and often, telling him privately and regularly the bad news as well as the good. Roosevelt responded warmly. He admired Britain's lonely stand. He wanted her to win.

Towards the end of the war and particularly during the conferences at Teheran and Yalta, which determined the political future of eastern Europe, Roosevelt sided with the Russians. He was being realistic rather than disloyal. Roosevelt recognized – as the British themselves did not – that the war and other factors had already reduced Britain's status in the world. Roosevelt recognized that after the war the USSR would be the only country comparable in economic and military power to the United States, and he acted accordingly. Also he still suspected the British of imperialist designs. He had grounds for this. During the 1930's one of Churchill's main political ambitions had been to prevent the granting of self-government to India. In fact Churchill's successor, Attlee, made haste to grant self-government to India and Pakistan as soon as the war was over, whereas the Russians made haste to occupy and dominate the countries of eastern Europe. Roosevelt suspected Britain of an imperialism she was about to abandon while forgiving the USSR for the imperialism of another sort which she was about to practice.

Coolness between the Allies at Teheran and Yalta did not, however, produce any comfort for Hitler. Anglo-American military co-operation was on the whole close and generous throughout the war. Roosevelt knew from Churchill's messages how serious Britain's position was, and he also knew that until 1940 America had to some extent relied upon Britain to keep the peace in the Atlantic and, therefore, to protect the United States. When France fell Britain became not simply a friend in trouble but also a bastion threatened – a bastion which America needed. The US navy was not then ready to fight a war in two oceans at the same time, and at his back Roosevelt could already hear warlike noises coming from Japan. Already in 1940, long before Hitler declared war on America, the defence of Britain was an important element, perhaps a vital one, in the defence of the United States.

Roosevelt understood this but the American public and Congress did not. American public opinion, still largely isolationist, was not then ready to accept the alarming prospect that the United States itself might be threatened by a European war. Roosevelt was engaged in his third presidential election campaign. Until he won it, in November 1940, he could not afford politically to give much practical aid to Britain. He did, however, give Britain fifty old but good destroyers in return for base facilities in the West Indies.

Once elected Roosevelt acted quickly. Britain's first need was money, not destroyers. Since 1939 she had been buying increasing quantities of arms and other war materials in America. By November 1940 Britain's stock of dollars was almost exhausted. Roosevelt proposed lend-lease, the arrangement under which the United States for the rest of the war was to supply her Allies with arms which were technically 'on loan'. 'We must', Roosevelt said, 'be the great arsenal of democracy'. The

44. May 1944: Indian troops in Italy prepare to attack across the River Garigliano

45. Italy again: 4·2″ mortars in action in May 1944 during the 8th Army's assault on the Gustav Line

46. November 1943: the Teheran Conference, where the three leaders, Stalin, Roosevelt and Churchill, met for the first time

47. *Left to right:* General Ironside, Winston Churchill, General Gamelin, Lord Gort, January 1940

48. President Roosevelt and Winston Churchill attend service during the conference at Placentia Bay, at which they signed the Atlantic Charter, August 1941

49. Generals Patton, Bradley and Montgomery chat together after the latter had presented the two Americans with medals, July 1944

50. General Eisenhower and his party at Julich, Germany. Next to
Eisenhower is General Simpson, Commanding General of the 9th Army

51. Stalin, Truman and Churchill at the Potsdam Conference, 17 July 1945

lend-lease bill, passed by Congress in March 1941, authorized him to offer arms and supplies to 'the Government of any country whose defence the President deems vital to the defence of the United States'. To ensure that the arms would be available Roosevelt also established the Office of Production Management which represented unions and employers and which was to build, organize, and spur on the largest programme for the manufacture of arms, ships, and aircraft that the world had ever seen. The Americans astonished the world and themselves. Their genius for organization and production, nurtured and guided by the Office of Production Management, produced an arsenal that was indeed un-matchable.

The first and one of the most useful Anglo-American conferences of the war was organized by scientists and its purpose was to exploit American production-potential. The scientific adviser to the British air attaché in Washington, Professor A. V. Hill, a distinguished physicist, had been deeply impressed by the Americans' capacity for large scale production and by their technical ingenuity. Soon after the fall of France and nearly eighteen months before the Americans were themselves at war, Hill urged the British Government to offer to the United States the advanced and still-secret war devices which had been invented by British scientists. Hill wrote from Washington to his chief, Henry Tizard, in London that 'we could get much more help in the United States and Canada if we were not so damnably sticky and unimaginative'.[1] Tizard persuaded the government to take Hill's advice. In August 1940 Tizard went to Washington, taking the secrets with him. They included a new 'proximity' fuse for anti-aircraft shells and, above all, the cavity magnetron, the device which made short wave radar possible. The Americans seized upon all these devices, gratefully and eagerly, and began to produce them in quantities which British industry could never have achieved.

In many effective ways the most important wartime conference of all did not include a single senior politician. The conference – known under the code name A.B.C.1 – met in Washington in January 1941 and was composed of British and American Staff Officers. They made two decisions of high importance. Joint Anglo-American military planning staffs were to be established in London and Washington and were to work together on the firm assumption that if the United States found herself at war with Germany and Japan she would concentrate on defeating Germany first. This was a decisive undertaking by the Americans which they honoured to the end.

Immediately this meant that there was an additional and urgent reason why America could not afford to see Britain defeated. Victory in the Battle of the Atlantic became even more important to America than it had been before. In the spring of 1941 the United States declared that the Azores, the eastern coast of Canada, the Bahamas, the Gulf of Mexico, and the Caribbean belonged to a zone for whose defence the United States had assumed responsibility. Greenland, which belonged to occupied Denmark, became an American protectorate. In July US Marines replaced a British garrison in Iceland. In the Battle of the Atlantic, at least, the United States were committed on the British side.

By then also the United States were committed to help the Soviet Union. Hitler had invaded that country on 22 June 1941. Roosevelt, like Churchill, at once promised to send all the aid that he could. Russia, like Britain, was to be a 'country whose defence the President deems vital to the defence of the United States'.

By the end of the war the Soviet Union had received through Iran and, to a lesser extent, through the Russian ports of Archangel and Murmansk, more than 11.3 billion dollars worth of supplies from America and £428 million worth of supplies from Britain. These included 22,000 aircraft and 13,000 tanks. This aid was only a fraction of the Soviet Union's own war production. But no one knew in 1941 when the Soviet Union was going to be down to its last shell.

Placentia Bay

The first wartime meeting between Churchill and Roosevelt took place at Placentia Bay, Newfoundland, in August 1941, six weeks after Hitler's invasion of the Soviet Union and four months before Japan's attack on Pearl Harbor brought America into the war. At Placentia Bay Churchill and Roosevelt confirmed the joint arrangements which had been made already and – in what was meant to be a solemn statement of the Allies' war aims – they proclaimed and signed the Atlantic Charter.

This said that the Allies would 'seek no aggrandizement, territorial or other'; that they desired 'to see no territorial changes that do not accord with the freely expressed wishes of the people concerned'; that they respected 'the right of all peoples to choose the form of Government under which they will live'; 'that they would try to further the enjoyment by all States, great or small, victor or vanquished, of access, on equal terms, to the trade and to the raw materials of the world'; that they wished 'to bring about the fullest collaboration between all nations in the economic field, with the object of securing for all improved labour standards, economic advancement, and social security'; that after the final defeat of Nazi tyranny the Allies hoped 'to see established a peace which will afford to all nations the means of dwelling in safety within their own boundaries, and which will afford assurance that all the men in all the lands live out their lives in freedom from fear and want'; that the peace the Allies would establish 'should enable all men to traverse the high seas and oceans without hindrance'; and finally that the Allies believed 'that all the nations of the world, for realistic as well as spiritual reasons, must come to the abandonment of the use of force'. 'Since no future peace can be maintained', the Charter concluded, 'if land, sea or air armaments continued to be employed by nations which threaten, or may threaten, aggression outside of their frontiers, they believe, pending the establishment of a wider and more permanent system of general security, that the disarmament of such nations is essential'.

The Charter was a brave statement of impeccable intentions. Both Churchill and Roosevelt believed in what they had signed. They hoped that the Charter would bring encouragement to the peoples Hitler had enslaved. The other Allied governments, including the Soviet one, endorsed the Charter too. The Polish and Czechoslovakian Governments, who also signed the Charter and whose lands were to be dominated by the Russians, were putting their faith in nothing more serious than a piece of paper.

The Arcadia Conference

By the time Churchill and Roosevelt met again Japan had attacked Pearl Harbor and the United States had been at war for a fortnight. The Arcadia conference took place in Washington, lasted three weeks, and sealed the Anglo-American alliance by establishing a combined Anglo-American general staff. This important decision was inspired by the Chief of Staff of the United States Army, General George Marshall, one of the chief architects of the Allies' victory. From December 1941 until the end of the war the combined Chiefs of Staff, based in Washington, were responsible for all the Allies' main military decisions. The establishment of the combined Chiefs of Staff as a permanent institution for the duration of the war helped mightily to win it.

At Arcadia Churchill and Roosevelt also reaffirmed their joint determination to concentrate first on the defeat of Germany even though, only fourteen days before, Japan had annihilated the American Pacific Fleet at Pearl Harbor. In spite of this Roosevelt was steadfast. He did not abandon his European friends even though his country had just been stabbed in the back by the Japanese, and United States forces were in peril throughout a hemisphere. At Arcadia also the United Nations was conceived, though not born. Twenty-six governments endorsed solemnly the principles of the Atlantic Charter and promised that they would not make a separate peace with Hitler until the alliance had achieved total victory.

While Churchill and Roosevelt were re-endorsing the Atlantic Charter in Washington the British Foreign Secretary, Anthony Eden, was discovering in Moscow that the Russians had no intentions of respecting the Charter's solemn promise that the Allies would 'seek no aggrandisement'. Sir Alexander Cadogan, Eden's Permanent Under-Secretary of State, who attended the Moscow meeting, wrote in his diary[2] on 17 December 1941 that Stalin 'wants us, here and now, to recognize Russia's 1941 frontiers – i.e. including a bit of Finland, Baltic States and Bessarabia'. 'We told him', Cadogan continued, 'we couldn't do this (and he had given no warning of this requirement to us). Argued, inconclusively, till 3 a.m. and then left without anything settled'. On 20 December Cadogan records that it was 'pretty clear' that the Russians would sign no treaty with the Allies 'if we don't recognize their 1941 frontiers'. Even then, with the Germans at the gates of Moscow, Stalin had decided what the map of post-war Europe was going to look like. Russia would take eastern Poland, part of Rumania, and the Baltic States. Poland would take East Prussia. Germany would be partitioned. The British had been warned and the warning was accurate. All those frontier changes came to pass when the war was over.

The Russian Foreign Secretary, Molotov, travelled first to London and then to Washington partly to negotiate further about a treaty of assistance and about Russia's post-war frontiers but mainly to ask for the opening of a 'second front' in western Europe. Russia wanted her Western Allies to invade occupied Europe as soon as possible. From Russia's point of view this was a reasonable and indeed an urgent demand. The Germans were on the offensive in southern Russia, were about to launch a major offensive against the Caucasus, and were presently to besiege Stalingrad. The Soviet army was under heavy pressure. Anything that could be done to divert German resources would help.

But Molotov's request could not be met. In July 1942 the British Chiefs of Staff decided that even in 1943 a landing in France would be impossible. In August the disastrous failure of the Anglo-Canadian assault on Dieppe confirmed this gloomy view. The American Chiefs of Staff did not agree but they were over-ruled by Roosevelt. Roosevelt was, however, determined that the Western Allies should do whatever they could to relieve the pressure on the Russians. Churchill agreed with him. The result was a decision to invade north-west Africa. The decision was taken in July 1942. The landings were to take place in November. The Commander-in-Chief was to be Major-General Dwight D. Eisenhower.

In August Churchill went to Moscow to break the news to Stalin that there would be no second front in 1942 or in 1943 either but that there would be a landing in North Africa instead. It was an angry meeting. Stalin denounced the British army's 'cowardice'. Churchill retorted in what seems to have been a rage. But there was nothing that either of them could do to alter the military facts.

Casablanca

The next meeting between Churchill and Roosevelt was at Casablanca in Morocco on 14 January 1943. The landings in north-west Africa had succeeded and the campaign was going well.

It was the last campaign in which the British contribution was larger than the American. The armies which had invaded north-west Africa had been transported mainly in British ships because the Americans had not yet succeeded – as they were later to succeed brilliantly – in mass-producing the so-called Liberty ship. On land, too, the British effort still was bigger than the American one. This was one reason, probably the main one, why – for the last time at Casablanca – the British won an argument with the Americans. Marshall wanted to drive the Germans and Italians out of North Africa and then to invade France from Britain. Churchill had always wanted to attack occupied Europe from the south. Marshall thought that this would divert resources wastefully. Roosevelt overruled him. In any case the Allied armies in Africa could not be kept idle. It was decided to attempt both operations, but not simultaneously. Sicily was to be invaded from North Africa initially in order to safeguard the Mediterranean route but possibly also as a prelude to an invasion of Italy or southern France. In the meantime, America would build up her forces in Britain in preparation for a landing in northern France.

At Casablanca also, Roosevelt proclaimed the 'unconditional surrender' doctrine – the doctrine that Pershing, the American Commander-in-Chief, had urged upon the victorious Allies at the end of World War I. Pershing's aim had been to make it impossible for the German army to claim that it had never been defeated and had only been betrayed by politicians. Roosevelt's purpose may have been the same. 'Peace can come to the world only by the total elimination of German and Japanese war power', Roosevelt said. 'The elimination of German, Japanese, and Italian war power means the unconditional surrender of Germany, Italy and Japan'.

This statement has been criticized on the grounds that it left no room for a negotiated peace. In practice, the unconditional surrender doctrine made no difference. Before the end of the year the Italians had negotiated a peace settlement with the Western Allies and nobody even mentioned unconditional surrender. What mattered was that the Germans and the Japanese should surrender unconditionally, and in the end they did.

De Gaulle v. the Anglo-Saxons

The north-west African landings led to the angriest of many exhausting quarrels between the Free French leader, de Gaulle, and the British and Americans. In 1940 the United States had recognized the Vichy Government and maintained relations with it. De Gaulle regarded this as akin to treachery. When the British and Americans landed without his knowledge in what he regarded as French territory in north-west Africa he was furious. His fury grew when he learned that the Americans were anxious to come to terms with General Giraud, a former French army commander who had escaped from German captivity. De Gaulle suspected Giraud because he had taken over command of the Vichy forces in North Africa from the deeply suspect collaborationist Admiral Darlan, when the latter was assassinated on Boxing Day 1942. The Americans, whose chief and reasonable concern was to conquer north-west Africa as cheaply as possible, were prepared to collaborate with any Frenchman who did not actually attempt to bar their way. Unlike Churchill, whose dealings with de Gaulle had begun in 1940, Roosevelt does not seem to have anticipated de Gaulle's resentment at the very notion that any Frenchman except de Gaulle could speak for France.

Having come to terms with Giraud the Allies tried to bring him together with de Gaulle. De Gaulle sulked in London. He sulked until even Churchill, who understood better than anyone de Gaulle's need to protect the name of France, threatened never to have any personal dealings with him again. The quarrel over Giraud was a serious matter. The Vichy French forces in North Africa were numerous and their allegiance was in doubt. The British Foreign Office summarized Roosevelt's and Churchill's dilemma in a message to the Cabinet:

In accordance with the American policy, de Gaulle was not informed in advance of the North African operation. He deeply resented this treatment. In public, however, he rose to the ocassion well, made no reproaches, and on the evening of 8 November (the day of the landings) welcomed the Anglo-American action in a broadcast appeal to Frenchmen. The understanding with Darlan, the retention of Vichy elements and the continued persecution of de Gaullists disgusted him, but he held the Americans rather than ourselves responsible.

When Giraud succeeded Darlan on the 26 December, an early understanding between him and the National Committee (de Gaulle's supporters) seemed possible. The first step was to get the two generals to meet and the Anfa (Casablanca) conference provided a good opportunity for this. Accordingly the President and the Prime Minister invited both generals to meet them. Giraud agreed readily, but de Gaulle, although prepared for a meeting in principle (he had already suggested one to Giraud) did not want it to take place under Anglo-American auspices. He regarded his dealings with Giraud as a French internal matter and revolted at the idea of conducting them under outside pressure. He therefore made every sort of difficulty about going. He actually said: 'If the President wants to see me, I could always call upon him in America, nor could there be any invitation to me to meet anybody on French soil.' He only undertook the journey after the Prime Minister had threatened to throw him over if he did not. When there his behaviour was arrogant and intractable, contrasting badly with that of Giraud, and serious progress towards an agreement was rendered impossible. The President and the Prime Minister were much incensed by his conduct, and after his return the Prime Minister gave him to understand that he did not wish to have any more personal dealings with him, although HM Government would continue as before to treat with the National Committee.

During the protracted negotiations between de Gaulle and Giraud, which occupied March, April, and May, our relations with de Gaulle were again disturbed by the persistence of Free French propaganda against the French leaders in North and West Africa and against the policy of the United States. This caused protests to us from the United States Government, and it was difficult to convince the Americans that we were really unable to stop it, since de Gaulle remained dependent on us financially. Massigli (the French ambassador in London), to whom we made strong representations, deplored the propaganda but was powerless to stop it, and there is little doubt that those responsible acted with de Gaulle's approval. . . .[3]

De Gaulle was an extremely troublesome ally. There were many other rows. He felt deeply that his Free French forces and no one else ought to intervene to recapture French colonies dominated by Vichy. He wanted the Free French to liberate their own territory and their own country, even though they did not have the strength to do this. He was angry when the British invaded Vichy-held Syria and Madagascar because, as he saw it, they were interfering in the internal affairs of France.

De Gaulle's motives were noble, patriotic, and understandable – at least by Churchill. The elected government of France, unlike that of any other occupied country, had collaborated with the Germans. De Gaulle's overriding concern was to delete this stain, as he saw it, on French honour. He insisted at all times and even on the most awkward occasions that he and his Free French followers alone had the right to speak for France. Roosevelt never fully understood de Gaulle's motives. De Gaulle never forgave Roosevelt (or America) for this.

Cairo

Churchill and Roosevelt met again in Washington in May 1943 when they confirmed their joint decision to invade France from Britain in May 1944. In November 1943 they met again in Cairo at a conference which also included Chiang Kai-shek. It was really a conference between Roosevelt and Chiang Kai-shek. The British were more or less bystanders, although Churchill was dismayed to discover the extent of Roosevelt's faith in the Nationalist Chinese – a faith which Churchill did not share. The Cairo Conference accomplished very little apart from a final communiqué and a promise, never fulfilled, of an amphibious operation against the Japanese in the Bay of Bengal. But it was the prelude to the first of the two decisive conferences of the war in which all three major Allies – the United States, the Soviet Union and Britain – took part. From Cairo Churchill and Roosevelt flew to meet Stalin in Teheran. At Teheran in November 1943 and at Yalta in the Crimea in February 1945, these three men re-drew the map of eastern Europe and largely determined the future of the east European peoples.

By 1943 the probable fate of Poland had begun to trouble the conscience of the British Government. Britain had gone to war in 1939 with the honest intention of protecting Poland against German domination. This was the basis of Britain's understanding with the Polish Government in exile in London. But as the war proceeded it became more and more evident that when it was over Poland would not be liberated but would simply be dominated by Russia instead of Germany. Stalin had explained his intentions to Eden in Moscow in December 1941 when Russia was close to defeat. Now, in 1943, the Russian army was beginning to overcome the Germans. Stalin's intentions towards Poland had not changed.

In the meanwhile the bodies of 1,700 Polish officers had been found in mass graves in the forest of Katyn. The Germans said that they had been murdered by the Russians. The Russians said they had been murdered by the Germans. The Germans, this time, were probably right. The British Ambassador to the Polish Government in exile, Sir Owen O'Malley, told the Foreign Office in a moving despatch that the British Government must take into account the possibility that Britain's Russian ally had, in fact, murdered officers in the service of her Polish ally. The Polish Government in exile demanded an investigation by the Red Cross. Stalin severed relations with the London Poles. He had already released the surviving Polish prisoners of war captured by the Russian army in 1939 and had sent them via Iran to fight in the West.

Foreknowledge of Stalin's intentions towards Poland together with the news of Katyn troubled the minds of British diplomats as they prepared for the Teheran Conference. But they kept their misgivings to themselves. There was nothing that the Western Allies could do to prevent Stalin from dealing with Poland as he wished. Therefore there was nothing useful that the West could say.

The frontiers of post-war Poland were formally settled – in the absence of any Polish representative – at Yalta. But the decisions taken at Yalta had, in fact, already been accepted at Teheran. The western frontier that Stalin wanted for the Soviet Union was the one that he had negotiated with Ribbentrop in 1939. This is what he had told Eden in Moscow in December 1941. He said it again at Teheran. Neither Churchill nor Roosevelt argued. They also accepted the River Oder as Poland's western frontier with Germany.

Stalin told them, in effect, that he intended to move the western and eastern frontiers of Poland westwards towards Berlin and Warsaw respectively. The Poles would have to migrate westward and so would the Germans, whether they liked it or not. The casual diplomatic process by which several million Poles and several million Germans were made to migrate is described in a British Foreign Office Minute of a meeting between Churchill, Roosevelt, Stalin, Eden, Molotov, and officials at the Soviet Embassy in Teheran on 1 December 1943. Roosevelt wanted to know whether the Poles would be gaining as much territory in the west as they would be losing in the east. The Minute reads:

President Roosevelt asked if he might put a question. Did the frontier of East Prussia and the territory east of the Oder approximate to the size of the eastern provinces of Poland itself? Marshal Stalin said that he did not know and that it had not been measured. The Prime Minister (Churchill) suggested that the value of this land was much greater than the (barren and impassable) Pripet Marshes. It was industrial and it would make a much better Poland. We should like to be able to say to the Poles that the Russians were right, and to tell the Poles that they must agree that they had had a fair deal. If the Poles did not accept we could not help it. And here he made it clear that he was speaking for the British alone, adding that the President had many Poles in the United States who were his fellow-citizens. Marshal Stalin said again that if it were proved to him that any district were Polish, he would not claim it and here he made some shadowing on the map west of the Curzon line and south of Vilna, which he admitted to be mainly Polish. At this point the meeting again broke up and there was a prolonged study of the Oder line on a map. When this came to an end the Prime Minister said that he liked the picture, and that he would say to the Poles that if they did not accept it they would be fools, and he would remind them that but for the Red Army they would have been utterly destroyed. He would point out to them that they had been given a fine place to live in, more than 300 miles each way.

Marshal Stalin said that it would indeed be a large, industrial State. The Prime Minister said that it would be a State friendly to Russia. Marshal Stalin replied that Russia wanted a friendly Poland. The Prime Minister said to Mr Eden, with some emphasis, that he was not going to break his heart about this cession of parts of Germany to Poland or about Lvov. Mr Eden said that if Marshal Stalin would take the Curzon and Oder lines as a basis on which to argue that might provide a basis.

At this point Mr Molotov produced the Russian version of the Curzon line and a text of a wireless telegram from Lord Curzon giving all the place names. The Prime Minister asked whether Mr Molotov would object to the Poles getting the Oppeln district. Mr Molotov replied that he did not foresee any objection. The Prime Minister said that the Poles would be wise to take our advice. They were getting a country 300 miles square, and that he was not prepared to make a great squawk about Lvov, and (turning to Marshal Stalin) he added that he did not think that we were very far off in principle. President Roosevelt asked Marshal Stalin whether he thought a transfer of population on a voluntary basis would be possible. Marshal Stalin said that probably it would be. Here the discussion about Poland came to an end.[4]

After discussing the future of Finland the three leaders turned their attention to Germany. The future of Germany, unlike that of Poland, was not decided effectively and finally at Teheran but the principle of partition was accepted by Britain and the United States as it had already been accepted by Russia.

The British Foreign Office Minute records Roosevelt as having said that he thought Germany should be divided into five self-governing provinces and two United Nations trustee territories comprising the Ruhr and Saar in one territory and Hamburg, Kiel and the Kiel Canal in another.

. The Prime Minister [the Foreign Office Minute records] suggested that he might use the American idiom and say that the President had indeed 'said a mouthful' and that Mr Roosevelt's plan was a new one to him. In his opinion there were two things: one constructive and the other destructive. He had two clear ideas in his (the Prime Minister's) mind. First was the isolation of Prussia. What was to be done to Prussia after that was only secondary. Then he would like to detach Bavaria, Wurttemberg, the Palatinate, Saxony, and Baden. Whereas he would treat Prussia harshly, he would make things easier for the second group, which he would like to see work in with what he called a Danubian Confederation. The people of these parts of Germany were not the most ferocious, and he would like to see them live tolerably, and in a generation they would feel differently. South Germans were not going to start another war, and we would have to make it worth their while to forget Prussia. He did not much mind whether there were one or two groups, and he asked Marshal Stalin whether he would be prepared to go into action on this front.

Marshal Stalin said 'yes', but that he preferred a plan for the partition of Germany if Germany was to be broken up, something like the

President's plan which he preferred as being more likely to weaken Germany. When one had to deal with large masses of German troops one found them all fighting like devils, as the British and American armies would soon learn. The Austrians alone were different, and he described the way the Austrians surrendered. Germans were all the same. It was the Prussian officers that provided the cement. But fundamentally there was no difference between north Germans and south Germans: for all Germans fought like beasts. We should be careful not to include the Austrians in any kind of a combination. She (Austria) had existed independently and could do so again. So also must Hungary exist independently. After breaking up Germany it would be most unwise to create new combinations, Danubian or otherwise.

President Roosevelt said he agreed warmly. There was no difference between Germans, and Bavarians and Prussians were much the same. The Bavarians had no officer class, otherwise they were exactly like the Prussians, as the American troops had already discovered. The Prime Minister said that he did not wish to be represented as not in favour of the partition of Germany, but that if Germany were divided into a number of parts as suggested by the President, and these parts were not attached to other combinations, they would reunite. It was not a question of dividing Germany, so much as giving a life to the cut off bits and making them content not to be dependent on the greater Reich. Even if this were achieved for 50 years that would be a great deal.

Marshal Stalin said that it was important not to create dead States that could not be brought back to life. The Danubian combination would not be able to live and the Germans would take advantage of this by putting flesh on something that was only a skeleton and thus creating a new great State. Here he asked whether Hungary and Rumania would be members of any combination. He then reiterated his views about the advantages that this combination would present to Germany in the future. It was far better to break up and scatter the German tribes. Of course they would want to unite, no matter how much they were split up. They would always want to reunite. In this he (Stalin) saw great danger, which would have to be neutralized by various economic measures and in the long run by force if necessary. That was the only way to keep the peace. But if we were to make a large combination with Germans in it trouble was bound to come. We had to see to it that they were kept separate – that Hungary and Germans should not be coupled. There were no measures to be taken which excluded a movement towards reunion. Germans would always want to reunite and to take their revenge. It would be necessary to keep ourselves strong enough to beat them if they ever let loose another war.[5]

This was the rudimentary way in which the Allied leaders discussed – and later settled – the future of the eastern and central European peoples.

The decisions taken at Teheran altered the map of Europe but did not materially alter the course of the war. The Russians had first been promised a second front in 1942. Now they were to get one in 1944 when they would need it less badly. By December 1943 the Russians were probably, perhaps certainly, capable of defeating Hitler on their own and occupying the whole of western Europe. There is no evidence, however, that they actually intended to do this. Stalin wanted to defeat and dismember Germany. But he did not show any eagerness at Teheran or on other occasions to extend Soviet influence west of the line which later became known as the Iron Curtain.

The rooms occupied by the American delegation to the Teheran Conference were probably 'bugged' by the Russians. The Russians said that they had uncovered a plot to kill Roosevelt and his advisers in the American Legation. The Americans believed the Russians and moved into the Russian Embassy which was more closely guarded. The British did not believe in the plot. The British were probably right. The private deliberations of the Americans may well have been overheard by the Russians. It is unlikely, however, that if this happened it made any difference to the outcome of the Teheran Conference. Roosevelt was minded before he ever got to Teheran to let the Russians have their way in Eastern Europe.

Before, during, and after the Teheran Conference a rather more efficient piece of German espionage had enabled the German Ambassador in Ankara, von Papen, to frustrate a British plan to involve Turkey in the war on the Allied side. Von Papen's main agent in Ankara was the British Ambassador's valet. The British Ambassador, Sir Hughe Knatchbull-Hugessen, suspected nothing. His valet, known to the Germans as Cicero, had a key to the ambassador's safe. Von Papen received photographs of all the important despatches that Knatchbull-Hugessen received or sent. These included the minutes of the Cairo and Teheran Conferences as well as Foreign Office telegrams concerning Britain's desire to persuade Turkey to join the war against Germany. Von Papen shrewdly told the Turkish Government what was going on. The Turks, with equal shrewdness, decided to stay neutral until they were sure that the Allies were going to win. They joined the Allies in the end in the spring of 1945 when Allied victory was certain.

Quebec

After the conference at Teheran (and before the one at Yalta) Churchill travelled to meet Roosevelt at Quebec and then to meet Stalin in Moscow. The true motive for his first meeting at Quebec was probably economic. After five years of war Britain was close to bankruptcy. The country had reached its production limit and also its manpower limit. In September 1944 Churchill's first concern, whether he admitted it or not, probably was the maintenance after Germany had been defeated of American aid through lend-lease or by other means. Germany was not to be defeated for another eight months but even after that Britain would still need American help. Having endured a longer war than any other country except Germany Britain was badly in need of money, or at least of economic resources in some other form. Churchill hoped to secure them from Roosevelt by continuing the alliance in the Pacific war against Japan. He offered to send a British Pacific Fleet to help the Americans defeat the Japanese as soon as the war in Europe was over. The Americans did not need this. They had fought and had virtually won the Pacific war almost unaided. A so far unco-ordinated British contingent would have made their operations more difficult. Roosevelt nevertheless welcomed Churchill's offer. The US navy did not. The outcome was immaterial. The Pacific war was over long before the British could mount any important force in that ocean. The Quebec conference did, however, produce an Anglo-American agreement (of great significance) to convene conferences to discuss and organize the permanent structure of the United Nations as a peace-keeping organization and to set up a world monetary organization as well. Both conferences ensued, the first at Dumbarton Oaks and the second at Bretton Woods, and did much to influence post-war history.

In October 1944 Churchill went to Moscow to discuss eastern Europe with Stalin. The outcome was a formal carve-up. Churchill was then very probably in two minds about whether Stalin was a menace or not. 'It is by no means clear', A. J. P. Taylor has written, 'when Churchill's anti-Bolshevism came to the surface even in his own mind. With him one emotion easily eclipsed another, and affection for his "war-time comrade" Stalin was still strong'.[6] Churchill and Stalin came to a series of agreements about spheres of influence in Eastern Europe. Britain was to have '90 per cent' influence over the future of Greece. Russia was to have the main influence over the future of Bulgaria, Hungary, and Rumania. The future of Yugoslavia was left unclear, or at least undecided. Churchill and Stalin disagreed only about Poland. Poland's frontiers had been settled in effect at Teheran. What remained in doubt was the character of Poland's post-war Government. Churchill had a Government in exile sheltering in London. Stalin had another sheltering in Moscow. The London Government was mainly composed of anti-Communists. The Moscow Government consisted exclusively of Communists. Churchill tried to insist on free elections. Stalin prevaricated, but had no intention of allowing them. The two men parted having, in reality, agreed to disagree although neither would admit this.

Yalta

When Stalin, Roosevelt and Churchill met again at Yalta in the Crimea in February 1945 it was evident that the Russians were winning the war in eastern Europe whereas the Western Allies, checked in the Ardennes, were making slower progress. However, it was clear in any case that Hitler had been defeated. Only the defeat of Japan still seemed to be an open question; although the Japanese had been defeated already, no one was to know this.

At Yalta Roosevelt was eager to enlist the Russians' help in defeating Japan. He supposed, realistically, that the British Pacific Fleet when it came into being would not be able to give decisive help. He also believed, unrealistically, that Russian help could and would be decisive. He imagined that Russia and the United States could strike mortal blows at Japan – Russia from Vladivostok and America from the Philippines. The potential Russian threat to Japan was far less serious than Roosevelt supposed, if only because of the enormous length of the trans-Siberian railway and the difficulty of transferring armies and air force support units from European Russia to the Pacific coast. Roosevelt was nonetheless determined to secure a pledge of Russia's intervention in the war against Japan. He was anxious also to secure from Stalin a promise that Russia would join the United Nations. Stalin agreed to declare war on Japan as soon as he could after Germany had been defeated. In fact Russia declared war on 8 August 1945, two days after the first atomic bomb had been dropped on Hiroshima and six days before Japan surrendered. Stalin also agreed to join the United Nations. The first promise was empty. The second did not mean what Roosevelt had hoped it would mean. The United Nations had acquired an awkward member.

The main outcome of the Yalta conference, however, was a re-affirmation by all three Allies of the decisions taken at Teheran about Eastern Europe. By this time Churchill, like Roosevelt, had accepted Stalin's proposals for the future of Poland. He had no alternative anyway. By the time he returned to London from Yalta he was convinced, or had convinced himself, that they were in the best interests of the Polish people. Reporting to the British Cabinet on 19 February 1945 Churchill said:

So far as Premier Stalin was concerned he (Churchill) was quite sure that he (Stalin) meant well to the world and to Poland. He (Churchill) did not himself think that there would be any resentment on the part of Russia about the arrangements that had been made for free and fair elections in that country. On arrival in the Crimea he (Churchill) found that the situation had undergone an extraordinary change. In three weeks the Russian army had fought its way from the Vistula to the Oder; almost the whole of Poland had been liberated; in many parts of the country so reconquered the Russians had been warmly welcomed, and great cities had changed hands very nearly intact. In his discussions at the Crimea Conference he had been at pains at all times to press the policy that had been approved by the War Cabinet viz. a free and independent Poland, sovereign in her own territories; with a government more broadly composed than it had been, and with the principles of free and fair elections maintained. Whatever criticisms there might be of the arrangements that had been reached he felt no doubt that they were on any broad and statesmanlike view the best practicable and that they were truly in the interest of Poland. Premier Stalin, at the beginning of their conversations on the Polish question, had said that Russia had committed many sins [the word was so translated but the actual word used might have been crimes] against Poland, and that she had in the past joined in the partitions of Poland and in cruel oppressions of her. It was not the intention of the Soviet Government to repeat that policy in the future. He (Churchill) felt no doubt whatever that in saying that Premier Stalin had been sincere.

He (Churchill) had a very great feeling that the Russians were anxious to work harmoniously with the two English-speaking democracies. Premier Stalin was a person of great power in whom he (Churchill) had every confidence.[7]

Churchill went on to express his satisfaction at the way his Moscow agreement with Stalin about the Balkans was working. Under the agreement the Russians were to have a free hand in Bulgaria, Hungary, and Rumania while Britain had a free hand in Greece. Stalin honoured this agreement even to the extent of curbing the Greek Communists who were waging a moderately successful civil war against the British-supported Greek Government.

As regards Greece [Churchill reported to the Cabinet] the Russian attitude could not have been more satisfactory. There was no suggestion on Premier Stalin's part of criticism of our policy . . . the Prime Minister added that Premier Stalin had most scrupulously respected his acceptance of our position in Greece. He understood that the emissary sent to the USSR by the Greek Communists had first been put under house arrest, and then sent back. There had been no shadow of criticism in the Russian press at any time, and the conduct of the Russians in this matter had strengthened his view that when they made a bargain, they desired to keep it.

As far as Greece was concerned this was true. It was not true, however, of Poland. Stalin had no intention of allowing the Poles to choose their own government and they never did. The agreed term 'free elections' meant one thing to Stalin and something quite different to Churchill and Roosevelt.

Truman takes the Presidency

In April 1945 a decision taken almost casually at what had become by then a half-forgotten conference suddenly assumed world significance. In 1944 the American Democratic Party Convention had chosen a Missouri politician, Harry S. Truman, to be Roosevelt's running-mate in the presidential elections of November 1944. Roosevelt won easily; but on 12 April 1945, crippled as he had been for many years by polio and having led a great but independent-minded nation through twelve years of economic upheaval and war, Roosevelt died. Vice-President Truman, with very little apprenticeship to guide him, immediately assumed responsibility for America and for the war she was fighting. The Democratic Convention of 1944 had chosen casually but wisely. Truman guided the United States through some of the weightiest

H

decisions in its history. Within months of taking office he was to face the decision whether or not to drop the atomic bomb on Japan. In the meanwhile he was to face Stalin for the first time at the next major inter-Allied conference at Potsdam, a suburb of Berlin and the former home of the kings of Prussia.

Chapter 12

The Reconquest of Western Europe

The Allied invasion of Normandy from Britain on 6 June 1944 was the greatest amphibious operation of all time. The naval commander, Admiral Sir Bertram Ramsay (who had a fine English distaste for high-flown language) told some of his captains on 3 June that he was sorry about the superlatives but that this time they were true.

Overlord, the code name for the invasion, had to be different both in scale and character from any previous amphibious assault. The Germans then had 59 divisions stationed in France. Many of them, it is true, were below strength or of doubtful military value. On the other hand the rate at which the Allies could land troops was limited.

The original plan, conceived by General Sir Frederick Morgan, foresaw a simultaneous first-day landing by three divisions. Later, General Eisenhower, the Supreme Commander, and General Montgomery, the Field Commander, decided that a three-division front would be too narrow. The plans would have to be expanded so as to put five divisions ashore on the first day. This called for the accumulation of more landing craft which, in turn, led to the postponement of the Normandy landings by a month and rendered impossible the original plan for a simultaneous landing in the south of France.

The reason that Eisenhower and Montgomery wanted more men landed on the first day on a broader front was that in theory at any rate the Germans would be able to send reinforcements quickly to attack a landing force which, to begin with anyway, they would probably out-number. The danger was that the first Allied troops, however successfully they had conquered their bridgehead, would be overwhelmed before they could advance far enough inland to make room for their own reinforcements.

To guard against this possibility the Allied planners first mounted prolonged and heavy air attacks on the French communications systems.

They also arranged to build artificial harbours off the Normandy beaches to ensure that supplies would not be held up by bad weather. They devised a way of laying pipelines under the English Channel to hasten the supply of fuel.

The preparations were elaborate and meticulous. Although some of them went wrong – one of the artificial harbours was wrecked – the scheme worked. When the test came the Allies were able to reinforce their troops in Normandy more quickly by sea than the Germans were able to reinforce theirs by land; and this was the first essential condition for success.

The second was to keep the enemy guessing. The Germans were defending the whole coast of France. But it was essential that they should have no grounds for concentrating their troops more thickly in Normandy than elsewhere. Partly by imposing very strict security measures in Britain, partly by subterfuge, and partly because they were lucky, the Allies kept the Germans guessing till the end.

It was of course impossible to conceal from the Germans that the invasion would be launched sometime in 1944 somewhere on the coast of France. The invasion as such had been more or less publicly announced, and a large army had assembled in southern England. But by using the strictest censorship, extending even to diplomatic telegrams, the Allies succeeded in concealing completely its actual destination.

By this stage of the war Allied air superiority had made it impossible for the Luftwaffe to carry out systematic photographic reconnaissance over Britain, or indeed any air reconnaissance at all west of Kent. To the extent that the Germans expected the invasion to come in one place rather than another their expectations were based on hunches. Von Rundstedt, their Commander-in-Chief in the West and by now a Field Marshal, thought that the Allies would invade across the Straits of Dover because the distance at that point was shorter. He therefore fortified the coast of the Pas de Calais more strongly than any other sector. Left to himself he might not have fortified the other sectors at all.

But he was not left to himself. In January 1944 Hitler sent Rommel, also by now a Field Marshal, to take command of Army Group B in northern France and with orders to repel the expected invasion. Rommel foresaw correctly that the Germans would not be able to reinforce the invaded sector of the coast, wherever it was to be, at all easily or quickly. He appreciated, as von Rundstedt probably did not, that Allied air superiority over France had robbed the German army of mobility. The railways were being bombed. The roads were usable only by night. Rommel decided that von Rundstedt was living in the past and began vigorously to fortify all the beaches. Rommel believed that the period during which the Germans were most likely to defeat an invasion would be within forty-eight hours of the first landing. But he still did not know where the first landing would be.

The Allies put a good deal of effort into ensuring that his ignorance continued. During the spring of 1944 British intelligence baited several hooks and got several bites. Montgomery's headquarters were at Portsmouth but his command radio transmitter was some 100 miles to the east in Kent. This simple subterfuge was to help to confirm von Rundstedt in his mistaken view that the main Allied invasion would take place in the Pas de Calais. Dummy gliders were parked on aerodromes in southeast England, the only part of the country that German reconnaissance aircraft could photograph. Dummy landing craft were moored in southeastern harbours. Hints were dropped in places where the Germans would hear them about 'Army Group Patton', and its readiness to cross the Straits of Dover.

Thus misguided, the German commanders constructed a number of theories all of which were wrong in different ways. Hitler believed that the main invasion would be in the north into the Pas de Calais but that there would probably be a feint attack first in Normandy. Von Rundstedt stuck to his theory that it would be the Pas de Calais and the Pas de Calais only. Rommel agreed with Hitler's theory about a feint in Normandy but surmised that it would be a big one. At no time, however, did the Germans waver in their conviction that sooner or later there would be a major attack in the Pas de Calais region, or at any rate north of the Somme. To this end they kept their entire 15th Army in the Pas de Calais, idle but on guard, until well after the real invasion had started.

While the 15th Army was preparing to defend the Pas de Calais to the death and while the Luftwaffe was allowed to take the occasional peep at the Kentish airfields, the real invasion forces were being assembled in south-west England, south Wales, and the Southampton-Portsmouth area where the Luftwaffe could not penetrate.

As Rommel fortified the beaches with obstructions designed to stop landing craft, to blow up tanks, and to hamper the infantry, Montgomery and Eisenhower were changing their plans to meet the new hazards. Rommel's underwater obstacles lay between the high and low water marks. The danger was that if the landing was carried out at high tide a large number of landing craft might be lost. If, on the other hand, the landings were made at low water or at half tide so that engineers could clear a way through the obstacles (which they would then be able to see) the infantry would have to cross a wide stretch of open beach almost certainly under fire from the defenders. To meet this hazard Montgomery decided that the first assault should be carried out by tanks. But for this to succeed he needed a new kind of tank – a tank that would swim.

The man who provided it, Major-General Hobart, was one of Britain's most ingenious soldiers whose genius and delight was to teach old machines new tricks. His DD tank could propel itself through the water as well as on land. His flail tank carried a monstrous rotating carpet-beater on a frame ahead of its own tracks to detonate land mines harmlessly before the tank itself ran over them. Hobart also invented and produced a tank which could lay its own solid carpet of matting to give it traction over soft sand or clay. These were the strange new machines which, for the most part, broke through Rommel's defences on 6 June.

The chosen landing place was the bay of the Seine. If Rommel, von Rundstedt, and Hitler had been able to settle their differences and over-come their prejudices they would have realized that it was the only place on the coast of France where the Allies could have landed five divisions. The entrance to the bay, from Cape d'Antifer to the Point of Barfleur, is 58 nautical miles wide. The bay is clear of natural obstructions, except for the Saint Marcouf Islands near the western shore. The tidal streams are weak. Although the east shore from Cape d'Antifer to the mouth of the Seine is backed by commanding heights most of the land behind the beaches at the head of the bay where the landings were to take place, is comparatively flat.

In the spring of 1944 the Royal Navy began preparing the bay with an almost loving regard for the terrain on which the troops were to fight. The crews of midget submarines and commandos landed unobtrusively by night to inspect the defences and also to collect samples of sand and clay to guide General Hobart in his work of preparing the tanks. During the second half of May, motor torpedo boats (MTB's), working from Portsmouth, laid a series of minefields from Cape d'Antifer to the seaward end of the Seine entrance channel and another round the Point of Barfleur to prevent the German Navy from attacking the invasion force from Le Havre, from Cherbourg, or from other ports further up or down the Channel. The mines were adjusted to go active on 5 June, the date which had been set for the invasion. The MTB's had been laying mines undetected in enemy waters since 1941 and this time also the enemy never knew that the mines were there.

The final task was to clear a gap in the large German minefield which ran up the middle of the English Channel from south of the Isle of Wight to the meridian of Calais. Most of this field was about two years old. It had been laid in sections, each section representing one night's work by the German minelaying flotillas. There were gaps between the sections because the German minelayers had not been confident enough of their own navigation to resume work exactly where they had left off the night before. British coastal force flotillas, whose operational areas were all on the Continental side of the Channel, had discovered these gaps and had been using them ever since 1942. But the gaps were unmarked and none was more than a mile wide. This is wide enough for an MTB flotilla but not for an invasion force of 5,000 ships. The navy would have to make them wider.

This was a major operation which could not be done without the enemy's knowledge, or at least without the grave risk that the enemy would detect the mine-sweeping operation and draw the right conclusion from it. Moored mines, which these were, must be swept in daylight because once their cables have been cut they float to the surface and have to be sunk by rifle fire if they are not to become a drifting menace instead of a stationary one. The mine-sweepers were therefore obliged to start work during the afternoon of the day before the actual invasion. They swept ten broad channels from the assembly area off the Isle of Wight to the beach-head, arriving within sight of the French coast before dark. No one seems to have noticed them. Or if they were seen, no one drew the correct conclusion. This was the Allies' first piece of good fortune.

Ramsay could prepare the ground but he could not prepare the weather. The main requirements for the landing were that half-tide on the beaches should occur forty minutes after first light, that the cloud should not be so thick as to prevent bombing, and that the surface wind should not exceed 13-18 miles per hour so that the sea would be relatively smooth. The limitations were severe. The tidal requirement was met on only three days in each lunar month. The joker was the weather.

Ramsay's preparations had been favoured throughout most of May by a stable high pressure area over the Azores which had helped to keep the Channel weather calm and dependable. Eisenhower had chosen Monday 5 June for the invasion date, one of the three days when the tide would serve. But on 2 and 3 June the Azores high began to dis-integrate. Eisenhower's meteorologist, Group Captain Stagg of the RAF, advised a postponement.

The outcome of one of the Allies' mightiest operations of the war depended then upon the skill and judgment of Group Captain Stagg. It must, for him, have been a moment of appalling tension. Especially as the weather in Portsmouth was marvellous. The weather systems whose behaviour he was trying to predict were still hundreds of miles away over the Atlantic. But Stagg was right. By the evening of Sunday 4 June it was blowing hard in Portsmouth and the invading forces which had already sailed from the most distant bases in Scotland, Wales and the West Country, had to return to shelter in the face of a strong westerly. By Sunday night, however, the worst of the weather – the front – was passing Portsmouth. That evening Stagg promised Eisenhower five-tenths cloud for the night of Monday to Tuesday and a falling wind. Stagg expected that that would be the best weather of the week.

Wednesday's tide would be no good anyway. Eisenhower's choice then was to go on Tuesday or to wait three weeks. He went on Tuesday. During the night of 5–6 June he launched a first wave of 60,000 men onto the beaches, two parachute divisions, one of the biggest air operations of the war, and a final, elaborate, and successful attempt to deceive the enemy into expecting the invading forces to land north of the Somme.

Now that the time had come and the invasion was under way it was impossible for the Allies to pretend that 5,000 ships were not at sea. All night a sizeable force of aircraft to the north of Cape d'Antifer dropped 'window', small sheets of silver paper whose dimensions were multiples of the enemy's radar frequencies. 'Window' blankets reception by producing a magnified and misleading response. The purpose was to try to persuade the enemy that a large force of ships was proceeding under air cover to the east of Cape d'Antifer to invade from there and that the air force was trying to prevent its detection by radar. Below the aircraft about thirty small warships flew balloons to simulate the radar echoes caused by large ships, broadcast a stream of simulated radio traffic, and even 'waged sonic warfare' with loudspeakers. Similar deceptions were practised further north off Boulogne. There were concentrated bombing attacks on communications between Dieppe and Calais.

All these deceptions helped to cause uncertainty although Stagg's sure prediction of the weather may have helped most of all. His German opposite number in Paris, Major Lettau, had also noted the breakup of the Azores high. He also foresaw correctly that the weather would be impossible on the night of Sunday 4–5 June. On the strength of this report Rommel left his headquarters in Paris to spend the weekend at home with his family near Ulm. Lettau did not foresee, as Stagg had foreseen, that the weather would be better on Tuesday. On the Monday, even as the invading force was weighing anchors, Rommel's staff reported no indication of an imminent invasion although they admitted that there had been no air reconnaissance over any south British ports except Dover. The deceptions practised north of Cape d'Antifer also produced results. The German radar men said that their sets were being jammed. Late on Monday 5 June, as the ships and aircraft off d'Antifer were beginning their deceitful radio performance, Rommel's staff ordered the 15th Army to stand by to repel invaders. But the 15th Army was centred in the north of France, in the Pas de Calais. The invaders were indeed on their way, but to another place. The warning did not go to the German 7th Army, the one which was about to meet the invaders as they came ashore in the bay of the Seine in the morning.

For invasion purposes the south shore of the Bay of the Seine had been divided into five beaches. Reading from west to east their names were Utah, Omaha, Gold, Juno and Sword. The capture of Utah and Omaha was the responsibility of the 1st United States Army, commanded by General Omar Bradley. The United States 7th Corps, under General Collins, was to take Utah. The United States 5th Corps, under General Gerow, was to take Omaha beach.

The British and the Canadians, united as the British 2nd Army, were to take Gold, Juno and Sword. General Dempsey, commanding the 2nd Army, had assigned the British 30th Corps, under General Bucknall, to take Gold beach. The British 1st Corps under General Crocker was to occupy Juno and Sword beaches.

The first objective of the invading forces was to secure the bridgehead's two flanks by dropping troops from the air. The first forces in action were the 6th British Airborne Division on the eastern flank and the 101st and 82nd American Airborne Divisions on the western flank. The tasks of these three divisions were complicated, hazardous, but crucial. The 6th British Airborne Division, commanded by General Gale, had orders to capture the two bridges leading eastward from the bridgehead across two parallel water courses – a canal and the river Orne – which run north-eastward from the town of Caen to the sea near Ouistreham. The division was also required to destroy a German coastal defence battery at Merville close to the mouth of the Orne, to take possession of high ground east of the Orne and, if possible, to destroy the bridges in the next valley to the eastwards, that of the river Dives.

This intricate task had to be accomplished during the four hours between midnight and a June dawn. In spite of appalling difficulties (the 9th Parachute Battalion, assigned to destroy the Merville battery, found itself widely dispersed on landing) all these objectives were reached and achieved on time. It was an important, brave, and ingenious feat of arms in which the airborne troops, landing by parachute or in gliders in the darkness, lost many men. But by acts of daring they secured the eastern flank of the bridgehead against the first immediately expected threat – a counter-attack from the east by the 21st German Panzer Division which was known to be quartered in the area.

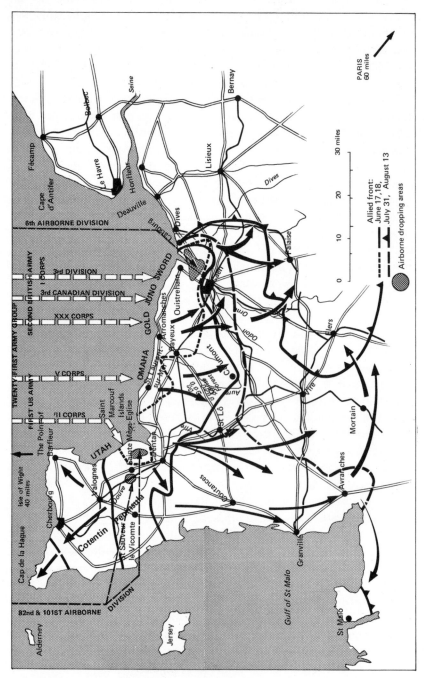

The Normandy Landings, June 1944

The American airborne landings on the right flank were not so neat. By dawn only about one sixth of the 101st American Airborne Division had reached their assigned positions. The 82nd Division was more nearly united but its gliders, carrying guns and jeeps, were widely scattered. The task for both divisions was to ensure that when the troops landed from the sea on Utah beach they would be able to move inland. The Germans had flooded a large area of country about eight miles inland comprising the valleys of the rivers Merderet, Douve, and Vire. There was another flooded area immediately behind the sand dunes which backed the beach and which stretched south-eastwards from Quineville to the Vire estuary, the southern extremity of Utah beach. The two airborne divisions were to seize the bridges and causeways which still spanned the flooded areas, so that the main landing forces would not be trapped on what would have amounted to an artificial island; but their success was only partial.

In the north the 82nd Division succeeded in capturing the important road junction at Sainte Mère Eglise on the main road from Cherbourg to Carentan and the rest of France. The 82nd failed, however, to secure the bridges over the Merderet river. Because the landings were so scattered the American paratroopers who actually reached their objectives west of the river were too few in number to seize the bridges in the face of stern opposition from the German 91st Division onto whose territory they had dropped.

The 101st Division was able to carry out all its tasks except for the destruction of the bridges across the Vire estuary and Carentan canal which runs parallel with it. The objective here was to hamper any counter-attack on the southern flank of Utah beach which might develop. But in spite of all mishaps the airborne landings – two American and one British – were a success, and an essential one. Without them the main landings would have fared very differently.

An extremely heavy naval bombardment of all the beach defences began shortly before the seaborne landings. Venerable battleships, cruisers, destroyers, and rocket-firing assault craft all joined in a precisely targeted firing plan.

The landing on Utah beach was the smoothest of the five partly because of the weather. Group Captain Stagg had said that the weather would be possible but had not promised a millpond. There was a brisk wind from the west which distressed the soldiers if not the sailors and which caused the leader of a German E-boat (MTB) flotilla based at Cherbourg to return to harbour. All Allied vessels, MTB's included, kept the seas. Utah beach, at the western end of the bay, was more sheltered than the others. In spite of the weather the landings went well on the three British and Canadian beaches at the eastern end of the bay. Only at Omaha beach did the invaders suffer what was very nearly a serious reverse.

There seem to have been several reasons for this. Omaha was a difficult beach in any case, being steeper than the others. It was more heavily defended than the Americans had expected. And, worst of all, most of the landings at Omaha were inaccurate so that the units landed in the wrong places. This was due partly to the weather but mainly to the US navy's decision to launch its assault craft from a position twelve miles from the coast instead of eight.

The naval bombardment was less effective at Omaha than elsewhere and several strong points and batteries which should have been put out of action were still firing when the men came ashore. The assault craft were under heavy fire for the last half mile of their approach. Once ashore the Americans were pinned down by continuing fire from at least two undemolished strong points. The 116th Infantry Regiment, leading the assault at the western end of Omaha, suffered heavy casualties. Some soldiers took cover in the sea. Others were drowned when their landing craft were hit and sunk or when they jumped overboard in deep water. Because of the firing, the demolition teams had not been able to work either, so that many underwater obstacles had not been cleared.

General Bradley was deeply anxious especially about the western end of Omaha.

> The 1st Division lay pinned down behind the sea wall while the enemy swept the beaches with small-arms fire. Artillery chased the landing craft where they milled offshore. Much of the difficulty had been caused by the underwater obstructions. Not only had the demolition teams suffered paralysing casualties, but much of their equipment had been swept away. Only six paths had been blown in that barricade before the rising tide had halted their operations. Unable to break through the obstacles that blocked their assigned beaches, craft turned toward 'Easy Red' [a beach further east] where the gaps had been blown. Then as successive waves ran in towards the cluttered beachhead they soon found themselves snarled in a jam offshore.[1]

At one time Bradley seriously considered diverting the follow-up forces destined for Omaha to other beaches. Faithful to Ramsay's plan, an unstoppable stream of soldiers and ammunition was arriving in the crowded sea off Omaha to reinforce a landing which had not yet been made effective.

During the forenoon, however, the survivors of the leading elements of the 1st Division began to make slow progress up the heights and off the beach. By nightfall after bitter fighting the 1st Division had occupied a beachhead one and a half miles deep and perhaps eight miles long. The 1st US Division was in France to stay.

Eisenhower's decision to assault the Utah beach in spite of its flooded hinterland paid off. The beach itself was comparatively lightly held. The assault forces made contact with one of their parachute divisions by early afternoon. By the evening more than 20,000 men had landed at Utah.

At Sword beach in the east the British 3rd Division tried but failed to capture Caen on the first day. Caen had been a town that Montgomery had hoped to capture at once, although his hopes were higher than his expectations. What beat the 3rd Division was that they found themselves opposed by a German Panzer Division in full working order before they had been able to land enough tanks of their own. The British knew that the 21st Panzer Division was stationed in the neighbourhood. What they did not know was that it was garrisoned in Caen itself. The King's Shropshire Light Infantry advanced boldly but mainly on foot and with minimal armoured support down the road from Hermanville towards Caen, but were stopped before they got there by elements of the 21st Panzer Division. However in spite of this the three British–Canadian bridgeheads had all been united by the evening of 6 June. Bayeux, Creully, Douvres and Ouistreham were all in Allied hands. Hitler's Atlantic wall had a hole in it.

The Allies' task now was to build up enough strength to break out from their bridgehead. The Germans' task was to contain them. The country was on the Germans' side. The 'Bocage', as that part of Normandy is called, consists of small fields divided by thick hedges growing on and binding together strong banks of earth. The lanes between the fields are sunken. The ditches around the fields are deep. It is country in which a bold defender can stay hidden until his adversary has approached to within yards. Tank crews could not manoeuvre freely. If they were able to move at all they could not see far enough to spot the German defences.

This country was being defended by a German army which was being reinforced steadily, albeit slowly. The French railwaymen had sabotaged their own railways. The bombing had done serious damage. Nevertheless the Germans soon had three Panzer divisions in Normandy and were gathering infantry from all over France. The Germans decided – as Montgomery had hoped they would – that the main threat to their position would come from the eastern end of the bridgehead. Once the Allies were past Caen and out of the Bocage they would have a clear run across territory that suited tanks and extended all the way to Paris. The Germans' first concern was to protect Caen from the British 3rd Army.

Meanwhile the Allies strove hard to make their bridgehead continuous. They achieved this on 12 June when the 101st American Airborne Division captured Carentan, which commands the estuary of the Vire. This closed the last gap in the Allied front – the one between Omaha and Utah beaches. 'On our seventh day ashore', Bradley wrote, 'we had linked the Allied forces together in a beachhead 42 miles wide. We would now force our way across the Cotentin [Peninsula], then choke it off and capture the port of Cherbourg'.[2] The Americans captured Cherbourg on 27 June and the Allies had gained their first port.

Although Cherbourg had been extensively sabotaged and mined by the Germans and proved to be less useful than had been hoped its gain was nevertheless a relief to the Americans. The American artificial harbour off Saint Laurent had been destroyed by a gale on 21 June. The commander of the American 7th Corps which took Cherbourg, General Collins, developed a hedgecutter for fighting in the Bocage on his way north up the Cotentin Peninsula. Compared to the jungles of Guadalcanal (which is where this formidable soldier had been before) the Bocage was pleasant, open country.

The bridgehead, though secure, was strongly encircled. The Germans had recognized by now that once the Allies broke out of it there might be no holding them anywhere in France. United now in the conviction that the Normandy beachhead was the real thing, the main invasion, Hitler, Rommel and von Rundstedt reinforced their besieging divisions as fast as the ruined French railways would allow. At SHAEF (Supreme Headquarters Allied Expeditionary Forces) Eisenhower and others became uneasy. They began to fear that the Allied armies might become penned into a bridgehead already full to bursting point with supplies for the advance that had not yet happened. Because it had not yet happened some members of Eisenhower's staff (notably General Morgan, who had conceived the original plan, and Eisenhower's Deputy, Tedder) were openly critical of Montgomery. They believed that he was being over-cautious. There were even suggestions that he ought to be relieved. An ugly fog of misunderstanding (to put it mildly) drifted between SHAEF in England and the commanders in the field.

It seems likely that Eisenhower, and perhaps Tedder also, never fully comprehended Montgomery's plans at the time. Had they understood them they might not have agreed with them. But these were, in fact, the plans that the invading forces followed, and with proud success.

Most American generals believed that in most military situations the right time to attack was always and that the right place to attack was everywhere. Montgomery's general belief was more subtle. He was a consistent seeker-out of weak places in the enemy line. If no weak place existed Montgomery would try to create one. Time and again he would tempt his opponent to reinforce one part of his line at the expense of another. Montgomery would then attack the weaker part. He had done this at Alamein and had prevailed. He was doing it again in Normandy, and was about to prevail.

He wanted first to trick or persuade the Germans into reinforcing the eastern end of their besieging line at the expense of the western end. He planned to keep the best German units busy at Caen so that the Americans, on the right, could carry out a swift encircling movement against light resistance. Montgomery was consistent about this. He refused to abandon his plan even under considerable pressure from his superiors.

Probably the most important outcome of the Allies' operations during the seven and a half weeks that they were in the Normandy bridgehead – more important even than the capture of Cherbourg – was the heavy over-concentration of German strength, induced by Montgomery, at the eastern end of the line. The day before General Collins began his success-ful breakthrough in the west, seven German Panzer divisions and four heavy tank battalions were facing the British armies at the eastern end of the bridgehead. Only two Panzer divisions and one division of Panzer grenadiers were in a position to meet the main American attack in the west. The tactical situation which Montgomery set up for Collins was as favourable as he could make it.

It was much more favourable than the one which had faced the Ameri-cans when they first tried to capture the communications centre of Saint Lo at the base of the Contentin Peninsula during the first half of July. After suffering heavy casualties in the Bocage, the Americans were in Saint Lo on 18 July but could get no further. On the same day the British 8th Corps under General O'Connor, back on duty after his escape, advanced southwards on the east side of Caen in an attempt to take the heights to the south-east of the town. It was a very heavy attack and had been preceded by a very heavy aerial bombardment of the German positions. Partly because the bombing had not obliterated all the German defences, partly because the area for manoeuvre was restricted, the attack did not gain all the hoped-for objectives. What it did, however, was convince the Germans that the British and the Canadians now constituted a direct and immediate threat to the whole area between Caen and Paris. The Germans, therefore, did not dare to weaken their defences east of Caen.

The Germans' best troops were still there, in the wrong place, seven days later when 2,400 Allied bombers dropped 4,000 tons of bombs close to Saint Lo to open the road south for the Americans.

Collins began his main attack on 26 July. By 1 August the Americans had cleared the whole of the Contentin Peninsula as far as Avranches; and south of Avranches there was nothing much to stop them. The American 8th Corps was sent to capture Brittany, which it did in less than a week. The main force drove south to Le Mans and then east. Generals Patton, whose forces were in the lead, Bradley and Montgomery agreed that the chances of encircling large numbers of the enemy at Falaise were now good and that it would also be worth trying to trap those that escaped in a second encirclement on the Seine.

Hitler helped them by ordering a forlorn German counter-attack westwards towards Mortain. The attack not only failed, it ensured that more German troops were further from safety than would otherwise have been the case. The Mortain attack may have ensured, finally, that the Germans would be driven out of France.

General Crerar's 1st Canadian army attacked from the north towards Falaise and reached it on 16 August. The Canadians in the north and the Americans in the south were then only fifteen miles apart. The gap between Falaise and Argentan was closed on 20 August. 50,000 German troops were trapped inside the so-called Falaise pocket. Those who escaped – mainly the remnants of the 5th and 7th Panzer Armies – made their way north-east towards the Seine, hoping to hold a line there. But Patton had reached the Seine before them. Those Germans who got across had to leave virtually all their equipment behind. The Allies had not just broken the siege which had kept them in their beachhead since 6 June, they had also captured some of their most resolute besiegers.

One month before the Allies reached the Seine a group of German army officers had tried to kill Hitler. On 20 July 1944 they left a time bomb in his eastern headquarters. The attempt failed and its immediate consequence was to strengthen Hitler's position. There was some public sympathy for Hitler and a good deal of wonderment at his escape. Rommel was one of the generals who had been approached by the plotters. On 20 July he was in hospital, having received wounds three days earlier when his car was machine-gunned by Allied aircraft. He never returned to the front. In October he was offered the choice between

52. A Japanese plan of Pearl Harbor, raided 7 December 1941

53. A small boat rescues a seaman from the *West Virginia* during the Japanese raid on Pearl Harbor

54. The light cruiser *Helena* belches smoke following a torpedo hit during the Pearl Harbor raid

55. A Marine gives cover while men from the Medical Corps tend to a wounded soldier during the attack on Eniwetok Atoll, Pacific, 1944

56. The USS *Hornet* from which in 1942 Col. Doolittle led the first strategic bombing attack on Japan using B25 Aircraft

57. Landing operations on Rendova Island, Solomon Isles, 1943, as the Americans go in for a dawn attack in heavy rain

58. A Japanese suicide plane attacks an American ship; Pacific, 1945

standing trial along with the other conspirators before a people's court or of taking poison. He took the poison. Hitler had shot his own best pianist.

From early July onward the German commander in the west was Field Marshal von Kluge, von Rundstedt having been sacked. But von Kluge agreed with von Rundstedt and Rommel that retreat was the only course open to the German armies in France. Hitler insisted on a firm stand. On 18 August he sacked von Kluge. Von Kluge wrote Hitler a letter urging him to end the war immediately and then committed suicide.

His successor was General Model who at last succeeded in persuading Hitler to see sense. Model had made mistakes in his time (notably at the tank battle of Kursk against the Russians) but he did not mind standing up to Hitler and he was a generally competent and popular general. Hitler was going to need him badly.

Model had scarcely taken over before the Allies landed in the south of France. On 15 August one French and three American Divisions commanded by the American General Patch landed without much difficulty at Saint Tropez on the French Riviera. Two days later the main German forces in the south of France were ordered to retreat northward. Resistance continued, particularly in the ports of Toulon and Marseilles; but in most directions, and particularly northward, the Allies' progress was swift. By 3 September they had captured Lyon and on the 11th they had joined forces with Allied troops driving east from Brittany. The advance from the south ended temporarily in the Vosges mountains, partly because the Germans had decided to defend them, partly because Patch had run out of supplies.

The northern invaders had also been on the move. Once they were across the Seine there was little that Model could do to stop them until they, too, ran short of supplies. First, however, the Allies were obliged to take Paris. Eisenhower, who had now (by previous arrangement) replaced Montgomery as the Field Commander of all Allied troops, had intended simply to by-pass Paris in order to spare lives and because he considered that the German garrison was impotent and could safely be left alone until later. Eisenhower's plans did not, however, suit those of the Paris Liberation Committee – the capital's Resistance Organization – which was preparing to liberate its own city in an armed uprising on 17 August. By this time General Patton was already east of Paris. General de Gaulle asked that the 2nd Free French Division under General Leclercq should be sent to help take the city lest the Paris Resistance Movement should be wiped out by the remaining Germans. The German Military Governor, General von Choltitz, disregarded Hitler's

orders (which were to destroy Paris if he could not defend it) and surrendered to Leclercq on 24 August. De Gaulle entered his country's
capital in triumph on 25 August.

Meanwhile, the main Allied armies were racing north-eastwards
towards Germany. On the left the Canadians seized all the channel ports
except Dunkirk. Further inland, Montgomery headed straight for
Antwerp. This was the port which the Allies were going to need because
it was big enough to handle all their supplies. The British captured
Antwerp undamaged on 4 September, although the Germans still held
positions on the banks of the River Scheldt which prevented Antwerp's
immediate use.

On Montgomery's right the American 1st Army captured Liége on
7 September and Luxembourg three days later. Further south Patton
and Patch were threatening Metz and Nancy. The speed of the advance
had been sensational. The Allies were now several months ahead of
their own forecast timetable. But they had come close to the main defences
of Germany itself, the first thoroughly prepared defensive positions they
had encountered since they crossed the Normandy beaches. Moreover
Antwerp was not yet open to traffic and most of their supplies still had
to be hauled in lorries all the way from Normandy to the front. General
Bradley had the additional task of feeding the Parisians.

As the Allied advance gathered speed and force so did another debate
between the Allied generals. Eisenhower had always intended to advance
into Germany on a broad front. He wanted all his armies to keep in step
with one another. Montgomery favoured a concentrated thrust on the
left of the front. He argued that the Germans had a long front to defend,
that they did not have the forces to defend it at every point against a
really heavy attack, that the place to deliver such an attack would be
the northern end of their line where the German fixed defences were
non-existent or feeble, and that the soldiers to do the job were those
serving in the British 21st Army Group under his, Montgomery's,
command. General Bradley's 1st US Army was to be at his side. Montgomery contended that the Germans were now short of fuel, transport
and air cover, that they would need time to recover, and that if the Allies
by a strong thrust could surround and neutralize Germany's industrial
base in the Ruhr it should be possible to shorten the war considerably
or even to win it by Christmas.

A different alternative to Eisenhower's plan to have all the armies
advance in step until they reached the west bank of the Rhine together,
was to hold Montgomery back in the north and allow General Patton to
advance in the south. This (naturally) was what Patton wanted to do.

Eisenhower, sitting in the chairman's chair, knew that he did not have enough fuel to allow both Montgomery and Patton to advance simultaneously. He also knew that both generals would fight hard for their own proposals. The chairman's chair became a hot seat.

Politics came into the decision too. The Americans were by now providing and sustaining the largest proportion of the Allied effort in western Europe. Patton was a national hero in the United States (besides being an immensely able general). The popular judgment of Montgomery (which was superficial and was based on his tactics at Alamein and in the beachhead) was that he tended to be over-cautious. This was not true, as his swift advance to Antwerp was to show. What was true, however, was that Montgomery's relations with some of his American colleagues – Bradley probably excepted – were distant and sometimes bad. The American generals combined efficiency with matiness. Montgomery combined it with asceticism. The Americans found Montgomery a difficult man to understand.

Eisenhower, who owed loyalty to his own generals as well as to the whole Allied cause, probably could not have given Montgomery the fuel and held Patton back even if he had wanted to. (Patton would probably have stolen it.)

In the end Eisenhower compromised. Under his original broad-front plan the British and the Canadians were to have advanced through Belgium and Holland between the Ardennes forest and the sea. All remaining forces were to have advanced south of the Ardennes. Eisenhower's compromise was to send the 1st US Army north of the Ardennes at Montgomery's side, thereby reinforcing the northern drive as Montgomery had suggested, but to insist also that there would be no immediate attempt to envelop the Ruhr.

It was not a bad compromise. For one thing it almost certainly enabled the 21st Army Group to capture Antwerp sooner than would otherwise have been possible. And at this stage Antwerp was the Allies' most important objective by far. While the main body of the British troops were being welcomed in carnival in the streets of Brussels the 11th Armoured Division was making its way swiftly, and less obtrusively, towards Antwerp.

The Fall of Antwerp

The 11th Armoured Division was able to capture the Port of Antwerp intact partly, perhaps mainly, because of the courage and ingenuity of a

Belgian resistance man, a civil engineer called Robert Vekemans. He had been an engineer lieutenant in the Belgian Army. In 1945 he was employed by the Belgian 'Ponts et Chaussées', the public works department. He had a special pass to enable him to do his work which also enabled him to move freely around Antwerp. Alastair Hetherington, who was an officer with the 11th Division, and later editor of *The Guardian*, has described what Vekemans did for the Allied cause:

> Robert Vekemans, illegally listening to the B.B.C. in his flat in Antwerp, learned on the afternoon of 3 September that the British forces were already close to the Belgian border. He deduced, correctly, that they were probably across it. In fact, the leading tanks and armoured cars had crossed near Tournai at about that time.
>
> He had a brief meeting with the harbour master, whom he knew well. He learned that the Germans had called for pilots and crews for five block ships, which were to sail if possible by the first tide next day to be sunk across the harbour entrances in the River Scheldt. He told the harbour master that a delay of even one tide (12 hours) could be vital and he suggested that it would be useful if the pilots failed to arrive in time. Fail they did, and the block ships were never put into position.
>
> Vekemans then left the city at about 5 p.m. using the tram to the town of Boom, about seven miles south of it. Again he had correctly deduced that this was the line of advance likeliest to be taken by the Allies, because a direct approach from the west would put them the wrong side of the Scheldt, which is more than half a mile wide at Antwerp.
>
> On leaving the city he observed that the German guns, barbed wire, and minefields were manned on the defence belt to the south but that the last mines had not yet been laid to block the road. Farther out, at Boom, there was another defence belt. Here the main road crossed the River Rupel, a major tributary of the Scheldt.
>
> The great bridge across the Rupel, here about the width of the Thames at Westminster, again had guns, wire, mines and booby traps to defend it; and 200 yards further south, across a canal, German infantry were dug in along the forward defence positions.
>
> Having taken a final look at the Germans on the main bridge – and been chased off by a guard – Vekemans walked about 400 yards up the Rupel to another, smaller bridge. This was wide enough only for one vehicle and was in poor condition, but the Germans themselves were still using it. He found it less well guarded, though demolition charges

were in position. He also noted that the electric cable leading to the charges in the centre of the bridge ran from a defended villa on the bank and had been tied to the bridge's balustrade. Although again challenged by a guard, he was able to show his official pass and talked the soldier into letting him walk across the bridge.

His reconnaissance completed, Vekemans walked on to the village of Willebroek, two miles or so farther south. Here he collected his bicycle, which he had previously left at the house of a shipyard worker (a former corporal in his engineer unit). He then bicycled in the dusk to his mother-in-law's house, which was not far away. He spent the night there, again listening to the B.B.C., and at dawn on Monday bicycled back to the main road south of Boom. . . .

Only after dawn on Monday, 4 September, did the first tanks turn northwards towards Antwerp. At about that time Vekemans had placed himself in a cafe beside the main road. Its shutters were closed, but he persuaded the proprietor to open one window where he could watch the road from the south. He expected a long wait. But, to his astonishment, only half an hour after he had settled down he saw a column of tanks coming up from the south.

He had chosen his place after carefully calculating the field of view from the forward German positions. If his plan was to work, however, he had to stop the leading tanks before they moved onwards to where the German defenders south of Boom could see them. Could he stop the tanks? He was not sure.

He stood in the road with his arms raised up – a lonely civilian figure in a grey mackintosh. The first tank was coming rumbling up quickly, its turret closed. It was covered by the guns of two more tanks behind. It refused to stop, by-passing Vekemans and moving on.

The second tank slowed down, and its commander stuck his head out and pointed back to the fourth in the group. This, in fact, was the Squadron Leader's tank – that of Major John Dunlop, of the Third Royal Tanks. Dunlop, dark and bearded, gestured with his pistol that Vekemans should climb up and say what he had to say. . . . Vekemans was convincing. He immediately asked Dunlop to stop the advance of the leading tanks, before the Germans could sight them. Then, speaking in English, he quickly told Major Dunlop what lay ahead. More than that, he put forward a plan. He said that if the tanks drove straight up the road the defenders at Boom would see them, the bridge would be blown, and they would come under heavy fire.

Instead, he suggested, they should turn off by a small side road. He

would guide them if they were willing. About 400 yards upstream
from the main bridge, he said, there was the smaller bridge. Why not
try that first? He believed that it could be rushed. . . .

Vekemans had the kind of quiet determination that is convincing,
and he had given a detailed account of what lay in front. So while
some of the regiment waited, John Dunlop's squadron turned off.
Vekemans was put in a scout car and led the way.

They went, as he suggested, down a rather dusty side road and
through the village of Willebroek. They crossed the canal in Willebroek
leaving three tanks to guard the crossing. The other turned north,
along the canal bank; and a thousand yards from the lesser Rupel
Bridge, they stopped behind a factory wall. There the leading tanks
turned their guns to face backwards and put camouflage nets over their
British markings. There, too, they were given their final briefing by
Vekemans.

Three tanks then went ahead with Lieutenant Gibson Stubbs in
the lead; Vekemans followed close behind in the scout car; and John
Dunlop was behind him. The tanks went flat out for the bridge,
kicking up as much dust as possible. Vekemans says that he was
scared stiff by the noise and dust, and by the expectation of being
shot at. He thinks that they must have been going at about 50 miles
per hour, although in truth the tanks cannot have exceeded 30 to 35
miles per hour. He does not know how the scout car driver managed
to follow so closely.

The ruse worked. The German soldiers beside the bridge thought,
in the dust, that these were German tanks retreating. The first
tank was across the bridge and into the houses on the far side before
a shot was fired. The second and third, as soon as they were across,
opened fire on the defended villa and on the soldiers round the
bridge.

Vekemans in the scout car wanted to stop in the middle of the
bridge; the scout car driver didn't. As they passed it Vekemans seized
him by the collar shouting: 'Stop, I must destroy the wire'. The scout
car stopped; Vekemans jumped out, carrying a big knife that he had
borrowed beforehand from the driver. With machine gun fire now
coming from both sides of the bridge, and with the fear that the
bridge would blow up at any moment, Vekemans sliced through the
wire in two places.

He then ran back to where the demolition charges were, to make
sure there was no hand primer. (As an engineer officer, concerned
with demolitions in 1940, he knew what to look for.) Having found

none, he returned to the scout car which quickly joined the tanks on the north shore.[3]

Having gained the further bank the tanks turned downstream to capture the main bridge intact. From then on, guided by Vekemans, British tanks were able to race through the streets of Antwerp to the main lock gates and sluices. They had no detailed maps because they had been advancing so fast through France that they did not yet have them. But with Vekemans and other resistance fighters to guide them, they had captured the port of Antwerp by the evening. And it was undamaged. The Allies now had a usable major port, but could not use it. Elements of the German 16th Army, by-passed in the Channel ports by Montgomery, held on firmly to positions on both sides of the estuary of the Scheldt which connects Antwerp with the North Sea. The Scheldt remained impassable till the end of November.

On 17 September Montgomery launched a new assault from the territory he had won in north-east Belgium. The fixed defences that the Germans had prepared did not extend into the Netherlands. Montgomery proposed to outflank them and to cross the Rhine over the Dutch bridge at Arnhem; but he had two other rivers to cross before he could get there – the Meuse (or Maas as it is called in the Netherlands) at Grave and the Waal at Nijmegen. He planned to have the British 30th Corps drive straight up from one river-crossing to the next and then on to the Zuider Zee (or Ijsselmeer, as it is now called). He would then have isolated the German 16th Army which had been cut off in the Pas de Calais by the British advance from the Seine to Brussels and had since begun to make its way by ferry across the Scheldt and into western Holland. In addition the 21st Army Group would have crossed the Rhine, would have outflanked the main German defences, and would be in a position to swing right and envelop the Ruhr. It was a big prize and worth a big effort.

The main difficulty was that the ground between Belgium and Arnhem was marshy, intersected by canals, and for practical military purposes impassable except along a single road. The drive could not begin until the 30th Corps could depend upon being able to use the road and the bridges which carried it across the Meuse, the Waal, and the Rhine. At first three and later four airborne divisions were assigned to capture and hold these and other essential bridges in the biggest airborne operation of the war. The American 101st Airborne Division landed south of the Meuse after penetrating heavy anti-aircraft fire. The 101st managed to capture intact all but one of its target-bridges and secured the route from the

Meuse south to Eindhoven. The American 82nd Airborne Division secured the crossing of the Meuse at Grave but could not at first capture the crossing of the Waal which was protected by the heavily fortified town of Nijmegen. 30th Corps, led by the Guards Armoured Division, set forth up the road from Belgium to Eindhoven and on to Nijmegen. The Germans attacked ferociously from both sides of the road. But by 21 September, after a joint attack by the American paratroopers and the British Guards Division tanks, Nijmegen was in Allied hands and Montgomery had a bridgehead north of the Waal.

The third of the three parachute divisions – the 1st British – had been dropped at Arnhem, the furthest target. It also proved to be the best defended. The advance guard of the division was able to assemble comparatively quickly in its chosen dropping zone about six miles west of Arnhem and to the north of the Rhine which, at this point, flows from east to west. Unfortunately, however, some of the division's gliders, including most of those carrying armoured jeeps to be used against the bridge defences, did not arrive.

There were two bridges across the Rhine at Arnhem, a railway bridge to the west of the town and a road bridge leading straight into the town itself, which lies on the northern bank of the river. As the 2nd Parachute Battalion approached the town from the west the railway bridge was blown up. By the time they had reached the northern end of the road bridge a strong German detachment had established a position at the southern end. The Germans had artillery. The parachutists had none.

While the 2nd Battalion and the Germans confronted each other from either end of a bridge that they both coveted, but which neither could capture, the rest of the division was becoming more and more heavily engaged west of the town. The British parachutists had been unluckier than they knew. They had landed within two miles of the headquarters of General Model, the man best qualified to organize counter-attacks. Had they landed two miles further east they might have captured Model himself, who, as Commander-in-Chief, immediately took personal charge himself of the defence of Arnhem. The forces at his disposal were stronger than the parachutists knew; and they were closer.

Two SS Panzer Divisions, the 9th and the 10th, had been ordered into Holland. So had a large number of German airmen. (By then the Luftwaffe was seriously short of fuel and although this was generally to the Allies' advantage because the planes were grounded it also meant that the airmen could fight on the ground.)

The landing at Arnhem was gallant but in vain. The 2nd Parachute Battalion, though isolated, held the northern end of the road bridge

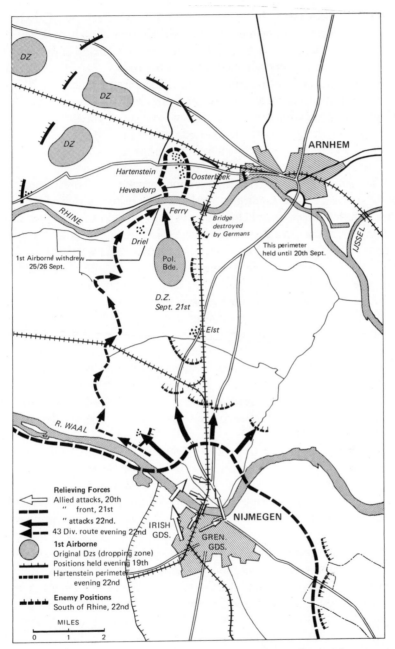

DZ

DZ

DZ

ARNHEM

Hartenstein

Oosterbeek

Heveadorp

RHINE

Ferry

Bridge
destroyed
by Germans

Driel

This perimeter
held until 20th Sept.

IJSSEL

1st Airborne withdrew
25/26 Sept.

Pol.
Bde.

D.Z.
Sept. 21st

Elst

R. WAAL

Relieving Forces
Allied attacks, 20th
  "   front, 21st
  "   attacks 22nd.
43 Div. route evening 22nd

IRISH
GDS.

NIJMEGEN

GREN.
GDS.

1st Airborne
Original Dzs (dropping zone)
Positions held evening 19th
Hartenstein perimeter
  evening 22nd

Enemy Positions
South of Rhine, 22nd

MILES

0   1   2

Arnhem, September 1944

against the heaviest odds for four days until the afternoon of the 20th when they were overwhelmed. During all this time they had denied the Germans the use of the bridge to carry reinforcements southward to counter the Guards division's advance up the road.

The rest of the British airborne division suffered cruelly too. Heavily besieged in their perimeter west of the town, their position was hopeless. Montgomery ordered them to withdraw southward across the river on the night of the 25th-26th. Only 2,400 men out of 9,000 got away, in boats. An attempt by the Polish airborne brigade to come to their help was delayed by bad weather. The Poles arrived too late.

The planning of the Arnhem operation, though not its execution, has been criticised with hindsight. Perhaps the British airborne division should have landed troops close to both ends of both bridges instead of landing in a concentrated group some distance away from their real targets. There were also communication failures. The weather interfered badly with support operations. But the attempt was bold and gallant and the prize was worth winning. The Rhine was still the main barrier between the Allied forces and the heart and homeland of the Germans. Arnhem would have been a good place to cross it. As it was, the Allies had reached Nijmegen and had driven a wedge nearly 60 miles deep into the German lines. But they still had one more river to cross – the big one.

The Allies' failure to capture Arnhem was not really relevant to the main strategic dispute between Eisenhower and Montgomery. Montgomery had not, in fact, needed more than his share of scarce supplies. Nor would he have had room to use them. But the generals' debate was, and still is, unfinished.

Both before and after Arnhem Montgomery maintained that what had been needed was a really strong thrust into north-west Germany or a really strong thrust elsewhere sustained by all the supplies that the Allies could muster during the autumn of 1944. He never concealed from Eisenhower his conviction that the broad-front strategy was wrong.

The proper development of Allied strategy north of the Seine [Montgomery said] will become one of the great controversies of military history. In the end it was the Germans who benefited from the argument. At the time I was, and I remain, of the opinion that in September 1944 we failed to exploit fully the German disorganization consequent on their crushing defeat in the Battle of Normandy in August. The quickest way to end the German war was not merely to have the free use of Antwerp, as some have alleged. It was to act quickly in the middle of August using the success gained in Normandy as a springboard for a hard blow which would finish off the Germans and at the same time give us the ports we needed on the northern flank. To do these things we had to have a plan and concentration of effort; we had neither. I am still firmly convinced that had we adopted a proper operational plan in the middle of August, and given it a sound administrative and logistic backing, we should have secured bridgeheads over the Rhine and seized the Ruhr before the winter set in. The whole affair if properly handled would not only have shortened the war; it would also have held out possibilities of bringing it to an end in Europe with a political balance very much more favourable to an early and stable peace than that which had actually emerged. . . .

The trouble was that Eisenhower wanted the Saar, the Frankfurt area, the Ruhr, Antwerp and the line of the Rhine. I knew how desperately the Germans had fought in Normandy. To get *all* these in one forward movement was impossible. If Eisenhower had adopted my plan he could at least have got Antwerp and the Ruhr, with bridgeheads over the Rhine in the north, and would then have been very well placed. Or if he had adopted Bradley's plan he could have got the Saar and the Frankfurt area, with bridgeheads over the Rhine in the centre and south. . . .

When I think back I am more and more convinced that the arguments, and difficulties of understanding, about the strategy after crossing the Seine have their origin in terminology. The matter has been argued under the labels 'narrow versus broad front'. My plan was described by Eisenhower as a 'pencil-like thrust', and on another occasion as a 'knife-like drive'. But a strong thrust by forty divisions can hardly be described as 'a narrow front'; it would represent a major *blow*. I was expounding the doctrine of the *single punch* against an enemy who was now weak on his pins. . . .

We did not advance to the Rhine on a *broad* front; we advanced to the Rhine on *several* fronts which were unco-ordinated. And what was the German answer? A single and concentrated punch in the Ardennes, when we had become unbalanced and unduly extended. So we were caught on the hop.[4]

Eisenhower saw things rather differently from Montgomery:

The task in the north comprised three parts. We had to secure a line far enough to the eastward to cover Antwerp and the roads and railways leading out of it toward the front. We had to reduce the German defences in the areas lying between that city and the sea. Finally, I hoped to thrust forward spearheads as far as we could, to include a bridgehead across the Rhine if possible, so as to threaten the Ruhr and facilitate subsequent offensives. As a first requisite our lines had to be advanced far enough to the eastward to cover Antwerp securely, else the port and all its facilities would be useless to us. This had to be done without delay; until it was accomplished the other tasks could not even be started. Equally clear was the fact that, until the approaches to the port were cleared, it was of no value to us. Because the Germans were firmly dug in on the islands of South Beveland and Walcheren, this was going to be a tough and time-consuming operation. The sooner we could set about it the better. But the question remaining was whether or not it was advantageous, before taking on the arduous task of reducing the Antwerp approaches, to continue our eastward plunge against the still retreating enemy with the idea of securing a possible bridgehead across the Rhine in proximity to the Ruhr.

While we were examining the various factors of the question, Montgomery suddenly presented the proposition that, if we would support his 21st Army Group with all supply facilities available, he could rush right on into Berlin and, he said, end the war. I am certain that Field Marshal Montgomery, in the light of later events, would agree that this view was a mistaken one. . . . I explained to Montgomery the condition of our supply system and our need for early use of Antwerp. I pointed out that, without railway bridges over the Rhine and ample stockage of supplies on hand, there was no possibility of maintaining a force in Germany capable of penetrating to its capital. There was still a considerable reserve in the middle of the enemy country and I knew that any pencil-like thrust into the heart of Germany such as he proposed would meet nothing but certain destruction. This was true no matter on what part of the front it might be attempted. I would not consider it.

It was possible and perhaps certain, that had we stopped, in late August, all Allied movements elsewhere on the front he [Montgomery] might have succeeded in establishing a strong bridgehead definitely threatening the Ruhr, just as any of the other armies could have gone faster and further, if allowed to do so at the expense of starvation elsewhere. However, at no point could decisive success have been attained and meanwhile on the other parts of the front we would have got into precarious positions, from which it would have been difficult to recover.[5]

Eisenhower went on to say that Montgomery 'was acquainted only with the situation in his own sector'. Eisenhower said that Montgomery understood that his proposal would have meant 'stopping dead for weeks' the advance of all units except those of the 21st Army Group but that Montgomery did not understand the impossible situation that would have developed if, having outrun the possibilities of supply, the 21st Army Group had been forced to stop or withdraw. Eisenhower said that he had told Montgomery that he wanted Antwerp in working order and that that port should be protected and that he also believed it possible to seize a bridgehead over the Rhine near Arnhem to outflank the Siegfried line. But Eisenhower also remembers saying that this operation – which was to be the attempted thrust towards Arnhem – 'would be merely an incident and extension of our eastward rush to the line we needed for temporary security'.

Eisenhower was, nevertheless, well pleased with the operation when it was over. He said that the attack would unquestionably have been successful except for bad weather. 'We did not get our bridgehead but our lines had been carried well out to defend the Antwerp base. . . . When, in spite of heroic effort, the airborne forces and their supporting ground forces were stopped in their tracks, we had ample evidence that much bitter campaigning was still to come. The British First Airborne Division, in the van, fought one of the most gallant actions of the war and in its sturdiness materially assisted the two American divisions behind it, and the supporting ground forces of the 21st Army Group, to take and hold important areas. But the division itself suffered badly; only some 2,400 succeeded in withdrawing across the river to safety.'[6]

Like General Gamelin four years earlier, Eisenhower had left the Ardennes comparatively weakly defended. It was here, as Montgomery put it, that the Allies were caught on the hop. The terrain was no easier or harder than it had been when General Guderian forced his way through to the surprise of the French in 1940. Eisenhower, concentrating his thoughts on an advance on a broad front, had nevertheless dismissed an advance through the Ardennes by either side as impossible or at any rate as an undesirable option. Only six American divisions held a front seventy miles long from the latitude of Malmedy to that of Trier. On Hitler's orders the Germans concentrated twenty divisions, eleven of them armoured, and with a reserve of five more divisions, for an assault on this sector. Partly because bad weather interfered with air reconnaissance, partly because the war was now being fought on German soil (so that the information about German troop concentrations which had been so promptly and accurately provided in France by the Resistance Movement was no longer coming in), the Allies were unaware of this formidable concentration. In fact it comprised the entire German reserve in the West. Even when they began to realize how strong the forces against them were, the Allies remained sceptical about the true intended scope of the attack.

Hitler's bold and simple proposal was to repeat Guderian's drive through the Ardennes to the Meuse and then to have his armies sweep north to recapture Antwerp. This would cut the supply lines of all the Allied armies in the Low Countries and to the north of the Ardennes, and turn the tables on Eisenhower.

To achieve this Hitler risked all he had. The Allies, confident by now that they could reinforce indefinitely their existing superiority in men and weapons, did not foresee the desperate grandeur of Hitler's plan. Bradley simply could not conceive that at this stage of the war Hitler could be so bold and so ambitious. When he first began to learn of the concentrations opposite the Ardennes, Bradley supposed that they were preparing to regain ground near the River Roer or else that, like the Allies, they were using the relatively unimportant Ardennes front for the training of raw, new divisions.

In fact the German divisions were fresh but did not need training. In the north the 6th SS Panzer Army, commanded by General Sepp Dietrich, attacked between Saint Vith and Malmedy. In the centre the 5th Panzer Army, commanded by General von Manteuffel, headed straight into the middle of the Ardennes forest making for Celles and Dinant where the Germans had made their initial crossing of the Meuse in 1940. From the Meuse both these armies were to sweep northwards across Bradley's and Montgomery's lines of communication to Brussels and Antwerp. Meanwhile the 7th German Army, attacking north of Trier under General Brandenberger, was to guard von Manteuffel's southern flank against counter attacks by Patton from the south.

The advance began on 16 December 1944, a day when fog and cloud prevented Allied air reconnaissance and support. In the event Dietrich's 6th Army quickly encountered stiffer resistance than had been expected. On the northern 'shoulder' of the front General Gerow's 5th Corps successfully defended the high ground – the Elsenborn Ridge – and the good roads that the Germans needed if they were to advance past Malmedy to the Ambleve river valley which would have led them to Liége from the south-east. A roaming German battle group called after its commander, Colonel Peiper, ranged ahead of the main force and temporarily took possession of the important communications centre of Stavelot only to lose it again the same day.

Supreme Allied headquarters and even General Hodges' army headquarters which was then at Spa only a few miles from Stavelot, failed at first to appreciate the weight of the attack. This seems to have been due partly to the Allies' general disbelief that Hitler would attempt anything so bold, partly to lack of reconnaissance through bad weather, and partly to German infiltrators dressed in American uniforms and driving American jeeps who had penetrated behind the lines and had cut many vital telephone wires.

Fortunately General Gerow, the stubborn conqueror of Omaha beach, was closer to the action and quickly realized what was happening. His 5th Corps held the northern shoulder stoutly. Dietrich could advance neither to the north-west towards Liége nor to the northwards to widen the breach in the Allied line.

But the breach had been made and was serious. Von Manteuffel plunged into the Ardennes forest as boldly as Guderian had done before him in 1940. But now the Ardennes were manned by forces more formidable than the Belgian cavalry. The Americans fought delaying actions on every road. They held on grimly to the town of Bastogne where five of the few main roads in the southern part of the Ardennes meet. To save time and in accordance with the German staff doctrine that an armoured thrust should never lose momentum, von Manteuffel by-passed Bastogne and drove onward boldly towards the Meuse.

This time, however, the doctrine proved wrong. This time the Germans were not dealing with the indecisive Gamelin. The American army, unlike the French one in 1940, possessed reserves, was in a position to deploy them, and was alert enough to act in time. The 101st American Airborne Division, with famous and hard-won experience behind it at Utah beach and in the Netherlands, reached Bastogne only hours after von Manteuffel's advanced units had begun to besiege the town. By the evening of 19 December, reinforced by the 101st Division, Bastogne had become a fortress surrounded by a moving stream of German tanks heading for the Meuse. In the last days before Christmas von Manteuffel's forces continued to advance towards the Meuse, though delayed continually by small American pockets of resistance.

This was von Manteuffel's undoing. The Germans could not move as quickly as he had hoped. Having failed to capture Bastogne and with it American petrol his advance units were running out of supplies. He needed the Bastogne road junction and the American supply dumps more than he had realized. Hopefully, on 22 December, von Manteuffel offered surrender terms to the Bastogne garrison. The American commander General McAuliffe, sent back the vernacular message 'nuts'.

On 23 December the weather improved and the Allied air forces were able for the first time to help the soldiers on the ground. On Christmas Eve von Manteuffel's most advanced unit was stopped three miles

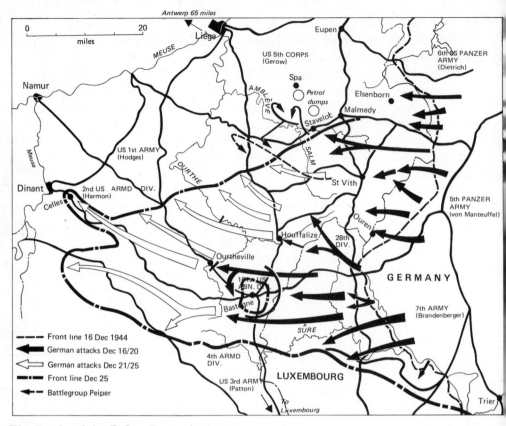

0   20
miles

MEUSE

Liège

Eupen

US 5th CORPS
(Gerow)

6th SS PANZER
ARMY
(Dietrich)

Spa

AMBLÈVE

Petrol
dumps

Elsenborn

Namur

Stavelot

Malmedy

Meuse

US 1st ARMY
(Hodges)

OURTHE

SALM

St Vith

Dinant

2nd US ARMD DIV.
(Harmon)

Celles

5th PANZER
ARMY
(von Manteuffel)

Ouren

Houffalize

28th
DIV.

Ourtheville

GERMANY

101st US
ABN. DIV.

Bastogne

7th ARMY
(Brandenberger)

SÛRE

Front line 16 Dec 1944
German attacks Dec 16/20
German attacks Dec 21/25
Front line Dec 25
Battlegroup Peiper

4th ARMD
DIV.

LUXEMBOURG

US 3rd ARMY
(Patton)

To
Luxembourg

Trier

The Battle of the Bulge, December 1944

short of the Meuse by the American 2nd Armoured Division. On the
26th the 4th Armoured Division dispatched northward by General
Patton fought its way through to relieve Bastogne. The Ardennes offensive
had been broken.

Patton's relief of Bastogne was a remarkable feat of arms. Within
forty-eight hours he had altered the course of an army through 90 degrees.
He then moved 133,000 vehicles seventy-five miles north from Alsace
to Bastogne and broke through to relieve McAuliffe. Meanwhile in the
northern shoulder, General Hodges contained very strong attacks which
continued for many days. At the Bulge's extremity the second US
Armoured Division under General Harmon decisively routed its German
opposite number in a three-day battle lasting over Christmas. When it

59. Pacific Fleet landing craft launch an attack against the beaches of Polelin Island in the Palau Group, 15 September 1944

60. American soldiers march into Paris in August 1944 after the Germans had surrendered

61. The ruins of Monte Cassino after the bombing

62. Hiroshima

was over the strength of the 2nd Panzer Division had been reduced to 1,500 men.

The Battle of the Bulge, as it came to be called, was a desperate thing while it was happening. On 19 December Eisenhower began to fear that communications between Bradley, whose headquarters then were at Luxembourg, and Hodges and the other commanders on the northern flanks of the Bulge would be cut. He decided that he could no longer risk leaving Bradley to command the forces on both sides of the Bulge. By then they were separated by an obviously large and menacing German force. Temporarily, therefore, Eisenhower put Montgomery in command of all forces to the north of the Bulge leaving Bradley in charge of the forces on the southern side.

Bradley was more confident than Eisenhower that the communications would hold. But he saw Eisenhower's point and accepted the decision, though with some reluctance. 'Had the senior British Field Commander been anyone else but Monty', Bradley wrote, 'the switch in command could probably have been made without incident, strain, or tension. Certainly it would never have touched off the Allied ruckus it subsequently did. But Montgomery unfortunately could not resist this chance to tweak our Yankee noses'.[7]

Bradley was sadly right. Montgomery and Hodges, who now was his immediate subordinate, did not see eye to eye about how the German advance should be contained. Hodges was eager to drive southward into the German-held Bulge. Montgomery was for allowing the Germans to exhaust themselves before attacking. He was also more concerned than Hodges about the possibility that the Germans would get across the Meuse. At this stage the difference between Hodges and Montgomery amounted to not much more than a difference of tactical emphasis. However, as Bradley had feared, the friction between them generated heat not light. Wilmot quotes one of Montgomery's staff officers as saying that the Field Marshal strode into Hodges's headquarters like Christ come to cleanse the Temple.

'It was perhaps too much to expect Montgomery to hide his feelings entirely,' Wilmot said, 'the wound was too deep. In the hour of triumph after Normandy the Americans, he felt, had spurned his leadership and had let slip the chance of gaining a decisive Allied victory. Now in defeat they had turned to him again to extricate them from a predicament which, he believed, would never have developed if he had been left in command of the ground forces. That afternoon [20 December] Montgomery did not endear himself to his American audience, for his confident tone seemed to carry a note of censure'.[8]

Despite the ruckus the Allies won the Battle of the Bulge and the victory was decisive. The Germans had used up all their reserves in the west. They were now desperately short of fuel. Much of their precious remaining stock of armour had been shot to pieces on the forest roads of the Ardennes. The men came back, for the Allies did not succeed in closing the mouth of the Bulge until nearly all the German troops had escaped. But by 31 January the Germans were back on their starting line. They had fought their last offensive in the west, and had lost.

Probably even Hitler – and Hitler was by now a deranged man – never hoped that the Ardennes offensive could bring a decisive victory in the west. The most that he had hoped for was the re-capture of Antwerp. The most that he could attain at that stage of the war was a delaying action and this, at great cost, was what the Battle of the Bulge achieved for Germany.

During the winter of 1944–45 delay was all that the Germans could hope for. In terms of time, in the number of days during which the Allies could have advanced but for German resistance, the stubborn German defence of the Scheldt Estuary was cheaper and in its way more effective than the Ardennes offensive. The German 16th Army, the army which Hitler had held too long in readiness to repel the attack which never came on the Pas de Calais, had been outflanked and by-passed when Montgomery's 21st Army Group advanced like a hurricane from the Seine to Antwerp.

Most of the 16th Army escaped northward across Flushing Roads into the Dutch islands and then to the north where they took part in the defence of Arnhem. But strong garrisons were left behind in the so-called Breskens pocket on the south side of the Scheldt estuary and in the islands of Walcheren and North Beveland, and in the south Beveland Peninsula. They sustained themselves on the stores left behind by an army. Their mission was to deny the Allies the use of Antwerp as a port.

For eighty-five days and against extremely heavy odds they succeeded. The Allies had captured Antwerp on 4 September. But they were not able to use it until 28 November. The Germans, under General Daser, held both sides of the commanding narrows at Flushing. The Breskens pocket was marshy, and made marshier when the Germans flooded it. Walcheren was flooded by the Allies, who bombed the dykes. A very considerable combined operation which included the battleship HMS *Warspite*, amphibious forces, and, above all, the relentless British and Canadian infantry, had to be mounted before Walcheren could be subdued. Even then three weeks' minesweeping was necessary before the port of Antwerp could be used. For nearly three months General Daser and his men denied the Allies the use of a port they needed and had actually captured. The defenders of Walcheren, whether they knew it or not, helped powerfully to ensure that the Russians and not the British or the Americans reached Berlin first.

In spite of delays the Allies were nevertheless now set to win. With Antwerp in working order Eisenhower proposed to clear the west bank of the Rhine of German soldiers during the second half of the winter of 1944–45. At the beginning of February the American 1st Army, now once more under General Bradley's overall command, set out to seize the dams over the River Roer south of Aachen. Simultaneously, the 1st Canadian Army drove south-westwards out of the bridgehead which the Allies had gained the previous autumn at Nijmegen. Their joint objective was the comparatively flat ground between the Roer (a tributary of the Meuse) and the Rhine which run parallel. The Germans delayed the American advance by blowing the dams and flooding the Roer valley. The Canadians made steady progress against stern resistance. After a month's fighting the two forces met on 3 March. From Düsseldorf to the Dutch frontier the Allies were emplaced along the Rhine.

All German resistance west of the Rhine was now collapsing quickly. The Germans were destroying the Rhine bridges well before the Americans came in sight of the river. By 6 March the US 1st Army was in Cologne. Further south Patton was sweeping through the Palatinate. Patton's 3rd Army and General Patch's 7th Army surrounded most of a German army group. In the centre of the front, on 7 March, a unit of the American 1st Army discovered to its amazement an undestroyed railway bridge across the Rhine at Remagen, some twelve miles south of Bonn. The bridge had been wired for destruction but the destruction had not followed. Delighted American engineers cut the wires. The bridge held. There now was one point at least at which the Allies could cross the Rhine dry shod. Hitler was furious. He sacked von Rundstedt and replaced him as Commander-in-Chief by Kesselring who was recalled from Italy. The major who had failed to blow the bridge was shot.

Further south, and without benefit of dilatory German majors, Patton crossed the Rhine on his own at Oppenheim on 22 March and south Germany lay before him. All west Germany, by now, was vulnerable. In delaying the Allies' advance to the Rhine the Germans had lost a quarter of a million men. The Allies now were unstoppable.

In the last week of March they surrounded the Ruhr as planned. Eisenhower decided to give priority to a drive through central Germany rather than against Berlin which was about to be captured by the Russians, then only thirty miles from the city. By 18 April the 320,000 German soldiers who had been surrounded in the Ruhr pocket surrendered and General Model committed suicide. By now the Allies were advancing along the whole front at the rate of about forty miles per day. Whether Hitler, crouching in his bunker in Berlin, knew it or not German resistance in the West had collapsed. By 25 April the Americans and the Russians had joined forces at Torgau to the east of Leipzig. Germany had been beaten.

Since the war the Western Allied leaders, and Eisenhower in particular, have been criticized for failing to launch a drive on Berlin instead of advancing into central Germany. Considering the length of the daily marches they were able to achieve during the last two weeks of the war in Europe it seems reasonable to suppose that they might, indeed, have reached Berlin before the Russians. Six months earlier the Western Allies had, tentatively, decided to go for Berlin first.

The argument was – and in some quarters still is – that central Germany did not matter politically but that Berlin did. If the Western Allies – Britain and America – had captured Berlin before the Russians got there their influence over post-war settlements would have been greater than it actually was, or so the politicians believed.

Churchill, for one, wanted Berlin. He said that if the Russians got there first they might see themselves as having been 'the overwhelming contributor to our common victory' and that this might generate future political difficulties; but Churchill was pleading for a gesture. Already in April 1945 the facts spoke against him. The Russians had lost 20 million dead. They had already shown themselves to be an 'overwhelming contributor to our common victory', and the political difficulties were inevitable in any case. The Allies' respective spheres of influence in Germany had been settled at the Yalta Conference. The inter-Allied bargain about the partition of Germany had already been signed and sealed. Whoever had got to Berlin first, the Russians were going to hold their Western Allies to the Yalta bargain.

In any case the military situation in the spring of 1945 was different from that which had been envisaged in the autumn of 1944 when the Western Allies first conceived the notion of a concerted drive on Berlin from the west.

By April 1945, the Western Allies were further from Berlin than they had expected that they would be. On the other hand the Russians were closer, much closer, than the Allies had supposed that they would be by April. The Berlin decision was left to Eisenhower. His soldier's answer was that he did not propose to risk the lives of his men to achieve a military objective (which the Russians were about to achieve in any case)

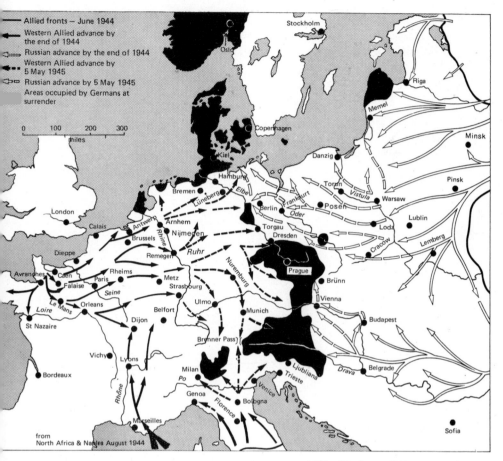

Allied fronts — June 1944
Western Allied advance by the end of 1944
Russian advance by the end of 1944
Western Allied advance by 5 May 1945
Russian advance by 5 May 1945
Areas occupied by Germans at surrender

0   100   200   300
miles

Stockholm
Oslo
Riga
Memel
Minsk
Copenhagen
Kiel
Danzig
Pinsk
Hamburg
Bremen
Lüneberg
Elbe
Toruń
Vistula
Warsaw
London
Berlin
Oder
Posen
Lublin
Calais
Antwerp
Arnhem
Nijmegen
Lodz
Lemberg
Cracow
Brussels
Torgau
Dresden
Dieppe
Remegen
Ruhr
Avranches
Caen
Rheims
Nuremburg
Prague
Brünn
Falaise
Paris
Metz
Vienna
Seine
Strasbourg
Le Mans
Orleans
Ulmo
Munich
Budapest
Loire
St Nazaire
Dijon
Belfort
Brenner Pass
Vichy
Lyons
Milan
Ljubljana
Drava
Belgrade
Bordeaux
Po
Trieste
Rhône
Genoa
Venice
Florence
Bologna
Marseilles
Sofia
from
North Africa & Naples August 1944

The Defeat of Germany 1944-5

simply in order to gain a political advantage over an ally. Without, as it
were, written orders from superior authority he was not prepared to risk
American, British or Canadian lives in order to give the British and
American Governments better debating positions at the inter-Allied
conference table. 'I regard it as militarily unsound', Eisenhower wrote to
Marshall 'at this stage [early April] of the proceedings to make Berlin a
major objective, particularly in view of the fact that it is only thirty-five
miles from the Russian lines. I am the first to admit that a war is waged
in pursuance of political aims, and if the combined chiefs of staff should
decide that the Allied effort to take Berlin outweighs purely military
considerations in this theatre, I would cheerfully readjust my plans and

251

my thinking so as to carry out such an operation.'[9]

The combined chiefs of staff did not so decide. The Western Allies did not march on Berlin. The Russians got there first and, as arranged at Yalta, stayed there.

Chapter 13

Death and Resistance in the Occupied Countries

The Jews

During the German occupation of Europe the people who suffered most were the Jews. Their hardships under German occupation were much more grievous than those of any other nation. When Hitler talked of their 'extermination' he was nearly right. The other peoples of occupied Europe suffered hideously too. About 20 million Soviet citizens died as a result of the war, the most grievous casualty total for any nation. But only about three and a half million – as far as incomplete figures can suggest – died in German-occupied territory. The Jews, who had nowhere to go, had no chance even to become collaborators. Hitler wanted them dead. His attempted extermination of European Jews was an unprecedented massacre.

Hitler's was not the only pre-war European regime that was anti-Semitic. The Polish and Russian administrations also were suspicious of Jews, but whereas the Poles and the Russians persecuted, Hitler exterminated – or tried to. Hitler's treatment of the Jews differed from his treatment of the other 'subject' races in Europe. The latter could be made to work and, perhaps, even to help the Germans as collaborators or mercenaries. But the Jews had to die.

Before the war began Hitler persecuted ferociously the Jews who lived in Germany. As soon as he came to power he began sending Jews to concentration camps, not because of what they had done but because of who they were. He encouraged his followers to destroy Jewish shops and businesses, to harass, to mock, and to denounce. In 1938, as an act of protest against the persecution of German Jews, a young Jew – Herschel Grynszpan – assassinated a member of the staff of the German Embassy in Paris. The Nazis reacted immediately. Within twenty-four hours they had wrecked 200 synagogues, had arrested 20,000 Jews in Germany, and had killed seventy who were already in the Buchenwald concentration camp. It was the first use by Hitler of vengeance and collective punishment to compel the obedience of a whole community. But for all his brutality to German Jews, Hitler was not yet ready to exterminate them systematically. It is possible that public opinion in other countries may have mattered to him before the war began and may have deterred him. At all events Hitler waited until he was alone in his dismal European fortress before building extermination camps with their gas chambers, their incinerators, and their ample and convenient railway sidings where victims could be unloaded. The killing of the Jews of Europe was a major organizational problem. When the war began there were only about 350,000 Jews in the German Reich, which by then included Czechoslovakia. When Poland had been conquered there were three million more. Their extermination was entrusted to four special Einsatzgruppen or special duty groups of the SS or Schutzstaffeln, the para-military force of dedicated Nazis who did Hitler's dirtiest work. In the beginning the Einsatzgruppen simply collected Polish Jews together, stripped them, and shot them. In Poland and occupied Russia the Germans did not bother to conceal what they were doing. In September 1941, someone blew up an hotel in Kiev and the Germans killed 33,000 Jews in revenge.

In the rest of occupied Europe the Germans were more circumspect, although the outcome was the same. In western Europe and in Germany itself, the SS did not think it right or prudent to kill Jews on the spot. It is true that they were herded together and taken away in cattle trucks, but the reason given for their deportation was that they were going to labour camps. To sustain this fiction the Germans made a grotesque rule – that no Jew should be put on a train unless he was in good health. In fact their health did not matter; they were going to die anyway.

Most west European Jewish victims of the SS were sent straight by train from their own countries to the extermination camps at Auschwitz, Belsen, Majdanek, Sobibor or Treblinka. The Einsatzgruppen had been obliged (mainly for sanitary reasons) to give up simply shooting Polish and Russian Jews in fields. Instead they confined the Polish Jews to ghettoes in the main towns. The Jews were kept by the SS in the ghettoes until there was room for them to be killed in the extermination camps. The extermination programme was extended to all the German-occupied countries. The slaughter was appalling.

According to figures collected by Calvocoressi and Wint[1] the SS killed 2,600,000 Jews from Poland; 750,000 from the Soviet Union; 500,000 from Rumania; 40,000 from Bulgaria; 60,000 from Greece; 58,000 from Yugoslavia; 700,000 from Hungary; 60,000 from Austria; 60,000 from Czechoslovakia; 104,000 from Lithuania; 70,000 from

Latvia; 180,000 from Germany, 65,000 from France; 9,000 from Italy; 40,000 from Belgium; 104,000 from the Netherlands; 100 from Denmark and 750 from Norway.

On the whole the native peoples of western Europe did their best to help the Jews escape. The safest occupied country for Jews was Denmark, whence Danes smuggled Jews across the sea to Sweden so successfully that virtually all the 6,000 who lived in Denmark escaped. The Norwegians did likewise. In the Netherlands, where the Jewish population was large, the Dutch tried to prevent their deportation by calling general strikes, by hiding Jews, and by a brave policy of non-co-operation. But the Jews in the Netherlands were too numerous and too concentrated to escape. Only 36,000 out of 140,000 seem to have survived. In Belgium 45,000 out of 85,000 survived. In France – the only country where the puppet government actually tried to help the SS to round up Jews – 235,000 out of 300,000 survived. Mussolini, who had no strong feelings about Jews, left them alone; but after his fall from power and the virtual occupation of Italy by the Germans the SS killed 9,000 Jews from Italy.

The exact Jewish death-role is not ascertainable. But the round figures suggest that about a quarter of a million Jews escaped from Germany to Britain and America before the war began, that when the SS extermination campaign began in 1941 there were about $8\frac{1}{2}$ million living in occupied Europe, and that the SS had killed about 5,500,000 of them before the war ended.

This fearsome deed was done solely because of Hitler's racial theories. 'The attempt to exterminate whole peoples was a logical consequence of Nazi ideology', wrote Calvocoressi, 'and the degree to which it succeeded was a result of the military conquests which placed millions of Jews within the Nazi grasp and of the reiterated propaganda which so transformed thousands of Germans that they were able to perform the cruellest of obscenities. Many thousands more witnessed them or were otherwise aware of them'.[2]

Military Casualties

The Nazi ideology also foresaw a need to kill 30,000,000 Russians. In Hitler's book Slavs were only slightly less obnoxious than Jews. But it would not be possible to eliminate all Russians. Some of them, anyway, would make useful slaves. Hitler gave orders that Russian prisoners of war were not to be treated like other prisoners of war. Political commissars (and it was up to his German captor to decide whether a man was a commissar or not) could be shot on sight. The Germans were not especially interested in the health of Russian prisoners unless they could be usefully employed in factories. About 2,600,000 Russian soldiers probably died in captivity. About 7,000,000 Russian civilians died on both sides of the line as a result of the war. About 6,000,000 Poles died as a result of the war, most of them under German occupation in their own country. About 1,700,000 Yugoslavs died as a result of the war. So did about 600,000 Frenchmen.

Allied losses were much lower outside occupied Europe. The Americans lost about 405,000 men. Britain lost 357,000 of whom 32,000 were merchant seamen and 60,000 were civilians killed by air raids. The British Commonwealth outside the United Kingdom lost 109,000 men. These figures explain why hatred of the Nazis burns more fiercely in Eastern Europe than elsewhere. The Nazis came to kill their fellow Europeans on an unprecedented scale. Their chief legacy to the continent they tried to dominate was death itself.

The Nazis governed their non-Jewish fellow Europeans as colonial peoples to be used if they were useful and to be starved if they were not. For more than four years the Germans managed to subdue many proud nations partly by starving them, partly by deporting men and women to work in German war factories, but mainly because they did not hesitate to impose collective punishment. If a telephone wire was cut or a railway line displaced the Germans would simply arrest the first 100 people they could find as hostages. They were prepared to kill them. In France they burnt the entire population of Oradour-sur-Glane in the village church as punishment for an act of sabotage which had been committed somewhere else. German reprisals were ruthless, swift, and did not pretend even to punish the guilty. Anyone would do. There is strong evidence that the people of Oradour-sur-Glane were burnt by mistake. The Germans had intended to massacre the inhabitants of another village with a similar name. But they lost their way. So it was Oradour-sur-Glane.

Hitler's Expanding Reich

Hitler's original plan for the government of Europe or most of it by Germany had been upset by the intervention of Britain and France in 1939. He had intended to incorporate Austria, the Sudetenland, northwest Poland and a small area on the Belgian frontier into the German Reich itself. Other territories, Alsace-Lorraine, Luxembourg, and north-west Yugoslavia, were seen as candidates for inclusion in the Reich but were not to be given this so-called privilege at once. Most of eastern Europe including the rest of Poland, the rest of Czechoslovakia, White Russia, and the Ukraine was to become a German colony. Germany would run this colony and would also dominate, through puppet governments, the Balkan States. Hitler's plan for Europe was to have a large, monolithic German Reich inhabited only by true, Aryan Germans in the middle surrounded by colonial or subject territories inhabited by less important Aryans or even, in the case of the Russian territories, by 'subhuman' Slavs. This neat plan was upset in 1940 when Hitler unexpectedly came into possession of Norway, Denmark, the Netherlands, Belgium, and France. It was upset again in 1941 when the Germans, coming to the aid of their incompetent Italian allies, occupied Yugoslavia and Greece. Hitler had no clear, preconceived plan for the government of these countries. In most of them he simply appointed a Reich Commissioner to run the country as best he could with instructions to ensure that nothing happened to impede the German armed forces and that each country should contribute whatever was available, either in the form of labour or raw materials, to the German war effort. But the practice varied from country to country. Denmark, for example, retained the odd status of a neutral country under German occupation with the King and his Cabinet still in nominal control. This arrangement did not last. The activities of the Danish resistance movement became too obnoxious and in 1943 the SS imprisoned the King, dissolved the Danish Parliament and disbanded the (still existing) Danish army. Norway had a Reich Commissioner. So did the Netherlands. France was divided into an occupied zone governed by the Germans from Paris and including the entire Channel and Atlantic coastlines, and an unoccupied zone governed from Vichy by Marshal Pétain and Pierre Laval.

In each of these countries the Nazis had hoped to find useful, like-minded friends. There were Fascist, semi-Fascist, Nazi, or semi-Nazi parties in existence in all of them. Most unfairly, in the light of subsequent events, the most famous of these was the Norwegian Nazi party led by Vidkun Quisling. It was also the least effective. Quisling did the Nazis more harm than good in Norway. The comparatively large Dutch Nazi party was mistrusted by the Germans. The French Fascists turned out to be less useful to the Germans than the Vichy Government which could lay some claim to having been elected.

As a general rule the Germans governed these territories simply by giving orders to existing public officials who had to carry them out. They applied this method both nationally and locally. Mayors could be ordered to provide supplies or labour for the German armed forces just as the Permanent Secretaries of National Ministries could be ordered to ration food more strictly, to identify Jews, or to round up workers and send them to Germany. As the war continued forced labour was what the Germans began to want from their conquered territories. The task of public servants in occupied Europe was complicated by the deliberate untidiness of the German system. The SS operated alongside the Reich Commissioners and sometimes independently of them. The administrators often found that they had two masters. Alternatively the SS would spy upon them to ensure that they were doing what they had been told to do.

However unwillingly, European public servants did what the Germans wanted them to do for four years and more. They had very little option. If your conqueror is prepared to take hostages and shoot them, to impose collective punishments on whole communities, or to deport them to Germany, the administrator must think first of his own people. Taking orders from an occupying power is not the same as collaboration with it. The borderline between the two activities can never be clear. But there is a difference between taking orders from the Germans while, at the same time, doing your best to protect your own people, and actively helping the Germans by pursuing policies of your own which will support theirs. Most European public servants, alone with their consciences, chose the first course. Here and there a few chose the second. They were ill-rewarded. In practice the Germans did not treat the local Nazis well. Quisling was virtually ignored by the German administration in Norway. The Dutch Nazi leader, Mussert, was allowed to strike postures and to recruit his followers for service with the German army. But that was all. The Dutch resistance movement, valiant in the defence of Dutch Jews, certainly did the Germans more harm than Mussert did them good. In countries where all the news was censored, where all parliaments and public debate had been stopped, where even the music had to be of Aryan origin, where hostages could be taken without warning, and where the SS was the ultimate authority, every man when faced with a German demand had to make his own lonely decision.

Resistance Movements

The resistance movements – the men and women who offered active opposition to the Germans – weighed the importance of an act of sabotage against the likelihood of reprisals and their extent. Each situation differed from the next and well-meant help sent adventurously from Britain was sometimes counter-productive or even fatal. Two Anglo-Norwegian raids on the Lofoten Islands destroyed a great deal of shipping but left the islanders open to savage reprisals. In 1941 a Czech and a Slovak were flown from Britain and parachuted into Czechoslovakia where they assassinated the SS chief, Reinhardt Heydrich, by throwing a bomb into his car. The Germans killed 15,000 Czechs immediately, sent 3,000 Jews to their deaths in the gas chambers, and obliterated the Czech villages of Lidice and Lezaky, killing the men and sending the women into concentration camps. The Dutch resistance movement who worked hard and ingeniously to protect Jews from the Germans, suffered badly when the code in which they communicated with London was betrayed to the Germans. The Dutch believed it had been compromised. London disagreed, and continued to use it. There were some hideous mistakes. But they were the exception, not the rule.

Clandestine operations launched from Britain against north-west Europe and later in the Adriatic against German-occupied Yugoslavia were, for the most part, successful and often extremely daring. Raids on a heavy water plant in Norway enabled the Western Allies to monitor German progress towards the manufacture of a nuclear weapon. Communication between Britain and Norway and between Britain and France was more or less continuous in spite of the Germans. The Norwegian navy, exiled in Britain, operated the 'Shetland bus' which was virtually a ferry service home. From time to time Norwegian MTB's would operate for as long as their fuel would last in their native fjords. Many men landed in France by parachute, by boat, or even by aeroplane to bring supplies to the resistance there. As the time for the invasion approached many brief raids by British and French commandos on the coast of France yielded much information about the defences. At great risk to themselves the French resistance developed and maintained a highly efficient escape route for Allied airmen who had been shot down or for commandos who had been cut off. The route ended in neutral Portugal or North Africa whence the rescued pilots were flown back to Britain.

Yugoslavia was the only occupied country whose people liberated themselves from the Germans. They achieved this distinction under the leadership of a Communist, Josip Broz Tito, whose partisans defeated not only the German forces of occupation but also a rival group of Yugoslavs led by Draza Mihailovic in a civil war. To a large extent geography was on Tito's side. Yugoslavia is mainly mountains. The partisans, 20,000 strong by 1943, survived encounters with much larger German forces because they were able to take to the hills. They suffered many casualties and much privation. But their greatest assets were their hardy determination and the leadership of Tito. They were strong enough to fight and win pitched battles against German forces but not strong enough to win them all. But they survived to win the last one.

At first the Allies sent supplies to Mihailovic who was the agent of the exiled Yugoslav Government. Mihailovic tried to take over command of the partisans from Tito. The partisans resisted. After a while Mihailovic began to collaborate with the Italians who were occupying north-west Yugoslavia. Relations between Tito's men and those of Mihailovic deteriorated and there was fighting between them for possession of the partisans' arms factory at Uzice. The partisans won. Mihailovic became, in effect, a guerrilla leader with pro-Italian and pro-German leanings. Neither the Western Allies nor the Russians realized that this had happened until sometime afterwards.

When a further British mission reached Yugoslavia at the end of 1942, the Allies learnt definitely that Mihailovic was, in fact, collaborating with the Germans. From then on Tito received all the aid that the Allies could despatch to him. In 1943 he fought and lost a pitched battle against the Germans and Mihailovic's men in Bosnia. But he recovered. When Italy surrendered they were in a strong position to take advantage. They quickly occupied the Dalmatian coast and came to control most of north-western Yugoslavia. Their numbers grew. They drove the Italians out of Fiume. In 1944 they were ready to go on the offensive, besieging the Germans in Sarajevo, Zagreb and Ljubljana. By the end of the war Tito's army was a quarter of a million strong and had recaptured its own country.

The only other resistance comparable in scale and effectiveness to that of Tito's partisans was that of the Russians operating behind the German lines in occupied Russia. The Russian resistance was all the more effective because it was unexpected by the Germans. The Soviet peoples defended their country bitterly, not so much because some of them were Communists as because all of them were patriots. Early in the war Hitler (oddly enough) had predicted correctly that if Germany invaded Russia – as Hitler fully intended that she should – Stalin would rally the Russians by an appeal to their patriotism. Hitler did not think that this would make much difference. He believed the Russians to be 'sub-human'. Sub-humans are incapable of patriotism. Therefore, Hitler argued, Germany had nothing to fear. The peoples of the Soviet Union proved him wrong and their resistance fighters rubbed the lesson home.

By January 1944, the Russian partisans operating behind the German lines had became a fearsome menace. According to one German estimate the German Army Group Centre, which was holding the line between Newel and Korosten, was threatened from the rear by 144,000 Russian partisans organized in sixteen or perhaps seventeen different commands. Sustained by the forests, by a climate they were used to, and by effective radio links with their own army commands, the partisans embarrassed the Germans hugely. In a single night in March 1943 the Briansk Forest partisans killed 353 Germans, took 246 prisoners as well as capturing two German tanks in running order. The Briansk partisans were only one example among many. From the northern to the southern end of a long front – from Leningrad to the Black Sea – Russian civilians in German-occupied territory harassed their conquerors effectively and fiercely.

Resistance fighters fought, suffered, and died throughout occupied Europe. The German resistance movement, though unsuccessful, was in its way even more heroic than the others. The German resistance was, after all, seeking the overthrow of the German Government and State, of its own terrible dictatorship which, though wicked, was also German. The German resistance movement, unlike most of the other European ones, did not, however, have much of a popular base. Its leaders tended to be professional army officers, bishops, leading politicians who had formerly belonged to the Social Democratic Party, and senior trade unionists. They were sadly unco-ordinated. But they were brave. The police State which Hitler founded discovered and executed virtually all of them before the war was over. They laid various plans but each of them involved the assassination of Hitler. Count von Stauffenberg, a colonel attached to the German general staff, made two attempts to kill Hitler, both of them unsuccessful. In his second attempt Colonel von Stauffenberg left a time bomb in Hitler's headquarters in East Prussia shortly before Hitler was due to attend a conference there on 20 July 1944. The bomb went off but Hitler escaped without serious injury. Von Stauffenberg and his colleagues had planned a military takeover. But, having escaped death, Hitler took charge again and at once ordered ferocious reprisals. Stauffenberg was arrested and executed.

The usefulness of the European resistance movements to the Allied cause as a whole is difficult to assess. The Russian partisans certainly helped the Russian army to advance more quickly and safely than it could otherwise have done. The Yugoslavs liberated themselves and, together with Greek partisans, kept twenty-one German divisions busy which would otherwise have been used on the fighting fronts in Italy, Russia and Normandy. When the Allies landed in Normandy the Germans had no less that fifty-nine divisions stationed in France, Belgium, and the

Netherlands; but only some of them were there because of the French, Belgian, and Dutch resistance movements. The rest had been moved to France to counter the expected invasion. The eighteen German divisions in Norway and Denmark had, however, been stationed there largely – perhaps solely – to contain the resistance fighters in those countries. Hitler boasted often enough that he had subdued a continent. But this was only self-deception. He knew that he had not really conquered the European peoples. If he had been sure of himself and of his conquests he would have disposed his divisions differently.

Chapter 14

Strategic Bombing

The Second World War was the first war in which the combatants possessed bomber aircraft capable of carrying large bomb loads long distances. When the war began the long-range bomber had been developed but had not been tried. No one knew from experience how to use heavy bombers or what the effects of using them would be. There were theories, but there had been no practice.

The most widely accepted theory was that there could be no real defence against bombing. 'The bomber', it was said, 'will always get through'. Having got through the bomber would then be able to wreak such destruction that the nation under attack would simply give up the struggle and sue for peace. All that was necessary to win a war was enough bombers. These theories were first put forward by the Italian General Giulio Douhet and his American counterpart, William Mitchell. The British Air Force Commander, Sir Hugh Trenchard, favoured a balanced RAF (whatever his critics may say) in which it was hoped that the bombers would be able to get through to Germany whereas the fighters would be able to defend Britain. In the event only Britain and America out of all the belligerent countries practised strategic bombing – as it was called – and in the event also the theories of Douhet and Mitchell proved incorrect, at least in their purest form. The bomber did not 'always get through'. The German nation did not surrender when a thousand bombers bombed Cologne. The Japanese did not surrender when the Americans set fire to Tokyo, night after night. The inhabitants of bombed cities suffered serious casualties, but they did not stop working.

One reason why this still untried weapon did not fulfil the hopes of its champions was that the bombers were unable, by and large, to hit their targets. The bomber did not always get through and, with the invention of radar, bomber crews faced mounting difficulties. Anti-aircraft defences improved steadily as World War Two went on. The bombers that did get through were often so harassed by fighters or by anti-aircraft fire that they were unable to take careful aim. When the war began both the British and the Americans were convinced that their bombing would be accurate. In fact it never was. The Americans believed devoutly in the efficiency of the Norden bomb sight which, they contended, enabled them to hit 'a pickle barrel' from a vast height in daylight. The British came to believe that they could do likewise by night with the aid of new and sophisticated radio navigation aids. But these were suppositions. As long as the defences were strong the bombers were unable to bomb with accuracy because they could not afford to fly straight and level for long enough to take aim.

The consequence was that the bombers often failed to hit the precise targets – factories and war installations – which actually were vital to the enemy's war effort, and destroyed houses and people instead. When World War Two began the principle that civilians should not be killed was generally accepted. When the bombing began this principle was forgotten. About half a million Japanese civilians and about 300,000 German civilians were probably killed in air raids during World War Two. About 60,000 British civilians died also, of whom nearly 9,000 – or 15% – were killed in a comparatively short period during 1944 and 1945 by flying bombs or missiles. These successful German weapons were totally indiscriminate. Unlike bombers, whose crews would try their best to hit the designated targets, the missiles – V-1s and V-2s as they were called – were simply aimed at London.

Although much the heaviest weight of bombs was dropped by Bomber Command and the United States Army Air Force, the first bombing that could be called strategic was carried out by the Luftwaffe. By British or American standards, the Luftwaffe was ill-prepared relying, as it did, on comparatively small Heinkel III bombers which could only carry a fraction of the ten-ton loads which the British Lancasters were later to drop on Germany. The Germans began to bomb London on 7 September 1940, partly in retaliation for the isolated raids which Bomber Command had by then carried out over Germany, partly – apparently – in preparation for the postponed invasion of Britain.

From 7 September until early November, the Luftwaffe bombed London almost nightly. The raid on 7 September caused much damage and killed one thousand Londoners. The East End of London suffered most. So did the City, and bombs fell on Buckingham Palace and the House of Commons. In November, the Luftwaffe switched its attacks to provincial cities and then to west coast ports, and even to Belfast in

Northern Ireland. Coventry, a major engineering centre, suffered heavily, perhaps the worst damage of any British city, but production was back to normal within five days. The bombing of Britain destroyed many homes – officially three million – and killed about sixty thousand civilians. But it did not seriously interfere with Britain's capacity to continue the war. Even as the bombs fell, factories were being dispersed. By comparison with the subsequent achievements of the RAF, the German raids were small. The Luftwaffe was seldom able to drop more than one hundred tons of bombs in one night. Although the Germans were to achieve more effective results by dropping incendiary bombs, they never came close to achieving the same degree of destruction by night as the RAF was later to achieve. Moreover, the morale of the British was not affected. London, which was raided more often than any other city, could 'take it'. The courage and tenacity of civilians under attack from the air surprised the British Government which had feared mass hysteria, much heavier casualties, and a possible break-down of the services of administration. None of these things happened, either in London or in other cities which later suffered far heavier attacks. Later in the war, faithful to the theories of Douhet, the staff of Bomber Command remained confident that their admittedly much heavier attacks on German cities would destroy not only houses, but civilian morale as well. They do not seem to have reflected that if London could 'take it', Hamburg could probably 'take it' as well. In the event, night bombing never interrupted war production for very long, either in Britain or in Germany. In general the longest period that British workers stayed away from work after an air raid was one week, and then only if their house had been destroyed. The Ministry of Labour observed that this did not seem unreasonable.

The Germans stopped serious attacks on Britain on 16 May 1941. By then, British defences and night fighters had become more efficient, largely with the help of radar, but were not then nearly as effective as the German night fighters were to become later in the war. The Germans did not abandon the night bombing of Britain because they had been defeated in the air – as they had been in daylight in the Battle of Britain – but because they were about to invade Russia.

The British were to some extent misled about the usefulness of bombing by two experiences early in the war. During the winter of 1939–40 two-engined Whitley bombers of RAF Bomber Command made repeated sorties over Germany to drop leaflets by night. They returned more or less unscathed. On the other hand a daylight raid by Wellingtons on

Wilhelmshaven had been a disaster, in which twelve out of twenty-two aircraft were shot down by German fighters. In August 1940 the Battle of Britain – in which German bombers suffered heavily in daylight even though they were escorted – helped to confirm Bomber Command in the view that night bombing was the best policy. The gap in the argument, however, was that although the night bombers had been getting through no one knew where the leaflets had gone. The Whitleys had been getting back all right but no one knew whether they had dropped their loads of paper in the right places.

Bomber Command flew night missions over Germany during the winter of 1940–41 in the belief that the bombs dropped had fallen within a reasonable distance of their targets. The first hint that this might not be the case came on Christmas Eve 1940 when the RAF flew a daylight reconnaissance mission over Gelsenkirchen where two oil refineries had been attacked by a total of nearly 300 aircraft which had dropped 262 tons of high explosive bombs. The photographs showed the oil refineries to be intact, or nearly so.

Bomber Command had assumed till then that the average bombing error was about 300 yards. This figure was plainly wrong. A new assumption was made. The average error, the RAF decided, was 1,000 yards. This meant that Bomber Command could not be expected to hit targets as small as oil refineries. Therefore it should be asked to aim at something larger. Bomber Command was looking for targets which were both large and vital. Railway marshalling yards met these requirements, or so it was thought at the time. In practice, however, railway lines can be replaced and repaired much more easily and quickly than most industrial installations. Dr Noble Frankland, a Bomber Command navigator and co-author with Sir Charles Webster of the British official history of the strategic air offensive, has summarized the dilemma in which Bomber Command found itself in July 1941:

. . . Bomber Command had started the war with the intention when the time was ripe of attacking precise and highly selective targets in daylight. Early experience had shown that day bombing was impossible. Bomber Command turned with the same plans to night attack. Experience then indicated, though for a time the indications were ignored, that at night only semi-precise targets as large as marshalling yards could be hit and these only when the weather was clear and the moon was out. When the weather was not clear or the moon was in, the only thing which could be hit was a large industrial area. . . . In effect this position amounted to a policy of area bombing. It only required a thorough investigation of the limitations which darkness imposed upon bombing accuracy and a development of night fighter tactics, which would make bombing yet more dependent upon darkness to make it [the area bombing policy] absolute.[1]

In the autumn of 1941 an analysis of night photographs taken by the bombers as they dropped their bombs showed – though not yet conclusively – that only one-third of the bombers had dropped their bombs within five miles of their assigned targets and that, over the Ruhr, only one-tenth had done so. These findings, as Frankland points out, showed that Bomber Command did not yet have a bomb-aiming problem. 'The navigational problem, to which scant attention had been paid, was, to a substantial extent, preventing it from reaching its targets at all.'[2] This conclusion led to the development and introduction into Bomber Command of three new radio aids to navigation which, it was hoped, would enable the bombers to determine their positions accurately at night.

Although Bomber Command as a whole was generally unable to hit anything smaller than a large town, specialized squadrons could do a great deal better. 617 Squadron under Wing Commander Gibson accomplished what Frankland calls 'perhaps the most accurate bombing attack ever carried out in the whole of the Second World War', when they bombed the Moehne and Eder Dams in May 1943. These, together with other dams, were thought to control the water supply for the Ruhr Valley. The mission was to breach the dams. Gibson's nineteen Lancasters faced the problem of dropping special bombs from a height of sixty feet into the water behind the dam. The attack was successful, but eight of the nineteen Lancasters were lost. The dams were destroyed, but the consequential damage to the Ruhr was less than had been expected. Gibson's 'dam-busting' raid was, however, an exceptional operation carried out by exceptional crews. Bomber Command's main business was area bombing.

Bomber Command's first new navigational aid was a radio position-finding system known as Gee, which was the ancestor of the modern Decca navigator. Gee depended on the use of a cathode ray tube and other devices to measure very short intervals of time. If signals transmitted simultaneously by a pair of radio transmitters on the ground are received simultaneously in an aircraft the pilot knows that he is on a line which bisects the line joining the two stations. If one signal arrives before the other the pilot knows that he is closer to one station than he is to the other. If the two signals can be separately identified and if the time difference can be measured the pilot has a position line – that is to say he knows that his aircraft is over a point somewhere on a line drawn on the map between the two transmitters. This line will be a curve, a hyperbola in mathematical terms. A second pair of transmitters or a third transmitter linked to one of the first two can generate another pair of signals offering the pilot another set of hyperbola. He then knows that his aircraft is on two position lines and that his exact position is where the two lines intersect.

Gee was an immense help to Bomber Command, as it later was to the Royal Navy. It was accurate. It was passive, in that it did not require the ship or aircraft to reveal its position by transmitting radio frequency. But its range was limited and it could be jammed. In practice Gee was useful only as far as the Ruhr. Gee came into service in March 1942. Oboe, the next navigational aid, came into service in December 1942. With Oboe an aircraft could fly along a hyperbola as if it were riding a directional radio beam – the pilot receiving coded instructions from the ground to tell him whether he was off his track. Another ground station would read the aircraft's range. When the pilot reached the point on the beam at which he should release his bombs the second station would signal him to do so. Oboe was even more accurate than Gee but, like Gee, its range was restricted.

The third navigational aid was H2S which was an airborne radar set directed at the ground. H2S did not depend on ground transmissions. Its range, therefore, was unlimited. But it was itself a powerful transmitter. Aircraft using H2S could be detected by the Germans. Another limitation was that a radar picture of the ground can be extremely confusing. H2S worked best over Hamburg where the broad waters of the Alster Lake contrast comparatively sharply with the returns from the built up area around it. H2S was less useful, however, over towns without lakes and, in particular, over Berlin which does not possess so large and distinctive a lake as the Alster.

To exploit these devices Bomber Command developed a new technique. A special group of bombers, known as the 'Pathfinders', would precede the main bomber force and, equipped with Gee, Oboe or H2S, would mark the target for the mainstream of bombers behind. The Pathfinders, flying light, fast, high-level Mosquito aircraft, were thus able to provide aiming points for the heavier and slower Lancasters of the main force. This technique enabled Bomber Command to cause great destruction in the Ruhr, in Hamburg, and to a lesser extent in Berlin. But while the bombers were achieving a greater measure of success in finding their targets the German night fighters were having more success in finding the bombers. Metric or comparatively long wave radar was by then an open secret and in wide use. Bomber Command's losses to night fighters mounted steadily throughout 1943. By March 1944, Frankland states,

The German air defences had got on top of the night bombers and were inflicting an insupportable casualty rate upon them. In March 1944 Bomber Command was no longer in a position to sustain a major night offensive against German cities. In fact, the tactical conditions of daylight had invaded the night to the extent where the cover of darkness had been fatally compromised. The night bomber never had the capacity to fight. It now also had an inadequate capacity to evade . . . In the thirty-five major actions between November 1943 and March 1944, German night fighters destroyed the majority of the 1,047 British bombers which failed to return. The daily average of bombers available for operations in the front line during this period varied from just over 800 to just under 1,000, so that, within five months, the German air defences, and principally the German night fighter force, destroyed more than the equivalent of the whole front line of Bomber Command. This happened in spite of the most brilliant tactics of evasion through radio counter-measures and other methods which could be devised.[3]

Bomber Command suffered badly. The crews did not fly in formation but they flew in uncomfortably close company and their experiences were often hideous. Flight-Lieutenant William Reid, VC has described one mission to Düsseldorf:

Just after we crossed the Dutch coast I felt a terrific bang in my face and the windscreen was shot away. We lost probably something like 2,000 feet. . . . I had been wounded in the forearm and shoulder and head and the plane went out of control temporarily. . . . I checked up with the crew and seemingly everybody was all right so I didn't see any sense in saying I was wounded in case they all thought he'll pop off any minute now. We flew on again and set the same course again but I had no windscreen in the front and in some ways this was lucky because my head had been cut up here above my helmet and it was bleeding pretty badly but the cold air coming in – it was minus 28° – made it chill up quickly and it stopped bleeding so this helped.

Fifteen minutes further on towards Düsseldorf a night fighter scored hits depriving Reid of both his compasses and a part of the aircraft's control surface and, though he did not know it, killing his navigator.

The elevator that keeps the plane straight and level each side of the tail had been shot off and this meant that you had to hold the stick right back as if you were going to climb to keep the plane straight and level because you're only using half the surface. . . . It was a matter of keeping the stick back by clasping my hands in front. The engineer held it with his other hand, his good arm. . . . The four engines kept flying so this was the main thing. . . .

If we had had any engine cuts I would have thought, well we can't get any further. But another factor here was, had I turned back we'd have another six or seven hundred planes more or less in the same track in a stream something like eight or ten miles broad and maybe four to six thousand feet deep. You're turning right back into them and you're heading right down through this lot to get back. Then again, had I turned off ninety degrees to try and avoid them, you're still turning across quite a number of them.

Using the Pole star to guide him Reid went on to drop his bombs on Düsseldorf before returning to Britain. When Reid made his emergency landing the undercarriage collapsed beneath him. 'It was only then', he said, 'that I knew the navigator was killed because he'd slipped forward beside me'.

Later, in another crowded sky, Reid's aircraft was disabled by British bombs falling from above. 'One of the bombs', he recalls, 'went through the port wing and the engine started to fall out. Then another bomb must have gone between the cabin and the mid upper gunner because it severed the controls that lead back to the tailplane. They just went sloppy. The rudders went sloppy. Of course as soon as I felt this one hit and saw this engine falling out I shouted stand by to bail out and to bail out, and the plane started to fall'.[4]

They were over France. Reid survived, but most of his crew were killed.

The American 8th Army Air Force joined the strategic air offensive against Germany in 1942. They began their operations convinced that daylight bombing, after all, would be possible provided the bombers were well enough armed. The Americans equipped their B-17 Flying Fortress bombers with 50-calibre machine-guns, they developed formation flying techniques designed to produce the maximum combined fire power, and they set forth hopefully from Britain to bomb German targets with precision and in daylight. They were escorted as far as possible by fighters. But in 1943, when the Americans set out to attack objectives deeper into Germany, the bombers outranged their fighter escorts. At this stage they began to suffer very heavy casualties. The combined fire power of the American formations was no match for the German Messerschmidts and Focke-Wulf 190's. The Americans decided to concentrate their attacks on the aircraft factories producing the German fighters. This tactic did not work. It amounted, says Frankland, 'to an attempt to make a difficult task possible by attempting a more difficult one. Nevertheless, the bombers were committed to a race between the destruction of the German fighter force in production by the bombers and the destruction of the bombers by the German fighter force in being. The result was a decisive victory for the German fighters in being.'[5]

The tactic was abandoned after the spectacular failure of a series of American daylight raids on Schweinfurt, the main centre of production for ball-bearings. On 14 October 1943, 60 out of 291 flying fortresses were shot down mainly by German fighters during the last major raid on Schweinfurt. The formations had been obliged to fly for about 400 miles – from Aachen to Schweinfurt and back – without fighter cover. For the 8th Air Force the result was disastrous. The Americans suspended daylight raids. They were not equipped in any case to bomb by night. For the time being the mighty 8th Air Force could do nothing.

If they were to bomb by day over Europe, what the Americans needed (and had always needed) was a long-range fighter. They had reached the same point of frustration that the Luftwaffe had reached at the end of the Battle of Britain. The bombers were vulnerable in daylight unless escorted by fighters. But the fighters did not have the range to stay with the bombers. The Allies, unlike the Germans, found a solution. It was the North American P-51B Mustang fighter, powered by an Anglo-American Rolls-Royce Packard version of the Rolls-Royce Merlin engine. The Mustang was probably the most remarkable combat aeroplane produced during World War Two. It represented the ultimate development of the highly-stressed internal combustion piston-engined aeroplane. The Mustang had originally been ordered by the RAF in 1940 direct from the American manufacturers. When it was first delivered equipped with an American Allison engine its performance was disappointing. Rolls-Royce believed firmly that what it needed was more power. Equipped with a new engine the P-51 turned out to be the best single-seat fighter in the world. Its performance was considerably better than that of the Messerschmidt 109 or that of the Focke-Wulf 190. Above all it could be equipped with long-range fuel tanks and could reach Berlin. For the first time the American B17's were able to count on an escort all the way out and all the way back. After their defeat at Schweinfurt the Americans ordered an immediate expansion of Mustang production. They were in action with the 8th Air Force by December. By February 1944 the 8th Air Force was back in business. The deployment of the Mustang was a turning point not only because it possessed the hitherto undreamed of capacity to stay with the bombers all the way but also because the Americans used it more intelligently than the Germans had used their escort fighters during the Battle of Britain. General Meyer pioneered a new escort tactic.

When I was first over there [Britain] we had quite clear directives that the first job of the 8th Air Force fighters was to protect the bombers. The commitment was that we would fly close to the bombers where they felt comfortable by seeing us and where, the notion was, we could do a better job at protecting them from enemy attack. Shortly after General Doolittle took command of the 8th Air Force, we in the fighter business made a plea to him that that was not the correct general tactic, that we could do a better job at defending the bombers by getting out further away from the bombers where we could engage the fighters before they had a chance to get in so close. This was due to the high speeds that were involved. When we were flying close escort to the bombers, the German fighters moved so fast that by the time we could drop our tanks and take any particular action, they had already fired at the bombers, had had whatever degree of success they might have attained, and were on their way home, on their way to the deck.

We prevailed on General Doolittle to agree to change our directives . . . We started moving away ahead and quite a bit higher than the bomber stream. In this way we were able to engage the enemy fighters while they were forming up to attack. We had considerable success in doing that, and it turned out to be a very significant tactical advancement in our ability not only to wreak more havoc on the German fighter force but also in actually protecting the bombers. . . .

We finally came to the conclusion . . . that we would be in a group formation very much like the Royal Air Force started in the Battle of Britain. We would fly a high squadron, a medium squadron, and a low squadron, with the squadrons in visual sight of each other but each squadron fairly intact. When we rendezvoused with the bombers we would divide up in the three squadrons, one going well ahead of the bomber force and usually high, and another one fairly well behind the bomber force and about level with it. And then the other squadron, that we had called a 'roving squadron', would usually break down into two flights of eight ships and fly around the bomber force and a little closer than these other two formations. Generally speaking, the squadron that went high and up-sun and way out would always keep the bombers in sight, but almost out of sight. And that was the squadron that had most of the successes. We would find that the Germans would be coming up through the overcast, they'd be forming with other units getting ready for the attack. And we would have altitude advantage, we would have the advantage of the sun and we would have the advantage of being organized and ready . . . The other two squadrons would pick off those that did get through. . . .[6]

The Mustang gave the 8th Air Force superiority in the air over Germany in daylight. The 8th Air Force used this and so did Bomber Command by night to wage a bombardment campaign which came as close to being decisive as anything that was achieved by air bombardment throughout World War Two. In June 1944 the Allied air forces launched a concerted attack on the centres of German oil production and on the refineries. The object was to immobilize the Luftwaffe and if possible also the German armies. The campaign was an immediate success, although this was not apparent until later.

In May 1944 the Germans produced 156,000 tons of aviation gasoline and the Allied air forces dropped 5,100 tons of bombs on German and Rumanian oil installations. In June the Allies dropped 17,700 tons of bombs on the installations and the output of aviation gasoline by the Germans dropped by two-thirds to 52,000 tons. In July the Allies dropped 21,400 tons of bombs and aviation gasoline production dropped to 35,000 tons. In August the tonnage of bombs dropped was 26,300 and the tonnage of gasoline produced had dropped to 17,000. By January 1945 aviation gasoline production in Germany had fallen to 11,000 tons. By March it had ceased altogether. What is more the production of gasoline for road vehicles had dropped from 134,000 tons in March 1944 to 39,000 tons in March 1945. The production of diesel oil had fallen from 100,000 tons in March 1944 to 39,000 tons in March 1945. Even if the Luftwaffe had been able to overcome the Mustangs by day the German pilots would not have had the fuel to do so. The still-formidable German night fighters were not only short of fuel but their ground control organization and many of their aerodromes had been overrun by the British and

American armies advancing eastward from the Normandy beachhead. From the autumn of 1944 until the end of the war in Europe in May 1945 the British and American strategic bombing forces were able to operate much more effectively than ever before because effective opposition in the air had been eliminated or starved of fuel. During this period the 8th Air Force and Bomber Command were able to help the Western Allies' armies on the ground by disrupting German communications. They were also able to mount one of the most devastating area bombing attacks of the war when they raided Dresden in south-east Germany on 14 February 1945. Dresden was thought to have been, and may have been, an important communication centre for the German armies resisting the Russians on the eastern front. But this was the secondary reason for the attack on Dresden which, by itself, almost certainly killed at least 60,000 people and probably many more. The main reason for the attack on Dresden – by the RAF at night and by the Americans during the day – seems to have been mainly that the Commander-in-Chief of Bomber Command, Sir Arthur Harris, faithful to Douhet's theory, was determined to let loose one more major area bombing attack. Harris, still ignorant of its real effects, did not have much faith in the attacks on the oil installations. He did not welcome instructions from Tedder, Eisenhower's deputy as commander of the invading ground forces, to attack German communications. Harris, to the last, believed that bombing could and would by itself somehow destroy the enemy's morale and his will to continue the war. The main reason that Dresden suffered rather than some other German towns seems to have been that it was about the right size and that it had not been attacked before. The raid on Dresden was the last major one of the strategic air offensive against Germany. Two months later, three weeks before Germany's final surrender, the offensive was formally called off.

The first strategic bombing attack on Japan was launched from the aircraft carrier *Hornet*, and led by US Army Air Force Colonel (as he then was) James Doolittle, flying the first of sixteen twin-engined B-25 bombers. The raid was an act of defiance. In April 1942 the Japanese were still advancing everywhere. In the Philippines the Bataan Peninsula had surrendered. The island fortress of Corregidor was about to be overwhelmed. America's fortunes were low.

Besides being an act of defiance, the Doolittle raid was also an act of skilled airmanship and courage. No one had ever flown a B-25 off an aircraft carrier. No one had ever supposed that it would be possible. In conventional aeronautical terms it was not possible. The heavily-laden

B-25s were theoretically and in practice unable to attain their designed flying speed – that is to say the speed at which the flow of air across their wings would lift them – before they left the flight deck of the *Hornet*. What Doolittle and his pilots did, and had to do, was to 'stall the aircraft off'. That is to say, they were obliged to point the noses of their aircraft into the sky and lift them off the *Hornet's* deck with the power of their engines before they were, aeronautically speaking, ready to fly.

> The idea [Doolittle said] of taking off a land plane with the tail down and stalling it off the runway . . . was somewhat foreign to the air force type. . . . We had only one real worry – that there would be a dead calm. The carrier would have been able to make, perhaps, thirty knots, so our effective take-off wind would have been about thirty knots. Under these conditions, taking off from the carrier deck with the heavy loads that we had, would have been, at best, precarious. However, we were very fortunate. There was a thirty-knot wind. The carriers were able to make twenty knots into this wind, so we had an effective wind of fifty knots across the deck which made our only serious problem a very simple one – that was, take-off with heavy loads with these aeroplanes from the carrier deck.[7]

In the event, the *Hornet* was able to penetrate to within six hundred miles of Tokyo before being intercepted and identified by two Japanese patrol ships. Doolittle and his pilots took off successfully. They dropped sixteen puny tons of bombs on Tokyo and flew on to friendly China. The raid itself did little material damage. Its main consequences, however, were considerable. It heartened the people of the United States who had been digesting nothing but bad news since Pearl Harbor. It bothered the Japanese authorities who believed that Japan was impregnable to bombing. It caused the Japanese to retain fighters at home to repel further attacks. For the first time, some Japanese began to doubt whether victory was certain.

It was more than two years before the US army air force again bombed Japan. In June 1944 the American 21st Air Force, commanded by General Le May, began a series of daylight raids mounted, first of all, from bases in the Szechuan province of China. The aircraft he used were Superfortresses, advanced versions of the B-17 Flying Fortress, with longer range and better armament, and with a heavier bomb load. The first raids from China, though successful, did not achieve Le May's objective. It proved impossible to supply the B-29's in China with enough fuel and bombs to carry out the concentrated assaults which Le May desired. He withdrew the China-based B-29's to the Mariana Islands where the

US Army Air Corps had, by then, constructed a series of bases. The real and telling aerial assault on Japan was launched from the Marianas. Up till March 1945, the 21st Air Force attacked Japan exclusively in daylight, and from a high altitude. Le May – who had himself flown on the Schweinfurt mission – decided to change his tactics. During the night of 9–10 March 1945 more than three hundred B-29's flew low over Tokyo dropping two thousand tons of bombs, many of them incendiaries. The Japanese defences were overwhelmed. This one raid killed eighty-three thousand people, injured forty thousand, and destroyed about one quarter of Tokyo. Le May mounted similar raids on Yokohama, Osaka, Nagoya and Kobe. The effects on these cities were similar to the effects in Tokyo. By the end of June 1945, most of Japan's war industry had been laid waste.

During July the Japanese made tentative and, to the Western Allies, incoherent statements which suggested that they might sue for peace. However, the Japanese were not of one mind. The messages they sent were far from clear. They never responded with clarity or decision to the Allies' demand, agreed at the Postdam Conference, for their surrender. In the end, Truman decided to drop the atomic bomb and Le May's men did so on 6 August. Truman's motives were probably mixed, but certainly sincere. He did not want to risk more American lives. He did not want to allow the Japanese to blur the fact that they had been the aggressors and had been defeated. Probably, also, he wanted to demonstrate to the Russians that the United States could beat the Japanese on their own and that they had developed what was then the ultimate weapon – the atomic bomb. At all events, it was one of Le May's B-29's which dropped it. The ultimate cause of Japan's surrender was bombing from the air. But the reason why the bombing was possible was that the US navy, the army, and the marines had secured the bases from which bombing became possible.

None of the major strategic bombing campaigns of World War Two proved the correctness of Douhet's theory that the bomber could, by itself, defeat an enemy. Even Le May's campaign in the Pacific, which brought Japan to its knees, was not an independent operation. It depended for its success on work done by maritime and ground forces. The bombing campaigns in Europe showed that aerial bombardment could, indeed, subjugate a country and a nation, but not until that country's air defences had been neutralized. One military lesson that emerged from the mists of World War Two was that, in those days anyway, the bomber by itself could not prevail. The RAF could destroy large parts of the Ruhr, but could not, in the event, dispirit the people of the Ruhr to the point at which they ceased working, any more than the Luftwaffe had been able to dispirit the people of London or Coventry.

The 8th Air Force inflicted grievous damage on the ball-bearing factories of Schweinfurt, but did not prevent the production of German fighter aircraft any more than the Luftwaffe had been able in 1940 to inhibit the production of replacements for the losses sustained by Fighter Command.

At the same time the bombing of communications and oil installations in Europe was, in the end, one of the decisive war-winning factors. Before the war Trenchard had insisted that communications and fuel supplies would be Bomber Command's proper targets and that the place to fight and win the war in the air would be over the enemy's territory and not over your own. By 1944 and 1945 events were proving him right. But by then, also, Bomber Command and the 8th US Army Air Force had served a long and hard apprenticeship and the RAF as a whole had had time to make good the numerical deficiency from which it had suffered when the war began. The strategic air offensive in Europe forced the Germans to build fighters (instead of bombers which could have bombed Britain), to spend scarce resources on air defence, to delay their rocket programme at Peenemünde, and to move their armies – in the end – largely with the aid of horses.

Chapter 15

The Legacies of War

World War One was supposed to be the war to end all wars, but it wasn't. The resentments and injustices that it generated were one cause of World War Two, which followed it twenty-one years later. For all their imperfections and fresh injustices, the peace settlements that followed World War Two were more effective in preventing another worldwide conflict. Another outcome of World War Two, perhaps more important than the peace settlements themselves, was the invention of nuclear weapons. The partition of Germany, the establishment of Russian satellite States in eastern Europe, and the bomb, combined to prevent the outbreak of a third world conflict. This is not to say that the World War Two settlements were morally defensible. The bomb was a weapon of terror. The absorption into an extended Soviet empire of the east European States violated the principle of self-determination (by which peoples are supposed to be allowed to choose their own form of government) and contravened directly, specifically, and unashamedly the provisions of the Atlantic Charter which all the major Allies had signed. Nevertheless the bomb and the Yalta and Teheran agreements about eastern Europe did help to keep the peace.

The bomb helped to keep the peace because it multiplied hideously and enormously man's power to destroy his own kind. It made the likely consequences of another world conflict so horrifying that even the most ruthless statesmen were afraid to risk one. It was only necessary for one bomber to get through if it was carrying a nuclear weapon. For the first years after World War Two ended only the United States possessed this new power of destruction. Later, when the Russians acquired it too, these two super powers came to realize in mutual fear that the risks involved in armed conflict were now so much greater than they had ever been before that no cause could be imagined that might justify full-scale war. The 'deterrent', as it was called, did in fact deter.

63. General de Gaulle returns to Paris, 25 August 1944

64. The Japanese, represented by their Foreign Minister, Namoru Shigemitsu, surrender to the Americans on board the USS *Missouri* in Tokyo Bay: 2 September 1945

65. The people of Brussels welcome British and Belgian troops, September 1944

66. May 1945: the war is over. Londoners in Picadilly Circus

When the Russians decided to blockade and threaten the Western Allied garrisons in Berlin along with two and a quarter million Berliners in 1948 they refrained from taking the city – as they could have done – for fear of American nuclear reprisals against which they had no defence. In the 1950's China, by then a Communist country, refrained from committing the full weight of her immense armies to the conquest of South Korea, then being defended by the United States and other members of the United Nations against the North Korean puppet Communist State. In 1962 the Russians began to install rockets with nuclear warheads on sites in Communist Cuba from which they could have threatened the mainland of the United States. President John F. Kennedy, communicating directly with the supreme Russian leadership, made it plain that these rockets would be seen as a direct threat to the United States which that country would resist if necessary by using nuclear weapons against Moscow. The Russians understood the risks, weighed them, and withdrew the rockets.

The Yalta and Teheran agreements – which gave Russia a free hand in Eastern Europe and which partitioned Germany – were like the nineteenth-century agreements between the European colonial powers, Britain, France, Germany and Belgium, to respect each other's 'spheres of influence' in Africa. The proposition that the great powers had any right to claim dominion over smaller ones, let alone to make a bargain among themselves about which smaller power should be dominated by which larger one, ran counter to the spirit of the Atlantic Charter. Nevertheless the deals were made. Perhaps the clearest and most candid was Churchill's deal with Stalin under which the Soviet Union undertook not to interfere in Greece in return for a British pledge not to interfere in Rumania. The bargain was kept. So was the much larger bargain between the Western Allies and Russia about the future of eastern Europe as a whole. The 'iron curtain', as Churchill called it, divided a Russian sphere of influence in eastern Europe from an Anglo-American one in the West. Bulgaria, Rumania, Czechoslovakia, Poland and eastern Germany were to be Russian satellite States whose governments, however chosen, were to be subservient in all things to the Soviet Union. Western Germany and the western part of Berlin were Allied spheres of influence. Turkey, which had been neutral in the war, was left to itself. So, in effect, was Austria.

There were two exceptions to this European carve-up – Berlin and Yugoslavia. Yugoslavia's position was different from that of the other east European States in four ways. It was the furthest Communist State from Russia; Yugoslav territory was not occupied by the Red Army and the leading Yugoslav Communists had not been trained in Moscow. Above all, however, the Yugoslavs did not owe their liberation to the Red Army or to any other ally. They owed it to their own efforts. The Yugoslavs were the only people whose country had been totally occupied by the Germans and the Italians and who had, by themselves, chased their enemies out. It is true that they had received aid from Britain, principally, and from the other Allies, but they had done their own planning, their own fighting, and their own suffering. It is also true that Yugoslavia was governed by the Communist parties of the various States of the Yugoslav Federation, united behind Tito. But, Communists or not, the post-war rulers of Yugoslavia supported by the people saw no reason why they should exchange German domination for Russian. In 1948 the non-conformist Yugoslavian Communists were expelled from the Cominform, the international organization of Communist parties through which at that time the Soviet Union sought to impose its will on other European countries. The Russians denounced the Yugoslavs bitterly and continuously, and cut off all commercial ties with their country. The tame Communist governments of eastern Europe followed suit. Yugoslavia was isolated but undaunted. The Russians could do nothing to bring it to heel.

Berlin produced a tenser situation. It lay well within the agreed Soviet zone of occupation in Germany, therefore well within the Soviet sphere of influence. The westward displacement of both Polish frontiers had put Berlin within forty minutes' drive of Poland. Nevertheless it had been the capital of Prussia and of Hitler's Reich. So on paper, at any rate, the Allies agreed at their Potsdam Conference to establish a four-power council – representing the Soviet Union, the United States, Britain, and France (which had, through the efforts of de Gaulle, been accorded great power status) which would rule Germany from Berlin. This meant that each of the four powers must have a 'presence' there. The city was divided into four sectors each of which, initially, was under the direct control of an Allied military government. The British, French and American sectors constituted a Western island in the middle of the Soviet sphere of influence. But the Russians on the one hand and the three Western Allies on the other had different ideas about how to govern Germany in the immediate post-war period. The Russians demanded and got reparations. They did not encourage or allow the East Germans to raise their standard of living which, at this time, was miserable. The Western Allies, while demanding reparations initially, were genuinely concerned that the West Germans and the West Berliners should be able to recover economically and to raise their standard of living. There was thus a direct conflict between Russian policy towards Germany and the policies of the Western Allies. Berlin, deep in the heart of the Soviet zone of Germany, became an embarrassment to the Russians. West Berlin began to prosper more than East Berlin, and West Berliners enjoyed greater liberty. The attempt to govern Germany jointly broke down. The Russians decided to try to get the Western Allies out of their sphere of influence.

In the early summer of 1948 the Western Allies put into operation a British plan for the reform of the West German. currency. The Germans were still using Hitler's money which had lost virtually all its value. The West German 'currency reform' was to lay the foundations for West Germany's post-war recovery and for its subsequent prosperity. The introduction of the new money – the Deutschmark – cured inflation at a stroke and began almost immediately to widen the gap in prosperity between West and East Germany and between West and East Berlin. Without waiting for this to happen the Russians made the introduction of the new currency an excuse for blockading Berlin.

Under the agreements which had established four-power rule the Western Allies had rights of access from West Germany to Berlin through air corridors, along specified super highways, by rail, and along specified canals. The Russians cut all these surface links. It was easy for them to do this. They had seventeen divisions stationed between Berlin and the Western zones of occupation. Short of declaring war on Russia and fighting their way through, there was nothing the Western Allies could do to restore land communications. The Russians did not, however, interfere with the air corridors to Berlin. These were West Berlin's only link with Western Europe, and, to most people, they appeared inadequate. In 1948 no one supposed that it would be possible to supply two and a quarter million city-dwellers with food, fuel, and raw materials for their industries by air. But two Western statesmen in particular thought it could be done – President Truman and the British Foreign Secretary, Ernest Bevin. Truman and Bevin were right. American, British, Australian, French, and Canadian pilots succeeded in supplying a city by air for nearly one year – a year which included an inclement winter.

The blockade of Berlin lasted until the spring of 1949 and it failed. The Russians could not drive the Western Allies out. They reopened the surface communication routes. West Berlin could breathe again. But it remained for the Russians a dangerous gap in the Iron Curtain. Through it the people of East Germany and of East Berlin could observe another, more prosperous, freer society. And for the next eleven years they were able themselves to pass through the gap as refugees. It was not until

*These countries, together with the USA and Canada, were founder members of NATO (which was ratified on 4 April 1949), with the exceptions of Greece and Turkey which became members in 1952 and West Germany which joined in 1955.

Europe in 1949

1961 that the puppet East German Government, with Russian approval, built the Berlin Wall not to keep the West Berliners out but to keep the East Germans in. The stream of refugees from East to West represented a drain on East German manpower which the East German economy could not sustain. The Berlin Wall expressed in concrete the inadequacy of the East German economy, and the Communists' fear of contact between the people they oppressed and people who were being given democratic rights.

The blockade of Berlin marked the active beginning of what became known as the 'Cold War' between the Soviet Union and her satellites in East Europe, and the Western Allies and their friends in the West. It was a period of suspicion and of hostility short of war during which the Soviet leaders strengthened their hold over their satellite States. In 1948 as they were preparing to blockade Berlin the Moscow-trained Communists in the Czechoslovakian Coalition Government brutally threw out the Social Democrats. Jan Masaryk, a Social Democrat who had been Ambassador in London during the war and who had become Foreign Secretary, was killed. The Communists say he fell out of a window. No one believed them. Either way, Masaryk died, and with him the illusion that Moscow-trained Communists would allow Social Democrats any real power in a Coalition Government. The Red Army intervened, again brutally, to suppress the aspirations towards independence of the Hungarians in 1956. In 1968 the Russians intervened in Czechoslovakia for the second time, disposing ruthlessly of liberals among the ruling Czechoslovakian Communists. The Russians did not hesitate to assert their domination over their own sphere of influence. World opinion made no difference. Eastern Europe was Russia's vassal.

On the other hand the Russians made no serious attempt to interfere in Western Europe. They may have intended to interfere, but in the event they did not act. They did not encourage the strong French and Italian Communist parties to foment revolution. They maintained diplomatic relations which were formally cordial with the French and Italian Governments. To the extent that the Teheran and Yalta Agreements constituted a bargain sealed by the Iron Curtain, the Russians kept their side of it.

Eastern Europe had been one potentially dangerous source of renewed conflict. The colonial empires of the European powers were another. World War Two was followed by many small colonial wars and by a few larger ones. By the 1940's the colonial empires won by the European powers in the nineteenth century were no longer tenable. World War Two had been about liberty. The Indian Army, for example, had fought valiantly with the British to liberate Italy, France, and the other enslaved European countries. British and French African colonial troops had fought for the same cause. Why, when the war was over, should India, Burma, and the African colonial empires remain subject to European masters?

World War Two did not of itself bring about the end of colonialism but it was the catalyst which started the process and which hastened it. The man who probably first saw most clearly what the war had done to the colonial concept was Lord Mountbatten. As Supreme Allied Commander in South-East Asia it fell to him to accept the surrender of the Japanese forces in what had been French Indo-China. In a despatch[1] to the British Foreign Office (which was kept secret for a number of years) Mountbatten warned that the French could not simply return to Saigon and resume colonial government as if nothing had happened. He found the country being governed not by the Japanese but by the Vietnamese themselves, led by the North Vietnamese Communist, Ho Chih Minh. Mountbatten found a similar situation in Indonesia. Again he warned the Dutch that they could not expect to resume business as if the war had never happened. The French and the Dutch paid no heed, though the Dutch were quicker to learn from experience and soon gave up trying to restore colonial rule in Indonesia. The French, more stubbornly, continued the struggle until their defeat at the hands of the Vietnamese at Dien Bien Phu in 1954.

The British, meanwhile, had resolved to grant self-government to India and Burma. The decision to do this was taken by the new, post-war Labour Government led by Clement Attlee and executed with despatch by Mountbatten himself in 1947. The outcome was the birth of three new Asian States – India, Burma, and Pakistan, which last comprised the Muslim areas of what had formerly been British India.

Colonialism died more slowly in Africa and more slowly still in the Middle East where, in the 1960's, the British were still fighting to retain control of Aden. But the process that began with the granting of independence to India, Burma, and Pakistan was unstoppable. In 1962, under the firm leadership of de Gaulle, who had been recalled to power, the French came home from Algeria. Colonialism ended in a welter of small, bitter wars which the colonial powers lost, not necessarily for lack of military might but because they did not have the will to sustain an untenable situation for ever.

Surprisingly, in view of their strong anti-colonial traditions, the Americans fought the longest, bitterest, and most bloodthirsty colonial war of all in Vietnam. Believing it to be their duty to suppress Vietnamese Communism they took up the cause which the French had abandoned. Having allowed themselves to become more and more deeply involved in the fighting between the non-Communist South Vietnamese and the Communists in the North, they eventually withdrew their ground forces in 1973. China and Russia helped the North, but not with men.

In Europe World War Two left behind the nucleus of two organizations – the North Atlantic Treaty Organization and the Warsaw Pact – which sustained a balance of power of a sort on either side of the Iron Curtain but which also, and much more importantly, involved non-European powers in the defence of Western Europe. When the war ended Britain, the United States, Canada, and France all were providing sizeable contingents of troops in Western Germany. As time wore on and Western Germany became self-governing, the 'occupying powers' and their forces were transformed into Allied powers and Allied forces. The North Atlantic Treaty was a mutual defence pact between the United States with its nuclear arsenal and America's World War Two Allies and some other countries. NATO's stated purpose was to defend democracy. Its main and guiding principle was that an attack on one member of NATO would be deemed to be an attack on all and that the 'all' included the United States with its power of nuclear retaliation. In practical terms, however, the Treaty was probably less important as a peace-keeping instrument than the fact that American, British, and Canadian soldiers remained on guard against a Russian attack on West Germany. It meant that any Russian attack on West Germany would count as an attack on North America and Britain and would therefore invite retaliation which might be nuclear.

The United Nations Organization, a direct descendant of the Atlantic Charter Agreement, did not of itself play a peace-keeping role in Europe but it was occasionally effective elsewhere. The United Nations was more efficient than its predecessor, the League of Nations, for two main reasons. The United Nations' constitution does not assume, as the League's had assumed, that a majority of small, peace-loving nations can coerce a minority of larger, more bellicose countries to abandon their war-like plans. The second main difference is that the United States was a founder member of the United Nations and did not abdicate its place in the nations' councils as President Wilson's America had done in the 1920's. From the beginning the constitution foresaw a Security Council consisting of the five most powerful (as they were then) military nations in the world – the United States, the Soviet Union, Britain, France and China. In the first instance the China in question was Chiang Kai-shek's, who was even then losing a civil war to the Communists. The inclusion of Nationalist China in the UN Security Council was originally part of a bargain between Roosevelt and Stalin. It was, however, soon to become an unrealistic arrangement. As Chiang Kai-shek and his forces were driven back from the Chinese mainland to Formosa (Taiwan) it became evident that Nationalist China's membership of the Security Council was a pretence. Nationalist China was not a major world power. Mao Tse-tung's Communist China was. For more than twenty-five years this fiction was maintained, and the UN looked the sillier for it.

In practice the existence of the Security Council as the UN's supreme decision-making body meant that the UN did not on the whole try to solve problems which it was incapable of solving. Each of the five Security Council members had the right to stop any decision. When an international quarrel involved the interests of one of the great powers one of the great powers would, more or less inevitably, use its veto in the Security Council. The great powers, with the bomb at the back of their minds, settled their own disputes. The Security Council tackled the others. When the quarrel was comparatively small and when it did not involve directly the interests of the great powers the UN was able, as often as not, to soothe things down.

When the United Nations was unequal to the job one or other or both of the super powers – the United States and the Soviet Union – intervened to prevent or restrict conflict. In 1956, the Egyptian Government nationalized the Suez Canal, thereby offending the British Government, then led by Sir Anthony Eden. Together with the French and the Israelis, the British made war on Egypt. Almost simultaneously the Russians, acting in their own agreed sphere of influence, intervened to get rid of a liberal Government in Hungary. The United States made no move to stop the Russians but intervened effectively to oblige Britain, France and Israel to desist from the Suez war.

It was easily done. The Egyptians, under attack, had blocked the Suez Canal (it was to stay blocked for many years), and deprived Western Europe of its main supply of oil which came from the Arabian fields. North America was the only other possible source of oil. In effect the United States rationed Europe's oil supplies until Britain, France and Israel desisted.

The Suez war demonstrated for the first time clearly and publicly the extent to which Britain's economic power and therefore her influence had diminished. There were many reasons for this decline but one of them – a main one – had been the effect of World War Two on the British economy. The British were at war for longer than any other nation. They also organized themselves better and more completely for war than any other nation. The British devoted everything they had to the fight. But they themselves did not realize the cost until later.

Towards the end of 1943 the British Government was dismayed to learn from a private report by its chief economic adviser, John Maynard Keynes, that Britain was running out of money. Victory – or something like it – would have to come in 1944 or the war effort would have to be curtailed. British resources, human and other, were fully stretched. In spite of lend-lease and the sale of her foreign assets, Britain was virtually a pauper whereas the United States had become an economic giant.

The United States was large enough and rich enough to take World War Two in its economic stride. America, for the first time, had measured its own economic and industrial strength and had found it to be vast. The American standard of living actually rose during World War Two, partly because more people were employed, partly because under the stress of war the Americans had discovered new resources to exploit. In 1945 Keynes compared the losses suffered by the two nations. British casualties were two and three quarter times as great as those of the United States, with losses in killed and missing three and a half times as great. 55% of Britain's total labour force was engaged in war production by June 1944, compared with 40% in America. Britain had lost 35 times as much capital invested overseas as had the United States. The consumption of goods and services by civilians decreased by 16% in Britain whereas it had increased by 16% in the United States. British and British Commonwealth merchant shipping losses had reduced the total size of the fleet from 40 million tons to 19 million 500 thousand tons, whereas American merchant shipping had increased fourfold to 50 million tons.[2]

The United States emerged from the war stronger than she had gone into it. In 1945, rather to their own surprise, the Americans discovered that they were richer than any other nation had ever been before. The Americans' reaction to this discovery was imaginative and generous. General Marshall, by now Secretary of State, secured Congressional approval for the plan which bears his name. The United States offered aid to those countries which needed it, Germany included, because of losses suffered during the war. Roosevelt's lend-lease principle was extended for peaceful purposes in peacetime. The offer was open to all. Only the Soviet Union and the East European Russian Satellites refused it.

Marshall Aid was a great act of national generosity but it was also sensible. By giving away her wealth, the United States was able to avoid the slump which would have followed an abrupt cessation of her vast war production. In the event, American wealth was re-distributed widely and generously while, at the same time, the United States continued to prosper. Inevitably, too, the United States became the dominant economic power in the post-war years. Americans became involved commercially as well as diplomatically with the rest of the world to an extent that had no precedent in American history. The new circumstances in which the

United States found itself, including its new wealth, had made isolationism impractical as well as out of date. One of the things that World War Two did to America was to introduce that rich and resourceful country into a new role as the generally benevolent regulator of the economies of the Western world.

Notes on Sources

1. Beginnings

1. Adolf Hitler, *Mein Kampf* (London, 1972).
2. British Cabinet Records* CAB 24 139 paper 4298.
3. Lecture at University College, London; reported in *The Guardian*, 1.11.72.
4. A. J. P. Taylor, *The Origins of the Second World War* (Harmondsworth, 1964), p. 147.
5. BCR CAB 23 68.
6. BCR CAB 24 series.
7. Jacobsen & Dollinger, *Der zweite Weltkrieg in Bildern und Dokumenten* (Munich, 1968), p. 28.
8. Iain Macleod, *Neville Chamberlain* (London, 1961).
9. Ian Colvin, *The Chamberlain Cabinet* (London, 1971), p. 265–6.
10. BCR CAB 23 series, vol. 94 onwards.†
11. Letter to Ida Chamberlain, 19.9.38.
12. A. J. P. Taylor, *English History 1914–45* (Oxford, 1965), p. 449.

2. The Phoney War

1. Jacobsen & Dollinger, *op. cit.*, vol. I, p. 43.
2. *Ibid.*, p. 71.
3. Donald Macintyre, *The Naval War against Hitler* (London, 1971), p. 26.

3. The Fall of France

1. H. Guderian, *Panzer Leader* (London, 1952), p. 90.
2. Charles de Gaulle, *The Call to Honour* (London, 1955), p. 18.
3. *Ibid.*, p. 26.
4. *Ibid.*, p. 28.

* Hereafter abbreviated to BCR, followed by the appropriate reterence number.
† This reference applies to all the following quotations from Cabinet papers in this chapter.

5. H. Guderian, *op. cit.*, p. 96.
6. Charles de Gaulle, *op. cit.*, p. 49.
7. J. R. Colville, *Man of Valour: The Life of Field Marshal The Viscount Gort* (London, 1972), p. 212–13.
8. BCR CAB 65 13.
9. BCR CAB 65 13.
10. BCR CAB 65 13.
11. Iain Macleod, *op. cit.*, p. 280.
12. Charles de Gaulle, *op. cit.*, p. 79.
13. *Ibid.*, p. 75.

4. The Battle of Britain

1. Chester Wilmot, *The Struggle for Europe* (London, 1971), p. 38.
2. *Ibid.*
3. Thames Television interview.
4. Thames Television interview.

5. The Battle of the Atlantic

1. Thames Television interview.
2. President Roosevelt, radio broadcast.
3. Jacobsen & Dollinger, *op. cit.*, vol. V, p. 140.
4. John Deane Potter, *Fiasco* (London, 1970).
5. BCR CAB 98/22 3830.
6. BCR CAB 98/22 3830.

6. The War in the Desert

1. Thames Television interview.
2. Thames Television interview.
3. Thames Television interview.
4. Thames Television interview.
5. D. Kahn, *The Code Breakers* (London, 1966), p. 473–6.
6. Montgomery of Alamein, Field Marshal the Viscount, *El Alamein to the River Sangro* (London, 1948), p. 25.

7. The Campaign in Italy

1. Ewen Montagu, *The Man Who Never Was* (London, 1953).
2. Peter Calvocoressi & Guy Wint, *Total War* (London, 1972), p. 510.
3. Fred Majdalany, *The Monastery* (London, 1945), p. 8.
4. *Ibid.*, p. 8.
5. F. von Senger und Etterlin, *Neither Fear Nor Hope* (London, 1963), p. 231.
6. *Ibid.*, p. 202.
7. *Ibid.*, p. 202.

8. Victory in the USSR

1. Jacobsen & Dollinger, *op. cit.*, vol. III, p. 14.
2. *Ibid.*, p. 82.
3. Thames Television interview.
4. Jacobsen & Dollinger, *op. cit.*, vol. III, p. 114.
5. Thames Television interview.
6. Thames Television interview.
7. *The Diaries of Sir Alexander Cadogan, 1938–45* (London, 1971), p. 423.
8. V. I. Chuikov, *The Beginning of the Road* (London, 1963), p. 71–2.
9. *Ibid.*, p. 72.
10. *Ibid.*, p. 79–80.
11. Jacobsen & Dollinger, *op. cit.*, vol. VI, p. 21.
12. V. I. Chuikov, *The End of the Third Reich* (London, 1967), p. 41.
13. *Ibid.*, p. 66.
14. *Ibid.*, p. 52.
15. *Ibid.*, p. 245.
16. *Ibid.*, p. 258.

9. The Struggle for the Pacific

1. Thames Television interview.
2. D. Kahn, *op. cit.*, p. 33.
3. *Ibid.*, p. 3.
4. *Ibid.*, p. 33.
5. Thames Television interview.
6. Thames Television interview.
7. BCR CAB 66/3.
8. Winston Churchill, *The Hinge of Fate* (London, 1951), p. 43.
9. S. L. Falk, *The Bataan Death March* (Washington, 1952), p. 27.
10. Thames Television interview.
11. Thames Television interview.
12. Burke Davis, *Get Yamamoto* (London, 1971), p. 163.
13. S. E. Morison, *A History of United States Naval Operations in World War II* (Boston, 1970), vol. 12, p. 228.
14. *Ibid.*, p. 273.
15. Thames Television interview.

10. Burma Regained

1. Barbara Tuchman, *Sand against the Wind: Stilwell and the American Experience in China* (London, 1971), p. 220–2.

2. Thames Television interview.
3. William Slim, *Defeat into Victory* (London, 1956), p. 311.
4. Thames Television interview.

11. The Politics of War

1. Guy Hartcup, *The Challenge of War* (Newton Abbot, 1972), p. 28.
2. *The Diaries of Sir Alexander Cadogan, op. cit.*, p. 422.
3. BCR CAB 66/50 8210.
4. BCR FO 371 34577.
5. BCR CAB 66/45 8206.
6. A. J. P. Taylor, *English History 1914-45, op. cit.*, p. 587.
7. BCR CAB 65/51 8244.

12. The Reconquest of Western Europe

1. Omar H. Bradley, *A Soldier's Story* (London, 1951), p. 271.
2. *Ibid.*, p. 285.
3. Alastair Hetherington, *The Guardian*, 1.9.69.
4. *The Memoirs of Field Marshal Montgomery* (London, 1958), p. 263-5.
5. Dwight Eisenhower, *Crusade in Europe* (London, 1948), p. 333-6.
6. *Ibid.*, p. 340-2.
7. Omar H. Bradley, *op. cit.*, p. 477.
8. Chester Wilmot, *op. cit.*, p. 592.
9. *Ibid.*, p. 693.

13. Death and Resistance in the Occupied Countries

1. Peter Calvocoressi and Guy Wint, *op. cit.*, p. 233.
2. *Ibid.*, p. 220.

14. Strategic Bombing

1. Noble Frankland, *The Bombing Offensive against Germany* (London, 1965), p. 59.
2. *Ibid.*, p. 61.
3. *Ibid.*, p. 72-3.
4. Thames Television interview.
5. Noble Frankland, *op. cit.*, p. 76.
6. Thames Television interview.
7. Thames Television interview.

15. The Legacies of War

1. Lord Mountbatten, *Report on Post Surrender Tasks* (HMSO).
2. *New York Times*, 21.9.45.

Chronology
of the War

	W. Europe	E. Europe	Italy & Mediterranean	Burma & China	Pacific	Atlantic
1939						
March 15		Hitler's troops enter Prague, & Czechoslovakia is dismembered				
March 31	Chamberlain announces Anglo–French guarantees to Poland					
April 7	Germany, Italy, Spain & Japan sign Anti-Comintern Pact		Italy invades Albania			
May 22	Germany signs 'Pact of Steel' military alliance with Italy					
Aug 23	Germany signs Nazi-Soviet Pact, containing clauses about the partition of Poland					
Aug 25	Anglo-Polish Mutual Assistance Treaty signed					

		Poland & annexes Danzig		Germans sink 26 British merchant ships
Sept 2	Britain sends ultimatum to Germany			
Sept 3	Britain, France, Australia & New Zealand declare war on Germany			
Sept 17		Russians invade Eastern Poland		
Sept 29		Germany & Russia sign the agreement partitioning Poland. Russia signs pacts with Estonia & Finland		
Oct 12	Chamberlain rejects Hitler's peace plans			
Nov 3		Stalin presents territorial demands to Finns		Cash & Carry clause introduced in US Statute of Neutrality
Nov 30		Russia invades Finland		
Dec 13				Battle of River Plate

1940	W. Europe	E. Europe	Italy & Mediterranean	Burma & China	Pacific	Atlantic
Mar 12		Russo–Finnish Pact signed in Russia				
April 9	Germany invades Denmark & Norway					
April 13	2nd Battle of Narvik					
May 1	Norwegians surrender					
May 10	Germany attacks Low Countries. Churchill becomes PM					
May 15	Holland overrun. The French are defeated at Sedan					
May 27–8	Allies evacuation from Dunkirk. Belgium capitulates					
June 10			Italy declares war on Britain & France			
June 14	Germans enter Paris					

June 22	Franco-German Armistice signed at Compiègne				
July 3		RN attacks French fleet at Oran & Mers-el-Kebir			
July 10	Battle of Britain begins				German submarine base established at Lorient
July			British start closing Burma Rd		
Sept 13–14		Italians invade Egypt			
Sept 27	Germany, Italy & Japan sign Tripartite Pact	Tripartite Pact signed		Tripartite Pact signed	
Oct 28		Italians invade Greece			
Nov 5					Roosevelt re-elected President
Nov 11		British attack Italian fleet at Taranto			
Dec 9		First British offensive in desert begins			

1941	W. Europe	E. Europe	Italy & Mediterranean	Burma & China	Pacific	Atlantic
Jan 22			Allies take Tobruk			
Feb 2			Rommel arrives in Tripoli			
March 8						US Senate passes Lend-Lease Bill
March 28			Battle of Cape Matapan			
April 5			Wavell sends troops to Greece			
April 6			Germans invade Greece and Yugoslavia			
April 13			Rommel encircles Tobruk		Stalin signs neutrality pact with Japan	
May 21			Germans take Maleme airfield, Crete			
May 24						*Hood* sunk

June 22		Germany invades Russia				
July 12	Anglo-Soviet Treaty of Mutual Assistance					
July 28				Japanese troops land in Indo-China		
Aug 5		Soviet resistance at Smolensk eliminated			US & British impose embargoes on sale of raw materials to Japan	
Aug 12		Army Group North advances on Leningrad				Churchill & Roosevelt sign Atlantic Charter at Placentia Bay
Aug 19		Army Group South captures 650,000 Russian soldiers at Kiev				
Aug 29		Russians evacuate Karelian Isthmus				
Sept 5		Germans occupy Estonia				

	W. Europe	E. Europe	Italy & Mediterranean	Burma & China	Pacific	Atlantic
Sept 8–9		Leningrad's land communications with rest of Russia severed				
Sept 28						First Arctic convoy to Russia leaves Iceland
Oct 17					Tojo succeeds Konoye as PM of Japan	
Oct 20		Germans take Bryansk				
Oct 30		Germans break through in Crimea and attack Moscow				
Nov 18			8th Army launches 2nd Western Desert campaign			
Dec 5		Hitler abandons Moscow offensive for winter				
Dec 6		Russia mounts counter-offensive				
Dec 7					Japan attacks Pearl Harbor, the Philippines, Hong Kong & Malaya, having sent war ...	

Dec 8	Allies declare war on Japan. USSR remains neutral			
Dec 9		China declares war on Japan & Germany		
Dec 10	Japanese capture Guam			
Dec 11		Japan attacks Burma		Germany & Italy declare war on USA
Dec 22				First Washington Conference begins
Dec 23	Japanese capture Wake			
Dec 24			British retake Benghazi	
Dec 25	Hong Kong falls to Japanese			
1942				
Jan 1				UN Declaration signed by 26 countries
Jan 2	Japanese occupy Manila		British retake Sollum	
Jan 11	Japanese attack Dutch E. Indies			

	W. Europe	E. Europe	Italy & Mediterranean	Burma & China	Pacific	Atlantic
Jan 28		Timoshenko advances into Ukraine	Germans retake Benghazi		RAAF bombs Rabaul	
Feb 8						*Scharnhorst, Gneisenau* & *Prinz Eugen* steam through Straits of Dover to Germany
Feb 12				Japanese capture Rangoon		
Feb 15				Japanese capture Singapore		
Feb 19					Japanese bomb Darwin	
Feb 26-28					Battle of Java Sea	
March 2					Japanese take Batavia	
Apr 8					US surrenders Bataan	
Apr 29-30				Japanese take Lashio		
May 1				Japanese take Mandalay		

Date	Western Europe	Russian Front	North Africa	Pacific	Arctic
				renders all forces in Philippines. Japanese take Corregidor	
May 15		Russians under Timoshenko try to retake Kharkov		Battle of Coral Sea	
May 27		Germans surround Timoshenko's troops & take ¼ million prisoners			
May 30	First RAF '1,000 bomber' raid on Cologne				
June 3–4				Battle of Midway	
June 5		Germans besiege Sebastopol			
June 24			Rommel advances to Sidi Barrani		
June 25	Eisenhower appointed C-in-C Europe		8th Army retreats to Mersa Matruh		
July 3		Sebastopol falls			
July 4		Germans reach the Don			PQ 17 attacked
July 23		Germans take Rostov			

	W. Europe	E. Europe	Italy & Mediterranean	Burma & China	Pacific	Atlantic
Aug 7					US start landings on Solomon Islands	
Aug 12		Stalin & Churchill meet in Moscow				
Aug 17					Henderson Field completed	
Aug 31			Battle of Alam El-Halfa			
Sept 13		Battles for Stalingrad begin				
Sept 21				Arakan Campaign begins		
Oct 23			Battle of El Alamein begins			
Nov 1					Marines launch attack in Guadalcanal	
Nov 3–5			Axis troops start retreat from El Alamein			
Nov 8			Operation Torch			

Nov 11	Darlan surrenders to Allies. Germans occupy S. France		Germans occupy Tunisia 8th Army takes Bardia		
Nov 13			Allies take Tobruk		
Nov 17			Anderson's 1st Army meets Germans at Tabarka		
Nov 19		Russians attack Rumanians north of Stalingrad			
Nov 20			Allies take Benghazi		
1943					
Jan 2					Japanese resistance at Buna collapses
Jan 2–3		Germans start withdrawal from Caucasus			
Jan 14	Casablanca conference begins				
Jan 23			8th Army enters Tripoli		
Feb 2		Von Paulus surrenders at Stalingrad			

	W. Europe	E. Europe	Italy & Mediterranean	Burma & China	Pacific	Atlantic
Feb 8		Russians recover Kursk		Wingate's Chindits make first expedition into Burma		
Feb 14		Russians take Rostov	Rommel attacks at Faid	Chindits cross Chindwin		
March 6			Rommel attacks 8th Army at Medenine			March was worst month of the war for the Allies in the Atlantic with 43 ships sunk in first 20 days
March 29			Battle of Mareth Line			
April 18					Yamamoto shot down by USAF	
April 19		Jewish uprising in Warsaw ghetto begins				
April 21			8th Army attacks Enfidaville Line			
May 7			Tunis & Bizerta fall to Allies			
May 11					US begins liberation of Aleutian Islands	

Date		Eastern Front		Pacific	
May 13			Germans & Italians surrender in Tunisia		2nd Washington Conference begins
May 16		Warsaw uprising suppressed			
May 17	RAF attacks Ruhr dams				No Allied ships sunk by U-boats from now until September
June 29				US landings in New Guinea	
July 4		Battle of Kursk begins			
July 9–10			Allied invasion of Sicily		
July 22			Americans take Palermo		
July 25			Mussolini is imprisoned & Badoglio becomes PM		
Aug 17	US daylight raids on Regensburg & Schweinfurt		Allied armies reach Messina & Sicilian resistance ends		SE Asia command under Mountbatten set up at Quebec Conference
Aug 23		Russians retake Kharkov			
Sept 3			Allies land in Calabria. Armistice signed but not announced		

	W. Europe	E. Europe	Italy & Mediterranean	Burma & China	Pacific	Atlantic
Sept 8			Italians announce their surrender & Germans move to occupy Rome			
Sept 9			Allies land at Salerno			
Sept 12			Mussolini rescued			
Sept 25		Russians recover Smolensk				
Oct 1			5th Army captures Naples			
Oct 13			Italians declare war on Germany			
Oct 25		Russians recover Dnepropetrovsk				
Nov 1					US Marines land on Bougainville	
Nov 6		Russians recover Kiev				
Nov 18	RAF makes heaviest raid yet on Berlin					
Nov 20			8th Army crosses S			

begins

Nov 28			Teheran Conference begins		
1944					
Jan 12			Juin attacks near Cassino		
Jan 19		Russians take Novgorod			
Jan 22			Allies land at Anzio		
Feb 15			Cassino monastery destroyed		
Feb 16			Kesselring launches counter-attack at Anzio		
Feb 17-18					US destroys Truk base
Feb 22					US take Kwajalein, Engebi, Eniwetok & Parry
March 18	RAF drops over 3,000 tons of bombs on Hamburg				
March 29				Siege of Imphal begins	

	W. Europe	E. Europe	Italy & Mediterranean	Burma & China	Pacific	Atlantic
April 2		Russians enter Rumania				
April 17				Japanese renew offensive in China		
April 22					US make unopposed landings in Dutch New Guinea	
May 9		Russians recover Sebastopol				
May 18			Poles capture Cassino monastery			
June 2				Chinese besiege Myitkyina		
June 3				Battle of Kohima ends		
June 4			Rome falls to Allies			
June 6	D-Day Invasion of Normandy					
June 15					US Marines land on Saipan	
June 18		Russians break through Manner-	8th Army takes Assisi			

July 3	Cherbourg				
July 4		Russians capture Minsk	French troops take Siena	Japanese defeated at Imphal	Saipan falls to Americans
July 9	2nd Army takes Caen				
July 18	US troops reach St Lô				Tojo & Cabinet resign
July 20	Attempt on Hitler's life				
July 21					US Marines land on Guam
July 24					US Marines land on Tinian
Aug 1	US troops reach Avranches	Warsaw rising against Germans begins			
Aug 3				Stilwell & Merrill take Myitkyina	Tinian falls to US
Aug 15	Operation Anvil begins				
Aug 24	Choltitz surrenders Paris to Leclerq				

	W. Europe	E. Europe	Italy & Mediterranean	Burma & China	Pacific	Atlantic
Aug 27				Last Chindits evacuated to India		
Aug 31		Russians capture Bucharest				
Sept 3	2nd Army liberates Brussels					
Sept 4	Allies capture Antwerp undamaged					
Sept 5		Russia declares war on Bulgaria				
Sept 17	Arnhem operations begin					
Oct 2		Warsaw patriots capitulate to Germans				
Oct 14	Allies liberate Athens					
Oct 20		Tito's partisans & Russian troops enter Belgrade			US landings in Philippines begin	
Oct 23-26		Russians enter East Prussia			Battle of Leyte Gulf	
Nov 18	2nd Army crosses					

Dec 26	Patton relieves Bastogne					
1945						
Jan 9					US landings on Luzon	
Jan 17		Russians liberate Warsaw				
Jan 22				Burma Road re-opened		
Feb 4		Yalta Conference begins				
Feb 9	British & Canadian reach Rhine					
Feb 13-14	Dresden bombed	Budapest surrenders to Russians				
Mar 6	Allies take Cologne					
Mar 16					Iwo Jima falls to US	
Apr 1	Allied troops encircle Ruhr				US landings on Okinawa	
Apr 12						Roosevelt dies, Truman is President

	W. Europe	E. Europe	Italy & Mediterranean	Burma & China	Pacific	Atlantic
Apr 13		Belsen & Buchenwald camps taken by Americans. Russians occupy Vienna				
Apr 16		Russians begin offensive towards Berlin				
Apr 28			Mussolini killed. 5th Army takes Venice			
Apr 29	7th Army liberates Dachau		German unconditional surrender signed at Caserta. 5th Army enters Milan			
Apr 30	Hitler commits suicide					
May 2	Berlin held by Red Army					
May 3				Allies capture Rangoon		
May 8	Churchill & Truman proclaim					

	...ance in Czechoslovakia		
June 21		Okinawa falls to US	
July 17	Potsdam Conference begins		
July 27	Attlee becomes PM		
Aug 6		Atomic bomb dropped on Hiroshima	
Aug 8		Russia declares war on Japan	
Aug 9		Atomic bomb dropped on Nagasaki	
Aug 14		Japan agrees to unconditional surrender	
Sept 2		Surrender signed on USS *Missouri*, Tokyo Bay	
Sept 13			Japanese surrender in Burma signed

Biographical Notes

Harold Alexander (1891–1969) went to France at the beginning of the war as commander of the 1st BEF division and was responsible for commanding the last troops evacuating Dunkirk. After a period at Southern Command in the UK, urgently training new troops, he went to Burma in 1942 to command the retreating British forces. In August 1942 he became C-in-C Middle East, directing the major campaigns in North Africa during which Rommel's Afrika Korps was defeated. When Eisenhower became Supreme Allied Commander in N. Africa in January 1943 Alexander was appointed his deputy and commander of the 18th Army Group, which comprised all the Allied forces in N. Africa. Having driven all Axis troops from Africa, Alexander was field commander of the troops which invaded Sicily and later the Italian mainland. In December 1944 he became Supreme Allied Commander Mediterranean Forces and his drive northwards from the Po Valley forced the Germans to surrender in May 1945. He was Governor-General of Canada 1946-52.

Clement Attlee (1883–1967) was leader of the Opposition from 1935 to 1940, becoming Deputy Prime Minister under Churchill from 1942 to 1945. It was largely due to his and Ernest Bevin's efforts that virtually the whole British nation was mobilized for war. He became Prime Minister in 1945, taking over from Churchill at the Potsdam Conference. The Labour party was defeated in 1951 and Attlee spent the next four years as leader of the Opposition.

Claude Auchinleck (*b*. 1884) was GOC-in-C Northern Norway and GOC Southern Command before being appointed C-in-C India in 1941. In June 1941 he succeeded Wavell as C-in-C Middle East. He forced Rommel to retreat beyond Tobruk, but in January 1942 Benghazi fell to the Germans. They continued their offensive in May and had taken Tobruk by mid-June. Auchinleck took over direct command of the 8th Army and by the end of the month held the El Alamein corridor, but could make no advance. After Churchill's visit to Cairo in August Auchinleck was replaced by Alexander (as C-in-C) and Montgomery (as commander of the 8th Army). Auchinleck returned to India in 1943 and remained there until 1947.

Eduard Běnes (1884–1948) under pressure both from Hitler and Chamberlain resigned his Presidency of Czechoslovakia in September 1938 after the Munich agreement. He set up a Czech Government in exile, first in Paris then in London where, in 1940, his Government was recognized. He had declared war on Germany in October 1939, and in England he was able to build up a Czech brigade, made up of Czech refugees, which fought in the British Army. Czech airmen also played a valuable part in the Battle of Britain. He gained an assurance from Churchill (and from de Gaulle's Free French movement) that the Munich agreement would be renounced. And in 1942 Molotov promised him Russian support. A Czech brigade was formed in the Red Army and in 1943 he and Stalin signed a treaty of mutual assistance promising close co-operation after the war. The Russian army reached the Czech borders in 1944 and on 16 May 1945 Běnes re-entered Prague to a rapturous welcome. He was President of Czechoslovakia until 1948.

Tadeusz Bor-Komorowski (1895–1966) was a professional soldier who from 1941 commanded the largest army in the Polish underground movement. In August 1944 he led the Polish Home Army in the Warsaw rising. The battle was against the Germans, but its political purpose was to assert the Polish people's sovereignty in the face of a double invasion – Rokossovski had by then reached the Polish border. Whether or not Bor-Komorowski expected help from Russia, he did not receive it and after two months of ferocious fighting, during which about 10,000 resistance fighters were killed, he had to admit defeat. The Germans immediately sought revenge on the people of Warsaw and on the city itself. Bor-Komorowski was imprisoned in the camp at Markg Pengau but was released by the Americans in 1945. After a period in the United States he came to London where in 1947 he became Prime Minister of the Polish Government in exile. He remained in London until his death.

Omar Bradley (*b*. 1893) was a protégé of Eisenhower, having graduated with him and Marshall from the US Military Academy, West Point, in 1915. In World War Two he served in Tunis, at first reporting back to Eisenhower on battle performances. Having taken over the US 2nd Corps from Patton, he captured Bizerta in May 1943, taking over 40,000 prisoners. He took part in the invasion of Sicily, where his forces met fierce German resistance and only reached Messina after 38 days. Eisenhower chose him to command the US landings in Normandy in June 1944. His 1st Army landed on the Omaha and Utah beaches, later storming inland to St Lô and Cherbourg and breaking through the gap between Mortain and Avranches. On 1 August Bradley was given command of the US 12th Army Group consisting of 1,300,000 men. Bradley and the 12th Army Group liberated Paris and were active at the Battle of the Bulge. They crossed the Rhine at Remagen and, after battling their way through Germany, met the Russian army at the Elbe on 25 April 1945.

Neville Chamberlain (1869–1940) became Prime Minister in May 1937 and for two years followed a policy of appeasement of Hitler while re-arming at home. He realized after the fall of Poland, Norway and Denmark that war was going to be total and refused peace moves. But it became clear that the Commons would not support a Cabinet associated with the failure of the Norwegian campaign and with Chamberlain's appeasement policy; a National Coalition became inevitable. Chamberlain resigned as Prime Minister in May 1940. He fell ill in July and died in November.

Winston Churchill (1874–1965) was British Prime Minister and Minister of Defence from May 1940, following Chamberlain's resignation, until July 1945. On becoming Prime Minister he immediately made the first of his many rousing and confidence inspiring speeches: 'What is our policy? I will say it is to wage war by land, sea and air. . . . Victory at all costs'. One of his first acts was to set up a Directorate of Combined Operations and throughout the war he kept in close contact with his Chiefs of Staff. He established a close alliance with America which resulted in the lend-lease programme and, after the Placentia Bay Conference, the Atlantic Charter. After the German invasion of Russia he promised every assistance, without retracting his anti-Communism. In July 1942, an over-whelming majority defeated a censure in the Commons for his war conduct. The many wartime conferences kept him in touch with the Allies. He was at Potsdam when his party was defeated in the 1945 General Election.

Andrew Cunningham (1883–1963) joined the Royal Navy in 1898 and by the outbreak of war in 1939 had become C-in-C Mediterranean Fleet. He secured the bloodless immobilization of the French fleet at Alexandria and under his command part of the Italian navy was put out of action at Taranto and, later, Cape Matapan. He spent six months in Washington in 1942 as Head of the British Admiralty Delegation, returning to Europe as Allied Naval C-in-C under Eisenhower. In September 1943 he received the surrender of the Italian Fleet and in October, on the death of Admiral Pound, he became First Sea Lord and Chief of Naval Staff, responsible for the central direction of the navy.

Charles de Gaulle (1890-1970) was a colonel in command of a tank brigade when the Germans invaded France in May 1940. Premier Paul Reynaud appointed him Under-Secretary of War, his first political post, the following June. A few days later, with the new Premier Pétain seeking an armistice, de Gaulle fled to London where he proclaimed himself head of the Free French and was recognized as such by the British Government. Following his broadcasts urging Frenchmen to resist the Germans, thousands left France to join the Free French forces in Britain and North Africa. By November 1940 he had over 20,000 troops, 20 warships and control of all French Equatorial Africa. However, when the Allies invaded North Africa, Eisenhower put Giraud in command of all French troops. At the end of a power struggle between the two, Giraud resigned and by the end of 1943 de Gaulle controlled all French colonies except the Japanese-occupied territories in Indo-China. He returned to France in 1944, a week after the D-day invasion and on 25 August he marched triumphantly into Paris with the Allies' forces. He was immediately installed as President of the Committee of National Liberation Government. He was not invited to the Yalta or Teheran conferences, at which post-war strategy was discussed. He spent eleven years in the wilderness until, in 1958, he was recalled to help settle the Algerian question. His French Constitution was accepted and in 1959 he became the first President of France.

Karl Doenitz (*b.* 1891) was, for the first half of the war, Flag Officer U-boats. He developed the concept of the 'wolf-pack' formation and urged the building up of a large fleet of submarines. By 1943, when he succeeded Admiral Raeder as C-in-C of the German navy, Germany had 212 U-boats operating in packs. He was convinced that U-boat activities could play a decisive factor in winning the war for Germany, but with the Allies' development of microwave radar much of their effectiveness was lost. In May 1945, as Hitler's nominated successor, Doenitz had to supervise the capitulation of Germany. He was sentenced to ten years' imprisonment at the Nuremberg trials.

Hugh Dowding (1882–1970) joined the Royal Artillery in 1900 and the Royal Air Force in 1918. By 1936 he was Air Officer Commander-in-Chief Fighter Command. In this position, which he held until November 1940, he was largely responsible for saving Britain from possible invasion. While a member of the Air Council (1930–36), he had encouraged the development of a radar early-warning system and of the monoplane fighter; two factors which helped Dowding to win the Battle of Britain.

Anthony Eden (*b.* 1897) was foreign secretary in Baldwin's Government before being appointed to the same post by Churchill in 1940. He had resigned in 1938 in protest against Chamberlain's equivocating attitude towards Mussolini. On a visit to Moscow in 1941 after the German invasion of Russia, he became aware of Stalin's ruthless ambitions, but in May 1942, in the interest of defeating Hitler, he negotiated the Anglo-Soviet mutual alliance against aggression. In 1943 he attended the Foreign Ministers' meeting, where he had the delicate task of reassuring the Russians about the Allies' intentions in invading the Continent. He was a highly skilful foreign secretary. He was again Foreign Secretary, 1951–5, and was Prime Minister from 1955 to 1957, resigning because of ill-health after the Suez war.

Dwight Eisenhower (1890–1969) was a divisional chief of staff at the time of the Japanese attack on Pearl Harbor. By June 1942 he was US Commander in Europe. He commanded the US forces that landed in North Africa in November 1942 and in the same month persuaded Darlan to co-operate with the Allies. In February 1943 he was appointed Supreme Allied Commander in North Africa and in this capacity he led the Allied invasions of Sicily in July and Italy in September. In December he became Supreme Allied Commander of the Allied Expeditionary Force in Europe with the task of uniting commanders of several different nationalities and mounting an invasion against the Western Europe mainland. The success of 'Overlord', launched on 6 June 1944, was due as much to Eisenhower's powers of diplomacy as his skill in logistics. It was his 'broad-front' strategy, which was strongly criticized by Montgomery among others, that forced the Germans behind their borders by 1945. Eisenhower was Chief of Staff US Army 1945-58 and Supreme Commander of the NATO forces in Europe 1950-52. He resigned his commission in 1952 on his nomination as Republican presidential candidate and was President of the USA from 1953-61.

Heinz Guderian (1888–1954) was one of the key commanders of the German armoured forces: he created, trained and led the Panzer units. His breakthrough at Sedan in May 1940 and dash to the Channel were decisive factors in the fall of France. In 1941 he led the drive to the East which almost resulted in the collapse of Russia. His strategic withdrawal in winter 1941 led to his dismissal by Hitler and he was only recalled when Germany's position was hopeless. He became Chief of General Staff in July 1944 and a member of the military court which expelled from the army hundreds of soldiers who were then sentenced as civilians in connection with the attempt on Hitler's life.

Franz Halder (1884–1972) became Chief of the General Staff of Germany in 1938 during the Sudeten crisis. He led a half-hearted conspiracy to arrest Hitler but this came to nothing after von Brauchitsch backed out. He directed the Polish campaign and later planned the proposed invasion of England which failed to materialize. Halder disagreed with Hitler's strategy in the Eastern campaign, although he took part in it, and in 1942, after his opposition to Hitler's plan to advance simultaneously on Stalingrad and the Caucasus, he was dismissed. He was interned in Dachau in 1944, suspected of being involved in the July attempt on Hitler's life. The Americans freed him in 1945 and he gave important evidence at the Nuremberg trials.

Arthur Harris (*b.* 1892) directed the RAF's Bomber Command in its massive bombing of Germany. An early advocate of concentrated bombing on selected targets, in February 1942, when he became C-in-C of Bomber Command, he stepped up its offensive and on 30 May 1,046 planes dropped an average of 31 tons of bombs per square mile, devastating a third of Cologne. In August he established a force of photo-reconnaissance aircraft and in September the first 'blockbuster' bomb was dropped on Karlsruhe. In 1943 Harris initiated the policy of night-bombing. Later that year he bombed Berlin with unprecedented intensity but without inflicting a corresponding amount of damage. He therefore began heavy bombing in addition to depth bombing, killing many civilians but not diminishing Germany's war potential. Although his policies were supported by Churchill at the time, Harris was almost the only war leader not to receive a peerage after the war.

Adolf Hitler (1889-1945) became Chancellor of Germany in 1933 and by the outbreak of war was also head of state and supreme commander of the armed forces. He made himself personally responsible for Germany's conduct in the war. At first, in Poland, Norway and France, he was successful. The limitations of his military strategy began to become apparent when he invaded Russia in June 1941. His intention was simply to absorb the whole of Europe into the German Reich. In pursuing this vision he listened less and less to advice and disregarded unpleasant information. In addition, he continually changed his mind. Nevertheless, it was not until 1943, when the German Empire was at its most expanded, that Hitler's mistakes became evident. It was clear by the beginning of 1944 that Germany could not win the war. However, he refused to admit defeat and withdrew increasingly from reality, refusing to see any but his closest associates. Meanwhile, in pursuance of his Aryan ideal, millions of Jews, as well as political opponents, were being killed in his notorious concentration camps. On 29 April 1945 he married his mistress, Eva Braun, and the following day they committed suicide.

Chiang Kai-shek (*b.* 1887) was Allied Supreme Commander in China throughout the war. China's war against Japan began in 1937 when the devastation of Nanking and Shanghai forced him and his government to retreat to Chunking. After the Japanese attack on Pearl Harbor Chiang received American support which prolonged his hold on power as well as his war potential. At the Cairo conference in 1943, by which time he was chief of state and the strength of the

Communist party was growing, he was promised more positive support from the Allies. Chiang and General Stilwell, Commander of Chinese and US troops in the China/Burma/India theatre, quarrelled bitterly about the unification of Chinese forces under American command, and in 1944 Stilwell was recalled. It was assumed in the USA that Chiang would be head of the fourth great power after the war, but this notion had to be abandoned after his defeat by the Communists and Mao Tse-tung came to power in 1949. However, his Government in Taiwan continued to receive American support.

Douglas MacArthur (1880–1964) first served in the Philippines in 1922. He, maintained his connection with the Pacific in various capacities and in 1942 was appointed C-in-C of Allied Forces, SW Pacific Area. Earlier that year he had directed the brave but unsuccessful defence of Bataan Peninsula. From his base at Port Moresby, New Guinea, he worked out his strategy of 'island-hopping' and managed to achieve his aims with comparatively low casualties. Soon after the Luzon landings on 9 January 1945 the Americans entered Manila, and in February constitutional government was restored to the Philippines. That April MacArthur was given command of all ground troops in the Pacific while Nimitz controlled all naval units. As Supreme Commander for the Allied Powers, a postion he held until 1951, he was the chief Allied signatory at the formal surrender of Japan on 2 September 1945.

George Marshall (1880–1959) joined the US Army as a 2nd lieutenant infantry in 1901 and became a general in 1939. In September that year he became Chief of Staff of the US army, a post he held throughout the war. At that time the US army consisted of under 200,000 men and one of Marshall's main tasks was to persuade Congress and the Senate to increase its strength. After the Japanese attack on Pearl Harbor Marshall insisted on the unification of the Allied Commands. In 1942 he simplified the US command structure to only three components: the army ground forces, the air forces and the services of supply. Marshall himself remained directly responsible for the war plans division. Considered one of the ablest strategic thinkers of the war, he attended most of the war's major conferences, including Casablanca, Yalta and Potsdam. He retired from the army late in 1945 and was succeeded by Eisenhower. While US Secretary of State, 1947-9, he initiated the Marshall Plan. He was Secretary of Defence from 1950-1.

Bernard Montgomery (*b*. 1887) commanded the 3rd Division of the BEF in France until the evacuation from Dunkirk. For the following two years in . England he developed and put into practice his rigorous training methods. In August 1942 he took over command of the 8th Army in North Africa, completely reorganized it and put it into the attack. The Alamein offensive began on 23 October 1942 and by January 1943 Montgomery had taken Tripoli. In April he met up with the Allied troops in NW Africa and in July he and the 8th Army invaded Sicily and, later, Italy, reaching the river Sangro in November 1943. Montgomery returned to England in January 1944 to help plan 'Overlord'. On D-Day he was field commander of all land forces with Eisenhower as his immediate chief. From August, when he took over command of the 21st Army Group, he was in disagreement with Eisenhower whose plan (which was put into effect) was to attack on a wide front. Montgomery thought this plan too defensive and advocated a 'pencil-line thrust on Berlin'. In September Montgomery took Antwerp and in February 1945 the 21st Army Group began its thrust to the Rhine. It reached the Baltic on 2 May and on the 4th, at Lüneburg Heath, Montgomery received the surrender of all German forces in the Netherlands, Denmark and NW Germany.

Benito Mussolini (1883–1945) had governed Italy for thirteen years by 1939. That year he concluded a pact with Germany, but, taken by surprise by Hitler's attack on Poland and disturbed by the German-Soviet pact, he declared Italy neutral. Impressed, however, by Germany's success in the Low Countries and France, in June 1940 he reaffirmed his commitment to the Axis cause and declared war. By December Italy had suffered defeats in North Africa and Greece and from then on became increasingly dependent on and an embarrassment to Germany. At a meeting of the Italian Fascist Grand Council on 24 July 1943 a motion was passed granting command of the armed forces to the King. The following day, Mussolini was arrested and imprisoned, and Badoglio became head of the new Government. On 8 September Badoglio surrendered to the Allies, but three days later the Germans seized Rome and daringly rescued Mussolini who immediately formed a new cabinet. Hitler allowed him little power and no army, and by June 1944 there were more than 82,000 Italian partisans fighting against him. While the German forces were being defeated in northern Italy in April 1945, he went to Como where partisans arrested him on 28 April. He and his mistress, Clara Petacci, were shot dead then hung upside-down in a Milan square, at the mercy of a vengeful public.

Chuichi Nagumo (1886–1944) was Commander of the Fast Carrier Striking Force of the Japanese navy for the first eleven months of the war. A torpedo rather than an aviation expert, he was not the best person to carry out Yamamoto's Pearl Harbor strategy. Against the advice of his air staff, he left the task incomplete. And at Midway his indecision led to all his four carriers being caught with their planes refuelling and all were destroyed. He achieved only partial success during the battles of the Eastern Solomons and was relegated to a less important command in the Marianas. When it was confirmed that the American assault there had succeeded, he committed suicide.

Chester Nimitz (1885–1966) was C-in-C of the US Pacific Fleet and Pacific Ocean Area from 1941, shortly after the Japanese attack on Pearl Harbor, until 1945 when he witnessed the Japanese formal surrender on board USS *Missouri* in Tokyo Bay. By skilful use of the intelligence gained from the breaking of the Japanese naval code, Nimitz won the Battle of Midway in 1942, and by the end of the year he held the initiative in the Pacific. His fleet and air arm were enlarged and used to push the Japanese westwards. By mid-1945 Nimitz was able to say, 'We have paralysed the will and ability of the Japanese navy to come out and fight'.

Henri Pétain (1856–1951), a hero of the 1st World War, became Prime Minister of France after Reynaud resigned on 16 June 1940. Pétain immediately offered Germany France's surrender and ordered a complete cease-fire pending an armistice with Germany, which he signed on 22 June. Under the terms, Pétain was to remain head of the Vichy Government, controlling the southern, 'unoccupied' zone of France. During the next four years, he became weaker both politically and personally, while French collaboration with the Germans became more blatant. In August 1944 he was arrested by the Germans and left France. He returned in April 1945 and was put on trial. His sentence to death was commuted by de Gaulle to life imprisonment. Even today French opinion about Pétain is extreme, some calling him a patriot, others, a traitor.

Konstantin Rokossovski (*b.* 1896) gained fame for his heroic defence of Moscow in late 1941 and of Stalingrad a year later. He commanded the forces on the Belorussian front in the south, reaching Poland and taking Lublin and Brest-Litovsk. He was probably in a position to help the Warsaw uprising which in July 1944 Radio Moscow had urged. However, he did not assist the Poles during their two months' desperate struggle. He marched across northern Poland, taking Danzig in April 1945 and, in May, meeting the British at Wittenberg. After the war he became Minister of Defence and Chief of the Armed Forces in Poland.

Erwin Rommel (1891–1944), best known for his action in the Desert, served in Hitler's bodyguard battalion in Austria, Czechoslovakia and Poland. His fine command of a Panzer division in France 1940 was rewarded with the command of the Afrika Korps in 1941. He inflicted a series of defeats on the British

8th Army and on his reconquest of Cyrenaica in 1942 was promoted Field Marshal. He was recalled from Africa after the evacuation from Tunisia and served in Italy during 1943. He was responsible for strengthening the 'Atlantic Wall' against the threatened Allied invasion and when the invasion came he commanded Group B in France where he was severely wounded. He was thought to be involved in the plot against Hitler's life in July 1944 and imprisoned. In October he was found dead from poison, undoubtedly self-inflicted.

Franklin Roosevelt (1882–1945) was President of the United States from 1933 until his death. He sponsored the lend-lease act which Congress passed in 1941 and which allowed the USA to help the Allies with virtually everything except troops. From August 1941, when he and Churchill framed the Atlantic Charter, the two leaders met frequently. After the Japanese attack on Pearl Harbor Roosevelt led his country whole-heartedly into the war and proved a far-sighted and inspiring war leader. Never entirely fit, ever since a severe attack of poliomyelitis, he died suddenly in April 1945 just as the war in Europe was ending.

Joseph Stalin (1879–1953), one of the less famous leaders of the 1917 Revolution, was Russia's ruler throughout the war (his Constitution was adopted in 1936), becoming Marshal of the Soviet Union in 1943 and Generalissimo in 1945. A ruthless dictator and opportunist, he disrupted negotiations with Britain and reversed his anti-Hitler policy in 1939 by signing the Nazi-Soviet non-aggression pact. He promptly occupied eastern Poland after its defeat by Germany and made an unprovoked attack on Finland. He expected ultimately to be attacked by Germany, but was unprepared in June 1941 when the invasion began. Churchill immediately allied Britain with Russia's struggle against Germany, but was unable to accede to Stalin's demands that a 'second front' in France should be created to relieve pressure on Russia. In July 1941 Stalin made his 'scorch the earth' speech which was obeyed literally – Germans reaching Kiev in September 1941 found the city already destroyed. Militarily, Stalin's strategy of forcing the enemy to diffuse his troops and then making an all-out attack was eventually successful, although at the cost of a great many Russian lives. Politically, he was successful too. At the Teheran Conference in 1943 his support for 'Overlord' made Churchill and Roosevelt think that his objective corresponded with theirs – simply to win the war. In fact, Stalin had diverted attention from those Balkan countries he intended 'liberating'. The Polish experience was repeated in other East European countries where liberation by the Red Army preceded their reorganization into Soviet Communist satellites. In Russia, Stalin's popularity reached adulatory proportions, largely due to his systematic and brutal purging of his political and personal opponents.

Semyon Timoshenko (1895–1970) served in the 1st Cavalry Army during the First World War. Created General in 1939, he conducted the Russo-Finnish campaign of 1940 and was Commissar of Defence from May 1940 to June 1941. When Germany declared war on Russia, Timoshenko took command of the front's central sector, fighting at Smolensk and preventing the capture of Moscow. In September 1941 he took over the southern sector, but his failure to prevent the German advance on the Crimea and Stalingrad led to his transference to a quieter sector and in July 1942 he was further downgraded to a position at Stalin's HQ.

Josip Tito (*b.* 1892) was Secretary-General of the Yugoslav Communist party when the Germans invaded Serbia. After the German attack on Russia in 1941 he both organized and led the Partisan Guerillas which rapidly forced the Germans to retreat in Serbia. Meanwhile Tito came out in open disagreement with Mihailovic, leader of the anti-communist, anti-Fascist resistance group called the Cetniks, and the Germans regained the ground they had lost. Tito and his Partisans went into the East Bosnian mountains, whence they fought northwards as far as the Croatian border. However in 1943 they were driven back. At the same time, Tito at last secured British aid and by May 1944 he was supported by all the Allies. By September the Germans were in retreat, Tito supervising operations from the island of Vis, and in October he marched triumphantly into Belgrade. At the Yalta Conference in February 1945 he was recognized by Britain, America and Russia as Prime Minister of Yugoslavia. He remained unmoved when the Yugoslav Communist party was expelled from the Cominform.

Hideki Tojo (1884–1948) was Premier of Japan in 1941 when the attack on Pearl Harbor took place. A military dictator, he was ambitious for Japanese expansion and directed troops throughout South-East Asia and the Pacific. When the Allies began to whittle away the newly acquired Japanese Empire, Tojo was blamed and after the fall of Japan in July 1944 was forced to resign. After the war he and six other Japanese leaders were sentenced to death. A suicide attempt in 1945 failed, and in 1948 he was hanged.

Harry Truman (1884–1972) was elected Vice-President in 1944 and became President after the death of Roosevelt (in April 1945), whose policies he carried on. Truman ended the 'hot war' by authorizing the dropping of the atomic bomb on Hiroshima. Japan surrendered on 14 August 1945. He remained President until 1952, conducting on behalf of the U.S. the 'cold war' which began in earnest with the Russians' blockade of Berlin, and the 'hot war' which began in Korea in 1950. He refused MacArthur's request to drop another atomic bomb and eventually sacked MacArthur.

Mao Tse-tung (*b.* 1893) became Chairman of the People's Republic of China in 1949, when his Communist army finally defeated Chiang Kai-shek's Nationalist party and drove Chiang to the island of Formosa (Taiwan). Mao's revolutionary struggle in China had begun in 1927 and from December 1941 he fought the Chinese Nationalist armies as well as the invading Japanese. The Americans supported Chiang militarily against the Japanese and politically against the Communists. They did not recognize Mao's Government until twenty-three years after his coming to power. Mao's Revolution did not end in 1949. He successfully launched the agrarian socialization programme in 1955 and the 'great leap forward', which culminated in the Cultural Revolution, in 1958.

Erich von Manstein (1887–1973) devised the plan to attack France through the Ardennes, the success of which was a decisive factor in the defeat of France in 1940. During that campaign he commanded the Infantry Corps. He fought with distinction in Russia in 1941, advancing on Leningrad in July. In September, as commander of the 11th Army, he defeated the Red Army in the Crimea, taking 430,000 Russian prisoners. In July 1942 he became Field Marshal with command of Army Group Don. He managed to gain Hitler's permission to retreat after Stalingrad and to the Dnieper after Kursk, but when he tried to persuade Hitler to allow a retreat in March 1944 he was dismissed and took no more part in the war.

Archibald Wavell (1883–1950) became, in July 1939, C-in-C Middle East, where he completed arrangements for the defence of the Middle East and North Africa. From December 1940 to July 1941 he and his Western Desert Force were engaged in driving first the Italians and then the Germans from North Africa. At the same time his troops conquered Ethiopia and took part in the unsuccessful defence of Greece and on the Iraq and Syrian fronts. On 2 July 1941 Wavell and Auchinleck swapped jobs, Wavell becoming C-in-C India. He was appointed Supreme Commander SW Pacific in December 1941 and, at a time when the German front was considered the more important, he had to fight a losing battle in Burma and Singapore with very little support. In June 1943 Wavell became Viceroy of India, an appointment he held until 1947.

Isoroku Yamamoto (1884–1943), though opposed to war with the United States, planned the Japanese attack on Pearl Harbor as the best method of gaining control in the Pacific. Following the success of that attack, he advocated the building of aircraft carriers and planned a rapid destruction of the American fleet and the capture of Hawaii by means of the base at Midway. However the Battle of the Coral Sea intervened, proving Japanese vulnerability. By

June 1942, when hostilities against Midway began, the Americans had cracked the Japanese naval code, and were expecting the attack. Under Yamamoto's command, the Japanese suffered a crushing defeat. He then ordered the occupation of Guadalcanal which lasted five months with no decisive outcome. In April 1943, following the interception of a radio message, the Americans shot down a plane in which Yamamoto was a passenger. He was given a State funeral.

Georgi Zhukov (*b.* 1896) was Russia's most powerful and successful commander. In 1939 he thwarted a Japanese attempt to invade Outer Mongolia. He became Chief of General Staff in January 1941 and was appointed C-in-C of all the Russian Western front in October 1941. In August 1942 he also became Deputy Commissar for Defence. He was personally involved in almost all the major Russian victories, including those at Stalingrad, Kursk, Belorussia and Moscow. In 1945 he directed the Russian capture of Berlin where, on 8 May, he was a signatory to the document formally ending the war. He was deputy Minister of Defence of the USSR 1953–5, and Minister of Defence from 1955–7.

Acknowledgements

For permission to quote passages of some length, the publishers would like to thank the following: Laurence Pollinger and Holt, Rinehart & Winston, *A Soldier's Story* by Omar Bradley; Faber & Faber, *The Bombing Offensive against Germany* by Noble Frankland; MacGibbon & Kee and Holt, Rinehart & Winston, *The Beginning of the Road* and *The End of the Third Reich* by V. I. Chuikov; Collins Publishers, *The Memoirs of Field Marshal Montgomery*; Collins Publishers and Simon & Schuster, *The Call to Honour* by Charles de Gaulle; Harper & Row, *The Struggle for Europe* by Chester Wilmot; William Heinemann and Doubleday & Co., *Crusade in Europe* by Dwight Eisenhower; Macmillan, London and The Macmillan Company, New York, *Sand against the Wind* by Barbara Tuchman; Macdonald & Co., *Neither Fear Nor Hope* by Frieder von Senger und Etterlin; Victor Gollancz, *The Chamberlain Cabinet* by Ian Colvin; The Arcadia Press and Barrie & Jenkins, *El Alamein to the River Sangro* by Field-Marshal Montgomery; Alastair Hetherington (article in *The Guardian*).

Quotations from Crown-copyright records in the Public Record Office appear by kind permission of the Controller of H.M. Stationery Office.

The publishers and Thames Television would also like to thank all those who have kindly allowed passages from their interviews, given specially for the television series, to be printed in this book.

Thanks are also due to the Imperial War Museum for permission to reproduce all the photographs in this book except for numbers: 1 (Camera Press); 50, 64, 66 (Keystone Press Agency Ltd); 52, 55, 57, 58, 59 (Navy Department, National Archives, USA).

Bibliography

Among the many detailed accounts of aspects of World War II the British Official Histories are based on contemporary official records. The Military Series, edited by Sir James Butler, includes *Grand Strategy*, a series of six volumes written by N. H. Gibbs, J. R. M. Butler, J. M. A. Gwyer, M. Howard, and John Ehrman; volumes on *The Campaign in Norway* by T. K. Derry, in *France and Flanders* by L. F. Ellis, in *The Mediterranean and Middle East* by I. S. O. Playfair (six volumes), in the Pacific (*The War against Japan*) by S. W. Kirby (five volumes), in North West Europe (*Victory in the West*) by L. F. Ellis (two volumes), three volumes on *The War at Sea* by S. W. Roskill, three volumes on *The Strategic Air Offensive* by Sir Charles Webster and A. Noble Frankland, and a volume on *The Defence of the United Kingdom* by Basil Collier.

In the Civil Series of Official Histories there are books on *The British War Economy* by W. K. Hancock and M. M. Gowing, on *British War Production* by M. M. Postan, and on *Problems of Social Policy* by R. M. Titmuss. All Official British Histories are published by H.M. Stationery Office, London. S. E. Morison's *History of U.S. Naval Operations in World War II* (15 volumes) is an important and detailed source of information mainly about the war in the Pacific and is published by Oxford University Press and Little, Brown in Boston.

Other important books about World War II, its origins and consequences, include *Munich: Prologue to Tragedy*, Sir John Wheeler-Bennett, London, 1964; *Hitler: A Study in Tyranny*, A. Bullock, London, 1965; *History of the Second World War*, Basil Liddell Hart, London, 1970; *The Second World War*, J. F. C. Fuller, London, 1954; *The Siege of Leningrad*, Harrison Salisbury, London, 1969; *Barbarossa*, Alan Clark, New York, 1965; *Middle East 1940-42*, Philip Guedalla, London, 1944.

Among the many volumes of war memoirs the most important is Winston Churchill's *Second World War* (6 volumes), London. *The White House Papers of Harry Hopkins*, London, 1948, edited by Robert E. Sherwood, is a first-hand account of American diplomacy by one of Roosevelt's closest advisers. *Conversations with Stalin*, M. Djilas, New York, 1962 (Penguin 1969) throws as much light as can be thrown on Stalin's behaviour.

General Index

Index of Names